Humanity must learn to activate an aspect of human behavior that has been somewhat dormant for nearly five thousand years—the ability to think for ourselves!

"In time all things will be revealed." To me this means that there will be a time when teachings and other information will be hidden and a time when they will be available again. There have been many historical reasons for hiding away knowledge. We live in a time when some of the ancient sources of knowledge are once again being made available.

I have long felt that some of the real teachings of Jesus have been pushed aside, sifted and selected in order to reinforce particular agendas and belief systems. There has been a substantial departure from the unique ministry and teachings of Jesus over time.

I set out to discover as much as I could about what Jesus was really like and what he intended to offer to those whom he taught. My goal was to find a spiritual path that honored both my Native American beliefs and my experience with Christianity. I found that there are many parallels between the teachings of Jesus and the writings of his earliest first century followers and my understanding of the earlier Native American philosophy.

I have found it valuable to have the courage to re-evaluate past experiences. I have learned to take those experiences and pass them by what I know as my Sacred Self or the Elder Within. Native wisdom has taught me to learn from the past; to give gratitude for all experiences; for within them is the very medicine needed to for balance. This process has helped me with spiritual balance and has restored my love for myself and for life.

The Ancient Roots Of Christianity

A Native American's Look *Through* Christianity

Rolland James "Rainbow Eagle"
Williston, M. S. in Ed, B. D.
With
Mary J. Williston
"Rainbow Snake Woman"
M. Ed, B. D.

Rainbow Light & Co,
Zanesfield, Ohio

Copyright 2009 by Rolland J. Williston

All rights are reserved. No part of this book may be reproduced, stored in a retrieval system, or transmitted in any form by any means, whether electronic, mechanical, photocopying, recording, or otherwise, without prior written permission of the copyright holder—except by a newspaper or magazine reviewer who wishes to quote brief passages in connection with a review.

Editorial, sales, distribution, rights and permissions inquiries should be addressed to Rainbow Light & Company, 1143 County Road 5, Zanesfield, Ohio, 43360, USA.

I acknowledge the tremendous help and loving fortitude of my wife, Mary Rainbow Snake Woman for her writing and editing. The cover of this book is one of Mary's beautiful paintings. Also I give my gratitude to Gentle Heart and Sky Jimenez for their assistance in editing. The review of Judaism by Rabbi Weinstein has presented additional balance to my research. It has been the constant presence of "Hosh-tah-le," the Oldest Elder, the Creator who has brought the necessary patience and enduring motivation for this material to be presented at this time.

First Printing, 2009

ISBN 978-0-9824919-0-4

Published by
Rainbow Light & Company
1143 County Road 5
Zanesfield, Ohio 43360 USA

Website: rainboweagle.com
Email: rainboweagle@juno.com

Table of Contents

Introduction—

    Personal Reflections—The Log Cabin Story
    Suggested Pathways for Studying This Book*
    Introduction of Some of the Contributors to This Study
    I am Okla-Choctaw and a First Century Christian

Chapter One: The Journey begins: Opening to Some Mysteries...17

Seven Signs for Writing This Book--"Manifest Destiny"--1452 Doctrine of Discovery--Today's Spiritual Revolution--The Michelangelo Mystery--The Parade Magazine Poll on Religion--**Definitions of Some Terms--Six Pathways of Study**--Old Medicine for New Times--A Grandfather's Story--Constantine and Christianity--Ancient Information is Available--Early Versions of the Bible--Sources of My Research-- --A First Look at the Study of the Hebrew, Aramaic, and Greek Languages

Chapter Two: The Colonization of the Americas and the World: It was Going to Happen!...65

Information Explosion and Native Prophecy--**Some of the Real Story of Colonization of America (1492 to 1800's)**--The Nature of Various Christian Groups--Vicious Attitudes and Actions of Christians upon Christians--Black Slavery--Some of the Myths About the Early History of the United States--Thomas Jefferson and His Beliefs, "The Jefferson Bible"--Some Notes About the King James Version of the Bible--**A Discussion of "Victim Philosophy"**-- Dealing with Victim Identity

Chapter Three: A Respectful Discussion of Christianity and Native American Spirituality..89

Religion Forced On Native Peoples—**The Christianizing of Native Americans**--Trail of Tears--1924 Native Citizenship--Genocide--Earth-based Philosophy--**The "People of the Book"**--Christianity in Review--**Christianity and Natural Spirituality: A Look at the Similarities**--Belief in One Great Source, the Great Mystery--Angels and Spirit Guides--Spiritual Stories, Parables and Wisdom Tales--The Use of Symbolism and Drawings--**"Native American Philosophy and What Came Across the Waters: One and One is Three"**--A Respectful Comparison of Native American Philosophy (A Way of Life) and Christianity--Relationship with the

Creator: Separation or an Ever-present Creator--Some Peace Shield Teachings--Personal Vision and Group Spirituality--Christian Worship and Native Ceremony--Human Condition and "Being Natural"--Purification, Cleansing and the Natural Condition--Male Dominance/Women's Guidance--"Growing Spaces"--The Role of Elders--Right/Wrong, Good/Bad and "Being Related to All"-- Concepts of Evil, the Devil and Natural Spirituality--The Cathars--Surrender, Suffering, Sacrifice and Participation With all of Life--Chosen People and Native Identity--Being Related to All--**A Finnish Legend--Summary of Natural Spirituality and the People of the Book**

Chapter Four: A Historical Glance at Christianity after the Ministry of Jesus..138

What This Study is *NOT* About and What *IS* My Intention—**Some Conflicting Scenarios—The Council of Nicaea and Roman Emperor Constantine**--Pagan and Roman Influences on Christianity -- **Searching for the Ancient Teachings** --An Aramaic Study of the Concept of Heaven----Original Sin--Sexuality and Spirituality--"To Be in the World But Not of the World"--Reincarnation Out...Death In!--Reincarnation and Karma--Access To God Through Jesus and The Church Rather Than a Direct Personal Relationship-The Trinity--"Son of God" discussion

Chapter Five: Understanding the Jewish Culture and the Story of Yeshua...172

The Nature of Judaism--Different Groups of Judaism--"Chosen People?"--Rabbi Kushner--Review of Judaism to this point of our Study--**Honoring Jewish History**--The Nature of Midrash--What About Satan?--The Essenes and Christianity--A Hebrew Study of Sin and Repentance—The Jewish Court of Law (*Mishna*)--**The Role and Status of Women in Judaism**

Chapter Six: Ancient Roots of Christianity--Yeshua and other Traditions..216

The Jesus Story and Other Ancient "Saviors", "In Time All Things Shall Be Revealed"--**Egyptian Stories--Zoroastrianism--Goddess Traditions--The Aryan Race, The Goddess Tradition and Christianity: From Unity, to Duality, to a Masculine Deity**--The Gnostics--**How and why: Reasons for changes in the Jesus story**—The Dark Ages--Father Thomas Doyle's sharing of the changes in Jesus' Identity: The Effect of the Barbarians Invasions on Christianity--Development of the Eucharist (Communion): the Role of Jesus

Chapter Seven: What are the "Actual" teachings of Yeshua?.....248

The Role of Native American Spirituality--To Seek Spirituality--The Role of the Church Today--**Getting to Know Yeshua**--Concepts Prominent at the Time of Jesus--What Did Yeshua Say About Himself?--Most Biblical Scholars Would Agree--Hebrew Tradition of the Messiah--Some Ancient Observations About Yeshua--Jesus and Nature--**The Hebrew Meaning of "Soul" and "Spirit"**—The Greek Philosophy of Separation of Spirit and Matter--What Does it Mean to Have Faith?--The Meaning of Salvation--Ancient Clues to Help Sift Out the Teachings of Yeshua--The Oldest Bible in the World--The Sinaiticus (Sinai) Bible--**A Church or a Gathering of "God's People"?** -Christianity Came to a "Y" in the Road!

Chapter Eight: AND YESHUA SAID............................280

*Bold designates a main heading.

Appendix A..301
Jewish Religion in the First Century

Appendix B..305
Jewish Mysticism

Appendix C..317
The Jesus Seminars

Appendix D..320
Recent Events: Writings, Movies and Resources to Consider

Appendix E..327
Historical Notes and the Catholic Popes

Appendix F..332
What's this about the Free Masons?

Appendix G 335
The Original Transcript of the Interview With Stephanie M.
Various Groups of Jews--The Bar/Bat Mitzvah--The Keep "Kosher"--Worship only one God not in Torah--"Yom Kippur"(most solemn Day)--The place for women in Judaism--"body movements during prayer"--The Letter of the Law over Spirit of Law--The meaning of Chosen People--Judaism and ritual cleanliness--The survival of the Jewish people--"The Sabbath Joy"--"Being Tempted"--"The Sacrifice of Isaac"--Adam *had known* Eve--Judaism and Conversion--Jewish Bloodline?--The concept of Sin--"Arguing with G-D?"--The Feminine Aspect of G-d—"Polytheism strikes again!"--The "whaling Wall"

Glossary-- with Ancient Hebrew, Aramaic, and Greek Terms........................347

Bibliography..353

Index..359

Introduction

When my twin brother Ralph and I were in our early twenties we learned the story of how the church refused to perform our parents marriage ceremony. This decision was based on the fact that it would have been seen at the time as an unconventional inter-racial marriage. My father, Henry Silas Williston, was a full-blood Native American of Okla-Choctaw heritage[1] ("Okla" is the oldest tribal name), and my mother, Mabel Rebecca Montgomery, was Caucasian. It apparently did not matter that they also were both part of the music ministry of the church. Their Christian wedding did take place, but it was relegated to the living room of Mom's parents' house. A daring long-time and loving friend who was a minister performed the marriage and a few church members attended. My father also knew that it was unacceptable to his people that he married a white woman. The taboo went both ways in those days. The devastation of Native village life and the mandatory tribal system imposed by the government has taken its toll on all Native peoples. This attitude was typical of small towns toward mixed marriages in the early twentieth century "Bible belt" in northeastern Oklahoma.

In the mid eighteen hundreds, many Native peoples were moved to Oklahoma during what is known as the "Trail of Tears." Shortly thereafter, several Christian denominations came to the territories in the west, intent on "saving" the primitives. Government documents show that in the late-1800's the U.S. government gave certain denominations the right to occupy specific reservations and Indian territories. This allowed each denomination to convert the Native population without interference or competition.

The next intrusion into the Native way of life was the turning over of supervision of Native peoples to government Indian agents. Children were removed from their parents and placed in government or Christian schools which were often very far from their homes. It was difficult for the Elders to be separated from the children since it was the

---

[1] It is my decision to refer to my Native heritage as "Okla/Choctaw." I am registered with the Oklahoma Choctaw Nation under my Christian name, Rolland James Williston. My father is registered as 4/4 (a full-blood Choctaw) with both the Oklahoma Choctaw Nation and the BIA (US Bureau of Indian Affairs).

Elders who passed on important parts of the culture to the next generation.

The prohibition of Native ceremonies and cultural traditions was painful also. As I have said in many classes, for all intents and purposes, it was illegal to participate in Native American ceremonies for at least two centuries. The devastation of village life and the mandatory tribal system imposed by the government has taken its toll on all Native peoples. In the 1970's, many Native people participated in political actions[2] that finally led to the passing of the 1978 Religious Freedom Act by the United States Congress. For years I have surprised many audiences with this information. Most Americans are unaware of this little known event. Why would there have been a need for such legislation in a land that was established to promote religious freedom?

Dad was a twin at birth, but he was the only one to survive. He became an orphan at the age of twelve. There was no birth certificate that recorded his birth. Both of his parents died as the result of alcoholism, but a wonderful Choctaw couple down the road took him in for awhile. The government ultimately found him and placed Dad in a government Indian boarding school. He was shamed and humiliated for his Indian heritage in an attempt to strip him of his culture. Dad quietly carried memories of this military style education and the impact upon his formable adolescent years lasted throughout his lifetime.

Native people reacted in various ways to the forced changes that occurred in such schools. My father never gave up his love of the Native culture and he carried the spirit of his people in his heart. He was, however, influenced by the military style of the school. He was not able to remember much about his tribal traditions. He did keep his language, but it was not used very often in our home so it was not passed on to us children.

There were two memories that Dad would speak of occasionally. He remembered his grandfather taking him on walks in the nearby woods. Speaking in Choctaw, his grandfather had said, "You see the trees, the creek there, and all the beauty around. Remember the sunshine will always be there!" Another memory that

---

[2] Various Native walks across the nation from the west coast to Washington DC; the National Guard surrounding a church on Pine Ridge Reservation; Native Elders speaking up about the rights of Native peoples to practice their ceremonies, go to ceremonial sites, regain possession of their tribal articles in museums and hold the United States government responsible for some 300 treaties.

my father held was of sitting quietly on the front porch near his mother, Melina Williston. As is the nature of mothers, when the moment was just right she planted a seed that would grow in his future. Speaking in Choctaw she told him, "You must always go to school." He later became one of the first Choctaws in his area to graduate from college. Dad became a music teacher at the local small town public school. He was the only music teacher for all grades. Later, he also taught at Chilocco Indian Government School.

We children silently respected the need for our parents' privacy in all matters. Because my older brother was born with Down's Syndrome, our own childhood memories already held enough baggage for us to deal with. Answers to all the family history questions will never be known; but it was obvious that my parent's union was made in Heaven, even though I can count on one hand the number of times I saw them hold hands.

Occasionally, we noted various negative attitudes of some members of the community, especially the town's Post Master. We later came to find out that he was the school board president during the year when my dad left halfway through the school year to go teach at the Indian school. The man was harboring some resentment about that. In time, as he got to know our family better, this Post Master softened his attitude.

Years later, Ralph and I made a visit to the local public school where Dad taught music in one small northeastern Oklahoma town. We wanted to see what Dad looked like when he was young! Very few pictures were taken in those days. We searched the school halls looking at the photos on the walls of past teachers. We discovered that in every picture dating from the time he taught there, Dad's image had been deliberately cut out! We didn't know the reason for the missing photos at the time. For some reason, in this all Caucasian community, memories of this very dark-skinned teacher needed to be removed. Also, at the time there was a lot of fear about TB (tuberculosis) and the American public health system often assumed that Indians were carriers.

Our pre-school and elementary years were spent in another small town called Wyandotte, Oklahoma. It was in this small community that we found a village, of sorts. This town of about 400 people would brace themselves each spring for the threat of tornados as well as rising flood waters. The local stores and school buildings bore the marks of past floods. A government BIA (Bureau of Indian Affairs) boarding school was located nearby on a hill. Every Sunday Native children from the school would walk into town to attend church services. Once a week, the local movie theater was reserved just for them. How often I wanted to be there with them. I really wanted to see Superman, Roy Rogers and The Road Runner cartoons.

I felt a lot of sadness from those children. Dad would invite us kids to go with him to music lessons at the school, but after a few times I could not bring myself to go back. I felt how difficult it must have been for Native children to be pulled away from their families and tribal people with the chance to visit their parents only a few times during the school year. It was too painful for me to be near the school and to keep seeing their sadness. It was many years later that I had the courage to take a job as a dormitory supervisor and bus driver at another Indian boarding school near the college I attended. Still later, I took a counselor's job at that same hometown school and as I drove around the boarding school property my heart was unburdened as I looked at the empty dormitories and school buildings. It has taken a long time for me to find some balance with those earlier experiences.

Our first home in this small town was across the alley from a very noisy church. Not even the quiet comfort of our living room was free of the sounds of people "getting religion." One summer our mother asked us if we would like to attend Bible school there and we said, "Sure." Mom was busy keeping the home settled and dealing with our older brother and Dad was often giving music lessons. It seemed like a way to have a new experience. Our decision was based more on our curiosity than really wanting additional Bible education. More importantly, we heard that they served treats like lemon-aid and chocolate chip cookies! Indian school kids were also in attendance at Bible School, so that was very interesting.

Everyone came in as usual and sat in the pews waiting for the schedule to begin. It was quieter than usual. I thought it must be because the other Native kids were there. A young man in his early twenties came in the side door near the front of the church and walked across in front of us carrying a large plywood cut-out of a man. He set it up at the front of the church. Then this very enthusiastic member of the church opened a small trap door in the chest area of the cut out man. Inside the door was a very red wooden heart. I barely remembered the previous Bible school lesson which was about how important it was to protect what, now I know to be, the center of this church's spirituality—the heart. Many pictures on the church walls reminded members of this idea. The pictures I was used to seeing in our childhood church experience did not show an exposed, open heart.

A few more minutes passed in silence. Then from the back of the room came a very loud, booming rifle shot! The bullet obviously had to have passed over our young heads before accurately hitting the red heart of the plywood man! My twin brother and I (and others except for most of the Native children), jumped in utter surprise. The lesson hoped for was to impress upon the young people not to let the Devil get their hearts! We did not return the next day to that Bible school. We twins did continue volunteering to shovel the snow off their sidewalks in the winter, but now our curiosity was satisfied.

In our teenage years, we had summer employment working for Mom's parents at the only grain elevator around town. We never quite got used to the uncomfortable attention that being identical twins always brought to us. The town held the energy of complex social attitudes toward the unusual nature of our family. I began to realize that, more and more, my emotional bank was collecting weighty unexplained "deposits" that continued to influence me, even to this day.

My grandparents were beloved residents of this small farming community. Their position within community had developed slowly over time even though they had come as outsiders themselves years before. They had won the hearts and minds of the people by their hard work and lasting friendships. I have come to realize that religious change and tolerance happens much more gradually.

I watched a world of ethnicity pass through my Granny's house. My parents brought four half-Choctaw boys into the world and then they adopted two Native American girls. Our mother's brother married a Canadian lady. In our mid-teens Granny and Granddad Ralph opened their house to a fourteen-year-old girl from Korea who was brought to America by an American soldier. His family did not accept his decision to adopt her and consequently refused to take her in. "Chan" was able to finish high school, with much difficulty, and later became a licensed beautician. Granny set an example herself in her time, as she too received her high school diploma.

Years later, Granny and Grandpa made room for an African American man and his white girlfriend while they pursued a college education. No one else would rent to them! Eventually they got married in Granny's living room. Two Pakistani, Muslim young men needed a home-away-from-home so Granny made room for them too. By this time, the local community had literally thrown their hands up as if to say, "We can't keep the world from coming to this town!"

From these family roots, our mother's Christian religious faith was born. Her insistence on getting the family to church, attending church camps, and surrounding our lives with an extended family wasn't really appreciated until years later. It was the much needed emotional support of many of the church people that helped us kids deal with the special child in our family. When he changed worlds (died), I was thirteen. For the next two years we felt our mother's emptiness and sadness. That void in her heart would ultimately be filled when another extraordinary person came into our family.

One Friday evening Mom told us about a sixteen year old foster boy who had been turned away from a his foster placement. "He needs a place to live." She said. "No one wants to take him in." We saw what was coming next. A home owned by singer Dinah Shore had taken him in. One evening he came in late from a horseback ride and apparently that was the last of a series of behaviors and social problems. Mom shared that he had a tendency to place himself near where his mother was working—usually a local bar. To this day, I remember seeing this slender, slightly tall young teenager walking in the back door. Everything he owned was in the one cardboard box that he carried. That night a world of anti-social behaviors came into our lives. For example, every Saturday night he would leave to participate in a "rumble" in a nearby large town. His language, his smoking and his habit of manipulation were not welcome in the local school. All and all, he stayed with us longer than he stayed in any previous foster home. Our Mother continued to provide emotional support for him even when he went out on his own. His mother lost her job and left to live in northeastern Oklahoma. This young man located in the same town where Mom's parents lived, Fairland, Oklahoma. Some years later I traveled to a Kansas prison to visit him. As the years passed, his whereabouts became unknown to us kids. Our mother, of course, knew more about him, but we didn't ask her. I realized much later that this family experience prepared me for my life's work as a therapist for children and young people with severe emotional imbalances and antisocial behaviors. My first wife of twenty-two years and I hosted twenty-eight foster children of various ages and personalities over a period of sixteen years.

Often enough, we kids would be teased, but to hear adults refer to Dad as "chief" stirred a lot of repressed anger in us. It seemed like we never really fit in. We moved a lot to different schools and our ethnicity was always an issue. We learned to redirect many of our pent-up feelings and memories into sports and musical activities. We became very competitive in sports and successful musically. Our opponents, especially in football and track, became the legitimate targets of our unresolved feelings.

In my adolescent years I recognized Dad's feelings of isolation and estrangement from his Native roots. Sometimes quite unexpectedly, Dad would take off and drive alone to visit "Choctaw land" in southeast Oklahoma for awhile. When this happened it left us with memories of our mother's tears. It was difficult for us to fully understand all of this at the time. In our home such things were not discussed. Dad's experience at the government school did not provide him with appropriate male role-models much less an effective father figure. Thank goodness, for the sake of us boys Dad did learn on his own, along the way. Being a transient teachers' family, our security depended upon family unity and our church community. In our later years we children did understand Dad's need to reconnect with his "stomping grounds." Just being with the energy of the land and the people; even for a short time, helped bring an important balance back to him. Having a Christian community could not fully replace his yearning to speak Choctaw, sing the Choctaw songs and be near what remnants of his Native roots he still could find.

One summer Mom and Dad announced that we were all going to take a trip to Choctaw land. On the first night we set up our tent and prepared our camp. Dad was occupied with some kind of activity nearby. Later, he informed us that we had put our tent next to a den of copperhead snakes! We picked up and drove to a nearby church parking lot and spent the night there. It was late in the day when we finally located Dad's old home place. The only visible indication of where his old house once stood was the foundation. It was on the porch of that house where Dad had heard his mother's words about going to school. We watched as Dad looked in the direction of the woods where he once walked with his grandfather. He just stood there silently looking all around. There was no woods there anymore; just a four lane highway passing through their back yard! Dad told the story of his grandfather's words once again many months later when he was speaking to a group in church. "Remember, the sunshine will always be there," he reminisced, "no matter what changes may come, something will always anchor our thoughts and remind us of what we can count on; those ideas and beliefs that can ground us."

In Okla-Choctaw traditions we always face in the direction of the sun when offering a prayer. Not that the *Great Hushtalee*[3] was in the skies, but as a reminder that the love and presence of the Creator blesses us with warmth and constancy.

* * * * * * * * * * *

My journey to connect with my Native roots began with storytelling during my college years. As people began to express more interest in the Native culture and began approaching me with questions, I had to confront the fact that my knowledge base and cultural experience were lacking. Like my Father's yearning for his roots, I longed to go where my Native blood was pulling me. My journeys, however, were a bit different. It was the Native Elders who were calling me. There were few Native authors for me to consult and most of the books written about Native peoples had historical or cultural perspectives. While my father's journey was to retrieve any pieces of his earlier life as a Choctaw, mine was to seek out what could be remembered about the spirituality and beliefs of the many Native cultures by visiting the living Elders. Sorting out those pieces would turn out to be a lifetime job.

My personal efforts and the Christian organization that I was connected with at the time made it possible for me to visit and sit with Native Elders and Native communities. I have always been thankful for the experience of my childhood Christian church even though I began to walk closer and closer to Native ways in my mid-forties. That decision created tension in my marriage after twenty-three years. I was making changes that affected the rest of our family. All of our lives began to change. When the marriage came to an end, it was the first time there had been a divorce in my family. Of course, that was a difficult time for all of us. Although I had held many professional positions, finding my *real* self was like being pulled over Niagara Falls.

---

[3] The Okla-Choctaw word for the Great Mystery.

After that, I distanced myself from Christian congregational life, but never from my relationship with Jesus. In my current marriage of many years, personal and spiritual balance has come into my life. I can now more fully walk within the vision given to me by the Creator many years ago.

Over the years I have been with many Grandfathers and Grandmothers of North, Central and South America. I have also visited with indigenous people in Sweden and Finland. Those experiences have helped me gain a broader perspective. The loss of ancient knowledge and the intense impact that Christianity has had on the lives and traditions of First Peoples all over the world is just beginning to be realized.

All of my life experiences have been steppingstones to my present journey. I have seen many others embrace natural ways. People who have participated in the Native ceremonies that we conduct express how they, feel it in their bones. I am more confident than ever before that the ancient Native beliefs, spiritual practices and traditions will continue into the future. These ways will once again be a choice for those who seek a spiritual path.

As we consider this study just know that I am offering this material for contemplation; I am not trying to place blame or to build up a history of wrong-doing. I present the following example as a metaphor to help frame this journey as we seek out the original teachings of Jesus.

Down the lane from our house lives a family who has built a wonderful addition around an old one-room log cabin. From the outside one would not see the original cabin, only the front porch side of the log house. Around what used to be the original home place, holding all of the family's memories and experiences, more living space has been constructed. The reconstructed house is now seen as the new reality. The old cabin is still there, but most observers from the outside would not be aware of its presence.

Additional space and intent has changed the dwelling. There might be other changes over time with the addition of a dining room, more bedrooms, an in-house toilet, perhaps even a garage that weren't even considered as important 150 years ago. All of this reminds us that a current frame of reference is not always complete if it leaves out contemplation of previous historical perspectives. We would not be able to say that, "This house has always been this way"...or "The original house cannot be found or understood." Neither would we find fault with the changes that have occurred as the result of accommodating the needs and desires of the inhabitants.

I think that something wonderful can come from recovering the original "log cabin" memories of the Christian movement that can add more beauty to the present representation of Christianity. Also, as we reexamine what we can find of the original teachings of Christianity, I hope that we can come to honor and even appreciate the changes that have occurred with an attitude of understanding rather than fault-finding and blaming.

Suggested Pathways for Studying This Book

With the explosion of information available to us, we have the opportunity to avail ourselves of much knowledge. I often refer to the blessed times we live in today as a "spiritual smorgasbord." Many spiritual traditions are being placed on the table for us to taste and to choose from. As we discern which to bring into our spiritual body, hopefully it will be with less racial, tribal, religious or social restrictions. Accordingly, this spiritual food becomes a source of energy that can be useful and applicable to every step of our journey.

Like a spiritual buffet, each person if they wish can select what truths or ideas match his or her own spiritual appetite. As an individual encounters new information, it is essential to first pass it through their personal frame of reference. Then, one can find others who share similar truths. I once met Dennis Weaver, the actor and environmental activist, in Denver. He has such a beautiful way of speaking about the responsibility of applying our knowledge:

Ignorance is the worst. None of our problems can be solved without knowledge. Knowledge is power. But only if it is coupled with action guided by wisdom. We can have all the information in the world, but if we are not willing to do something with it, to use it in a constructive way, it's worthless.[4]

Having more of an opportunity for personal selection can be conducive to confidence and optimism. It behooves community to develop an environment of tolerance and respect for personal choice and growth.

---

[4] Weaver, Dennis. *All the World's a Stage*, 187-188.

This book can be constructive using any of the following strategies:
- Taking a slow read through the text; reading each chapter in sequence. You might want to make some notes in the margins and/or at the end of the chapter to refer back to. Highlighting some of the text (including footnotes as they come up), will facilitate coming back to the information later for more study.
- Reading and studying the information in the appendixes.
- Looking at the footnotes as a resource for discussion. I have intentionally placed the footnotes on the same page to make further study and discussion easier.
- Finding specific entries in the index that appeal to you.
- Focusing on the italicized words in the text.
- Just opening to some part of the book and reading for awhile.
- You may want to email the author (a few inquiries at a time, please), for clarification and further discussion.

Please keep in mind that my selection of various texts and references does not always mean that I agree with what is written. I feel that you, the reader, can decide for yourself and/or check out the information on your own. I am interested in encouraging thoughtful investigation of the topics and personal reflection as to the meaning it has for you.

Having pursued this particular study, often in private, for some twenty years, I hoped that a time would come when more people would have the courage to look deeply into the more simple forms of spirituality. I have been very encouraged to sense among many people a sincere craving to step outside of spiritual "boxes." There are some who have continued to urge me to present my research. I am not a graduate of any theological institution, but this book is a sincere effort to lay out some interesting thoughts I have encountered as I have studied the ancient roots of both Christianity and Native American spiritual traditions, especially as reflected in old materials.

Introduction of Some of the Contributors to This Study

"I am a historian of religion" is how *Elaine Pagels* speaks of herself. She holds a Ph.D. from Harvard University and is currently a professor of religion at Princeton University. Dr. Pagels is often asked to participate in panel discussions, television documentaries and guest lectures regarding Christian history. Her father was Catholic, but converted to Darwinism. "I was told that religion was for people who were insufficiently educated,"[5] she says. She joined an evangelical Christian church when she was fourteen, out of enthusiasm and respect for the commitment she observed. When Pagels entered college, she decided to learn Greek so that she could read the New Testament in its original language, in the hope that she could "discover the source of its power." Her studies of pagan writings led to the realization that they are "...also religious literature, but of a different religious sensibility." Like myself, Elaine Pagels decided to look more deeply into the "...earliest Christian sources, composed soon after Jesus and his disciples had wandered in Galilee."[6] Pagels speaks about the gospels which were discovered in Upper Egypt and date to the beginning of the Christian movement: "They completely changed, transformed and complicate our picture of what Christianity is."[7]

Another one of my main sources is Episcopal Bishop *John Shelby Spong*. He grew up in Lynchburg, Virginia, in the Bible Belt. His father was an Episcopalian who rarely attended church and, as he writes, his mother was, "...from a very fundamentalistic Presbyterian family, rigidly moralistic; yet is her own way, she was very loving." He writes that in high school it never occurred to him to question his faith. Spong finished college and then seminary as a very promising twenty-six year old minister. It was the reading of John Robinson's *Honest to God* that "let the cat out of the bag" for him. Spong resolved that from there on he would be completely *honest* in his search for truth. His Sunday School class became more popular than his sermons. Spong says, "It is interesting that in that class I almost never roamed out of the Hebrew scriptures...I literally put myself on notice that the days of hiding were at an end."

I have greatly appreciated the insights of those who have grown up within conservative ideologies and those who have studied ancient manuscripts and Hebrew resources. It has also been important to recover information about the Jewish culture and the customs that

---

[5] "America the Spiritual" series (webcast), For the Betterment of Humanity, Boston, Mass. A part of a panel of participants—Women and Spirituality: Breaking the Code.
[6] Pagels, Elaine. *Beyond Belief: The Secret Gospel of Thomas*, 31.
[7] "America the Spiritual" series, op. cit.

surrounded Jesus' ministry. A look into the Aramaic language that Jesus would have used to speak his words is paramount. In that regard, the work of *Neil Douglas-Klotz* in interpreting the words of Jesus in Aramaic has been an invaluable contribution to the research of this book. While part of his family comes from a Jewish background, he was raised as a Christian. He went on to study Islam, including Sufism. He holds a doctorate in both religious studies and psychology.

As can be seen, there are many resources that have contributed to the writing of this book. Recently, I had the privilege of sitting with several rabbis who offered their wisdom to me. Also, I want to give particular appreciation to Stephanie M. for her insight as a woman who grew up and was educated within the Jewish tradition. She was born of Jewish parents, practiced as a Conservative Jew, was educated in a Hebrew school and then later in life chose to step away from some, but not all, aspects of her Jewish heritage. Her personal knowledge and reflections have contributed much to my understanding of the Jewish culture and I have indicated her expressions with footnotes. Although she gave permission to include her full name, I have decided to refer to her only as "Stephanie M." in the footnotes. In the main text, I have edited her comments only for grammatical clarity and I have included the unedited version of the interview in "Appendix G." This is how she introduces herself:

I grew up a Conservative Jew, studied Judaism extensively through high school and lived in Israel for a time. I speak some Hebrew. Both of my parents were born Jewish and we celebrated all of the holidays in our household. My brother and I attended Hebrew school three days a week from age 5 until we each took our Bar or Bat Mitzvah. I continued on to a Jewish high school for more intensive study. Now I am a practicing Wiccan, but refuse to give up all Jewish practice. I still keep kosher and observe a number of the holidays.[8]

As we talked, she mentioned that she had pretty much dragged her family into the traditions. She explains:

Well, if you're 16 and still living at home and suddenly you're keeping kosher, and your mother is willing to encourage and accommodate your increasing observance, she might begin to cook kosher food more and more often. It makes life easier on you, and hey, the whole family really should be keeping kosher anyway, right? This is what happened in my household. I wanted to be going to synagogue more

---

[8] The interview with Stephanie M. from California took place from July 30-August 1st, 2009. She has given permission for her expressions to be included in this book.

often, and I didn't have a driver's license yet. That means someone has to go with me. I was at a Jewish high school, and coming home and talking about what I was learning. Studying Judaism is a big part of Jewish observance. We are very big on study, so just me coming home and talking about what I was learning brought my parents farther into the tradition. I started observing the Sabbath – not working or writing or using electricity, etc. My parents did not ever join me in this, but they were aware for the first time of what it actually meant to observe the Sabbath (called being Shomer Shabbat), and why a person would want to. It was part of their awareness of the week, the difference between Shabbos and all the other days, for the first time, that sort of thing.
Side note: a man once asked Rabbi Akiba, one of our greatest rabbis, if he could summarize the Torah while standing on one foot. Rabbi Akiba said, "Love thy neighbor; now go study."

I asked her how other Jews would react to her decision:

It's bad. It's a betrayal of our people, particularly because I am an educated Jew and kept such a strong practice for so long. It is not important for my sake, but rather for the sake of my children. If I am now a Pagan (which is a term with serious stigma attached), surely my children will not continue our religion and traditions. Because I have such a solid Jewish education, this is a major waste. My parents and teachers invested a lot of time in me, thinking that I would carry on the religion very strongly. Our survival and continuity as a people is tremendously important to the Jews.
There is a Jewish saying, "It is a betrayal of our murdered ancestors to abandon the tradition now."

I must give my heart-felt gratitude to my long time friend John Pratt for his assistance in helping me balance the research for this book. He has been an avid and obsessive reader of history for some forty years. He claims, and I mostly believe him after knowing him for some thirty-years, that he reads a book a week and can remember everything he has read! Though his specialty is American History (the Civil War in particular), he also has a deep, and sometimes fanatical, interest in the pursuit of the "truth and nothing but the truth." He has greatly assisted in the editing of this book for historical accuracy (from his "point of view"), and I appreciate his insights. One more thing: if John Pratt was writing and not just editing this book, it would **probably** have become three times longer!

Several people have contributed to the editing of this book. I am sure it took a great deal of patience and skill! My special thanks to Sky Jimenez and Jane "Gentle Heart" Walsh for their many hours of commitment.

My selection of reference materials for this book represents many writings that have "fallen into my lap" from a multitude of sources. Some of them represent more liberal Christian viewpoints. Some information will certainly challenge the Christian ideology you may be familiar with. I would encourage you to proceed with an open mind and pay attention to your own spiritual sensitivities as you explore the material.

* * * * * * * * * * * *

In my role as a spiritual advisor of sorts, I have found it valuable to have the courage to re-evaluate past experiences. I have learned to take those experiences and pass them by what I know as my Sacred Self or the Elder Within. Native wisdom has taught me to learn from the past; to give regard and even gratitude for all experiences. Often hidden within them is the very medicine that is needed to balance the experience. This process has helped me with spiritual balance and has restored the love I needed to develop toward myself.

In the material to come, I will try to offer some suggestions for study, but it will not be a full accounting. Some of the subjects I will explore more completely and others may seem to be pieces of information that I throw out for your further study. I provide exhaustive footnotes, appendices and an index so that the reader can pursue additional information depending upon interest. **It is not my intent to cross all the *t*'s and dot all the *i*'s.** I want to plant some seeds of information that can lead, I believe, to potential personal growth. By giving you the benefit of my extensive study, I hope to awaken within you the courage to journey with me and beyond. I will try to draw some conclusions, perhaps more for me than any attempt to persuade you! As I have said often at the beginning of classes, I'm not here to convince or convert. My hope is to present enough material for adequate conversation. It will be up to you, the reader, to decide what, if anything, to do with it.

I consider myself blessed in this lifetime to be a Native American. I more often refer to myself as a "natural" person. My wife and I both feel privileged to be walking on the Native path, as we understand it. I am regularly invited to teach and speak in many Christian settings. Respect for all Christian circles is important to my wife and me. In recent years we both have been ordained in an interfaith ministry. This particular ministry allows us to integrate our Native American ceremonies with service to the various communities we connect with.

In addition to my Native journey I would also call myself a *First Century Christian*[9] rather than a member of any particular Christian denomination today. I like the description Lola A. Davis gives of the term "Christian": "A Christian is any person who reveres Christ and tries to follow his teachings as *that person understands them.*"[10] This writing is hopefully reflective of both my Native American and my Christian spiritual traditions and experience. They are both meaningful to my spirituality. Now the journey begins, and I hope to be an informed and conscientious tour guide for you!

Relevant to our discussion, I am reminded of an expression by the Peace Shield teacher, Ervin Romans, who invited me into his home place many years ago. He continues to teach from the "other side":

"Strip away the story book tales and false teachings and search for your true identity with the Great Spirit and your past. Otherwise you are like a canoe, drifting in a stream. Search your legends and teachings from the past and the true Spirit Lodge that was taught by the teaching Shield, the Peace Chiefs. For there is the Key that will give you back what no one can promise you. Find your identity as a people. Remember your Grandfathers."[11]

---

[9] I have stretched the meaning of Christian here because in the first century those who followed Jesus did not call themselves *Christian*. My studies and others indicate that that term was not in common use within the Church (or gatherings) until clearly into the second century. Instead, the early followers were known as "belonging to *the Way.*" (Acts 9:2)

[10] Davis, Lola A. *Toward a World Religion for the New Age*, 122. (italics are mine)

[11] Eagle, Rainbow. *Native American Spirituality: A Walk in the Woods*, 129.

Chapter One

The Journey Begins—Opening to Some Mysteries

"Reverence is one of man's answers to the presence of mystery's." –Abraham Joshua Herschel[12]

Joseph Campbell writes: (the period of Egyptian history is richly represented in architectural and hieroglyphic remains) "...yet there is no notice anywhere of anything like those famous biblical plagues, no record anywhere of anything even comparable."[13]

"If it is ever possible to discover any profound knowledge or truth in the heart of Christianity, it will only be by rejecting obvious counterfeits that have been considered so sacrosanct as to be untouchable, and by turning to the true, pure teachings of Jesus and the real essence of Religion."[14]

In my late thirties, I began to realize that I must seek the ancient roots of my Christian heritage, just as I have done with my Native American roots. Surprisingly, I discovered that each new bit of information I uncovered created a spark of excitement within me and inspired my resolve to dig for more. As I received encouragement for this journey, mountains of anxiety began to loom in front of me. What attitudes would be stirred up; what spiritual foundations shaken; what resistance would be met, and what changes would happen for me?

There seemed to be no end to the information falling into my lap. One interesting fact led to another and then another. Finally, I had to realize that I could not completely present all of the many facets that I found of the Jesus' story. It is a story that is coming gradually and purposefully to light. My intension in this writing is to offer pathways toward further study as one is led by their own intuition and by the Great Creator.

---

[12] Herschel, Abraham Joshua. *Man is Not Alone: A Philosophy of Religion.*
[13] Campbell, Joseph. *Myths to Live By*, 8.
[14] Kersten, Holger. *Jesus Lived in Indiā: His Unknown Life Before and After the Crucifixion*, 29.

My layman's research into the early writings of Christianity has revealed a deep reservoir of interest that I didn't know existed within me. My connection with Christianity was introduced by my mother. It has been nurturing to me for most of my life. Many genuine, loving people encircled our family and gave me the spiritual community that I needed in my early years.

Then, like the opening of Pandora's Box, I began to recognize issues of power, management, politics and personal ambition within the organized institutions of the Church. However, I have found a way to have an appreciation for Christ without being a member of a church. Many Christian institutions do not represent my understanding of Jesus' genuine spiritual contribution. Often, when I have made this expression in class I have witnessed affirmative nods. As history reveals, religious leaders and institutions have rationalized the use of violence, torture and death in order to justify their causes. Yet many, me included, have benefitted from the relationship we have had with the spirit of Jesus that was celebrated in the first century. My hope is that there can be room for those who want to include the real essence and spirit of what Jesus taught into their lives.

I have come across seekers of spiritual teachings who tell me that one of the reasons they have distanced themselves from Christian institutions is that their questions have often not been addressed. Others felt their spiritual needs were not being met. Years ago I began to hear the expression that religion isn't the same as spirituality. This has become a rather common expression lately!

Other reasons given for the exodus of people from the institutional church ar: the lack of empathy and love for the non-compliant and the utilization of fear and guilt tactics by those in positions of power. Some also have mentioned the exclusive role of the masculine within many churches and the de-emphasis of the importance of women. There has been a long history of Christian attitudes toward the "lost," the "unsaved," the "sinful," as well as toward females in general.

My suspicion, when I began to dig into the written research about the history of the Christian Church, was that there might have been some deception that has been applied to the Jesus' story. I wanted to speak up for the Jesus that I felt was being misrepresented. Unfortunately, I did not know enough at the time to put into words what my intuition was communicating to me! And my thoughts would not have been accepted by my family or my community. I felt a growing compulsion to increase my knowledge of Christianity. From a Native American perspective, Christianity, along with the influences of the American system, had done so much to change our Native life. But I grew up with a true appreciation of Jesus. I needed to reconcile these two aspects of my spiritual life.

Seven Signs

There were at least seven signs within the span of six months which pointed me toward the writing of this book. The first occurred while traveling with my good friend John Pratt. We were doing our usual: passing the time away with conversation about everything under the sun. John, an avid reader and a civil war buff, has a tendency to focus upon matters of justice and issues of "good" over "evil." After a moment of silence John blurted out, "Something terrible happened in Southern France; something that has puzzled me for a long time and I don't like that!" Then he posed this question, "Did you ever hear about the massacre in Southern France by the Crusaders in A.D. 1209 that lasted for thirty-four years?" Later, I found out that it was called the Albigensian Crusade. This presents a bit of a mystery, because the crusades which went into the Bible lands only lasted for about seven years! I was not one who was particularly educated on the subject of history and I wasn't familiar with historical events in old Europe. So, I responded with ignorance of the topic. When we travel together I usually welcome most conversations, even if they are about things that don't appeal to me. It fills in the time and I often actually learn something! It was nice to sense an air of frustration and puzzlement in my good friend, who usually has done his research and has a firm grip on the facts. Consulting "Wikipedia" I found this for starters:

The Crusades were a series of religion-driven military campaigns waged by much of Latin Christian Europe. The specific crusades to regain control of the Holy Land were fought over a period of nearly 200 years, between 1095 and 1291. Other campaigns in Spain and Eastern Europe continued into the 15th century. The Crusades were fought mainly against Muslims, although campaigns were also waged against pagan Slavs, Jews, Russian and Greek Orthodox Christians,

Mongols, Cathars, Hussites, Waldensians, Old Prussians, and political enemies of the popes. Crusaders took vows and were granted an indulgence for past sins.[15]

Since that inquiry I have found the following information. When the Crusades came into the town of Beziers in Southern France, the crusade leader was asked how his men would distinguish Catholic from Cathar.[16] He supposedly replied with the words that had been conveyed to him by the Roman Catholic Pope, Innocent III, "Kill them all. God will recognize his own!" Also, "The same papal representative, writing to Pope Innocent III in Rome, announced proudly that 'neither age nor sex nor status was spared'."[17] History records that at least 15,000 men, women, and children were killed in this action and, in many cases, within the walls of the church. Some estimate that the Albigensian crusade resulted in the deaths of from many thousands to as many as one million people. This included not only the Cathars, but also much of the population of Southern France.[18]

John had a suspicion that something was amiss. With his knowledge of historical accounts he offered his reply, "This is just wrong; things just don't add up!" This bit of trivia remained stuck in his mind for a long time, like a tick that won't let go. There had to be more to the story. My reflection at the time was that I thought the Great Crusades had more to do with recovering the Holy Lands from the invading Turks! Authors of the book **Holy Blood, Holy Grail** write that by 1127 the "...western armies had already conquered the Holy Land and established the Kingdom of Jerusalem..."[19]

What threat did Southern France present to the Roman Catholic Church that led to some thirty thousand knights and foot soldiers from northern Europe occupying this area for thirty-four years? What did the church officials know that would cause them to send the Crusades into a place so far from the Holy Lands? In 1145, just before the

---

[15] http://en.wikipedia.org/wiki/Crusades.
[16] "The *Cathari*, 'the pure ones,' traveled in pairs throughout southern Europe...were living the Christian principles of voluntary simplicity, love of neighbor, and generous service to the poor...They maintained that theirs was a church...based on personal enlightenment rather than indoctrination." "...both boys and girls were taught to read...women were accepted as ministers. Garbed in dark blue robes, they traveled in pairs..." Margaret Starbird, *The Feminine Face of Christianity*, 78-79.
[17] Baigent, Leigh, and Lincoln. *Holy Blood, Holy Grail*, 49.
[18] Ellerbe, Helen. *The Dark Side of Christian History*, 74.
[19] Baigent, Leigh and Lincoln. *Holy Blood, Holy Grail*, 65.

Church directed the Crusaders to "kill them all…" Saint Bernard, a spokesman for the Church, went into Languedoc, France with the intent to preach against the heretics. However, it is written that after being with the Cathars he ended up speaking in their behalf! "No sermons are more Christian than theirs," he declared, "and their morals are pure."[20] One issue might have been the Cathars attitude toward women. In *Holy Blood, Holy Grail* we read:

In general the Cathars subscribed to a doctrine of reincarnation and to a recognition of the feminine principle in religion. Indeed, the preachers and teachers of Cathar congregations were of both sexes.[21]

To add to the thorn in the side of the Orthodox Church was the Cathars belief in "direct and personal knowledge… [that] took precedence over all creeds and dogma." The Church had declared for a long time that the priests were the "official and ordained intercessors between man and God."[22] The Cathars were referring to all humans, including women of course, as recipients of divine messages!

While I was teaching and visiting in Central Sweden, a beautiful eighty-three-year-old grandmother asked me to come visit her. She had written some twelve books in Swedish and she gave me her third book entitled, *"Legenden om Issa."*[23] Mariana Stjerna talked privately with me for two hours about her research on the legends of Jesus living in India. Known as "Issa" in the legends of India, he is said to have lived there during those lost years between ages twelve and twenty-nine, before he began his ministry at approximately the age of thirty.[24] She said that this book didn't stir people's thinking much because, as she related, "Most of the European people already know about these things and are not so surprised about stories that didn't get into the Bible."

---

[20] De Rougement, *Love in the Western World*, 78. (quoted in *Holy Blood, Holy Grail*, 56)

[21] Baigent, Leigh, and Lincoln. *Holy Blood, Holy Grail*, 52.

[22] Ibid.

[23] "According to local belief, Yuzu Asaph [*Saint Issa*] was a Jewish prophet who had come from another country two thousand years ago preaching in parables like Christ." William Bramley, *Jesus Goes to Hollywood*, 135-138, 227.

[24] "At about the age of thirty…Buddha starts his spiritual career. While keeping fasts… he is tempted by…the devil after his forty days' and nights' fast. A similar temptation story is known about Zoroaster…" Kersten, op. cit., 76.

In 1973 a report appeared in a major German weekly[25] about a professor who claimed to have found the tomb of Jesus Christ, apparently in the Kashmirian capital of Srinagar.[26] Some years ago, I had seen a TV program called "Unsolved Mysteries" which related that Kashmir had claimed for a long time to host the grave of Jesus and that he died there in his eighties!

A writer, Andreas Faber-Kaiser, wrote, "It has been suggested by some that Jesus traced Thomas the Apostle's footsteps into India, and…died at Srinagar, Kashmir[27] where a tomb has been attributed to him."[28] Gardner presents in *Bloodline of the Holy Grail* that, "This resulted from a Kashmiri suggestion in 1894 that Jesus was synonymous with a prophet called Isa, to whom the tomb[29] was originally dedicated…"[30]

Soon after I first began to explore the topic of early Christianity, I received an email from a highly regarded rabbi and author, Gershon Winkler. He knew a Jewish woman who had attended one of my classes in northeast Ohio where I had spoken about my feelings that many ancient and original teachings from various traditions had been altered or added to over time. Gershon sent me his latest book, "*Sacred Secrets: The Sanctity of Sex in Jewish Law and Lore*." Rabbi Winkler illustrates in his book that the Torah and other medieval rabbinic literature actually celebrated some pretty uninhibited attitudes toward

---

[25] Der Stern Nr. 16, 1973.
[26] Kersten. opt. cit., 32. Abdul Ahad Azad writes: "The language of Kashmir derives from Hebrew. According to tradition, in ancient times Jewish people settled here, whose language changed into the Kashmirian of today. There are many Hebrew words that are quite obviously connected with the language of Kashmir." (Addul Ahad Azad, Kashmiri Zaban Aur Shairi, Vol. I, p. 10 (Jammu and Kashmir Cultural Academy) Quoted in *Jesus Lived in India*, 69.
[27] "Kashmir hosts a monastery that claims to hold the rod of Moses; according to a regional legend, he had gone there to die. Many people of Kashmir wear their hair in the Jewish manner, and Kashmir boatmen still use a heart-shaped paddle that was only found elsewhere in the Middle East." William Bramley, op. cit., 141.
[28] Andreas Faber-Kaiser. *Jesus Died in Kashmir*, Abacus/Sphere, London, 1978.
[29] "The tomb of the prophet Yuz Asaf [Issa] in the middle of what is today Srinagar's old town, in Anzimar in the Khanjar quarter…The sarcophagus containing the earthly remains of Yuz Asaf points from east to west, in accordance with Jewish custom! This is clear proof that Yuz Asaf was neither an Islamic saint nor a Hindu." Kersten, op. cit., 206.
[30] Gardner. *Bloodline of the Holy Grail*, 95.

sexuality and sensuality. Here is an excerpt from the *Dictionary of the Jewish Religion*:

SEX. Judaism takes a frank and open attitude toward sex, and recognizes the strength of the sexual drive. It believes sex is not intrinsically sinful or shameful but should be confined to marriage and governed by certain set rules. Sodomy, pederasty, adultery, and incest are branded as capital offenses...Celibacy was discouraged by the Rabbis.
...Judaism does not look upon the body as inherently evil... [found within the word ASCETICISM, on page 19]

Stephanie gives this insight: "Married couples are actually expected to have sex on the Sabbath, as part of honoring it and keeping it holy. It is part of "the Sabbath Joy."[31]

Rabbi Moshe ben Nachman (Ramban), in his sex manual *Iggeret HaKodesh,* or "Epistle of Holiness," gives us an idea of the Judaic perception of sex:

No one should claim that sex is ugly or repulsive. God forbid! For sexual intercourse is called 'knowing' in the scriptures (Gen. 4:1), and not in vain is it called thus...If we were to say that sex is repulsive, then we blaspheme God Who created the genitals...All body parts are neutral; the use we make of them determines whether they are holy or unholy.[32]

The Judaic perspective was that the sex act is "worthy, good, and beneficial even to the soul. No other human activity can compare with it...There is nothing impure or defective about it, rather there is much elation."[33] I began to wonder, if there was healthy regard for sexuality and one's body within the Jewish religion, then how did these ideas change later in Christianity and why? Jesus[34] taught within the Jewish culture and eventually Christianity grew out of Judaism. I wanted to know what Judaism practices and teaches today. Christianity seemed to have a long history of separating sexuality and spirituality. Early in Christian history the Church began indoctrinating its members with the

---

[31] Stephanie M.
[32] Rabbi Moshe ben Nachmon (Ramban), *Iggeret HaKodesh*, 175.
[33] Rabbi Yaakov Emden in *Mor Uk'tziah*, no. 240.
[34] "...Christians have always had to deal with the fact that Jesus...was himself not a Christian but, indisputably, a Jew. From the earliest years of the Christian movement, followers of Jesus have tended to handle this fact in various ways...As time went on, however, Christians tended to ignore or minimize Jesus' Jewishness, and many denied that he was Jewish at all." (Tolston & Kulman, *The Real Jesus: How the Jewish reformer lost his Jewish identity*, U.S. News and World Report, 40)

assertion that the human body was unclean and not to be honored. Physical desire, especially sexual desire, was an evil manifestation of our "fallen natures." There were so many voids in my spiritual education that I wanted to fill.

Another sign came to me as I was finishing a weekend seminar in St. Louis, Missouri. A friend of mine revealed that some years ago she had chosen to leave the confines of a wonderful, nurturing monastery. After class she explained:

I left a life that I loved, which was my monastic life as a Benedictine monk. I left there because I felt called. I was told that I needed to bring what truth and spiritual power there was in the monastery out into the world...Because, there would be a time when the world would be desperate for the truth that was taught there behind the monastery walls.

When she received her confirmation at the age of eight, she chose the name "Mary," honoring Mary Magdalene. As I listened to her story I had to ask myself, "Just what were those truths that she referred to?"

I intentionally postponed this book until the release of a book called *Chasing the Magdalene: A Journey of Discovery in Provence and Languedoc,* which I helped publish. Cynthia Ploski had made actual journeys into Southern France and wrote about her research in her fictionalized story about the Mary Magdalene traditions that are very prevalent there. She asked me to review her manuscript. According to her, Southern France still held legends about Mary Magdalene coming there after the Crucifixion of Jesus. A tour guide had told her that there was historical evidence indicating that shortly after Jesus' Crucifixion, Mary Magdalene and others brought the Holy Grail to France. It was indicated that Joseph of Arimathea then carried it to England and it might have been buried in a well at Glastonbury.[35] The legends say that she arrived with a child and it is widely believed there that the girl was the child of Mary and Jesus!

I must admit, just reading about this set my mind to spinning! Slowly, I read her manuscript and more questions flooded my mind. Apparently there existed a long-standing tradition of honoring Mary Magdalene, not only for her connection with the Master[36] Jesus, but as

---

[35] Ploski, Cynthia. *Chasing the Magdalene*, 3.
[36] In Jewish traditions a rabbi had to be married, according to the Jewish Mishnaic Law that "An unmarried man may not be a teacher." W E Phipps, ***The Sexuality of***

a significant person herself. Her arrival date is said to be in 42 AD[37] and she died in 63 AD, in a place now called Saint Baume (in Southern France) at the age of sixty.[38]

Margaret Starbird, in her excellent book, *The Feminine Face of God*, presents this about Mary Magdalene: "Among the Gnostic Christians of the first three centuries of the Christian era, it was Mary Magdalene who was honored as the incarnation of the 'Sophia'."[39]

Starbird adds another detail to this legend:

Surviving in the town of Saintes-Maries-de-la-Mer is the story of Saint Sarah the Egyptian, an adolescent child who accompanied three Marys on their journey to exile...Every year, a festival is celebrated in honor of Saint Sarah and the three "Marys": Mary Magdalene, Mary Salome, and Mary "Jacobi"...[40]

Here is more of what she writes:

The bones of Mary Magdalene...were rediscovered in 1280 in an obscure tomb in Provence, kept secret during the extended period of the Moors' occupation of the Mediterranean coast of France. These sacred relics were later transported to her basilica, "La Madeleine," at Vezelay for safekeeping...pilgrims flocked to Vezelay, many climbing the town's hill barefoot to reach the grand Romanesque abbey church at its summit.[41]

Leonardo Di Vinci's painting of the Last Supper[42] has also caught the attention of an assortment of Christian believers, to say the least. A study of ancient paintings can offer some enlightening details that add more mystery to the Christian story. In addition, there are some interesting clues that can be found within the architecture of Europe. It is well known that the Freemasons placed ancient symbols into the design and construction of many medieval buildings. Some of the religious secrets and beliefs that were not accepted, or were actually

---

Jesus, 44. "...the occasional exception being the scholar who is totally absorbed in religious studies." (*Dictionary of the Jewish Religion*)
[37] Starbird. *The Feminine Face of Christianity*, "in a boat with no oars," 22.
[38] Taylor, John W. *The Coming of the Saints*, Covenant Books, London, 1969, ch. 7, 138, quoted in Laurence Gardner, op. cit., 97.
[39] Starbird. *The Feminine Face of Christianity*, 116.
[40] Ibid., 22, 121.
[41] Ibid., 64-65.
[42] "Ordinary [first century Jewish] meals were eaten in a sitting position, whereas festive meals or banquets involved "reclining," lying on one's side at a low table." Marcus J. Borg, *Jesus: A New Vision*, 144.

suppressed, by the Roman Catholic Church have been preserved to some extent by various secret organizations. If you are interested in the Free Masons, you will find a more complete discussion in "Appendix F" at the back of the book.

I have found that most present-day theologians believe that there is no foundation for the portrayal of Mary Magdalene as a prostitute in the sense that we define it today.[43] In A.D. 591 Pope Gregory gave a speech in which he claimed Mary Magdalene was a prostitute.[44] In 1969 the Vatican issued a statement that Mary Magdalene[45] was not a prostitute. My curiosity kicks in when negative images of a woman are promoted. What's being hidden and what is the motivation for doing so?

Roman Catholic nun and biblical scholar, Mary Thompson, writes in *Mary of Magdala, Apostle and Leader* that no place within the canonical gospels is that association between Mary Magdalene and prostitution made. She states that Mary is clearly shown as a leader in the apocryphal gospels. The term Apocrypha consists of fifteen Jewish books, or parts of books, written between 200 B.C. and A.D. 100 that were part of both the Greek Bible (Septuagint) and the Latin (Vulgate) Bible. Leaders at the time did not include them into the Hebrew Bible.[46]

After a class in Columbus, Ohio, the store manager walked up to me and said, "You need to have this book!" The book was called, "*Holy Blood, Holy Grail*," published in 1983. It offers a similar hypothesis that the Holy Grail is actually a metaphor for the bloodline of Jesus and a community of believers who gathered and resided in Southern France and not a literal chalice, as has been purported. The book further states that Jesus had been a "…legitimate king of Israel, that he had been married and had sired children, and that these children

---

[43] Baigent, Leigh, and Lincoln. *Holy Blood, Holy Grail*, 333.
[44] Picknett, Lynn. *Mary Magdalene*, 47-48.
[45] "In Western art, Mary Magdalene is almost invariable carrying her alabaster jar of precious nard, a fragrant and expensive perfume made from an exotic plant that is native to the slopes of the Himalayas." Starbird, *The Feminine Face of Christianity*, 20.
[46] Rovin, Jeff. *Fascinating Facts from the Bible: The New Testament*, 47-48.

had perpetuated his bloodline until, some three and half centuries later, it merged with the Merovingian dynasty of France."[47]

Was I discovering, as perhaps many others had before me, a new dimension to the Crusades? My childhood and adult Christian education did not prepare me for this information. Underneath my usual cool nature I began to experience a rise in my emotional temperature! I felt my curiosity growing; Jesus married? If he had children then he would have had…sexual experiences!

In recent years I saw a news story about research that had sought to create a portrait depicting the possible appearance of Jesus. When given the skeletal structure and skin color of the peoples of the first century,[48] he would have looked a lot like an African Muslim, not the typical image of a white-skinned, light-haired man with angelic qualities.[49] I could accept this picture of Jesus, however, the idea that Jesus had been married to Mary Magdalene and fathered children sent me on a personal journey to find out more. After researching this book I am now convinced that understanding the beliefs and practices of those communities that gathered to honor Mary Magdalene, will aid us in the quest to reconstruct the real teachings of Jesus.[50]

The next sign came while I was teaching in West Virginia some years ago. A big burly man sought me out in a restaurant where I was having a spicy egg omelet. He came directly to my table with an obvious mission in mind. It was as if he had been waiting a long time to finally get an opportunity to complete some unfinished business. I am usually ready to meet the curious public and I welcome people's comments. I enjoy all kinds of people, but I was not ready for this man's expressions. He caught me off guard in the middle of my breakfast. With respect and surprising gentleness he commented, "You

---

[47] Baigent, Leigh, and Lincoln. *The Messianic Legacy*, xii.
[48] Bishop John Shelby Spong gives this description of a first century Jewish man: "in all probability a brown-skinned Middle Easterner with cropped black hair, standing no more than 5 feet 4 inches to 5 feet 7 inches tall and weighing no more than 120 to 140 pounds." *Jesus for the Non-Religious*, 50.
[49] For example, as St Augustine said of Christ, according to the *Catholic Encyclopedia*, "in his time there was no authentic portrait of Christ, and…the type of features was still undetermined, so that we have *absolutely no knowledge of His appearance."* Joseph Wheless, *Forgery in Christianity*, 112.
[50] "In *Dialogue of the Savior* (c.AD 150) and the *Gospel of Thomas* (c. AD 50-140), Mary [Magdalene] sits with the Apostles as an equal while they ask Jesus questions. She is the only woman to do so." Bramley, op. cit., 177.

know if the Christians who came to America had really understood how the Indians believed, things would have been a whole lot different! The Indian beliefs were a lot like their own old beliefs." He shook my hand and left me nodding my head in mock agreement as he exited the restaurant. More to puzzle over!

My first take on what this man was saying was that Indian beliefs were closer to Christianity than the Europeans realized. Why I was so deeply affected and why did I continue dwelling on this man's statement? His words had truly lodged in my eagle mind and I couldn't release them. What did he know that I did not know? Could there be older Christian beliefs that I was not aware of or had missed along the way? This was an important sign for me to pay attention to. It came to have more meaning than I ever could have imagined at the time. I can now say, "thank you," to that man for helping me realize that I needed to take a journey to bring ancient Christian teachings and awareness forward.

Only recently have I come to fully understand the message that these signs brought to me. I now know that many of the ancient Christian beliefs, (or should I say Jewish/Hebrew beliefs) that Jesus taught, have changed through the course of history since the time in which he lived. So, the Christianity that came with the Europeans to North America was not completely indicative of the teachings of Jesus.[51] Before all this I was not particularly inclined to compare Native American beliefs to Christianity.

As some people know, the government encouraged and even financed Christian groups to make the first entry into Native communities after the years of removal from the 1820's to the 1900's. Native prophecy predicted that life was going to greatly change. Native peoples have had to adapt to different ways of life and adopt some of the new ways. Generally speaking, the attitude of the time was focused upon "Manifest Destiny". Researcher John Pratt gives this clarification: "Manifest Destiny was a term first used in a New York newspaper in the early 1800's. It was adopted politically as the idea that it was the God-given right and destiny of whites to take the North

---

[51] "It is a good thing," Albert Schweitzer wrote in *The Quest of the Historical Jesus* nearly a century ago, "that the true historical Jesus should overthrow the modern Jesus." 103.

American continent." This governmental doctrine essentially caused a drastic disruption of our way of life.

My studies have revealed to me that the drive for colonization of the world began with a 1452 Doctrine of Discovery. As found in *Sacred History and Earth Prophecies*:

In 1452 the Doctrine of Discovery was issued, giving religious sanction for the enslavement of indigenous peoples and the theft of their lands in newly discovered territories. This papal decree demonstrated Northern Stream arrogance by declaring all lands not owned by Christians to be considered vacant and thereby claimable for the Church.[52]

John adds this:

In 1455 a second encyclical was issued that said pretty much the same thing as the bull issued in 1452. In 1537 Pope Paul III issued a bull titled <u>Sublimus Dei</u> *in which he declared the previous bulls invalid and declared that Indians were men and should not have property or liberty taken from them. All three documents are worth reading.*[53]

The different denominations of Christianity that went onto the reservations made no room at all for the indigenous philosophy and culture. The purpose was to "Americanize" Native people. Children were removed from their Native communities and forced to abandon their language and customs. Their hair was cut and they were given white man's clothing and Christian names. They were forced to embrace American attitudes of competition, social appropriateness, patriotism, military service and the acceptance of male leadership. Dependency upon outside resources through the use of rations, welfare and the institution of governing structures completed the goal of assimilating Native people into the American way of life.

The seventh sign came from a fellow presenter at the Whole Life Expo in Atlanta, Georgia. His name is Gregg Braden, author of many books including *Awakening to Zero Point* and *Walking Between the Worlds*. My wife and I visited with him briefly and I came away from that experience more certain of my own path. I realized that many are taking courage to exercise their right to know the *real truth*.

During this time Gregg had been presenting his study of ancient texts called, *The Shift of the Ages*. In his book, *The Isaiah Effect*, he

---

[52] Dinawa. *Sacred History and Earth Prophecies*, 111.
[53] *1452 Dum Diversas, 1455 Romanus Pontifex, 1537 Sublimus Dei.*

had recovered *a lost mode of prayer* from the Isaiah scroll (part of the Dead Sea scrolls). This was intriguing to me. Being from a background in physics and geology, Braden sees how spiritual beliefs can be brought into a relationship with science. The natural world exists in relationship to old tenets and beliefs. He spoke about how, in the fourth century, much of the ancient knowledge was taken from the general public and contained within esoteric traditions, priesthoods and mystery schools and became inaccessible to common people. The recent discovery of ancient texts such as the Dead Sea Scrolls and the Nag Hammadi Library[54] have revealed information that enables us access today to healing techniques that modern science is validating.[55]

In the last twenty-five years America, and now the world, have experienced an information explosion. Access to material has become increasingly easier with the availability of the internet. World events are being experienced and monitored by the masses who are becoming more informed and growing a critical consciousness. For over two thousand years information has been in the hands of a few and used for the purpose of increasing dependency upon male dominated and fear-based powers. When access to information is controlled there is a heightened level of fear and uncertainty experienced by the masses.

It is less important to point a finger at the process, than to recognize it and then appreciate the lessons we can learn from having the experience. In our present situation we now have more personal choice and freedom to help us make decisions for ourselves. Nigel Leaves, Director and Dean of Studies of Wollston Theological College, Perth, Western Australia, writes in a publication known as *The Fourth R: An Advocate for Religious Liberacy:*

Today, there is a "spiritual revolution" taking place. It is being fuelled by those at the grassroots, by those ordinary folk who are moving away from the historical religions and forging a multitude of spiritual paths. There is a "smorgasbord of therapeutic spiritualities" from which people can pick and choose, and many people feel no need to cross the thresholds of the Church.[56]

---

[54] "The Gnostic Library at Nag Hammadi...has more saying of Jesus than we possess in the Bible." Hidden Stories, 16.
[55] Braden, Gregg. *The Isaiah Effect,* 2.
[56] Leaves, Nigel. *"The God Problem,"* The Fourth R. (May-June Issue, 1005), 3.

On February 18, 1564 Michelangelo died; but there's a mystery here. As reported in a 2009 PBS presentation[57] "At dawn the following day agents of the Pope arrived at his workshop to search for anything of value that he may have left behind. They find almost nothing. Before he died, Michelangelo set fire to all the drawings and private papers in his possession. Soon after, his corpse disappears; carried off in secret to Florence. The powerful Church Michelangelo had served for half a century is denied the opportunity to honor him with a state funeral." Some letters that Michelangelo wrote to another person have now revealed that he strongly disagreed with the Church's position on "indulgences."[58] The Church promoted the idea that one person can contribute money to the Church in order to pave the way for a deceased relative to enter Heaven. He believed that divine grace could not be bought! This aligned Michelangelo with the Protestant's belief that "only by faith" can one attain the Kingdom. The above presentation goes on to say, "We know from his contemporaries that the artist owned a Bible. Since he didn't read Latin, his copy was likely the illegal Italian Version…" The year that is being spoken of is 1541. You see, the possession of any Bible was considered a crime against the Church unless one was a member of the clergy.[59] This was news to me. How was one to know what to believe if access to any Bible was a crime?

In the last fifty years we have observed the instability of many institutional foundations, including religious denominations. Hidden agendas are being exposed. A part of the cracking of various foundations has been the opening up of secret information. We are living in a time when many things are being revealed. In natural beliefs what has been pushed down and hidden will ultimately rise to the surface. However, this has also created a dilemma. How does one determine the accuracy and the authenticity of the huge volume of information that is available today? Facts are constantly being presented and challenged. Scientific knowledge changes constantly. It

---

[57] PBS presentation: *Michelangelo Revealed: Secrets of the Dead*, 2009.
[58] "An indulgence is the extra-sacramental remission of the temporal punishment due…to sin that has been forgiven, which remission is granted by the Church…" "…the guilt of which has been forgiven." "An indulgence offers the penitent sinner the means of discharging this debt during his life on earth." www.newadvent.org/cathen/07783a.htm (Catholic Encyclopedia)
[59] PBS presentation: *Michelangelo Revealed: Secrets of the Dead*, 2009.

sometimes takes hundreds of years to revise religious attitudes, tenets and teachings, especially within the Christian community, and open them to change. Christian dogma is very entrenched within many denominations. Even in light of new discoveries and revelations about the early years of Christianity, change comes slowly. Some have become confused and have left the faiths that they grew up in. In a recent article in The New York Times (April 27, 2009) we read:

Polls show that the ranks of atheists are growing. The American Religious Identification Survey, a major study released last month, found that those who claimed "no religion" were the only demographic group that grew in all 50 states in the last 18 years. Nationally, the "nones" in the population nearly doubled, to 15 percent in 2008 from 8 percent in 1990. Not all the "nones" are necessarily committed atheists or agnostics but they make up a pool of potential supporters.[60]

The results of an on-line survey conducted by *The Parade Magazine* were presented in a news piece entitled, "A Matter of Faith," by the CBS News Sunday Morning program in October of 2009. The following are some of the conclusions:

- Twenty-five percent of the respondents say that they are not religious.
- Nearly seven out of ten believe in God.
- More than three quarters of the respondents pray.
- Half rarely if ever attend religious services.
- Barely half practice the religion they grew up with.
- Of the respondents nearly six out of ten believe that all religions have validity.
- More than one out of four practice no religion at all
- Six out of ten respondents still say that religion is an important part of their lives.

As presented in "Mysteries of the Bible,"[61] six in ten Americans believe that Jesus Christ will return to Earth one day and four in ten believe that Jesus Christ will return in the twenty-first century.

---

[60] THE NEW YORK TIMES. Vol. CLVIII, No. 54, 658, Monday, April 27, 2009.
[61] *Mysteries of the Bible*, QD3498, distributed by Questar Entertainment, ISBN 1-59464-065-3.

Definitions of Some Terms

Simple clarification is needed to define what is meant by "doctrine" and "dogma." My understanding is that a *doctrine* is that which is taught; *dogma* is a chain of doctrines which have been promoted and accepted by a group as being the truth. Further, Laurence Gardner states that, "Dogma is not necessarily truth: it is simply a fervently promoted *interpretation* of truth based on *available* facts."[62] It's a matter of who interprets, how it is interpreted and what biases and agendas are present.

I have conducted thousands of hours of reading and research and many people have gifted me with books relevant to my studies. Information has literally dropped into my lap and personal stories have been shared with me purporting to represent "inside" information. After all of that, I now know that it is important to explore and to make available some of the missing pieces of the Christian puzzle.

Just for the enjoyment of it let's look at a more ancient frame of reference for the word *religion*. Dr. David Moore says that the word religion has come to mean "...an organized, dogmatic approach which has orthodox beliefs as its foundation."[63] Its origin is from "...the Latin words *ligare* and *re*. *Ligare* means 'to bind' and *re* means 'back.' Therefore re-ligion means to 'bind back' or, in other words, to *'return to God'*."[64] Therefore, any group that has as its mission to be on a path back *toward* the Divine is a religion.

Many forms of religion call for self-sacrifice, obedience and suffering. Attitudes of surrender are promoted as well as beliefs about being "pitiful and helpless" humans. In these philosophies we are the victims of life experiences or we bear an ever-present guilt about our unwise choices thanks to the concept of original sin. We are hopelessly lost until we find our way "home" and join a community of like-minded persons who can help us see the light. Then we earn an eternal abode far from Mother Earth with the Creator. This philosophy

---

[62] Gardner, Laurence. Op. cit., 6. (italics by Rainbow Eagle)
[63] Moore, Dr. L. David. *The Christian Conspiracy*, 118.
[64] Ibid.

appears to limit any relationship with the natural creation[65] and makes it difficult to truly honor ourselves outside these constrictions. Please know that I am not finding fault with these spiritual concepts. Each of us has the right to choose our own spiritual beliefs. I believe the original philosophies of most ancient beliefs were housed within a relationship with nature. Sufi scholar Seyyed Hossain Nasr relates that "Nature itself is considered a holy book, the 'Quran of creation,' which inspires the ideas and archetypes of all human writings."[66] Joseph Campbell, an outstanding scholar and teacher of ancient mythology, tells a humorous story: "I once heard a lecture by a wonderful old Zen philosopher, Dr. D. T. Suzuki. He stood up with his hands slowly rubbing his sides and said":

God against man. Man against God. Man against nature. Nature against man. Nature against God. God against nature--very funny religion![67]

Six Pathways of Study

There are at least six sources that I believe point toward the actual teachings of Jesus. I will give more attention to some of these than others. Since my understanding of Christianity has been growing for over fifty years, I know that there is always more to be revealed. I appreciate the contributions of those who have been trail-blazers for me. I had originally planned to include my research into the development of Christianity in my second book, *A Walk in the Woods*. However, the chapter on Christianity was so long and extensive that I eventually decided to take it out and present it in a separate book. I

---

[65] Douglas-Koltz writes: "The Greek focuses on the human-to-human relationship and on saving time, whereas the Aramaic stresses coming into rhythm or timing *with nature* as an expression of Unity." *The Hidden Gospel*, 132.

[66] Nasr, Seyyed Hossain. *Man and Nature: The Spiritual Crisis in Modern Man*, 95ff, quoted in *The Hidden Gospel*, 35.

[67] Campbell, Joseph. *The Power of Myth*, 56. Daisetz T. Suzuki had this to say about the Western way of contrasting nature and the spirit as a pair of opposites: "God's own likeness (Man), God's own creation (Nature) and God himself--all three are at war." Nature here is an enemy to man and impedes his reach to God. He goes on to say that, "Man cannot be outside of Nature. I am Nature and Nature is me." From Daisetz T. Suzuki, *The Role of Nature in Zen Buddhism, in Olga Frobe-kapteyn, (ed.), Mensch und Erde*. Eranos-Jahrbuch, Vol. XXII (1953), Zurich: Rhein-Verlag, (1954), 294-5.

also had a dream a month before publication that confirmed that this was the right decision. Because Christianity emerged from many traditions around the Mediterranean Sea, **we must first look at the traditions that existed not only before, but during and after the life of Jesus**. This research is most important if there is to be a full understanding of the ideologies that were in the minds and hearts of the people of the region at the time.

As we will see, many pagan beliefs were still prominently part of the culture during the time of Jesus. Researchers Picknett and Prince have written that King David himself had been a goddess worshipper, as had King Solomon.[68] Walker relates an earlier version of the creation of humans:

The Sumero-Bablonian Goddess Aruru the Great was the original Potter who created human beings out of clay…The Goddess was worshipped as a Potter in the Jewish temple, where she received "thirty pieces of silver" as the price of a sacrificial victim (Zechariah 11:13)…[69]

It's revealing to know that there were various Gnostic,[70] Roman, pagan and Goddess practices going on even after Jesus' ministry.

A second area of exploration is to look at research into how the New Testament (specifically the Jesus story) came into existence. Most Christians do not understand that the vast majority of biblical scholars agree that *none* of the gospel writers *were eye witnesses* or people who actually walked in the presence of the Master. It might be helpful to look at the way the New Testament was put together. Biblical scholar Robert W. Funk gives his opinion:

Whether we like it or not, there are presently no fragments of any of the books of the New Testament older that about 125 C.E., and no copies of any substantial portions of any Christian writings that can be dated to a time before 200 C.E. And these are copies of copies made long after the originals…all copies of the Bible

---

[68] Picknett, Lynn and Prince, Clive. *The Templar Revelation: Secret Guardians of the True Identity of Christ*, 296-297.
[69] Walker, Barbara. *The Women's Encyclopedia of Myths and Secrets*, 815.
[70] "Gnostic Christianity—early sect encouraged 'knowing' God through personal enlightenment rather than 'organized'/mandatory sacraments, rituals, and prayers." Margaret Starbird, *The Feminine Face of Christianity*, 122. "More troubling to those who claimed to be orthodox Christians, Gnostic writers tended to view the virgin birth, the Resurrection, and other elements of the Jesus story not as literal, historical events but as symbolic keys to a "higher" understanding." U. S. News & World Report, *The Gospel Truth*, Dec. 2006.

were made by hand prior to the invention of the printing press in 1454 or thereabouts and consequently contain mistakes and inaccuracies.[71]

In the early part of the fourth century, Roman Emperor Constantine commissioned the Council of Nicaea to decide what texts were to be included in the Christian Bible. It is written that Constantine said of the true nature of the assemblers of Christianity, "...*They were "maddened."*"[72] We will broaden this study later. The Roman Catholic Church makes this statement about the origins of the New Testament writings in the *Catholic Encyclopedia*: "the most distinguished body of academic opinion ever assembled."[73] It then admits that much of the deliberation at Nicaea is "strangely absent from the canons."[74] And about the gospels we read: "We must begin to realize that these (Gospel) accounts are *not* biographies of Jesus and still less scientific history."[75] The authors of *The Missing Jesus: Rabbinic Judaism and the New Testament* make this very important and bold statement:

One of the most persistent failures in the study of Jesus in the modern period has been that scholars have not taken account of how the Gospels came into being...the Gospels are neither chronicles of history nor inventions of faith, but interpretations of Jesus for distinct communities.[76]

The *Catholic Encyclopedia* further reveals that "Our documentary sources of knowledge about the origins of Christianity and its earliest development are chiefly the New Testament, the authenticity of which we must, to a great extent, take for granted." What is meant by "the Gospels are not biographies of Jesus" or "...the authenticity of the origins of Christianity must be taken for granted?" Wait, wait there's more. In the same resource we find the Church acknowledging that the gospels[77] "do not go back to the first century of the Christian era."[78]

---

[71] Funk, Robert. *Honest to Jesus*, 25.

[72] *Life of Constantine,* Attributed to Eusebius Pamphilious of Caesarea, c. 335, vol. iii, 171.

[73] *Catholic Encyclopedia*, Preface.

[74] Ibid., Farley ed., vol. iii, 160.

[75] *New Catholic Encyclopedia*, Vol. XII; 1967, 43.

[76] Chilton, Evans and Neusner. *The Missing Jesus: Rabbinic Judaism and the New Testament*, ix.

[77] In contrast today most Biblical scholars place the writing of the gospels with some variation as follows: **Paul's writings (48-62 AD), Mark (65-70 AD), Matthew (80-85 AD), Luke/Acts (85-92 AD), John (95-100 AD).**

The Church further states that "the earliest of the extant manuscripts [of the New Testament] *do not date back beyond the middle of the fourth century AD.*"[79]

Thirdly, it is essential to the recovery of Jesus' contribution to consult the "earliest" writings. Biblical scholar William Bramley claims that "Only three known apocryphal gospels have a reasonable chance of being written prior to the New Testament gospels, namely the *Gospel of Peter*, the *Gospel of Thomas*, and the *Gospel of Mary.*"[80] I can understand why, if some of these descriptions were real, modern church historians had reason to suppress the facts surrounding this momentous event in Christian history. Only in recent years have ancient texts been found and compared with the King James Version of the Christian Bible.[81] Meticulous analysis of the early writings of the followers of Jesus' ministry has revealed a multiplicity of pre-Christian beliefs that existed among a variety of communities after the life of Jesus. Each group held onto their particular point of view about Jesus and some were attacked by the Church. In many ways these early Christian communities are reflective of today. Each denomination held onto their own set beliefs and there is as much variety within Christianity today as there was in the centuries after Jesus' ministry.

A fourth path is to reference recent studies by biblical scholars. A large volume of new research on early Christianity has appeared in the past fifty years that gives us a different perspective on the teachings of Jesus. This study has been facilitated by what is known as the Jesus Seminars.[82] Some 200 biblical scholars began to present their research and opinions in 1988. I will bring their courageous study into consideration later in this book. You can also refer to "Appendix C" for more information on the Jesus Seminars. Many of the writers whose work I have drawn on in researching this book have made invaluable contributions to the understanding of Jesus'

---

[78] *Catholic Encyclopedia*, Farley ed., vol. vi, 137, 655-6.
[79] Ibid., 656-7.
[80] Bramley. op. cit., 33.
[81] Emry relates "…when the Bible became the first book printed on the newly invented printing press, the second book was about Joseph of Arimathea!" Sheldon Emry, *Paul and Joseph of Arimathea: Missionaries to the Gentiles*, 7.
[82] "The Jesus Seminar, [is] a scholarly group founded by Robert Funk for the purpose of examining the Jesus tradition." Marvin Meyer, *The Gospel of Thomas*, 15.

teachings. A bibliography has been provided that will serve to facilitate further study if you wish it.

A fifth pathway for searching out the actual teachings of Jesus is **the awakening and activating of our own intuition and power of choice**. This requires a substantial amount of spiritual openness and personal maturity. When there has been so much educational programming based upon outside authority and instruction by seemingly qualified dispensers of the truth, it is difficult to trust internal validation of what our *personal* truth is. It often takes a great deal of courage to look for spiritual truth outside of the belief systems that we have been taught.

The sixth area that must be explored is to **consider how the Aramaic, Hebrew and Greek languages differed** in their interpretation and understanding of the words and teachings of Jesus. He would have spoken in his native Aramaic[83] tongue. He also would have understood the ancient Hebrew scriptures and writings. When these languages were translated into Greek later, they sometimes took on a more mental emphasis than would have been the case in their original forms. So, we will take a close look at some of the ways in which this occurred over time within the Christian journey.

Old Medicine for New Times

You may be aware that I have had many opportunities to be among various Native peoples and in recent years I have been able to walk more fully in my Vision to bring to the public original Native teachings. Ancient Native American spirituality has seemed destined to come forward during the time in which we live. We all are part of this season in which the recovery of personal spirituality and the quest for ancient wisdom is increasingly informing our journeys. Many are no longer satisfied with fear-based, institutionalized forms of spirituality, especially those that distance themselves from nature. Many desire to experience more joy and appreciation in their everyday

---

[83] "…few scholars had examined the ancient literature of Judaism in Aramaic, the common language of the Jewish people in the first century that Jesus spoke." Chilton, Bruce., op. cit., xviii.

life, and many want to experience blessings and lessons without fear and guilt.

Listening to Native Elders in their homes and around their fires, I have often heard expressions like, "You know, it seems that good people cannot treat other good people with respect for their beliefs." Or, "Nature is our classroom for understanding about the Creator and life. Respect for all life forms is our way." My Native blood and my early experiences with Christianity taught me that all life experiences are meaningful and purposeful. Each journey has a way of helping us to appreciate the beauty that surrounds us. There is a lot to be understood about the concept of *heaven on earth* and taking a walk in the Creator's beautiful creation.

For Native peoples, much of their original spiritual foundation has been shattered and disregarded; stereotyped and made fun of. The spiritual teachings of our traditions have not been available to us and certainly not to non-Native people until recently. Those old time-tested belief systems are now making their way back for us to consider. Native peoples, if they wish, can seek their older ways. It is an age-old Native American belief that we always have the right to our own personal choice of beliefs.

There is a story from my past that I hesitate at times to tell, because I am very sensitive to how information and ideas are presented and received. I try to discern what the make-up of a particular audience or class is. Once I perceive a group to be open to exploring some of the Christian concepts such as guilt, sacrifice and being saved, then I feel it is possible to plant some seeds that might enhance their understanding of Christian history and their personal experience of Christianity in general.

The story is about my experiences with Native peoples and a particular white friend whom I grew up with. Both of us were raised within a particular denomination, attending various church camps and later advocating for greater respect and understanding within the church of the spiritual gifts that Native peoples had to offer. This non-Indian man was always a supporter of the Native culture, and like me, he experienced some unsympathetic opinions from church members about his sensitivity to Native ways.

I want to begin this story with a personal appreciation for this long-time friend, although we have lost touch over the years as I have pulled away from the church. After he completed his educational degree he and his family intentionally located near an Indian reservation. His vocation for his entire life has been as a mortician. He was also a lay minister at a local church. Having had many conversations with the nearby reservation Natives, I often heard of their great respect for this man. When a person is called upon to assist families with their loss (and that occurs quite often around various Indian Reservations these days), you can understand that a personal connection might develop with such a person. That was the case with my friend who I will call "Chuck."

Over the years, I have met other very wonderful, courageous people who have intentionally located themselves and their families just off the reservations. I have many memories of people who, like me, have had lengthy "family" relationships with Native peoples on and off of various reservations. They have a special gift; an enduring love and willingness to be in relationship with Native people, over a long period of time. Such non-Indian people have helped bring about a greater respect for white people, in most cases, among Natives. I have witnessed a patient and genuine attitude of acceptance that looks beyond the unfortunate events of American history and racial prejudice.

Chuck tells a story that needs to be told. He remembers a particular Native friend who had opened his life to Chuck early on. Chuck values his own particular religion, but is very respectful of Native beliefs and traditions too. Knowing that he had a good relationship with the Native man, Chuck opened a discussion of Christianity. His Native friend told a story related to him by his grandfather many years ago:

(as his grandfather would have spoken it) "I was invited once to a "white guy's" house, who was very excited to "share religion" with an Indian. We had become very good friends, and being invited to someone's home is a very big honor, so I went. You can imagine the white guy's excitement. Once I entered his home, I was immediately shown lots of Christian pictures. Every room displayed a certain picture that was the main idea of this religion. I was respectful of this. After the visit, some years later, my grandfather told me about his feelings. It had to do with a particular picture that seemed to be in every room of the white man's house. What was that picture?...a picture of a man called a "savior" who had been severely tortured and nailed to a cross[84] to die. I didn't understand how this could represent

---

[84] "...Jesus' followers did not paint a cross—much less a crucifix—on the walls of the catacombs in Rome..." Pagels, *Beyond Belief*, 25

a religion. In Native traditions we honor everyday life, not death. We respect acts of courage and honor, but we see them as part of life, and it is more important to live life every day."

Needless to say, what his Native friend shared was a surprise to Chuck. When Chuck shared this with me we were both speechless and contemplative. Chuck wanted to bring the beauty of his religion to his friends, but he needed to rethink his religion and be willing to understand more of the Native way of thinking. I have never known Chuck to push his religion upon Native people, and he continues to love and serve Native people today, in his own way; not to Christianize them, but to personally and respectfully "become related."

Personally, I have embraced the ancient Native ways as much as is possible these days. I want them to become more and more a part of my life. On the other hand, aspects of Christianity have given me a special relationship with the Master Jesus as a divine messenger. However, I also believe that there are many other special messengers who have contributed their wisdom to humanity.

What I call finding "the bigger picture of life" is the gathering together of ancient information that can be found within many philosophies, religions and in old written material. Searching out the roots of human spiritual understandings has the potential of adding color, depth and meaning to the collage of spirituality. Yet, it can also add mystery. In Native ways there was always room for mystery. Using the name *Great Mystery* in reference to the Creator, reflected the importance of having patience and trust in the unknown; allowing for lessons to be realized in their own good time; and having faith in the divine plan for each person's life and for our collective life journey.

As you think about the information and recent revelations presented in this book, bear in mind that one must have respect for the developmental stages of your own sacred growth. Seek the guidance of our Elders of today and of ages long past. In time, ancient wisdom will become clearer and you will be able to use it as building blocks that will strengthen your loving relationship with the Great Source.

Elihu, who headed a school of prophecy some two thousand years ago in Zoan (Egypt), said of the coming times, "This epoch will understand but little of the works of purity and love; yet not a single word, no significant thought and no deed will be lost, for all will be preserved in God's chronicle."[85] I am confident that what is needed to bring back hope and optimism will find its way back.

As a Native person, I am very aware of the impact that Christianity has had upon the culture and spirituality of Native Americans. I now see the need to present a study of Christianity and its early origins from a Native perspective. I speak only for myself and not for other Native Americans. There are many religious and spiritual perspectives among the people of the various Native nations, just as there are in the general population anywhere in America. Each person has the right to choose for themselves. In Chapter Three I will discuss both the similarities and the differences between Christianity and American Indian[86] philosophy, as I have personally experienced those differences. A more representative presentation of Native philosophy can be accessed in my two preceding books.

Constantine and Christianity

I have come to the conclusion that if there had not been a gathering up of the many splintered groups following Jesus and the varied writings about him, especially by Constantine in the fourth century, Jesus' teaching might well have been lost. If it were not for the aggressive nature of the Roman Catholic Church in perpetuating the form of Christianity instituted by Constantine, Jesus could have become a faint memory.

Christianity survived because of being connected to the fourth century Roman Empire. The church adopted many of the traditions of Rome. Its emperors were seen as divine and many of them were given additional designations, including the title "son of God."[87] Emperors were given status and position by their titles, their brave deeds and their

---

[85] Levi. *The Aquarian Gospel of Jesus Christ*, London, 1908.
[86] This term became useful in the early 1970's as a general designation of indigenous people in America. It was required that Native grant writers use the term to give a general designation of U. S. indigenous people. In the mid-1990 the term "American Indian" was connected to Government documents, etc. Tribal people use either one according to their own choice.
[87] "The Romans not only obeyed the emperor, they worshipped him as God's son, *Divi filius.*" Bruce Chilton, *Rabbi Jesus: An Intimate Biography*, 19. Chilton is a scholar of early Christianity and Judaism with a degree in New Testament from Cambridge University, formerly a professor at Yale University, and now a Professor of Religion at Bard College.

heroic stories. Christianity likewise, systematically lifted Jesus to a place of royalty, referring to him as a "king." Jesus was consequently elevated and revered. Later, stories about him needed to have divine components such as miracles. Those who were to be leaders in the Christian movement had to look royal and majestic, and dress accordingly. It was important to posture themselves in king-like images, seated in royal chairs that were elevated and positioned in front of the people.

Before this time, most pre-Constantine Christian services were conducted "in the round" with officials in the center and on the same level as worshipers. Let's remember that for its continued survival it was necessary to expect obedience and loyalty to the Church, just as was true in the Roman government. For both the Roman Empire and the Church, it was imperative to claim that its' existence was somehow divinely blessed, carrying the full authority of God! This combination of being the *right* institution for the people and having the divine blessing of God was a successful way to marry religion with government.

I have always felt that some of the real teachings of Jesus have been pushed aside, sifted and selected to reinforce particular belief systems. I am suggesting that there has been a substantial departure from the unique ministry and teachings of Jesus. What has been brought forward by some was designed to support the establishment of religious empires and, sad to say, to facilitate the ambitions of men in general.

I feel that more is yet to be revealed and the complete story is somewhere in the future. In this book I am attempting to recover some of the pieces that can be fitted together to give us a more complete picture of whom Jesus was and what his teachings were about. In Chapter Eight I will offer my conclusions regarding what I think would be some of the teachings of the first century. If we look at any of the supposed sayings of Jesus we should know that they would have been spoken in Aramaic; because until the third century that was the common language of the people of Palestine and most of the Middle East.[88] It is my conclusion, and that of many others, that looking at Jesus' words in Aramaic reveals the real spirituality of his teachings.

---

[88] Douglas-Klotz, Neil. *The Hidden Gospel: Decoding the Spiritual Message of the Aramaic Jesus*, 5.

As we bring the beauty and wonder of the Aramaic language near to us, it is important to know that each Aramaic word has many facets or meanings. There are many possible ideas that can touch the minds and hearts of the listener. This language has an inherent closeness to nature and is loaded with images of animals, fertility, gardening and harvesting, and of harmony. Images that reflect awe of the cosmos are also a special gift of this language.[89]

For example, Douglas-Klotz, a well respected scholar of the Aramaic language gives this example of one interpretation of "Thy Kingdom Come": *"Come into the bedroom of our hearts, prepare us for the marriage of power and beauty."*[90] Also for "Give us this day our daily Bread": *"Animate the earth within us: we then feel the Wisdom underneath supporting all."*[91] This reminds me what Mother Earth means to me.

It is my prayer[92] that the wisdom that Yeshua planted in hearts and minds long ago will once again become a choice for us again. Yeshua's words resided in the hearts of his many followers. His teachings were very welcome in the midst of the controlling agendas and hurtful systems of his time. His insights led people toward hope and optimism. I want that for others and for myself today.

Ancient Information is Available

Among the sources of ancient information that I offer for consideration, some may certainly be perceived as myth and conjecture, but I hope will not be discarded all together. There is truth in all myths. That is why they survive and are retold generation to generation. So, look beyond the obvious. As I gently guide you toward some topics and information that might create tension or seem challenging, remember that you always have the option of relying on your own inner wise person as to what is meaningful for you.

---

[89] Ibid., 50. One possible Aramaic interpretation for "Blessed are the meek: for they shall inherit the earth" is *"Ripe are those who soften what is rigid, inside and out; they shall be open to receive strength and power—their natural inheritance—from nature."*

[90] Douglas-Klotz, Neil. *Prayers of the Cosmos,* 19.

[91] Ibid., 26.

[92] "Amen" in the Aramaic language means may this be "the ground from which a particular future growth will occur." Ibid., 39.

Often there is a sense of loss surrounding changes in our world view or our preconceived ideas. I like to refer to the pain of that loss as "birthing pains." There is light waiting at the end of many of the tunnels we will be exploring on our journey. I beckon you to travel toward new insights and ways of viewing history and your spiritual beliefs. I also encourage the strengthening of personal reflection, thinking for yourself, and honoring your intuition so that each one of you can deal with being exposed to new information, which I call "the rest of the story," in a balanced way.

Not having been a person who is particularly media savvy, I have been very amazed at how many sources of information are available today for anyone who wants to delve deeper into the topics I explore in this book. I found a lot of interesting information in the *Catholic Encyclopedia*, the King James Version of the Bible, and on some of the major television networks (including Discovery Channel, The History Channel, CNN, and The Biography Channel); not to mention Google and the world wide web! Some years ago Mary and I were gifted with a "TiVo" (digital recorder). This has made it possible to collect a significant cache of pertinent information and to develop a sort of contemporary library for myself. To keep my research in some kind of balance, I also considered various Christian radio and television presentations; not to find fault or to establish the correctness of my own spiritual philosophy, but to be more aware of, and to more fully understand, the spiritual choices that are available to people today. In "Appendix D" I have included many additional media and print sources for your consideration.

I need to emphasize that in my gathering of information, I do not include what could be called "channeled information." It is not that I don't believe it has value, but my vision is to gather the ancient studies and documents that are surfacing all over the planet. New discoveries and research are happening every day. Biblical scholarship is reflecting more diversity lately and there seems to be considerable courage to search for more of the *real and actual* facts concerning ancient times and even more recent history.

This explosion of information and attention on these topics intrigues me. I believe that I have recovered many meaningful pieces with which to reconstruct a more realistic picture of Christianity. The challenge before us is to put the pieces together in order to understand it. Can it be that our society is more open these days to a bigger variety of information than what was acceptable as I was growing up? I think so.

We live in a time when ancient documents and teachings are available to us. There aren't many topics that can't be "Googled!" With this renewed interest in learning more about the origins of Christian traditions, a new generation of archaeologists has surfaced. They are moving away from the beginning premise that the Bible is the irrefutable truth[93] and are forming hypotheses based upon *actual findings;* or more accurately, what has **not** been found. They are abandoning the old methods and are calling into question some of the findings in which half the world's population, in one way or another, believes.[94] Until we have the courage to ask questions about our spiritual roots, whether they are from Christian, Native American or some other tradition, we will remain separated from our true spiritual identity. As Christians we must ask, "Who was Jesus? What were his teachings?"

I believe we have a wonderful future as spiritual people ahead of us that will bring us more insights than we could ever have dreamed of. Edmond Bordeaux Szekely, who abandoned the priesthood and his faith as a result of documents he uncovered in the Vatican archives, reports that the secret Vatican Library consists of over twenty miles of bookshelves *"...of scrolls, parchments, paper manuscripts and codices...."* Szekely also says there may be as many as 10,000 unexamined documents in that library.[95]

Out of the blue in 1971, a man stepped in front of me and gave me a small book called *The Archko Volume: Or the Archeological Writings of the Sanhedrim & Talmuds of the Jews.* He said, "You will need this some day!" This book contains a number of letters allegedly written by eyewitnesses to Christ and was first published in 1887 by William D. Mahan of Missouri. Mahan was a Presbyterian minister who said that he came into possession of these documents when he

---

[93] "The Bible has noble poetry in it; and some clever fables; and some blood-drenched history; and a wealth of obscenity; and upwards of a thousand lies." (Mark Twain, *Letters from the Earth*) quoted in *Don't Know Much About the Bible*, Kenneth C. Davis, 1.
[94] Lazare, Daniel. *False Testament*, Harper's Magazine/March 2002.
[95] Reported by Tony Bushby. *The Crucifixion of Truth*, (Joshua Books, 2006), 26-27.

traveled to the libraries of the Vatican and St. Sophia Mosque in Constantinople.[96] The title page reads:

These are the official documents made in the courts during the days of Jesus Christ. Translated by Drs. McIntosh and Twyman of the Antiquarian Lodge, Genoa, Italy, from manuscripts in Constantinople and the records of the senatorial docket taken from the Vatican at Rome.[97]

Here is the brief story. In 1856, H. C. Whydaman was snowbound and stopped at the home of W. D. Mahan in De Witt, Missouri. Whydaman related that during a five year stay in Rome he had spent quite a bit of time in the Vatican and had seen and read records there of the Jewish Sanhedrin (Jewish Council of Elders). Among the records was an account of Pontius Pilate's report to Caesar that told of "the apprehension, trial, and crucifixion of Jesus of Nazareth." The document was part of the library of the Vatican containing 560,000 volumes. Mahan asked Whydaman to see if he could get copies of the documents. This was arranged and he paid a monk in Rome named Father Freelinhusen, "chief guardian of the Vatican," to write out an original Latin copy of some of the old dirty parchments. The Latin accounts were then translated into English. These accounts are now available in the *Archko Volume.* We will be referring to this material later.[98] In a translation by Drs. McIntosh and Twyman of the Antiquarian Lodge, Genoa, Italy, Mahan says:

Knowing there is not such a piece in history to be found in all the world, and being deeply interested myself, as also hundreds of others to whom I have read it, I have concluded to give it to the public…I found that there were many of such records still preserved at the Vatican in Rome and at Constantinople, that had been carried there by the Emperor of Rome about the middle of the third century.[99]

In the book, *Excavating Jesus: Beneath the Stones, Behind the Texts* we find a *Teaching (Didache)*[100] written in the second half of the first century and discovered in 1873. It's part of an eleventh century

---

[96] Bramley. op. cit., 12-13.
[97] Mahan, W. D. Records of the Jerusalem Sanhedrin, by Eliezer Hyran, B. 24. Taken in Constantinople, October 16, 1883. *The Archko Volume: or the Archeological Writings of the Sanhedrin & Talmuds of the Jews*, 9.
[98] Ibid., 9-14.
[99] Ibid., 13.
[100] Probably written (assembled by an unknown author) in the early second century in Egypt or Syria.

codex in a Greek monastery in Constantinople. There is "a small collection of Jesus' most radical sayings that appears at the very start of the document."[101]

Most researchers of the life of Jesus and the early writings about him rely heavily on a famous work by Flavious Josephus (A.D. 37-c. A.D. 100), entitled *The Antiquities of Jews*. It was published in A.D. 93 or A.D. 94 Since Josephus was born seven years after Jesus' death, he would have had to rely on second-hand accounts concerning information about Jesus.[102] He writes:

Now, there was about this time, Jesus, a wise man, if it be lawful to call him a man, for he was a doer of wonderful works—a teacher of such men as receive the truth with pleasure. He drew over to him both many of the Jews, and many of the Gentiles. He was [the] Christ; and when Pilate…condemned him to the cross…as the divine prophets had foretold…and the tribe of Christians, so named from him, are not extinct at this day.[103]

Josephus' original manuscript no longer exists, and all known versions are later translations. He refers to John the Baptist and "…when describing the stoning of a man called James, he mentions Jesus 'whom the people call Christ' as his brother."[104] Some researchers also do not consider Josephus as a credible source. Casting a shadow on this writing, John E. Remsberg points out that no Christian apologist[105] referred to the Josephus passage until the fourth century:

The early Christian fathers were not acquainted with it. Justin Martyr, Tertullian, Clement of Alexandria, and Origen all would have quoted this passage had it existed in their time. The failure of even one of these fathers to notice it would be sufficient to throw doubt upon its genuineness; the failure of all of them to notice it proves conclusively that it is spurious, that it was not in existence during the second and third centuries.[106]

---

[101] Crossan & Reed. *Excavating Jesus: Beneath the Stones, Behind the Texts*, 9.
[102] Bramley. op. cit., 42.
[103] Josephus, Flavius (trans. William Winston), *The Complete Works of Josephius* (1981, Grand Rapids), Kregel Publications, 379.
[104] Gruber, Elmer R. and Kersten, Holger. *The Original Jesus*, 5.
[105] "The term *Apologist* applies especially to early Christian writers (*c* 120-220) who took on the task of recommending their faith to outsiders." Cross, F. L., ed. The Oxford dictionary of the Christian church. New York: Oxford University Press. 2005.
[106] Remsberg, John E., *The Christ: A Critical Review and Analysis of the Evidence of His Existence*, 19.

However, there are other sources of early writings about Jesus. One of them is possibly speaking of Jesus, using a title that was believed to be the result of misspelling the word "Christ." A Roman writer named Suetonius (c. A.D. 69-130's) wrote a history c.A.D. 120 entitled *Lives of the Caesars*. In Book Five of *Lives*, Suetonius tells what Roman emperor Claudius did to the Jews: "He expelled the Jews from Rome [ca. A.D. 49], because of the rioting in which they were constantly engaging at the instigation of Chrestus."[107]

The translation of old Sumerian clay tablets by Zachariah Sitchen is also very thought provoking. He is one of a small number of people who have done such translations. These very ancient fired clay tablets easily date back some 7,000 years, before any of the Jewish writings or the Bible.

New evidence includes the discovery of the Dead Sea Scrolls[108] (which many believe were written by the Essenes), fourth century Gnostic gospels, excavations of the Temple of Jerusalem, and a number of Galilean settlements, including Nazareth and Capernaum. Starbird explains that The Qumran community[109] that authored many of the Dead Sea Scrolls, "...had long characterized the Temple cult and its priests as wicked and false to the teachings of the Torah[110] and the prophets. They had said the Temple itself was unclean, its worship defiled by association with pagans... a community that was radically anti-Roman, anti-establishment, apocalyptic, and messianist, expectant of the restoration of the Davidic line to the throne of Israel and they believed themselves to be the pure remnant of Israel..."[111] As we have seen, the ancient roots of Christianity are surfacing from formerly hidden places.[112]

---

[107] Harris, Murray J., *Three Crucial Questions About Jesus*, 22. Note: "The Sueonius passage is actually a problem to Christians and skeptics alike. It implies that Jesus was alive almost fifteen years after his crucifixion, and he went to Rome where he did some serious rabble-rousing." Bramley, op. cit., 44.
[108] The oldest known version of the Hebrew Bible was written on goat skins.
[109] This community was less than twenty miles from Jerusalem.
[110] According to the rabbis I have consulted, the Torah is considered feminine and Hebrew refers to it using the feminine gender.
[111] Starbird. *The Woman With the Alabaster Jar*, 56.
[112] Gardner writes that "the Templars...found [in Jerusalem]a wealth of ancient manuscripts in Hebrew and Syraic...that had not been edited by any ecclesiastical authority." *Bloodline of the Holy Grail*, 219.

The Nag Hammadi records[113] also have biblical scholars reexamining Christian theology. In December of 1945, just outside the village of Nag Hammadi in Egypt, two Egyptian brothers were digging for fertilizer and found several papyri in an ancient clay jar in a cave.[114] It has been spoken of as one of the greatest discoveries of Christian history. Probably translated from Greek, and now only written in the Coptic[115] language, most of the manuscripts are locked away in the Coptic museum in Cairo, Egypt.[116] They revealed a version of the Jesus' story that is attributed to the mid-first century; only some twenty years after the ministry of Jesus. Many biblical scholars, and I too, believe they revealed the core elements of Jesus' story.

The *Gospel of Thomas* is said, "to have been recorded by Judas Thomas the Twin."[117] The first line of the *Gospel of Thomas*[118] reads, "These are the secret sayings which the living Jesus spoke." Presented in the video *The Hidden Story of Jesus*: "Unlike the Gospels that made it into the New Testament there were no stories about Jesus' birth, life or death, *just his teachings!*...no mention of the virgin birth, no mention of Jesus as the Son of God, and no mention of the resurrection."[119] Just to emphasize the importance of this "heretical writing," as the Church tagged it, religious historian Elaine Pagels offers this summary of the *Gospel of Thomas*:

...those who later enshrined the Gospel of John within the New Testament and denounced Thomas's gospel as "heresy" decisively shaped—and inevitably limited—what would become Western Christianity.[120]

---

[113] Found in Upper Egypt in December 1945, written by the Gnostics. As Gregg Braden writes: "...Books such as the Gospel of Mary, the Apocalypses of Paul, James, and Adam, and the Book of Mechizedek survive today as a testament in the Gnostic wisdom of preserving rare teachings for future generations." *The Isaiah Effect: Decoding the Lost Science of Prayer and Prophecy*, 46.
[114] http://en.wikipedia.org/wiki/Nag_Hammadi_library
[115] "...the late form of the Egyptian language in use from the Roman period on." Marvin Meyer, *The Gospel of Thomas*, 9.
[116] Ibid.
[117] Ibid., 5.
[118] "The *Gospel of Thomas*, which most scholars now believe was also originally collected and composed by Eastern Jewish Christians in Syria in the first century." Neil Douglas-Klotz, *The Hidden Gospel*, 6.
[119] *The Hidden Story of Jesus*, Juniper Productions, YouTube, Executive Producer: Samir Shah.
[120] Pagels, Elaine. *Beyond Belief*, 29.

We can also look at the so called "Apocrypha" for insight into what early writers thought. The Apocrypha consists of fifteen Jewish books, or parts of books, written between 200 B.C. and A.D. 100. Some Hebrew leaders did not feel they should be in the cannons. They did accept the truths in these books and most of the writings are part of the Greek Bible (Septuagint) and the Latin (Vulgate) Bible.[121] Apocrypha originally meant *one too sacred and secret to be in everyone's hands.* It is my understanding that it is very difficult to find a complete collection of The Apocrypha.

We will be examining what is spoken of as the oldest Bible[122] in the world—The Sinaiticus (Sinai) Bible. Can you imagine, it was discovered in a furnace room at St. Catherine's monastery in 1859 at Mt. Sinai? It was written in Greek on donkey skins and dates to around the year 380. It includes both the Old and New Testaments!

Early Versions of the Bible

How did the Hebrew Bible[123] get translated into Greek? Remember Jewish tradition teaches that Moses[124] wrote the Bible from divine dictation. All copies are supposed to be handwritten, exact copies of the way that Moses wrote them! The original Hebrew Bible was a long narrative without the chapters we are familiar with today. During the translation to Greek, it was organized into sections in order to make it more like other literary works at that time. Because of this,

---

[121] Rovin, Jeff. Op. cit., 47-48.
[122] "There are complete Bibles in more than 40 European languages, 125 Asian and Pacific Island languages, and…more than 100 African languages." "The first Native-American translation, completed in 1663, was made into the language of the Massachusetts tribe, which the Puritan colonist then promptly wiped out." In English, there are more than 3,000 versions of the entire Bible or portions of the Bible." Davis, Kenneth, *Don't Know Much About the Bible*, xiv-xv.
[123] "…the original Hebrew Bible contains no chapter demarcations. To this day, it is just one long, continuous narrative…" Sheinkin, *Path of the Kabbalah*, 23.
[124] "…The Biblical name Moses is not from the Hebrew 'Moshe,' meaning '*coming out of the water*'(which would support the baby in the reed basket story) but is rather from the ancient Egyptian, meaning roughly '*born of*'…the baby in the reed basket,[is] borrowed from the Persian King, Sargon the Great…" Vayro, *Tears in Heaven*, 221. Another resource: "Like Moses, Krishna was placed by his mother in a reed boat and set adrift in a river to be discovered by another woman." Acharya S, *The Christ Conspiracy: The Greatest Story Ever Sold*, 241.

and the fact that it was later translated into English, it reads differently than the Jewish sages would have intended. "To a Kabbalist, such seemingly minor deviations from the text become very significant."[125]

In Judaism there are really two Bibles: the written "Law"[126] and the oral "Law." Some of the knowledge was taught to everyone and some was taught to some selected individuals. In our journey to sift out the first century teachings of Jesus, we need to have some knowledge about the Aramaic and Hebrew languages. Ancient biblical Hebrew and Aramaic are very similar. They have the same alphabet and the same number of letters. The Aramaic language has many meanings for each word. For example, *"ruha..."* when translated into the English "Holy Spirit" could mean all of the following: breath, wind, air, or atmosphere. The word *Paraclete* means Holy Ghost. It comes from the Greek word *Parakletos* which means "the Comforter" or the "one called to help" from *para* meaning "to the side of" and *kalein* meaning "to call."[127] How distant this is from the concept of an ever-present holy wind or breath! There is no separate word for body-soul-spirit-emotions—each is a part of the other. Stephanie gives this confirmation: "In Hebrew, the word is 'ru-ach,' and in modern Hebrew it still has all of these meanings."

Jewish scholar, Bruce Chilton, a member for over twenty-five years of a project to produce a *Comprehensive Aramaic Lexicon* has helped to analyze Aramaic texts. He states that "Aramaic is likely to cease to be spoken soon…" and that:

…Aramaic is a Semitic tongue, one of the world's oldest continuously spoken languages. Once as widespread in the Near East as Arabic[128] is today, it is now nearly extinct, except as kept alive by a few native speakers in Iran, Iraq, Syria, Turkey, and Azerbaijan.[129]

---

[125] Sheinkin. Op. cit., 23.
[126] Reformed Jew, Rabbi Samuel Weinstein, of *Temple Congregation Shomer Emunim* in Sylvania, Ohio informed me that Jews prefer to use the word Law in place of Bible. He also indicates that today there is more of a sense of openness regarding the teachings "…To be willing to address the changing and social environment of today regarding the teaching of Judaism, in general."
[127] Jewishencyclopedia.com-PARACLETE
[128] "The Quran was originally written in Arabic, and Muslims believe it can only properly be understood in Arabic." Mark A. Gabriel, *Islam and the Jews*, ix.
[129] Chilton, Bruce. *Rabbi Jesus: An Intimate Biography*, 3-4.

Mr. Chilton explains that even though not many could read Hebrew, there existed a kind of verbatim translation of the Hebrew text called a *targum* (Aramaic for "translation"): "...whole paragraphs were added and long sections loosely paraphrased by the *meturgeman*, a translator who handed on the local tradition of rendering scripture."[130] The *Dictionary of the Jewish Religion* gives this explanation of "targum":

Aramaic translation of the Bible. It was ordered by Ezra the Scribe because the everyday language of the Jews was Aramaic. The best-known translation into Aramaic was that of Onkelos, said to have been a proselyte, which is still found in many Bibles.

    Sheinkin in *Path of the Kabbalah* explains how the Hebrew Bible got translated into Greek. According to Jewish tradition, at one time an emperor wanted the Jewish scholars to translate the Hebrew Bible into Greek. This created a sticky situation for the scholars because they did not want to give him what they believed was a "*handbook to the universe!*" However, if they refused, they would likely be killed. They solved this dilemma by writing every word for "God" that appeared in the text, in Gold ink instead of black like the rest of the text. In this way, "...such a Bible would be spiritually voided and no longer powerful..." because it was an alteration of the original version given to Moses that was all in black letters![131]

    My Jewish friend Stephanie offers this reflection:

This reminds me of the Jewish custom of "building fences around the law." There is this sense in Judaism that the letter of the law is very important and must be strictly upheld – the letter of the law often over the spirit of the law. For example, it is forbidden to write on the Sabbath. So, observant Jews will actually put all of their pens and pencils in a locked drawer for that day, so that they are not tempted or do not forget and start writing by accident

    Jews do not play musical instruments on the Sabbath, not because it is in itself forbidden, but because, if it breaks, we will be tempted to fix it, and that will probably require actions that are forbidden (like tying knots).

    This translation of the Torah was accurate and complete, but because the name of G-d was written in gold ink, it was not holy and basically didn't count. (Side note: writing down the name of G-d is a bad idea, because if you ever want to get rid of the piece of paper or whatever, it has to be buried with ceremony in a special part of a Jewish cemetery. Even though the English word 'God' is not the

---

[130] Ibid., 4.
[131] Sheinkin. Op. cit., 19.

true name of the Deity and therefore does not have to be disposed of this way, modern Jews will often honor the Name by writing the word as 'G-d' instead.)

In Jewish tradition the *Septuagint* is the oldest existing translation of the Bible. The *Dictionary of the Jewish Religion* gives this important information:

> *...[the Septuagint is]believed to have been done in the 3rd century B.C.E. by some 70 scholars who translated the Hebrew into Greek in Alexandria...a few scholars believe it hastened the disappearance of Hebrew-speaking Jews in the then flourishing Jewish community of Alexandria.*[132]

Even the English translations that exist today are from the Septuagint, not from the Hebrew Bible. This concerns me, because I have to wonder how much of the original meaning has been compromised or altered; perhaps even added to.

In 1897, an ancient find known as the Oxyrhynchus Papyri surfaced revealing a range of writings about Jesus that had been excluded from the Church's canon. A great deal of excitement was experienced by scholars due to the fact that these papyri scrolls date to around A.D. 200.[133] After careful study it was determined that a lot of these writings were also from the *Gospel of Thomas*. One of the central themes was that "the true kingdom was within the believer, rather than a supernatural or apocalyptic state which was yet to come."[134] This concept would not fit the Church's dogma.

These new sayings (the Oxyrhynchus), led to the discovery of what some feel would be the earliest sayings of Jesus. Biblical scholars conclude that the *Gospel of Q* (rather, the early sayings of Jesus), was present at the time when the gospels of Matthew and Luke were written. It is believed by some that this book of sayings was influenced the writers of these gospels. Since there is so much similar content in the two gospels, it is assumed that there must have been a previous writing that they drew from. Jenkins states: "A significant overlap between the Oxyrhynchus Sayings and Q indicated a very early dating for the sayings, perhaps making them actually older than the canonical gospels."[135]

---

[132] *Dictionary of the Jewish Religion*, Entry "Septuagint," 145.
[133] Jenkins, Philip. *Hidden Gospels*, 32-33.
[134] Ibid.
[135] Ibid.

Burton Mack, in the book *The Lost Gospel: The Book of Q & Christian Origins*, suggests that the Book of Q was, for the followers of Jesus, a handbook for living in the present moment during a very confusing time for them. The people of the first century saw him as a teacher. They were not Christians. They were followers of his teachings. His death was not viewed as a "divine, tragic, or saving event" and the later idea that he was raised from the dead to rule the world at the side of God was unknown to them.[136]

If the Q information is closer to the real facts, the more accurate teachings, how does that affect our understanding of the teachings we have been aware of in our lifetimes? Are we who have a real appreciation for Jesus and his teachings ready to hear these sayings? What does the *Gospel of Q*[137] reveal? In addition to not containing any birth narrative and seeing Jesus as a teacher of wisdom, without a list of "don'ts," let's look at the following, also from Burton Mack:

In the Q information there is no hint of a select group of disciples, no program to reform the religion or politics of Judaism, no dramatic encounter with the authorities in Jerusalem, no martyrdom for the cause, much less a martyrdom with saving significance for the ills of the world, and no mention of a first church in Jerusalem. The people of Q simply did not understand their purpose to be a mission to the Jews, or to gentiles for that matter. They were not out to transform the world or start a new religion.[138] *...there [was] no reference to the death and resurrection of Jesus, no mention of Jesus as the Christ, and no instruction to Peter and the other disciples about continuing Jesus' mission and baptizing converts into the church...*[139]

We will be revisiting some of these topics in more detail later.

A First Look at the Study of the Hebrew, Aramaic, and Greek Languages

"I believe the time has come once again to introduce this world to the Hebrew concepts of biblical thinking, to lead the religious establishment toward looking at its Lord, its life, its faith with new eyes—Hebrew eyes. The Hebrew were life-centered,

---

[136] Mack, Burton. *The Lost Gospel: The Book of Q & Christian Origins*, 1-5.
[137] The *Gospel of Q* is not a narrative gospel; it is a series of sayings attributed to Jesus without narrative. Marvin Meyer, *The Secret Teachings of Jesus*, xviii.
[138] Mack. Op. cit.
[139] Ibid., 42.

not life-denying, people...Their passion was for life. Their call was not out of life, but into life." (Bishop Spong)[140]

As should be obvious to you by now, I have a passionate yearning to seek out and study ancient information. Those who have been in my classes know that I enjoy researching the ancient texts of many spiritual traditions, from which modern understandings have come. In this section I will be introducing a study of some of the prominent words that are commonly used in discussions of Christian doctrine, and we will explore their Hebrew and Aramaic origins. I will be expanding this study in the later chapters of this book.

For now, let's look at the word *heretic*. For some 1,500 years this word has been applied to people who did not comply with or agree to the accepted teachings and dogma of the Roman Catholic Church. A heretic often refers to someone who is defiant, disobedient, or a rebel; maybe disloyal to the accepted religious order. The first written language of the New Testament was Greek. To my amazement, I find that *heresy* is derived from the Greek word *hairesis* that really means choice![141] This applies to those people who valued their right to choose their own way of believing (or thinking). How did making a choice lead one to become an object of persecution? A papal bull[142] which instituted the Inquisition[143] was put in place in 1252 by the Roman Catholic Church. This led to the use of torture in order to get a confession of heresy.

In contrast to the Christian doctrine, we find that the word "confession" in Hebrew is *Vidui*. In Jewish thought, confession is made directly to God, either privately or as part of Yom Kippur (the most solemn day of the Jewish religious year).[144] This would come very close to the Native American idea that one's spirituality and

---

[140] Spong. *This Hebrew Lord: A Bishop's Search for the Authentic Jesus*, 55.
[141] Evrett, Ferguson, Michael P. McHugh, & Fredrick W. Norris. *Encyclopedia of Early Christianity* (New York & London: Garland Publishing, 1990), 420.
[142] The powers of the Pope's (Pope Innocent IV) inquisitors were increased in 1252 A. D. New Dawn Magazine. No 71, March 2002, 206.
[143] A devout Catholic is quoted as saying, "Jesus himself would have suffered and died at the hands of the pope's inquisitors, for he talked with heretics and sinners and he dined with publicans and prostitutes." De Rosa, *Vicars of Christ, The Dark Side of the Papacy*, 180.
[144] *Dictionary of the Jewish Religion*.

relationship with the Great Creator is a personal decision. Stephanie gives a nice explanation of Yom Kippur and confession:

Jews do "confession" once a year, in a big way, on Yom Kippur. The idea goes like this: G-d sits in judgment upon all people at the new year, Rosh HaShanah. He has before him the Book of Life, in which all people will be inscribed for a good life or a bad life for the year to come. On Rosh HaShanah, He reviews your behavior for the previous year, and inscribes you for good or bad. You then have ten days to change his mind.

The liturgy says, "On Rosh HaShanah it is written, and on Yom Kippur it is sealed: who shall live and who shall die, who in the fullness of years and who before, who by fire and who by flood, who by sword and who by stoning, etc…" At the end of that passage, it says, "But repentance, charity, and acts of kindness can remove the severity of the decree."

In the Ten Days of Awe, the time between Rosh HaShanah and Yom Kippur, we go to everyone we have wronged over the past year and apologize, and we make our apologies to G-d, we perform t'shuvah. On Yom Kippur, we fast, we pray all day, we wear white to symbolize that we are now as pure as the angels, having been absolved of our sins from the past year. This is the nearest thing to confession that we have in Judaism.

It does not go through a priest. The cantor, the person who leads the prayer chants for the congregation, does have a special prayer in the High Holiday services (Rosh HaShanah and Yom Kippur) in which s/he asks G-d to accept his/her prayers on behalf of the whole community even though s/he is unworthy…that's the nearest thing to confession via a priest.[145]

Due to the influence of Christian denominations upon Native people, some Native Americans have chosen to adopt the idea that there is a need for an intermediary in order to connect with the Creator. This philosophy is not the original belief of Native people. Another similarity between the original Jewish and Native teachings is that all people are loved by the Creator and there are no "chosen" people. The *Dictionary of the Jewish Religion* relates, "Although the Bible teachings are meant to transform the Jewish people into a holy nation, God is the Lord of all peoples, not of the Jews alone."[146] Rabbi Samuel Weinstein explained to me, "Traditional Jews would still hold to the concept of 'being chosen' by God. More liberal Jews would say that we are chosen in the sense that we choose to follow God's laws, etc. Judaism holds that all people because of 'human free will' have the choice to follow God's teachings in their lives."[147]

---

[145] Stephanie M.
[146] *Dictionary of the Jewish Religion*, 80.
[147] Reformed Jew Rabbi Samuel Weinstein, op. cit.

Another interesting comparison can be made between the earlier meaning of sin and the current understanding of it. In Christian theology, the concept of sin represents an action of disobedience to God's laws. One must then repent, confess, and seek forgiveness from God so that the sin will not stand in the way of getting to Heaven. According to this dogma, one's sinful actions are still recorded in the book of life. The Greek word for sin is *hamartia*. We know that Jesus' words were first written in the Greek language. What was the original Greek meaning of *hamartia*? In both Hebrew and Greek "to sin" means "to miss the mark" or "missing the mark"[148] which is an archery term referring to missing the target. As Bruce Chilton writes in his book, *Rabbi Jesus: An Intimate Biography*, "A rabbi's teaching showed how one could go right again, and only implied where one had gone wrong."[149] There appears to be less emphasis on being remorseful and more focus on adjusting one's aim.
Here's Stephanie's contribution:

The concept of sin in Judaism is very different from in Christianity. The word for sin means "missing the mark." It is like an archer who doesn't hit the target – a mistake, not a condemnation. There is a three-step process for clearing such a mistake from your record: you apologize to G-d, you apologize to the person you wronged, and you pass up an opportunity to do the same thing again. This is called t'shuvah, meaning repentance. It is as if each person has a plaster-board, and when you sin, a pin is pushed into your board. Apologizing to G-d removes the pin, apologizing to the person fills the hole, and passing up a future opportunity paints over it so it is entirely gone. The only unforgivable sins are the ones where you cannot perform full t'shuvah, like if the person is dead.[150]

Following this theme, Jesus' teachings encouraged changing ones behavior to attain a more desired outcome. The Jewish tradition teaches that "most sins are committed because of human weakness or lack of knowledge, not because of inherent wickedness."[151] This again reflects the Native idea that there are no mistakes, just opportunities to learn.

---

[148] "Sin in Jewish liturgy is fundamentally different from the popular (Christian-based) conception: it is not that human beings are flawed or essentially evil; rather, the Hebrew word for sin, *chyet*, means "missing the mark." Dr. Michael Lerner, *Jewish Renewal: A Path to Healing and Transformation*, 370.
[149] Chilton, Bruce. op. cit., 48.
[150] Stephanie M.
[151] *Dictionary of the Jewish Religion*.

In 1896 an ancient manuscript was found in Egypt known as *The Gospel of Mary Magdalene*.[152] Within that document is the following quote:

Peter said to him: "Since you have become the interpreter of the elements and the events of the world, tell us: What is the sin of the world?" The Teacher answered: "There is no sin. It is you who make sin exist..."

In this scripture Yeshua points out the source of the idea of sin. This passage implies that the source or initiation of the concept of sin (and the long journey to deal with it), comes from *human* thinking. The Christian notion of sin was a new spiritual idea for Native people. Changes have occurred in the original meaning of sin since Yeshua first spoke about it. So, there has been a mis-calculation.[153] The word (*hamartia*), labeled "sin" (disobedience to God requiring repentance and appeals for forgiveness by God), had quite another meaning in Greek. I think it crucial in the early portions of this book to contemplate the implications of the previous discussion. I'm not trying to find fault, but to encourage the recognition that another choice can be considered when evaluating life experiences.

Let's look at the concept of "being saved." The Exodus story has set a spiritual outline for the need to be rescued from a terrible circumstance. The Israelites were:

- *captured and held by the Egyptian rulers (the bad guys)*
- *a rescuer (savior) was needed to deliver them from their terrible living conditions*
- *a savior who was chosen by God performed miracles (which sometimes meant that enemies were killed with the blessing of God)*
- *the chosen people of God (the good guys) were given a promise land set aside by God just for them*
- *it was to take them a long time to reach that promised land*

The description of this journey has some parallels, in my mind, to the Christian life journey. Some denominations preach that this earthly experience is like being captured in a terrible place (the Earth) which is seen as a bad place; sometimes referred to as "the residence of

---

[152] Found in a jar unearthed at Nag Hammadi, Egypt. It had been found earlier in 1896 and now it is in the Egyptology section of the National Museum of Berlin.

[153] We will discuss this idea of "miscalculation" later in our study of Judaism and the Genesis story.

the devil." Good people are not able to escape the circumstance on their own. A savior is required to come and battle the evil[154] forces and to set the people free. Evil is defeated and the promise of a better land (Heaven), is fulfilled but it will take a long journey to get there. Is there an alternative meaning to "being saved?" In Hebrew, this concept is translated as *"to breathe freely."*[155] To me this would imply both a physical and emotional experience in the present moment. I interpret it to mean an unrestricted relationship with the Divine; a "peace that passeth all understanding." Perhaps it is possible for people to experience a freedom that can be available as near as every breath? To breathe freely can mean not feeling weighted down, imprisoned or victimized by terrible conditions. Bishop Spong puts it nicely:

...the Hebrews were life-centered, life-affirming, life-loving people who worshiped the God of life, creation, and history. They found joy in life...Hebrew worship celebrated the God of life.[156]

My Native roots enable me to have a daily experience with the Great Mystery that is as close as my "sacred breath."[157] I have trust and confidence that the Creator has a plan for all of life. Our physical body and our spirit have been designed to be capable of managing most situations that come to us. Our relationship with the Divine helps us have the inner power to respond to the dilemmas of life. Mother Earth is truly a beautiful home where we can learn many lessons.

The shift here is from an emphasis on personal liberty (the joy of freely breathing, which is in every moment), to a group experience of freedom (an event to wish for and wait for). The former is in the hands of each person and the latter is coming from outside the person and they are unable to bring it to themselves.

We will be exploring more of the original Hebrew[158] writings as we proceed through the chapters of this book. There is much to learn

---

[154] "The word for 'evil' in Aramaic means unripe or not at the right time…" according to Neil Douglas-Koltz. *The Hidden Gospel,* 79.

[155] Jean-Yves Leloup. *The Gospel of Mary Magdalene,* 52.

[156] Spong. *This Hebrew Lord: A Bishop's Search for the Authentic Jesus,* 29.

[157] An Aramaic interpretation for "God is a spirit" (John 4:24 KJV) is *"God is breath. All that breathes resides in the Only Being. From my breath to the air we share to the wind that blows around the planet: Sacred Unity inspires all.* Douglas-Klotz. *The Hidden Gospel,* 41.

[158] "…most scholars now agree that there were at least four or five main authors, or group of authors, of the Hebrew scriptures. They believe that they were composed

by delving into the meanings of original words and texts. Hebrew scholar Yacov Rambsel explains:

Did you know that 80 percent of the root words of the English language can be traced back many thousands of years to biblical Hebrew?...And not only is English overflowing with Hebraic origins, but there are hundreds of other languages and dialects enriched by Hebrew's influences.[159]

William Tyndale (1492?—1536) said: "The English agreeth one thousand times more with the Hebrew than the Latin or the Greek." Joseph Wild gives additional insight into the Hebrew language:

The Hebrew was a very limited language, not numbering more than 7,000 words. The English is now said to number about 80,000. In the English we have not less than 1,000 Hebrew roots, a large percentage. In names of persons and places in England, the Hebrew is very prominent.[160]

I have placed many of the Hebrew words discussed throughout the book into the final chapter. My hope is to frame out the parameters of what I believe can be a significant look at the real teachings of Jesus.

Some years ago I was waiting in an airport in Newark, NJ returning from Italy, and I became aware of the front page of a U. S. World & News Report. It said, "Secrets of the Bible." When traveling abroad, finally seeing English words is often a great relief. As I opened it, I was amazed to see these topics highlighted in the issue: "Jesus' Early Years, Searching for Eden, Christianity's Pagan Past, Sistine Secrets, and Michelangelo's Ceiling Frescoes..." In recent years various magazines are printing similar Christian-related stories. One of the articles was about how Eve was created in the Garden of Eden.[161] Here's what was written about the creation of Eve:

According to Christian translation and tradition, the Almighty created Eve, the mother of us all, from Adam's rib. However, the biblical Hebrew does not say this. The word used there is ha-tzelah, the side of Adam. The rabbinic sages explained that she was not made from Adam's head, which could have made her feel

---

over a long time, stretching from sometime around 1000 to 400 BCE." Davis, Kenneth, op. cit., 19.
[159] Rambsel, Yacov. *The Genesis Factor: The Amazing Mysteries of the Bible Code*, 17.
[160] Wild, Joseph. *Ten Lost Tribes*, 59.
[161] "In the Sumerian and Babylonian versions of the Garden of Eden myth, from which the Hebrew one is also derived, the original couple was created equal in stature by the great Goddess." Acharya S, op. cit., 184.

conceited and above her mate, and not from his foot, which could have made her feel downtrodden and want to run away, but from his side, to be his equal partner in life. For that reason, in the next verse after Eve is created and named, we read: "Therefore shall a man leave his father and his mother, and shall cleave unto his wife; and they shall be one flesh."(Genesis 2:24)[162]

I found out that in almost every non-Jewish picture of the birth of Eve, she is depicted as *rising* out of one of Adam's ribs. When we take a look at Michelangelo's ceiling frescoes, we see Eve *stepping out of the entire side of Adam!*[163] That depiction more closely matches Judaic tradition. Also, the forbidden tree of knowledge is more accurately painted as a fig tree not an apple tree![164]

Other cultures around the world would not agree with the concept that we can be separated from nature by some act of humanity or that the natural world is somehow evil. Dr. Alberto Villoldo[165] teaches that Westerners must turn away from the myth that we have been "kicked out of the garden." He says that we are alone in the world with this belief that we have been cast out of paradise.[166] What would lead this indigenous professor to make such a statement? Drunvalo Melchizedek includes an older version of the Garden of Eden story in his book, *The Ancient Secret of the Flower of Life*, which is 2,000 years older than Moses.[167] Joseph Campbell says that the Fall and the Garden of Eden are not well known in Japan and the Shinto texts express the thought that "...the processes of nature cannot be evil."[168]

---

[162] Blech, Benjamin and Doliner, Roy. *Sistine Secrets*, U.S News & World Report (Special Edition, copyright 2008), 76.

[163] "...a long-suppressed story about Adam's wife—not Eve, but his first wife, known as Lilith...formed at the same time... [she tells Adam] I will not lie beneath you...the two of us are equals..." For an extensive study of this "Lilith" see Hanson, Kenneth, Ph. D, *Secrets of the Lost Bible*, 79-86.

[164] "It did not become an apple tree until [Saint] Jerome translated the scriptures into Latin in the fourth century of this Common Era." Spong, *The Sins of Scripture*, 89.

[165] Director of the Four Winds Society, he has had various indigenous mentors and also is the author of many books. He is often invited to speak about indigenous topics.

[166] Gfere, J. L. *"Four Steps to Power and Knowledge*, 85. In my previous book, *"Native American Spirituality: A Walk in the Woods,"* I included an interesting older version of the Garden of Eden story. See Eagle, op, cit., footnote 447.

[167] Melchizedek, Drunvelo. *The Ancient Secret of the Flower of Life,* 83-84, 89.

[168] Campbell. *The Power of Myth*, 24.

Another Hebrew word jumped out in the text. It has to do with Noah's ark, the boat that held all the animals when the great flood allegedly took place.

There is a specific Hebrew word for "ark" in the original Torah text—teivah. The word teivah, however, does not mean a boat or sailing vessel. It really means "box"...on the Sistine ceiling, Michelangelo painted the ark as a huge box, once more following Jewish tradition to the letter.[169]

Recently I was reviewing a documentary about the apocalypse[170] and the end times. Unexpectedly, I saw the original meaning of the word "apocalypse"[171] being discussed by theologians who had studied the Greek language. To my surprise, here again was a different meaning than what I had been used to hearing. There was not an emphasis on the prophetic expectation of terrible events in present times. The word apocalypse, derived from the Greek *apokalypsis*, initially meant "an unveiling of hidden truth, hidden knowledge";[172] "secrets are to be revealed, the revealing of something kept secret."[173] Simon Pearson writes "to lift the lid off something."[174] Margaret Starbird elaborates: "The word apocalypse...means *lifting the veil.*"[175] These apocalyptic times *are* very anxious times when hidden secrets will be *uncovered and revealed!* My research and study is right on target! In the earliest written material in the New Testament (the gospel of Mark and the letters of the Paul), regarding the imminent return of Jesus and the coming of the Kingdom of God,[176] it was

---

[169] Blech, Benjamin and Doliner, Roy. Op. cit.

[170] "...*Apocalypse* from Greek by way of Latin means 'hidden'." "...after Emperor Constantine began to tolerate Christians in 313 CE, Greek was a dying language." Latin was the language of the Roman Empire. "Beginning in 382 CE, a priest named Jerome began the process of bringing both Hebrew scriptures and the New Testament into Latin...Jerome supervised the translation of a Latin Bible that was completed by 405 CE...known as the Vulgate Bible." Davis, Kenneth, op. cit., 29-30.

[171] In a 2002 *Time*/CNN poll, fifty-nine per cent of Americans believe the events prophesied in the *Book of Revelation* will occur in the future. See 'The Bible and Apocalypse,' *Time,* 1 July, 2002.

[172] History.com, Paul S. Boyer, Emeritus, University of Wisconsin. *God vs Satan: The Final Battle.*

[173] History.com, Jonathan Kirsch, Author of *A History of the End of the World.*

[174] Pearson, Simon. *The End of the World: From Revelation to Eco-Disaster,* 2.

[175] Starbird, Margaret. *Magdalene's Lost Legacy,* 85.

[176] "...the term 'God's kingdom' never actually occurs in the Hebrew scriptures, though it does occur in Wisdom of Solomon 10:10. The word 'kingdom' is also used,

indicated that there would be a bodily resurrection of the dead. However, as time passed the kingdom didn't come! Tom Krattenmaker, in USA TODAY (April, 2009), quotes Bart Ehman, professor of religious studies at the University of North Carolina:

With the passing of time about the apocalyptic notion of the resurrection of the body becomes transformed into the doctrine of the immortality of the soul. What emerges is the belief in heaven and hell, a belief not found in the teachings of Jesus or Paul, but one invented in later times.[177]

In my attempts to examine some of the ancient texts, and also to present theological terms within the framework of their original context, it is not my intention to give an in depth treatment of this subject. I am not a biblical scholar. However, I do hope to stir up enough curiosity to encourage you to explore further.

---

beyond Judaism, by the ancient author Epictetus to describe the Cynic life." In Sayings 3 and 113 of the *Gospel of Thomas* Jesus says, "the kingdom is inside you and it is outside you…the father's kingdom is spread out upon the earth, and the people do not see it." Meyers, op. cit., 16-17.

[177] Quoted in USA TODAY, April 13, 2009. "Fightin' Words," The Forum, article by Tom Krattenmaker.

Chapter Two

The Colonization of the Americas and the World—*It was Going to Happen!*

"In 1452 the Doctrine of Discovery was issued, giving religious sanction for the enslavement of Indigenous peoples and the theft of their lands in newly discovered territories. This papal decree demonstrated Northern Stream arrogance by declaring all lands not owned by Christians to be considered vacant and thereby claimable for the *Church.*"[178]

Bishop John Shelby Spong: "It was New York's late Senator Daniel Moynihan who said, '*Everyone is entitled to his or her own opinions, but no one is entitled to his or her own facts.*' Religion cannot hide from truth by seeking to accumulate its own facts."[179]

In the last fifty years, there has been an *information explosion.* Once we learned primarily from textbooks placed before us in our schools and churches, or from other family and cultural influences. Today there are many more sources of information. It has become easier to study and in some ways more fun. On the other hand this generation and those following will need to strengthen a skill that has not been exercised for many ages—thinking for ourselves!

Let's take a quick glance at how information has exploded. From one of the oldest human civilizations, the ancient Sumerians (circa 3800 B.C.), to A.D 1900, a given quantity of information was collected. Yet, from 1900 to 1950, our knowledge doubled in a mere fifty years. Amazingly, in the next twenty years, by about 1970, we doubled it again! "It took only ten years, to about 1980, to double *that!* Now it's doubling every few years."[180]

This explosion of information has not always provided us with accurate information. More information doesn't mean more truth! My studies confirm what most of us know by now, that the descriptions and explanations of some historical events have been "spun" in order to

---

[178] Dinawa. *Sacred History and Earth Prophecies,* 111.
[179] Spong, John Shelby. *Jesus for the Non-Religious,* 13.
[180] *Encyclopedia Britannica.*

support various institutional and governmental agendas. Not all records of the past are available to the general public. I feel that this generation, at least a portion of it, is ready to face the music and look at things more realistically. That which occurred in the past, even our own personal past, is beyond full understanding. So we must hold all of the clues and writings up for inspection and contemplation.

What we thought was history is now being reviewed and possibly revised as we look with more educated eyes. However, it is not always comfortable for the present older generation when we suggest that facts have been altered or even made up. Changing our understanding of history can be both a blessing and a curse. It also means extracting what is more authentic. What courage it will take to make this journey. I have listened to many Native people talk about untold stories that have not made their way into the general volumes of American history. There is something therapeutic and balancing about having an opportunity to fill in the holes of history. Especially for Indigenous peoples for whom there were actual prophecies that foretold of many difficult experiences that were going to happen.

I believe this is *the* generation that will open their minds so that the next generation might have access to more information than we grew up with. Yet, many are satisfied with what they are told without questioning. Considering the Doctrine of Discovery cited at the beginning of this chapter, not everyone is ready to hear the truth about how it was used to exploit indigenous people. However, no matter how revealing, no matter how agonizing, I believe many people are ready to have a more accurate picture of the facts of history.

Not all tribal nations had prophecies to prepare them for the great struggles and life altering changes that were destined to come. For most Native communities recovery has been extremely difficult and many are still facing extensive social and economic problems. However, I would say that many Native people today would also recognize the progress that was brought by those who came to this land.

Life is about change! A glance at the changing seasons, our physical body, technological innovation and the forces that drive the economy reveals the certainty of change. This reality demands adjustment and adaptability both personally and within communities if we are to survive. Reaching into my later years, I notice that my past physical abilities are destined to be compromised. It can be predicted that I will not play tennis as I did in the past. However, I can still carry self worth into the present and the future.

Revisiting what can be found of tribal prophecies is very important to those who want to step toward personal stability and power. A discussion of indigenous prophecy will disclose that—the colonization of all indigenous peoples around the world was *going to happen!* We as Native people, and those who are Native hearted, can either feel historically victimized or we can reach within our spirit and recuperate, heal and seek those spiritual beliefs that are meaningful to us today.

Some of the Real Story of "Colonization (1492 to 1800's)"

In this section I want to take a closer look at American history and maybe go to some places that many Americans may or may not want to visit. Personally, I have a great admiration for a particular radio *icon*, Paul Harvey. I have often borrowed his famous saying, "the rest of the story" to describe my own search for what lies behind some of the current understandings of history. Sometimes I will refer to myself as the "Native American Paul Harvey."

I feel it is time to dig deeper into the real experience of various historical events. Each year I have become aware of the public's need to hear directly from those who actually participated in current events. The twenty-four-hour news cycle has created the need to fill a lot of time on the cable channels. The tabloids and media are without mercy when it comes to examining every feature, every emotion, and every detail of any news event. The latest sensational story is reported in minute detail for weeks-on-end until it is pushed to the background by the next headline-grabbing story.

This appetite for more information must be viewed as a two-edged sword. It can effectively bring a feast of education about life, as well as cut life into small but distracting morsels! I want to present more of the "rest of the story" in a way that brings greater understanding. Therapeutically, it was important for me as a professional therapist to dig out as much of the details of a person's dilemma as possible. The more you know about the environment, the nature of each family member, etc., the more helpful the advice that is offered can be. I think many people are personally and spiritually mature enough to step back into historical settings and whittle out the real experiences of history for both Native peoples, for Americans in general, and for Christians specifically.

Let's step forward from the Doctrine of Discovery to some historical notes around the early colonization of America. Colonization in this part of the world has a unique history just as with other locations in the world. From the perspective of Native peoples at the time of initial interface with Europeans, early observations were very confusing and frustrating. As Steven Waldman, author of *Founding Faith*, relates in an interview with Terry Gross, host of *Fresh Air* on National Public Radio:

Most of the people who came here came because they wanted to establish a particular denomination; a particular approach to religion, often at the expense of other denominations.[181]

Watching the variety of newcomers must have been most interesting for the Native people. It surely was also difficult for the settlers in two ways: first to be ship-bound for months; and then to have to establish a new life in a wilderness that was so unlike their European homeland. There was a mix of those who wanted to come and those who had no other choice, such as released prisoners.

In Europe the Church (specifically the Roman Catholic Church), had wedded itself to various empires and kingdoms. There had been centuries of power struggles, loyalties, and heretical actions by the powers-that-be." It was inevitable that revolt by the people was going to happen and that some would search for new ways to escape the domination of the church in order to find a more free expression of their spiritual beliefs. Groups who later became denominations looked to America for that religious freedom. Again Steven Waldman:

It was usually protestant denominations; not Christian, but Protestants specifically, often as a way of fighting the spread of Catholicism. It was the reason that people left Europe. For a long time Catholics were viewed as "enemies of freedom."

---

[181] Waldman, Steven. *Founding Faith: How Our Founding Fathers Forged a Radical New Approach to Religious Liberty*. Steven Waldman is editor in chief, president, and co-founder of Beliefnet.com, not affiliated with any religion or movement.

The Catholic Church had a history for over a thousand years as the image of power and control. Many of the early colonists carried with them a negative attitude about Catholics. Also, there were strong opinions within each of the various colonies about *anyone* who didn't believe or think as they believed. Persecution was rampant, including Jews, Baptists and the Quakers to name a few:

What Americans don't realize is that in the first 150 years we had really horrible persecution as each colony experimented with having a particular religion in charge. In Massachusetts there was terrible persecution of Quakers to point of hanging, simply for the crime of being a Quaker. In Virginia there was horrible persecution against Baptists.[182]

Various groups with their religious focus set up geographic and theological boundaries within which they established civil rule. The Anglicans settled in Virginia, the Puritans in Massachusetts. Each location operated within a male-directed form of Christian commonwealth. The Pilgrims wrote the Mayflower Compact while sailing aboard the *Mayflower* in 1620, committing themselves to "ye glory of God, and advancement of ye Christian faith."[183] As Waldman says, "The Puritans believed that civil authorities, bound by the same Bible as they, could be responsible for creating a godly society…they had an obligation to create a kingdom of God on earth…"[184] This would have been viewed by Native peoples as quite the opposite of community harmony and compassion. In a 1703 book called *New England Judged by the Spirit of the Lord*, George Bishop, an English Quaker writes:

William Brend, "a man of years," was locked up in irons for sixteen hours and then whipped 117 times…Alice Ambrose, Mary Tomkins, and Ann Coleman had taken to preaching their gospel at the Piscataqua River. They were arrested, "stripped naked, from the middle upward, and tied to a cart, and after a while cruelly

---

[182] "In 1644, the Massachusetts General Court banned Baptists…" Waldman, op. cit. 9.
[183] Ibid., 7. "In earlier times, it didn't take 'faith' to believe *that* God existed—almost everybody took that for granted. Rather, 'faith' had to do with one's *relationship* to God—whether one *trusted* in God. The difference between faith as 'belief in something that may or may not exist' and faith as 'trusting in God' is enormous. The first is a 'matter of the head,' and second a 'matter of the heart'; the first can leave one unchanged, the second intrinsically brings change." (Marcus J. Borg, *Jesus: A New Vision*), 35.
[184] Ibid., 8.

whipped..., whilst the priest stood and looked on, and laughed at it...[Mary] Dyer was convicted of defying an order of banishment and sentenced to death along with two friends. She watched as her friends' necks snapped.[185]

Mary Dyer was given a last-minute reprieve, but a year later she defied the law again and walked to her hanging speaking these words, "Nay, man, I am not to repent. I do only what the Lord God requires of me. Do not mourn of my passing, for I am filled with happiness."[186] Many Quakers were executed by the Holy Commonwealth of Massachusetts—the very government that had been set up by Puritans who had fled England to avoid religious persecution![187]

Waldman further comments that, "Jews and Catholics and certainly atheists were not a part of the equation...they could not hold office[188] or vote, and other rights were denied." Native peoples were easily classified in a variety of ways: to be converted, removed, or exterminated. Generally speaking, indigenous peoples were not inclined to speak about their beliefs. They had no name for religion, as their spirituality was a *way of living*. They were not able to speak much English and were not at all used to explaining their ways in any case. Natives were seen as savage, primitive, pagan, and certainly LOST.

In early American history, what was witnessed by the Natives was white settlers watching, judging and killing each other. Courageous, pious white people were persecuted and tortured, and families were torn apart in the name of Christianity. The *colonists tried to enslave the Indians*, but there were too many of them. Even though they had superior firearms, if they massacred Indians they would face massacre themselves in return. As Howard Zinn writes:

The Virginians needed labor, to grow corn for subsistence, to grow tobacco for export...They couldn't force Indians to work for them, as Columbus had done....they could not capture them and keep them enslaved; the Indians were

---

[185] Ibid., 10-11.
[186] Ibid., 12.
[187] Much of the account of Mary Dyer's martyrdom is from Robert S. Burgess, *To Try the Bloody Law: the Story of Mary Dyer*, (Burnsville, NC: Celo Valley Books, 2000).
[188] "In 1640, it [Virginia] prohibited Catholics from holding public office unless they 'had taken the oath of allegiance and supremacy" to the Church of England. It decreed that any 'popish priest' who arrived in Virginia "should be deported forthwith." Steven Waldman, op. cit., 6.

tough, resourceful, defiant, and at home in these woods, as the Englishmen were not.[189]

The English decided to exterminate them. Edmund Morgan writes, in his history of early Virginia, *American Slavery, American Freedom*:

Since the Indians were better woodsmen than the English and virtually impossible to track down, the method was to feign peaceful intentions, let them settle down and plant their corn wherever they chose, and then, just before harvest, fall upon them, killing as many as possible and burning the corn...[190]

Europe already had an extensive history of enslaving Black Africans. Slavery existed in Africa, so the Europeans in the colonies were able to justify their own slave trade. However, it should be noted that the slaves in Africa could be described more like the serfs in Europe. They were servants, but they had rights.[191] When the slave trade began in the colonies of America the treatment of the slaves was more akin to the treatment of animals. First the Dutch and then the English dominated the slave trade. Zinn gives some of the horrible details surrounding Europe's capture and transportation of Black Africans:

...it was because they came from a settled culture, of tribal customs and family ties, of communal life and traditional ritual, that African Blacks found themselves especially helpless when removed from this...The conditions and sale were crushing affirmations to the black African of his helplessness in the face of superior force. The marches to the coast, sometimes for 1,000 miles, with people shackled around the neck, under whip and gun, were death marches, in which two of every five blacks died...packed aboard the slave ships, in spaces not much bigger than coffins [with blacks of other tribes, often speaking different languages], chained in the stench of their own excrement.[192]

By 1619, Zinn says, "...a million blacks had already been brought from Africa to South America and the Caribbean, to the Portuguese and Spanish colonies, to work as slaves."[193] In 1691, Virginia banished "...any white man or woman being free who shall intermarry with a Negro, mulatoo, or Indian man or woman bond or free...By 1763, [in Virginia]...there were 170,000 slaves, about half

---

[189] Zinn, Howard. *A People's History of the United States*, 25.
[190] Ibid., 13.
[191] Ibid., 27.
[192] Ibid., 28.
[193] Ibid., 25-26.

the population."[194] One more note regarding Black African History is provided: "…By 1800, 10 to 15 million blacks had been transported as slaves to the Americas…"[195]

Steven Waldman gently addresses his writing to some of the common myths of early American history. One myth, he says, is that *the United States was founded as a Christian nation.* He says that just isn't true! Even though there was some intention originally to establish a Christian land, by the time of the writing of the Declaration of Independence the founding fathers had become aware of the religious divisions that had been created within and among the colonies during the first 150 years and they were ready to create a different and more inclusive model. "They very explicitly and intentionally created a Constitution that was not Christian. The National government should not be thought of as a Christian government."[196]

Another myth that Waldman writes about is that "…*the Founding Fathers wanted religious freedom because they were devout Christians.* Most of them disliked much about organized Christianity, the clerical class, and its theology, especially the common Calvinist[197] doctrine…"[198] Waldman continues:

The ones we tend to focus on as the most important for religious freedom, George Washington, James Madison, Thomas Jefferson,[199] *John Adams, Ben Franklin;*[200] *none of them were orthodox Christians. Jefferson and Franklin*[201] *had turned*

---

[194] Ibid., 26, 32.

[195] Ibid., 29 .

[196] NPR (National Public Radio) presentation.

[197] "that salvation came only from expressed faith in Jesus (or from being among God's select) rather than through good works." Steven Waldman, op. cit., xi.

[198] Ibid.

[199] "But it does me no injury for my neighbor to say there are twenty gods or no God. It neither picks my pocket nor breaks my leg." (Thomas Jefferson, *Notes on Virginia*, 1782)

[200] "Franklin rejected claims that the Bible was penned by the Almighty and, although he admired Jesus' teachings, said that "I have, with most of the present Dissenters in England, some Doubts as to his Divinity." Franklin, letter to Ezra Stiles, Philadelphia, March 9, 1790, *The Papers of Benjamin Franklin.*

[201] "It would be difficult to exaggerate the importance of Masonry for the American Revolution…Many of the revolutionary leaders, including Washington, Franklin, Samuel Adams, Otis, Richard Henry Lee, Madison, and Hamilton were members of the fraternity." Gordon S. Wood, *The Radicalism of the American Revolution.* Also [Paul Revere, John Paul Jones]in Michael Bradley, *Secrets of the Freemasons*, 127.

away from the Bible as a literal document. They believed that Jesus was a great teacher, but they didn't think that Jesus was divine.[202]

Mary and I visited Monticello, Thomas Jefferson's plantation home some years ago. He established the University of Virginia and directed that no religious chapel be placed on campus. My knowledge of American history was enhanced as I viewed his extensive world library and his inventions, particularly his copying apparatus. As the tour continued, it became very apparent to us that Jefferson had a lonely and reclusive life. He spent considerable time reading and writing. I asked the tour guide about Jefferson's opinion of Jesus. He commented that Jefferson thought, "Jesus was the greatest teacher in the world and that Jefferson believed Jesus was not divine!" I had to ask if I had heard him right and he repeated the statement. I was not aware of The Jeffersonian Bible and the controversy that surrounded Jefferson because of it. Some referred to him as an "infidel and atheist."[203] Alexander Hamilton called Jefferson an "atheist and fanatic."[204] Then I found the following:

Numerous sermons were preached warning that if Jefferson was elected he would discredit religion, overthrow the church, and destroy the Bible. People in New England actually hid their Bibles to save them when Jefferson was elected president.[205]

I understand that this idea that Thomas Jefferson was non-religious, even an atheist, followed him throughout his life. Although the clergy of the established churches in New England and Virginia attacked Jefferson's beliefs, Henry Wilder Foote, a scholarly Unitarian minister of the twentieth century, believed Jefferson's "...knowledge of and admiration for the teachings of Jesus have never been equaled by another president."[206]

Waldman comments in an interview with Terry Gross that, Jefferson thought that the whole Bible was an exercise in covering-up the diamonds of Jesus' moral teachings with the "dung" that was

---

[202] NPR (National Public Radio) presentation.
[203] Sanford, Charles B. *The Religious Life of Thomas Jefferson*, 1.
[204] Ibid.
[205] Randal, Henry Stephens. *The Life of Thomas Jefferson*, 3 vols. (New York, 1858), 1:495, 2:547-68, 3:620-22; and Malone, 4:481.
[206] Sanford., op. cit. 3.

everything else!²⁰⁷ He writes, "Jefferson's task was to remove the artifice, to reveal that 'a more precious morsel of ethics [that] was never seen'."²⁰⁸ Hmmm, that sounds like one of the purposes of this book!

What about the Jeffersonian Bible? He cut and pasted what he selected as the more accurate images and understandings of Jesus from the Bible and created his own version of it. "Basically, he cut out the miracles. He cut out any sign that Jesus was divine. He basically cut out the Christmas story, and the Easter story."²⁰⁹ Waldman writes:

*In Jefferson's version, Jesus was not divine. The virgin-birth—gone. Christ's bodily resurrection—gone. The miracles of the loaves, walking on water, raising Lazarus—none of them made Jefferson's book. He transformed the Bible from the revelation of God into a collection of teachings of a brilliant, wise religious reformer—author of "the most sublime and benevolent code of morals which has ever been offered to man."*²¹⁰

Waldman says that in Jefferson's Bible the rock that covered Jesus' tomb was never moved away and that is the end of his Bible. His focus was on the character of Jesus.²¹¹ Jefferson really felt that Jesus' teachings were among the most inspirational and true in human history and he believed that the teachings had been "corrupted!" This is why he edited the Bible in this way. Jefferson was, in his own way, a very spiritual man.²¹²

In a letter to Samuel Kercheval, Thomas Jefferson wrote "year after year, priests managed to take the 'purest system of morals ever

---

[207] "...pulling 'diamonds' (the wisdom of Jesus) from the 'dunghill' (the conglomeration of lies and fiction that made up the rest of the Bible)." Steven Waldman, op. cit., 77.
[208] Letter to F.A. Van der Kemp, April 25, 1816, in Lipscomb and Bergh, editors, *The Writings of Thomas Jefferson*, Volume 15, 114.
[209] NPR Waldman interview
[210] Waldman. op. cit., 72.
[211] Jefferson's goal was to "justify the character of Jesus against the fictions of his pseudo-followers" in order "to rescue his character." Letter to William Short, August 4, 1820, in Lipscomb and Bergh, editors, *The Writings of Thomas Jefferson*, Volume, 15, 114.
[212] "...Jefferson's editing of the Bible flowed directly from a well-thought-out, long-stewing view that Christianity had been fundamentally corrupted—by the Apostle Paul, by the early church, by great Protestant reformers such as Martin Luther and John Calvin...Jefferson *loved* Jesus and was attempting to rescue him." Steven Waldman, op. cit., 73.

before preached to man,' and twist it into a 'mere contrivance to filch [steal] wealth and power to themselves'."[213] We conclude this exercise with a statement from Jefferson's great-grandson, who describes Jefferson's religion as that of a:

Conservative Unitarian…He did not believe in the miracles, nor the divinity of Christ, nor the doctrine of the atonement,[214] but he was a firm believer in Divine Providence, in the efficacy of prayer, in a future state of rewards and punishments, and in the meeting of friends in another world.[215]

I salute Thomas Jefferson's studies and his courage. I believe that religious freedom developed very slowly and is not very well described in twentieth century American history.

What was happening in Europe during these years? Maybe there is something about having the first name of Thomas!

- "In 1697 an eighteen year-old Scottish student named Thomas Aikenhead was hanged in Edinburgh for claiming that the Pentateuch was written not by Moses but by someone else eight hundred years later."[216]
- "In England in the early 1700s, Thomas Woolston, a professor at Cambridge, was put in prison for one year for claiming that the miracles of Jesus had not happened."[217]
- "Near the end of the 1700s, in *The Age of Reason* Thomas Paine of Revolutionary War fame denied the truthfulness of much of the Bible; his publishers in England were heavily fined and put in prison."[218]
- David Friedrich Strauss (1808-1874), when only twenty-seven years old published two volumes entitled *Leben Jesu* or in English *The Life of Jesus Critically Examined* (1834). [He]"used the notion of myth (or symbolic narrative) in his analysis of gospel texts…the miracle stories are religiously true, even though not factually true." He was seen by one reviewer as a "Judas" and he was fired from his teaching position at the University of Tubingen in Germany.[219]

---

[213] Letter to Samuel Kercheval, January 19,1810, in Andrew A Lipscomb and Albert Ellery Bergh, editors, *The Writings of Thomas Jefferson*, Volume 12 (Washington, DC: Thomas Jefferson Memorial Association of the United States, 1903) 345.
[214] "The doctrine of the atonement is the belief that the death of Jesus was necessary for human salvation." Robert J. Miller, *Literal Incarnation*, The Fourth R, May-June Issue, 2004.
[215] Coolidge, Thomas Jefferson, "Jefferson in His Family," Bergh, 15:iv.
[216] Borg, Marcus. *The Historical Study of Jesus and Christian Origins*, 127.
[217] Ibid.
[218] Ibid.
[219] Ibid., 128.

The King James Version of The Bible

An ABC News Primetime poll in 2004 found that six in ten Americans surveyed considered biblical accounts to be true; "word for word" from God.[220] The National Geographic Channel in July, 2006, reported that in the United States fifty-five percent of adults believe the Bible is the word of God, without error, and to be read literally.[221] On November 18th, 1965, during Vatican II, the Roman Catholic Church "declared...that God himself 'authored' the Bible...Everything written by the inspired authors is to be regarded as having been written by the Holy Ghost."[222] This book will probably appeal mostly to the other half of the population who are open to seeing the Bible from another perspective! I hope this will include those who read and consider the Bible to be important.

Biblical history indicates that the Bible is a translation, of a translation, of a translation. The original Aramaic[223] language that Jesus and his disciples spoke was first written in Greek, then placed into Latin, and then into many translations in English.

The King James Version is favored by many Christians. As I have implied, some of the more fundamental forms of Christianity and some individuals have chosen to embrace a literal interpretation of biblical teachings. Today's version of the Bible differs in a number of details from the King James Version of 1611:

- *"William Kilburne in 1659 found a total of 20,000 errors in six different KJV's."*[224]
- *The KJV "...was again re-written in 1881 and the committee responsible for the Revised Edition claimed to have made 36,190 changes that altered 1600 passages..."*[225]

Here are some notes about how the Bible has been used in earlier history and in the present:[226]

---

[220] Quoted in U.S. N & W Report, (Special Edition, *Secrets of the Bible*, 2008), 86.
[221] *Secrets of Revelation,* National Geographic Channel, 7/16/2006.
[222] Quoted in *Jesus Live in India*, Holger Kersten, 31.
[223] Aramaic is a Semitic language that is related to Hebrew but not identical with it. For a brief but helpful review, see Matthew Black, "The Recovery of the Language of Jesus," *New Testament Studies* 3(1956-57).
[224] Quoted in *Tears in Heaven*, 69.
[225] Ibid.
[226] This list is from Spong's book, *The Sins of Scripture*, from the dust jacket.

- *"...the Bible was used to oppose the Magna Carta and support the divine right of Kings,*
- *to condemn the insights of Galileo and Charles Darwin,*
- *and to support slavery and later apartheid and segregation.*
- *Christian leaders used the Bible to justify the Crusades and their...[actions against Muslim and Jewish people],"*
- *"...as well as the murderous behavior of the Inquisition and the virulent anti-Semitism of the Holocaust.*
- *The Bible is still quoted in the church to justify treating women as second-class Citizens.*[227]
- *Today it is the chief weapon of politicians and preachers seeking to deny justice for gay and lesbian people.*
- *In addition, the Christian Church, while claiming allegiance to this book, has encouraged the abuse of children*[228] *and supported environmental degradation."*

For this moment let's check out a brief summary of some of the awkward, humorous, and possibly uncomfortable events in the Old Testament, as outlined in a book called, *Don't Know Much About the Bible*:

There was Cain knocking off Abel. Noah's son cursed for seeing his drunken father naked. Abraham willing to sacrifice the son he desired all his life. The population of Sodom and Gomorrah destroyed for its wanton ways. Lot sleeping with his daughters.[229] *A tent peg driven through a man's head in Judges. King Saul asking young David to bring him a hundred Philistine foreskins as a bride price to marry his daughter. King David sending a soldier into the front lines so he could sleep with the man's wife. Then there is that ever-popular tale of wise Solomon threatening to cut a baby in half. But did you know that the two women who brought King Solomon that baby were prostitutes!*[230]

---

[227] "The patriarchs of Israel's history—Abraham, Isaac, Jacob and Joseph—*all had numerous wives.*" Ibid., 44.[italics by Author]

[228] "Reuter News Service in 2004 told the world of a Roman Catholic order of nuns in Ireland, known as the Congregation of the Sisters of Mercy, who had 'apologized unconditionally for the physical and emotional trauma its nuns had inflicted on children raised in its orphanages and schools'." Spong, *The Sins of Scripture*, 152.

[229] In the story of Sodom (Genesis 19: 4-8, KJV) "At last only Lot and his two daughters are spared. This man who has offered his virgin daughters for gang rape is nonetheless judged by God to be righteous and worthy of deliverance!" Spong, *The Sins of Scripture*, 131.

[230] Davis, Kenneth. Op. cit., xvi-xvii.

A Discussion of "Victim Philosophy"

Jesus said, "Let him who seeks continue seeking until he finds. When he finds, he will become troubled. When he becomes troubled, he will be astonished, and he will rule over all things."[231]

Considering the phrase, "Blessed are they that mourn: for they shall be comforted", "To mourn in Aramaic can also mean to be in confusion or turmoil, to wander, literally or figuratively… 'To be comforted' in Aramaic can also mean to be united inside, to return from wandering, or to see the face of what one hopes for."[232]

Those who have heard me say, "My fifth book will be about the spiritual lessons indigenous peoples can learn to appreciate from the last 500 years of the experience of *company*," surely thought that I was pulling their leg! I will carefully approach this big discussion hoping to create some fertile ground upon which hope and optimism can be planted. This is a journey that a few may not want to take. The idea is more relevant for people who can look beyond the admittedly sad personal and tribal historical injustices.

For many years I worked as a professional therapist. I was involved in the lives of people and all of the emotional dilemmas they faced. I witnessed many environments that facilitated the experience of people seeing themselves as "victims." In some cases, parental behavioral patterns formulated a child's anti-social conduct. I saw teenage manipulation and violence as they attempted to hold power over their parents and community systems. In the face of developmental disabilities, substance abuse, satanic worship, religious trauma and sociopathic behavior, I have listened to and walked beside people as they tried to understand their life experiences.

Although I attempted to serve a variety of people with various attitudes toward their circumstances, I was never quite able to see them as victims of life. Of course, I had tremendous compassion for their pain, but I also know that one can choose their reaction to any experience. I have previously written about the two attributes that greatly assisted Native people's survival during the last 500 plus years: the ability to adapt and adopt.[233] I will offer another: the potential to

---

[231] *Gospel of Thomas*, 32.14-19, in NHL (Nag Hammadi Library) 349-350.
[232] Douglas-Klotz. *The Hidden Gospel*, 49.
[233] Eagle, Rainbow. op. cit., 210.

strive for spiritual balance. Primarily, this means to have the courage to face what has brought us out of balance and to come into a relationship with those events and personalities that have pushed us off course.

A victim outlook by definition places responsibility in the outer world for what is occurring. Of course, in many situations people suffer greatly because of the actions of others upon them. It is important to acknowledge the devastating results of abuse, physical injury and disability, criminal behavior, cultural genocide and other such life experiences. Sometimes an individual is unable to move past these experiences and achieve some degree of healing. On the other hand, we all know of people who have experienced horrible events in their lives who have been able to survive, recover balance and in some cases even forgive and use the experience to help others. What accounts for these different responses?

As we step into discussions of victim philosophy, I remember a story about Victor Frankl who was a survivor of the Nazi war-camps during WW II. "On September 25, 1942 he, along with his wife, and his parents were deported to the Theresienstadt concentration camp… Though assigned to ordinary labor details until the last few weeks of the war, Frankl tried to cure fellow prisoners from despondency and prevent suicide…He later set up a suicide watch unit…"[234] He went on to become a world renowned psychiatrist and the creator of Logotherapy.[235] All aspects of life for those imprisoned in the concentration camps were controlled and severely dictated. The deprivation was unimaginable. Experiencing situations in which an individual has no control of most aspects of their lives certainly defines the meaning of victim. Frankl spoke about how he dealt with his imposed situation. He said, "I had no control over what was done to me, but I did have control over *my reaction to* those things." It was his attitude and response to those unfortunate and painful events that he **could** control.

---

[234] http://en.wikipedia.org/wiki/Victor_Frankl.
[235] Ibid. The following list of tenets represents the basic principles of Logotherapy: "1-Life has meaning under all circumstances, even the most miserable ones, 2-Our main motivation for living is our will to find meaning in life and 3-We have freedom to find meaning in what we do, and what we experience, or at least in the stand we take when faced with a situation of unchangeable suffering."

We must also realize that research on the human brain and child development has indicted that trauma, whether at an early age or later in life, can cause physical and psychological changes that are difficult to remedy. Frankl was an adult when he was in the concentration camps. Many children who have experienced developmental delays and/or trauma have what very well could be life-long changes in their brain function. Adults sometimes develop PTSD. So, I do not want to minimize the seriousness of these experiences. People are victimized through no fault of their own. The question is, can we continue to grow at our own individual pace in spite of our experiences and see ourselves as more than victims? Is it possible to gain balance in the now?

Somewhere in the vast history of humankind, we moved away from a focus on personal power and responsibility, toward an over-focus on external control and group power over us. This change took place, shifting individual worth that once was an inner resource, to a belief that one's fate is primarily controlled by external factors. This shift opened the door for the need for protection and guidance from people, groups, institutions, and governments. I am not suggesting that we do not need cultural and societal laws. I am concerned about the balance of inner and outer responsibility in the responses we have to life experiences.

Spiritual perspective has also changed. As I will discuss later, the concept of the *other force,* or evil and the devil, became part of theology and social thinking. In early cultures around the world, there was not this extreme polarity. In the "yin-yang" philosophy opposing energies were necessary parts of the whole. In indigenous cultures the relationship between humans and nature was primary. There was not the emphasis on good vs. bad. Everything and every experience were seen as part of the circle of life. At some stage in the evolution of human consciousness the integrity of personhood dimmed and self-assurance was slowly replaced by nationalism.

I will approach our discussion of victimhood in two ways. First, I will explore some of the circumstances that lead to a victim mind-set and second I will offer some suggestions about how a person might decide to respond. First let's look into some examples of circumstances that could induce people to see themselves as victims:

- *The Accident Victim*--One type of victim situation is a person who has suffered an injury like a car accident that was not caused by them. Sometimes the injury is life altering because of the severity of the physical injury. There may be a lengthy recovery. How a person processes the experience varies. In some cases, the emotional injury will not linger. In other cases, it could lead to a lifelong journey of feeling like a victim.

Some people in this situation will even turn on themselves with internal messages like: "I must have had something to do with it," or "If only I had done something different."

- *A Victim of a Broken Trust or Agreement-* There are situations in which a person is tricked, swindled, or deceived by the dishonesty of others. This involves betrayed confidence and trust. Mending the trust is a complex process. The experience of being the object of abuse where there has been physical, emotional or theological trauma can lead to severe complications. Lasting memories of being the victim of another's control are predictably pushed deep within one's psyche. The beginning of recovery is often some form of distancing from the circumstance. Sometimes, on the road to recovery a person is able to realize that the abuse was not their fault; that the abusive experiences were due to the nature or the dysfunction of the abuser. Some victims will blame themselves in some way. I do not subscribe to either the frequently heard idea that we choose all of our experiences before we come into human bodies or that we have no choice at all. I believe there is a divine plan and that we have lessons to learn; but there are some experiences that are just random and some that are for our lessons.

One's age, the level of experience and circumstantial factors all contribute to the response we choose after traumatic happenings. If a person's spiritual teachings are that it is selfish to feel good about oneself, then religion can impede full recovery in such victim producing situations.

- *A Victim of an Honorable or Voluntary Sacrifice-* One of the most complicated victim situations is when someone suffers injury, disease, loss or death as the result of a patriotic or justifiable cause that was entered into voluntarily. Some examples would include: service to country, to one's church, or to a social cause. Choice and commitment are involved. The decision to place oneself into a potentially harmful circumstance for the good of others can be based on certain assumptions and expectations about the reason for the service. The consequences of these voluntary commitments are both emotional and physical. The resulting injuries are often long-lasting for both the victim and those who are related to the victim. Sometimes there is doubt about the validity of the reason for the service on the part of the committed person, their family, or by others who express their opinions. This can lead to feelings of having been victimized, by either the dissenters or the institution one is committed to.

- Another victim experience that some would say is a recent condition is what could be called *"Victim Blaming."* This means that the victim of a crime is held to be completely or partly *responsible* for what has happened to them—such as a rape or assault. Victims are said to have "asked for it" or "unconsciously wanted the abuse." Today we are aware of legal proceedings in which the blame is placed upon the injured, not the perpetrator. I maintain that various religious dogmas have contributed to a long history of the victimization of women and indigenous people based upon the perceived right to act upon them in hurtful ways. Akin to this would be to hold the view that a person came into this lifetime having "agreed to a situation" before coming here. This thinking, in my view, reduces the potential for growth and encourages a victim identity. I feel similarly about the "caste" systems found in various cultures. The victim accepts their lot in life and the expected abuses as their destiny.

- *A Long-term Loss of Freedom-* This can refer to a person who has been forcibly extracted from their environment and placed into a role of total service to a person or to an organized system. It also includes those who have been imprisoned unjustly or forced into slavery. Unfortunately, such scenarios have been a part of human history for a long time. Some examples I can think of are: the Egyptians and the Israelites, the Romans and the Jews, kings and various peasant systems, and the American system of slavery. In each instance, a victim identity is the result. Today we still know of instances of what could be called "human trafficking." Persons, usually the young or women, are taken and placed into serving situations for economic profit. It is most difficult for the victims of such degradation to access a part of their psyche that helps them to survive this total loss of personal freedom. Reentry into the regular world is almost always an incredible challenge and for many an impossible reality.

- *A Victim of a Disability-* When a person is born with, or develops later in life, some inherent or perceived limitation that affects their ability to function in society, they can become a victim with a disability. It has been my professional experience with many young people who have genetic, physical, cultural or other debilitating limitations, that they do not always see their situation as a disability. If I would make an attempt to put words into their mouths, perhaps they would say, "I'm not disabled, I'm just *differently*-abled!" Many who perceive themselves as a victim of their circumstance have come to this conclusion with the help of social, familial and religious influences.

- *Victims of Alternative Life-style or Belief.* People who hold views that are not in alignment with the prevailing social or religious norms, who have a different sexual orientation or unpopular political views can be made to feel like victims if they are persecuted or made to feel less worthy.

Elaine Pagels presents sound research that tracks the social implications of the introduction of the figure of Satan into religious traditions and how that has allowed for the demonization of others.[236] Briefly, the concept of evil as embodied by the "guy in the red suit," has been changed from him being one of God's fallen angels to being the king of an army of attacking forces and having the power to possess one's soul. Pagels explains, "*Satan defines negatively what we think of*

---

[236] Pagels, *The Origin of Satan*, xviii-xix.

as human."[237] My research helps me to understand this viewpoint as professed by the Garden of Eden story. I do not believe in the philosophy that defines human nature as innately evil. However, this has been a very useful belief for placing the ultimate burden of guilt upon all of humanity.

The social impact of the supposed role of Satan throughout the millennia has been, in my opinion, a gradual but significant acceptance of a kind of collective victim mentality. As humanity embraced religious dogma, reinforced by political influences, the victim philosophy has now become enmeshed in the human psyche.

Ancient guidance reminds us that every experience holds a potential lesson. Developing a "learn from it" approach would call for patience and confidence and a belief that within each incident something life-supporting and life-strengthening could be discovered. In Native philosophy, we speak of placing an experience that we don't understand into a "mystery bag." The person would potentially learn something at a later time that was not understood in the present moment. It implies faith[238] in the Great Mystery's ultimate plan. Such guidance today presents a considerable challenge, since most have grown up with spiritual concepts that envision a "book of life" which records our every wrongdoing and ultimately leads to God's judgment.

Dealing With Victim Identity

What will it take to achieve a "learn from it" attitude? It can only begin as an individual resolve, and it will not be an easy task. My purpose here is to point the reader toward the first step which is awareness. It means **recognizing the strong tendency to justify one's actions using a victim philosophy.** Like a habit, or in stronger terms like a social addiction, victim consciousness is rooted within some of the major spiritual agendas. As our social structure has changed from a simpler life to an economically driven society, the idea that we can learn from all experiences has fallen by the wayside. It has been replaced, in some instances, with the idea that one can profit from every experience. Instead of using the mystery bag concept, there is a

---

[237] Ibid, xviii.
[238] One Aramaic interpretation for "Have faith in God." Mark 11:22 (KJV) is *"Remain within yourselves—live in a place of rooted confidence in Sacred Unity."* Douglas-Klotz, *The Hidden Gospel*, 27.

tendency to internalize the experience and the victim identity. In the old times, one identified with their vision, not with the circumstances of their life.

The second step towards benefiting from one's experience is personal honesty. That is, to determine what you can honestly take ownership of and what has been imposed upon you by outside influences. This includes looking at the validity of the concept that humans have an innately sinful nature. Sifting out the baggage that directly connects to our personal actions requires extensive personal resolve. As the old adage goes, "know thyself." Sounds simple; but since humanity has been influenced to believe for hundreds of years that our value is based upon outside validation rather than personal self-love, it gets really knotty. It is as if being human is something to overcome or guard against. Oprah Winfrey, the notable world-wide television host, gives this advice:

Always continue the climb. It is possible for you to do whatever you choose, if you first get to know who you are and are willing to work with a power that is greater than ourselves to do it.[239]

Sorting out what our true qualities are, and authentically expressing what we think and feel requires a willingness to take time for ourselves in reflection and the courage to own our shortcomings as well as our gifts. This self study will require us to examine our familial and social beliefs, our religious concepts, and how we love and respect ourselves. In the Aramaic language, the word for "neighbor" means both inside and outside, as if we are to love ourselves to the same degree as our neighbor. In an early manuscript known as the *Didache*, there is a unique reference to the so-called "golden rule" that is worth mentioning as we think of the Aramaic meaning for neighbor: "The Way of Life is this: First, you shall love the God who made you, and your neighbor as yourself; and whatever you do not want to have done to you, do not do to another."[240]

Third step is to see our past as the best frame of reference for self investigation. In Native philosophy everything happens in a cyclical pattern. Often, when we think we have overcome a particular behavior we find ourselves repeating that behavior in times of stress

---

[239] Hanson, Kenneth, Ph.D. *Secrets of the Lost Bible*, 45.
[240] *Didache* 1.2 quoted in *Beyond Belief* by Elaine Pagels, 15.

and this sometimes leads to us experiencing some shame, guilt or victim energy. We might chastise ourselves with thoughts like, "I went to confession about this. Here I go again. I am I bad person." It takes a lot of courage to accept and embrace repeating unwanted behavior and/or thoughts and move on toward growth. The truth is, we actually facilitate change when we are compassionate with ourselves and when we are able to learn from our uncomfortable experiences.

Fourth step is developing some measure of love and respect for oneself. So, I offer the idea that awareness can be a beginning step to self-love. This means learning to manage rather than seeking to get rid of what causes us pain. Each person has both strengths and weaknesses that must be honored. Managing means that *every* life experience is an opportunity to learn more about who we are and who we want to become. The spiritual skill involved is knowing that we can deal with everything, if and when it comes around again, if we can find meaning within the experience. What is the most constructive and life-enhancing thing we can do in the present moment, given the circumstances of our situation? Then, it means giving ourselves credit and compassion for doing our best. This essential foundation must be built slowly in order that self reflection will be beneficial rather than destructive. Once again, victim-consciousness and the accompanying remorse and regret often block people's ability and willingness to look within.

An understanding of the word *respect* can be useful here. The dictionary meaning for respect is to *re-look or to look again*. This means to revisit; to reconsider; to return to past events and reevaluate and reinterpret them in light of present understanding. We might need to say to ourselves, "I did the best I could at that time" or "My choices were based on conditions over which I had little control" or "I was in a different place then…" We can be supportive of our learning process instead of punishing ourselves.

It is my opinion that the concept of "karma," in its most often understood definition of "I am paying for mistakes I made in another lifetime," can be a block that stands in the way of the opportunity to learn and grow. It tends to contribute to the victim outlook because it seems like punishment. I believe we have an opportunity to try again until we learn from the experience what we need to integrate in order to move forward in our spiritual development. I suspect that this may be the older, more original meaning of karma. However, we all have the right to choose what is meaningful to our own spiritual practice and philosophy.

Distance can afford some perspective on experiences sometimes. Those who are still within an abusive environment will not always be able to successfully detach enough to identify what is meaningful in the experience. That's where the mystery bag can come in handy.

Step five is to take this journey with a good friend, partner, colleague or professional. A non-judgmental, compassionate, honest yet sensitive, co-journeyer who can be a constant and willing witness is crucial. It is good to seek out someone who can recognize growing experiences; as opposed to guilt-producing, victim-inducing ones. It is most difficult to be non-judgmental when one's spiritual up-bringing has fostered rigid rules about right and wrong.

A sixth suggestion is to take small steps. Most of us are pretty impatient with ourselves. Any new behavior or insight takes time to integrate. It is comparable to learning a new language or skill. We first have awareness, and then catch ourselves in the middle of the old behavior, and finally we are able to walk it into our life experience. All this take time, patience and practice. This needs to happen with as little focus upon shame, guilt or error as possible. An understanding of the consequences of holding onto a victim perspective can motivate us to move past our need to see ourselves in this way. It takes a lot of energy to maintain an attitude of victimhood. The price we pay for expending our energy in this way is to limit energy that could be expended to help us grow and develop spiritually. We then have much less joy in our lives.

Our desire to make a total change can sidetrack our efforts to start with tiny steps. However, each miniature step brings the likelihood of increasing our gratitude and our chances for success. Framing those intentional efforts requires substantial thought and discussion. As I suggested earlier, it is highly beneficial to have the support of fellow journeyers along the way. Then, there is the selection of the container (I see it as a "womb space"), which facilitates growth. Change will happen if you *intend* and *tend* it and have gratitude for the small changes along the way.

Chapter Three

A Respectful Discussion of Christianity and Native American Spirituality

"Good is that which promotes life, evil is that which destroys it."
Albert Schweitzer (1875-1965)

"...the concept of the 'love of God' appears many more times in the Hebrew Bible and Pharisaic literature than the concept of the 'fear of God.' " (Rabbi David Rosen)[241]

    I would now like to address some of the spiritual beliefs that have existed for many thousands of years around the world. It is my opinion that there has been a profound transition in the way people viewed life from early times to the present. This is not to indicate that life was necessarily better in the far distant past; unless you consider simple beliefs to be somehow more spiritual. My purpose is to make some comparisons between the beliefs held in ancient times and the prominent religious dogma of today.

    For those who have a great depth in theological discourse, this writing may not be satisfying. My hope is to simply lift up the old and the new concepts for discussion. It may surprise even some Native American people that the spiritual beliefs that were introduced by the European visitors did not exist in the old village tribal way of life. How did belief and religion come to be such an influence upon indigenous populations in the world? I think that there is a natural attempt to balance one's personal identity in relationship to whatever

---

[241] Tully, Mark. *Four Faces: A Journey in Search of Jesus the Divine, the Jew, the Rebel, the Sage*, 82. "The Hebrew verb for "fear" can be understood two ways. Occasionally it meant fear as we commonly think…But very often the biblical "fear" meant awe or reverence for someone of exalted position. In other words, Abraham was not necessarily "afraid" of God, as he was holding him in profound respect." Kenneth Davis, op. cit., 78.

group or institutional identity is present in a particular culture. My visits with many wonderful, and sometimes challenging, Elders have fulfilled a childhood longing as well as presented an assortment of adult lessons and journeys. All of these experiences have provided a springboard from which I am known to leap out into troubled waters! Having spent most of my life walking in two worlds, I take courage now to discuss the possible parallels that exist between Christianity and the spiritual beliefs of American Indians in general.

In this chapter I will first present an overview of the two philosophies with the intent of being both informative and respectful, and taking into consideration individual differences. Many more people are open to considering indigenous information these days. One could say better late than never about the emerging tolerance of ethnicity. I choose to believe that we walk in no better times for these discussions to occur. With an enduring faith and patience, our Elders have told us that when it becomes appropriate for "ears to hear and the eyes to see" the Ancient Ones will finally be given their due.

For many years I literally shed tears at the opportunity to be in the midst of Native Elders who wanted to share their teachings. In my first book I wrote of my experience of going to St. Paul's School of Theology near Kansas City, Missouri. Two Native Elders were invited by a panel of seasoned theologians to bring their understanding of Native teachings. It wasn't long before the discussion began to follow an outline designed to confront and challenge them about the validity of Native teachings. Clearly there was an agenda to discredit them.

I was so impressed at the quiet dignity of those Elders. Their opinions where expressed without anger and with tolerance, even though they had reason to feel otherwise. Those with impressive divinity degrees exchanged looks of futility. This dialog resulted in more listening than hearing and more rigidity than bridge building. As a young Native man however, I benefited greatly from this experience. The final words spoken by one of the Elders still ring in my ears, "Perhaps there was a good reason that the Creator gave human beings two ears and only one mouth!" I hope in this writing I can teach with Elderly integrity.

The Great Mystery has given me a vision and hopefully the skills to teach with diplomacy and to carefully keep the paths of knowledge open when possible. My affinity with such Peacemakers as Deganawidah, Tecumsah, Handsome Lake, the Morning Star Visitor, the Dala Lama, Gandhi, the Master Jesus and others gives me the determination to build bridges where I can. It is my hope to construct such bridges between people, ideologies and cultures. This is not at all to lessen the importance of any spiritual teaching, but to open passageways of understanding between them.

The Christianizing of Native Americans

Within my lifetime I have put together some of the history of the Christianizing and Americanizing of Native peoples. This journey has been painfully branded into Native memories for easily seven generations. My conversations with many Native Elders have helped me put the pieces together. I speak of this on rare occasions, because this story holds lots of anger and bitterness for some Native folks. My usual focus is on the gifts and lessons that are part of **every** life experience. However, I will touch on it here in order to initiate some discussion, because ancient voices have not always made it into historical accounts.

President Andrew Jackson signed the Indian Removal Act on May 27, 1830. The next year he went against a decision of the Supreme Court and ordered the removal of Native people from the eastern United States to the Indian Territories in Oklahoma. The ensuing forced migration is known as the "Trail of Tears." Land was offered to the Indians on a per capita basis to the enrolled members of each tribe. Choctaw Indians were relocated to southeastern Oklahoma. The old family names were discarded and English names were given. Unlike in the removal stories of other Native nations that were given tribal land called reservations, in the case of the Natives in Oklahoma 180 acres of land was deeded to each person. This is rather curious, given that Native Americans were not even citizens of the United States until 1924! The American concept of private ownership made it more convenient for land to easily slip out of the hands of Native people. Dad sold his 180 acres in order to have money to go to college. Many years later our family traveled to find his land and discovered that it was producing "black gold"—oil!"

There have been many Natives who have voiced their frustration and outrage over what happened to Native people. "What right did the 'company' have to take away our way of life? Look what has happened to our children, the Elders, and our culture! We had little chance to change the inevitable outcome of the genocide and the replacing of tribal beliefs. Now, with the increased interest in Native spirituality the white man wants to steal our spirituality too! How can we ever forgive the Europeans for the genocide, the injustices and the disrespect for our culture?" Let me say right up front that I recognize the pain that has been caused and I understand that there is certainly justifiable anger resulting from the cultural trauma that has occurred. Fortunately, we have some Elders who are providing guidance and prayers to facilitate the healing process. I carry memories of their expressions. I hope to share more of these expressions as we go along. As in olden days, I believe it is still possible for many peoples to come into balance with every experience.

Those who need to stand up for their beliefs and rights must be able to walk within their hopes and visions. Old wisdom tells us that all people have the right to choose their lessons. Everyone is exactly where they need to be for their own growth. It is not necessarily that they are calling such experiences to themselves as it is embracing the life experiences that do come along and learning from them. Remember the past, be vigilante in the present and be a part of the healing in the future. This involves not only a re-connection, human to human, but also participation in the healing process of our Mother Earth.

Earth-based Philosophy

A review of ancient history reveals that before the foundations of Judaism, Christianity, and the Islamic religions, indigenous communities around the world shaped their spirituality through their experiences and understandings of the natural world. Experiences inside the village, within the immediate environment and in nature were very helpful in forming and understanding life principles. Local tribal Elders, those who had long memories and held ancient teachings, were very willing to be available for consultation. Their expressions (some would say wisdom), were listened to and remembered. What was shared by an Elder was determined by the questions asked and the age and personality of the seeker.

Equally useful in the search for the answers to life's difficult questions were those who remembered the stories. The selection and sharing of specific stories, parables, or experiences was done with careful consideration for who was listening. Often such shared expressions were ideas and stories well-known to the community, but they would be aimed at indirectly addressing specific questions asked.

In some Native traditions, storytellers were easily recognized from a distance because of their appearance or apparel. For example, an elaborate, unique arrangement of their hair and the demeanor of the story teller in some Native traditions would identify a person as a storyteller with a specific vision. Some storytellers would arrange their hair in an assortment of knots! The selection and telling of certain stories had the potential to help untangle life's issues and problems.

In the old days, indigenous people would tell traditional stories to lay a spiritual foundation for living a joyous and meaningful life. Because storytellers were often welcome into any tribal circle, they would bring stories and experiences from faraway places. As I will discuss later, in old cultures and especially the Jewish culture, it was important for the listener and the teller that each piece of the story connected in some way with actual life experience. Stories were about the human experience of individuals as well as life within the community. It was not important that the story depict an actual occurrence. Referring to a story or event as a myth need not diminish the benefit it may have. The energy of the story brings meaning in layers that often take time to understand. There is always room for mystery and individual interpretation.

Some Native stories have strange characters that were known to act and speak in unusual ways. Sometimes known as "contraries" or "backwards people" ("hey-o-kah" in the Lakota language), they walked completely in their vision and were not seen to be doing things wrong. They served an important function in tribal life. They offered many possible ways of being and behaving, thus strengthening the ability to make choices. In the old days, it was important to learn from all experiences with an attitude that life is really about choices rather than making mistakes or doing the wrong thing.

It is my understanding that such religions as Hinduism, Sufism and Buddhism also still contain stories and expressions today that are spiritually helpful and applicable to life. The wisdom offered was not necessarily to be followed explicitly; but was only to be given consideration. Some examples would be:

- (Confucius) Adept Kung asked, "Is there any one word that could guide a person throughout life?"
  The Master replied: "How about 'shu' [reciprocity]: never impose on others what you would not choose for yourself?"[242]
- (Confucius) "When you have faults, do not fear to abandon them."
- (Confucius) "Respect yourself and others will respect you."[243]

That which could be called "wisdom," I believe, could more accurately be expressions that have endured the test of time. Often they were not written down. The deliverer offered the expressions with no expectation of a prescribed response. Under this philosophy the responsibility for making choices is placed solely into the lap of the listener. In most indigenous communities, the concept of "making a mistake" was not emphasized. Rather, the emphasis was on what could be learned from the experience.

Life was meant to be experienced as *part of the All.* Each person was aware of their unique place within the larger circle of life. All actions were viewed as connected to and influencing every aspect of life. Every action had an effect upon relationships in the environment. In Native terms, being related meant becoming more and more aware that every life form was intricately and mysteriously interconnected.

On the other hand, there was room for what can be called "growing spaces." I often describe these as "wombs." Every life form had experiences that defined these growing spaces, such as family, a close group of friends, home, certain boundaries in nature, etc. Allowing for personal movement within the womb meant that one had some liberties within the growing environment.

To balance this idea of flexibility of choice, each adult was watchful and was considered every child's relative. A *relative* was an older concerned observer, a gentle tribal intercessor. Rather than correcting and demeaning a child, the older members would provide a different perspective on a given experience. Respect for each person's personality and choice would be balanced with openness to hearing other ideas. Often when I present some of these concepts to parents, they will recognize the possible value these ideas might have in our present culture!

---

[242] Analects XV. 24, tr. David Hinton.
[243] http://en.wikipedia.org/wiki/Confucius.

An informed walk in life reflects a readiness to understand what can be learned from a walk in the woods. From early childhood it was important to develop the skill of awareness. One of the wombs where learning took place was the natural world[244] of animals and plants. They were members of the family too. As one grew within the more predictable confines of the home and village, another balance was added: gaining an understanding of the natural world. There was a sense of reciprocity in the attitudes of tribal people. Life was understood as interdependent. The actions and choices of each being were viewed as having some influence upon all of the rest of life.

Knowledge and personal experiences were to be placed alongside trust in the divine order of life. Just as personal knowledge was vital to survival, a deep-seated trust and belief in the Creator's plan was important. In Native terms, "we are all related." It's all about relationship. *All life is sacred.*[245] Life can be a mystery at times and life is about change. Each of these concepts pulls us toward a greater awareness of the divine nature[246] of everything in creation. Awareness brings us back into balance and helps us make room for trust in the great order of life.

Most tribal languages had no words for "belief," "religion," or "friend." Ideas and opinions were more important than beliefs that were to be adhered to by all. Instead of a religion, the Native perspective is best described as a way of life. The idea of a relationship is being interconnected and related to everything. So, the idea of friendship doesn't quite fit. That identity is used today to signify someone who is not family and therefore not related.

Regard for the feminine principle and for the grandmothers was a vital part of the community. The Creator in ancient times left little doubt about the significance of women. Some tribal systems varied in

---

[244] David Fideler in *Jesus Christ: Sun of God* relates that "Plato was initiated into the ancient mysteries and is said to have studied at Heliopolis, the city of the sun, a great center of scientific and priestly learning in ancient Egypt…he certainly did acknowledge the divinity of the natural world and the celestial bodies…", 8.

[245] "For the Irish, all life was sacred, all ground was holy ground." Margaret Starbird, *The Feminine Face of Christianity*, 44.

[246] Klotz, Neil –Doulas, *The Hidden Gospel*, pg 27. According to Klotz interpretation, in the Aramaic language "Blessed are the pure in heart: for they shall see God." (Matthew 5:8) KJV, is "Ripe are the consistent in heart; they shall see the Sacred Unity everywhere."

the roles women had, but none doubted the importance of the feminine aspect of life. The respect for grandmothers emphasized the importance of boundaries and of how the growing space and growing energy must be maintained. Generally speaking, life purpose and one's personal vision were recognized for every individual through ceremonies. The feminine energy within men and specifically within women was recognized to be the container for growth.

As nature demonstrates, the Great Mystery clearly intends that there be many life cycles or lifetimes. Each human lifetime brings more education and more experiences to be fully embraced. Native Elders refer to death as "the changing of worlds."[247] Also, each cycle creates a stronger connection to the divine.[248]

The "People of the Book"

This section addresses some of the beliefs and ideologies connected Judaism and Christianity, and how they influenced indigenous cultures and beliefs. Many of the theological tenets of these religions have been introduced to indigenous peoples around the world. History records that religions were systematically forced upon various cultures and ancient tribal systems, with little choice offered to them.

Followers of the three major religions, Judaism, Christianity and Islam have sometimes been referred to as "people of the book." One thing they have in common is that their tenets are recorded in sacred books: the Torah, the Bible, and the Koran [*qur'an*] respectively. From A.D. 661 until 1099, there were different dynasties that ruled Palestine. At that time, Jews and Christians were generally

---

[247] In the first century most Jews believed in life after death. "Every Jew desired to earn 'eternity in the World to Come.' The World to Come appears thousands of times in rabbinic literature but, curiously, it is never defined." Wylen, Stephen M., *The Jews in the Times of Jesus: An Introduction*, 92. "I was taught growing up that Jews believe in an afterlife but we do not talk much about it. We are to focus on *this* life, not the World to Come. We know we do not believe in a Hell, exactly, but reincarnation, Heaven, some kind of limbo state? Judaism does not explain. We are not supposed to worry about it too much. Our purpose is to make *this* world better, not to fixate on the next one." Stephanie M.

[248] In Judaism there was an awareness of the importance of individual relationship with God. As an individual would draw closer to God, this would be "independent of the communal covenant." Wylen, Stephen M., op. cit., 93.

well tolerated by the Moslem population.[249] One reason was that all of these religions were seen as "people of the book." The atmosphere of tolerance lasted until the Crusades. In this book, I will not specifically address Islam, since I have not conducted an in-depth study of that spiritual tradition as yet.

Christianity in Review

I realize the weighty responsibility of writing a summary of the tenets of Christianity, so this presentation will be a somewhat middle-of-the-road dialog rather than representing one end of the spectrum or another. Please know this cannot begin to do justice to all Christian communities and theologies. My humble apologies if I fail to adequately verbalize someone's belief system. I am not a theologian!

Looking into ancient texts that are not included in the Holy Bible has not been generally encouraged by many Christian spiritual leaders. Typical pastoral guidance is often to study, learn, and align spiritual actions and choices with scriptural interpretation. Some more rigid literal denominations give no credence at all to resources outside of the Bible.

Various forms of Christianity might include within their description of spiritual experience:

- *joining a church, being taught the doctrine and laws and responding with obedience*
- *seeking to obtain a heavenly reward and believing that this earthly existence of being removed from the presence of God was punishment for having disobeyed God*
- *participating in regular worship, service to community, and attaining a position of authority and stature within the institutional church.*

Baptism offers a path of salvation from a fallen condition resulting from disobedience in the Garden of Eden, into a blessed condition where the recipient is saved from eternal separation from God. Membership generally means accepting a body of beliefs and loyalty to the church as reflected in regular attendance at worship services. Baptism brings the saved into the fellowship of the chosen that are loved by the Holy Father. True believers often carry an attitude

---

[249] Mark A. Gabriel writes in *Islam and the Jews*, "…some Muslims became tolerant of Jews and Christians." Also the dates referred to in the text are supported. 126-127.

of repentance, submission and surrender. Many believe that adhering to this spiritual path will assure the acceptance and grace of the Heavenly Father through Jesus Christ and assure them of an abode in Heaven in the hereafter.[250]

Right actions will reward believers by finally freeing them from this Earthly prison. Within this context, the more rigid forms of Christianity recognize one's natural state, including the physical body, as an enemy to one's spirituality. Eve's disobedience and Adam's compliance in the Garden of Eden led to humanity's fallen state and a curse upon women in general. It then becomes mandatory to be saved from one's evil innate nature. Feelings of unworthiness and guilt are promoted. Believers strive to become more perfect and to be forgiven for being lost and sinful.

This opportunity to be forgiven is represented in the God-incarnated personage of Jesus Christ. Born of a humble Jewish Virgin Mother, Jesus was tutored as a rabbi[251] and teacher. Miracles are attributed to him and his teachings brought about the retaliation of both the Roman and Jewish authorities. Jesus accepted his lot, relinquished his own will to his Heavenly Father's will, and died painfully and sacrificially on the cross[252] in order to wash away the sins of the world and to afford believers a future reunion with Jesus and God in an afterlife in Paradise. Painted into the minds and hearts of believers are the images of the trial, Crucifixion and Resurrection of Jesus. The faithful are saved and enter into a blessed condition of direct relationship with God in which they are no longer in a fallen state. The final judgment will determine whether a person goes to Heaven or

---

[250] Biblical scholar Marcus J. Borg says, "It is important to emphasize that the Jewish tradition did not yet affirm an afterlife. Belief in a heaven and hell beyond death was still two or three centuries in the future. (about the time of the writing of Proverbs, 500 BCE)", *Reading the Bible Again for the First Time*, 151.

[251] "In the King James Version of the Bible, Jesus is called "Rabbi" thirteen times. In the Revised Standard Version, the word "Master" is substituted instead with an added footnote saying, 'or Rabbi'..." Moore, *The Christian Conspiracy*, 130.

[252] "The true sign of Christianity for the earliest centuries of church history was not a crucifix…In the catacombs, no figure of a man on a cross can be found for the first six or seven centuries of the era…Not until 692, in the reign of Emperor Justinian II, was it decreed by the church that the figure of the historical Jesus on the cross should supersede that of the lamb." *Recovering Christianity's Pagan Past*, U.S. News & World Report (Special Edition, copyright 2008), 50-51.

Hell[253] after life is over on Earth. They will return to the Holy Presence of God or go to the other experience away from the Divine Presence where they will be severely punished forever. This doctrine is exemplified in the Nicene Creed of the Roman Catholic Church:

Nicene Creed
We believe in one God the Father Almighty, Maker of all things visible and invisible; and in one Lord Jesus Christ, the only begotten of the Father, that is, of the substance [*ek tes ousias*] of the Father, God of God, light of light, true God of true God, begotten not made, of the same substance with the Father [*homoousion to patri*], through whom all things were made both in heaven and on earth; who for us men and our salvation descended, was incarnate, and was made man, suffered and rose again the third day, ascended into heaven and cometh to judge the living and the dead. And in the Holy Ghost. Those who say: There was a time when He was not, and He was not before He was begotten; and that He was made out of nothing (*ex ouk onton*); or who maintain that He is of another hypostasis or another substance [than the Father], or that the Son of God is created, or mutable, or subject to change, [them] the Catholic Church anathematizes.

Those who accept Jesus as a personal savior and Son of God are called into discipleship to follow the straight and narrow path. Discipleship is modeled in the scriptures with images of mostly male disciples whose writings are presented as the actual words of Jesus. Some denominations claim to be the actual church that Jesus established during his day. Often, denominations claim to be the right and correct church. Other churches are seen as misinformed and having beliefs that are wrong. The mission of the Church is to proselytize and convert the world to Christianity.[254]

Most Christians are to give respect and allegiance to church leaders. Ministers and priests are symbolic of what it means to be a servant of God, and to humanity. Some major institutions expect them to be an example of a suffering servant, celibate and self-sacrificial like Jesus was. Ordained ministers who are trained in seminary are to be given high regard and status. Often their attire and their titles are a part of their identity. Generally speaking, ideas such as experiencing

---

[253] Early writers of the Old Testament never mentioned Hell—"For the ancient Jews Sheol was a dark and melancholy place for departed souls who wander unhappy, but untormented. Eventually, Sheol took on the characteristics of Gehema, Hell in the New Testament, a place of punishment." *The Other Bible*, glossary--Sheol.

[254] A survey announced on National Public Radio indicates that more than eighty percent of the world's population (some six billion now and every year ninety million more are added), seek to embrace forms of spirituality other than Christian.

pleasure, self-care, having a connection to nature and having women in leadership roles are discouraged within the doctrine of some, but not all, Christian belief systems.

A church building or cathedral invites believers to worship indoors. Often there is the symbolism of a beacon in the night for the lost, the pitiful, the sinful and the unsaved. The structure is often referred to as the "house of God" or "the place where we come to worship God."

Prophecies in the Bible suggest that in the future the world and its people will experience the "end times," or "Armageddon" when an experience of rapture[255] will determine who God will choose to be with Him in Heaven. Those who are not chosen will be severely punished and will abide with the Devil in Hell[256] forever. This inevitable battle between good and evil precedes the return of Jesus Christ, the only son of God. Some teach of a Heaven on Earth reuniting chosen people who have been waiting for the Great Judgment Day. God and the Devil are viewed as battling for the souls of humankind.

I have heard a few Native Elders wonder, "How is it that so many nice and loving people treat each other with such disrespect? Why can't they come together and pray together? We are all sacred and have been born of Mother Earth, sharing a common walk as human beings. We have been given so much beauty to look at and appreciate. What is it going to take for us to become related again?"

---

[255] "Many believe that Jesus will reappear in the rapture. The concept of "rapture" is not in the Book of Revelations." (Rev. Dr. Barbara Rossing, professor, Lutheran School of Theology and Dr. Paul Samuel Boyer, Historian, University of Wisconsin) "In 1830 in northern Scotland fifteen year old Margaret McDonald had a vision not once but three times, Jesus comes and takes away believers to heaven before the Last Judgment. John Darby a British preacher, put various passages from the Bible and combined them with McDonald's vision to formulate a scenario of what's going to happen in the future which came to be known as the rapture. Early twentieth century Biblical Historian C. I. Scofield created an annotated version of the Bible. (The Scofield Reference Bible) placing Darby's notes about the rapture next to actual Bible passages. Over eleven million copies world-wide were sold. This further enmeshed the rapture idea and the book of Revelations. Today many people do not know that the rapture idea was not original to the Book of Revelations but was incorporated later." *Secrets of Revelation,* National Geographic Channel, 7/16/2006.

[256] The English word "Hell" is derived from a German verb meaning "to cover."(the one who is in Hell is hidden from God) Moore, *The Christian Conspiracy*, 94. "Hel" is also the name of a Germanic goddess of the underworld. Baring & Cashford. Op. cit., 582.

I remember sitting in a Blackfoot Elder's home outside of Calgary, Alberta, Canada. He asked me, "Can you explain why I must go through a building or a person to get to the Creator? In the old days we felt the Creator very near."[257] Others have said that nature is where we learn the original teachings of the Creator. Spiritual instructions were to be found here with Mother Earth. The Great Mystery made her our classroom for spiritual teachings. Standing Bear is known to have said: "The Old Lakota was wise. He knew that a man's heart away from nature becomes hard."

Christianity and Natural Spirituality: A Look at the Similarities

"The evidence of close similarities between Christianity and other ancient world faiths is massive, detailed, extremely specific, and quite far-flung, stretching from the Vedic wisdom of India to the Norse myths of Scandinavia, the legends of the Incas, and the original spirituality of the indigenous peoples of North America."[258]

Please understand that this discussion is based upon my personal experience, and my study and research into different forms of Christianity. There are many Christian denominations today. There are obvious differences in the rigidity of beliefs as well as the tolerance for open discussions within these various denominations. It is not my intention to focus on the specific variations between Christian churches. This is not to be exclusive; but to enable a more general discussion. There are some commonly held beliefs within the Christian tradition that will be the basis of my comparison with Native spiritual philosophy.

The same can be said of the Native spiritual beliefs. There are differences in the specific tribal belief systems. There are many resources available for further study of the cultures of individual Native nations. You can explore these if you wish. I speak for no one nation's belief system. When I describe "Native spirituality," I am referring to the philosophies that are generally common to Native people as I have

---

[257] "Cut open a piece of wood, and there I am. Pick up a stone, and you will find me there." *Gospel of Thomas* quoted in *Secrets of the Lost Bible*, Dr. Hanson, 31.
[258] Harpur, Tom. *Recovering Christianity's Pagan Past*, U.S. News & World Report, (Special Edition, copyright 2008), 47.

observed from my travels and visits with Native people over my lifetime.

It is my opinion that there has been a significant erosion of many tribal philosophies that has accompanied the cultural destruction experienced from the European presence. Few, if any, Nations are able to fully know and reflect their ancient cultural ways today; though many are making a huge effort to preserve what they can of their language, culture and spiritual traditions. As an Anishinabe Elder expressed to me, *"If the ancient wisdom is to come back, the Great Creator will see to it."*

My time with Elders and ceremony has assisted my understanding of ancient Native philosophies. Also, I greatly appreciate the contribution of an ancient drawing called the Peace Shield from the Anishinabe traditions. The teachings of the Peace Shield were shared with me by an Ojibwe Elder, Irv Romans, in the Upper Peninsula of Michigan in the 1980's. In response to the fulfillment of the Eight Fire Prophecy which is part of the Peace Shield teachings, I have written two published books containing some of the teachings of this Anishinabe Peace Shield.[259]

I am drawn to the ancient ways that I believe existed before the last five hundred years. Our current understanding of the original Native beliefs is based largely on the writings and interpretations of non-Native people. I confess that some idealism may exist on my part as I attempt to give a place for ancient wisdom to be brought forward and made available to *all* Earth Walkers.

Belief in One Great Source, the Great Mystery

For most Christians God is usually represented as a male fatherly figure. In most Native circles, the tribal name of the Creator had no particular gender identity. I have heard some references to "the Old Man" and "the One Above All" and even "Father Sky." These days the name "Creator" (an English word), is spoken more often than even the tribal names. Some Native words for God today are in masculine terms. In the Native way, the Great Source ("Hush-**tah**-le" in the Choctaw language), was ever-present and reflected in all life

---

[259] ***The Universal Peace Shield of Truths:*** *Ancient American Indian Peace Shield Teachings*, (1996), ***Native American Spirituality:*** *A Walk in the Woods* (2003).

forms. It was an understanding of being within the Oneness. In the Christian way, the Holy One was a great distance away.

Obedience and compliance, reward and punishment were represented in Christianity. Following the guidance of God was expected. Native beliefs reflected a choice of whether to be in harmony with "*All That Is*" or not. Every lifetime offered each sacred spirit the opportunity to find balance, unity and relatedness with the divine in all life. Each experience increased one's relationship with the Great Mystery. In both Native and Christian teachings a daily relationship with the Divine was the ultimate goal.

Angels and Spirit Guides

Whether the divine beings were special spirits with specific roles or, for Native people, those relatives who reach to humankind from the other side, each group believed in such beings.[260] Christianity honored positive angelic beings that could be called upon in times of need. Sometimes they offered role-modeling for humans. Some angels were previous prophets or spirits who attained divinity as they were recognized as having evolved to high levels of spiritual expression.

From the Native perspective, the relatives who reach to the people of Mother Earth have been here before. Each "spirit guide" apparition (not exclusively human-looking), has the same identity and attributes as when they were on Earth. They offer wisdom, thoughts or experiences for a person to reflect upon. Each spirit-energy has a gift of some kind. A spirit guide offers contemplation rather than an injunction of what one *should* or *must* do. Native philosophies of old had no opening for any spirit to possess someone's soul. Humans were always responsible for their actions.

Spiritual Stories, Parables and Wisdom Tales

In Christian stories there are specific lessons to be taught by heroes, story characters or exemplary persons. Often these stories and parables are useful to remind believers of the good qualities and actions that are to be exemplified in one's life. Some offer ideas that could be

---

[260] I understand that in the Moari traditions of New Zealand, in the older times there were no doors on their houses. This tradition allowed for spirits to come and go as they willed.

seen as undesirable and represent sinful actions. Most biblical angelic beings are masculine images and there are very few feminine role models. There are many biblical writings and stories that have their origins in much older myths.[261]

The characters within Native stories and myths have various purposes. They are intended to be reflected upon rather than emulated. These characters are not necessarily viewed as heroes or exemplary beings, but rather, participants in life processes. Stories are told to reach into the everyday life experiences and give the listener something to think about rather than specific guidance or instruction. Some stories have experiences of "shape shifting" which makes room for the unexpected and mysterious in life.

The Use of Symbolism and Drawings

Symbols like the cross, the guiding star, light[262] and the shepherd are among many meaningful images for Christians. Each symbol reminds believers of spiritual concepts that they hold dear. We find them within churches, in home places and worn on the body. Pictures are sometimes used to reflect events that are to be remembered and revered. There are Christian pictures and symbols that reflect devotion, compassion, allegiance, discipleship, sacrifice and protection.

A Native person might carry a stone, feather, shell, crystal, or some other symbolic object to remind them of a significant experience. These are not necessarily "power objects" but meaningful objects. We can add the following to our discussion:

1- Both groups make use of symbolic drawings. Religious figures are important to Christians; drawings such as medicine wheels, teaching shields, etc. for Native people.

---

[261] For example, in the ancient story of Egyptian Isis and Osiris, Osiris is killed, placed in a chest, goes underground, and is resurrected at sunrise. Anne Baring and Jules Cashford, *The Myth of the Goddess*, 228-243.

[262] My research has helped me to understand the meaning of the Hebrew word that was later translated as *light*. To Hebrew people it meant "knowledge" and what can be called "enlightenment" today. I believe that knowledge was more available in ancient times before information was placed into mystery schools and away from common people. Preservation was important, but this led to the initiated and selected becoming the holders of wisdom. I believe this opened the door to opportunities to change, modify and even add to original concepts.

2- Worship and ceremony are important. For Christianity, regular worship usually happens indoors. Native ceremonies, in the old days happened only when there was a need or a specific purpose. There are some annual, seasonal, or solstice gatherings which occur with both.
3- Prayer, fasting, quiet time, music and meditation are common to both traditions.
4- There is the use of incense by both Christianity and Native Americans (sacred herbs).
5- When it comes to spiritual leadership or the conducting of ceremonies, Christians usually have seminary-trained ministers. In most Native circles, ceremonial people might have a vision to do so or a long apprenticeship to qualify them to conduct ceremony. Unlike in Christianity, each individual Native person would choose the Elder that they wanted to ask to do a personal ceremony for them. Leadership was temporary rather than through a position or term of office. Native ceremonial people did not expect payment for ceremony. Most Christian ministers are salaried and have length of service based on being hired by a congregation.
6- In both groups there is some understanding of life after death. For Christians it is a goal to attain eternal life and reach Heaven.[263] For Native peoples the desire is to learn from each lifetime and to strengthen one's relationship with the Creator. Life is already eternal.
7- Christian prophecy has a linear perspective. Native prophecy could be viewed as a repeating cycle.
8- Both have stories about the memory of a flood or deluge.[264]
9- You can find stories depicting various special messengers, teachers, or prophets in both traditions. Christianity identifies Jesus as the one major divine source of their teachings. For Native people there were unique tribal messengers, but, generally indigenous peoples were open to even the most seemingly insignificant teachers of divine wisdom. A leaf, a twig, an animal, or really any part of the creation was deemed capable of imparting a lesson. Village Elders were always honored for giving their advice and ideas.

---

[263] "A Harris poll of our attitudes conducted a few years ago found that 94 percent of American adults believe in God, 89 percent in heaven and 73 percent in hell. For professing Christians, those numbers are even higher." http://www.msnbc.msn.com/id/14274572/

[264] "In the Sumerian Epic of Gilgamesh…written in cuneiform on slates of baked clay, [a Babylonian epic that predates the Bible] the hero Utnapishtim survives a flood…the flood is depicted as an arbitrary act of the gods…a man builds a ship according to the advice of the gods and thus survives a flood that destroys all life around him. Alexander von Humboldt mentions that the Peruvians have the same legend, and in an account of the flood from Polynesia, the hero is even called Noa. There are more than 250 accounts of the legend of the flood in the world." Holger Kersten, op. cit., 60-61.

Native American Philosophy and What Came Across the Waters: "One and One is Three"

Some who have read my previous book will recognize the concept of "one plus one equals three." This is an attempt to give some attention to the philosophies that came to indigenous people as new concepts, and to compare them to what was already present in Native life. The first *"one"* represents the new ideas and beliefs that came to America. The second *"one"* designates the indigenous philosophies of life that were already present. As Native people choose to bring these two *ones* into their belief system, each person forms his or her individual philosophy or spirituality, represented by the number *"three."*

Native peoples were unable to communicate the reality that they had no religion. Rather, they considered spirituality to be their way of life. Religious groups came to this land focused upon changing the lives of the indigenous people which left no room for hearing their side of the story.

With the lighting of the Seventh Fire,[265] there is now an opportunity for the ancestors of the "company" to become acquainted with indigenous understandings. I like to say that, "the ancient ones are speaking from the dust of the land." Although we might think that the audience for the information about indigenous ideology would be the non-Native, it must be remembered that many Native people are sorting out and researching their cultures too.

"Three" represents, in this discussion, what can be birthed from the union of one philosophy and another. For Native peoples it was universally important to honor each person's choices and individual life journeys (sometimes referred to as one's "vision"). From individual choices came unique lessons that would shape each person's spiritual journey. Knowing how to learn from every new experience and accepting change were facts of life. Part of learning the lesson was to consider what the previous experience or understanding was and then being willing to be open to a new perspective. That is the "three!" Perhaps a medical example will be helpful. A doctor is trained to view

---

[265] "A new people in the 7th fire will arise and seek out the Elders and ancient wisdom." Rainbow Eagle, op. cit., 145-149.

both the similarities of all human physiology, as well as the individual variables that exist with each individual patient. Both perspectives must be considered to come to a "three" consensus about the course of treatment.

I will focus on each "one" separately and then bring them into a relationship; as I have done with drawing the parallels. I will begin by reflecting on the general Christian concepts that were represented in most, but not all, forms of Christianity that came to the shores of America. The Christian concepts presented will reflect ideologies that came ashore and were fully formed by the twentieth century. The Native concepts discussed will mirror much more ancient times. Both the Native philosophies and Christian theologies present in the twentieth century were very diversified and had changed from earlier times. Although some church practices today remain the same, I am not trying to represent exact theologies, as there have been considerable changes within most denominations in the past one hundred years. Next, I will present an overview of the philosophy and spirituality that was common to most Native Americans at that time. For the sake of clarity, it is necessary to repeat some of what I have already covered. I hope you can bear with me.

Do keep in mind that my purpose here is to educate and not at all to present one as more valuable than the other. So, each "one" will be as important as the other. This facilitates the previously stated tenet of honoring choice amidst change. Subsequently, what can occur is a journey of deciding YOUR OWN truth rather than deciding what THE truth is. Author Karen Armstrong writes, "As the Koran [qur'an] had taught all truth came from God and should be sought wherever it could be found."[266] Neil Douglas-Klotz relates his views about how to understand the word "truth":

The word <u>sherara</u>, translated as "truth," has several meanings in Aramaic and Hebrew: that which liberates and open possibilities, that which is strong and vigorous, and that which acts in keeping with universal harmony.[267]

To me this means a sense of what is an **appropriate** choice *at a particular time* and strengthens or enlivens one's purpose rather than being a **right** choice. And at the same time, an appropriate choice takes

---

[266] Armstrong, Karen. *A History of God*, 230.
[267] Douglas-Klotz, *The Hidden Gospel*, 43.

into consideration being in harmony with all of life and natural principles. It is hoped that what is learned from each experience will facilitate the crystallization of one's own truth. Remember, I respect those who are not willing to take this journey. Some may feel that they have already made their choice and need not include other perspectives.

A Respectful Comparison of Native American Philosophy (A Way of Life) and Christianity

It is difficult to discuss Native spiritual concepts and practices using the present tense, since many Native ceremonies today do not reflect the older understandings. I will use the past tense here, and add that there is a mixed application of both the philosophy and the practice of rituals I will be describing among Native peoples today. It is my intention to incorporate these older principles into my own personal walk in life as much as possible.

All tribal groups had at one time a communal relationship with Mother Earth and the natural world. The teachings of the natural were more or less known within all Native circles. Such spiritual understandings as respect for diversity, honoring personal identity and a regard for territorial boundaries were well understood. A walk in the woods demonstrated these concepts, but Native people basically applied these natural teachings within tribal life and not always in their relationships with other tribes.

Native people were born into specific traditions and customs. Each person knew their specific vision. It could be a precarious and delicate balance to carry out one's vision in the midst of various tribal identities.

Marriages were to take place between clans within each tribe or nation. Cultural ethics demanded rigid boundaries that prevented relations outside the tribe or village. We are all related, as a concept, was reflective of a relationship with nature, but it did not always apply to relationships between nations. There was a respect for all of life, but sometimes there were boundary issues! Having said that, in the long-ago days it was not essential to actually be in relationship with other tribal groups because land was plentiful and tribes were generally located far apart.

Those natural ways of applying spiritual principles are greatly lacking now. The ancient Peace Shield drawing taught to me by the last Peace Shield Teacher, Irv Romans, an Ojibwe Elder, represents a pathway to balance. As tribal people choose, it is possible for them to relearn what I term as "natural spirituality." Until these principles are once again realized, our full relationship with Mother Earth, humanity, and all life forms will be delayed. Now let's consider the natural teachings that, more or less, existed in North America and discuss the new spiritual concepts that came across the waters. I will attempt to address this comparison in a respectful manner.

Relationship With the Creator: Separation or an Ever-Present Creator?

What was introduced to Native peoples was the Christian belief that humans had caused a separation from the Heavenly Father. In the Genesis' Garden of Eden story the first inhabitants disobeyed God, resulting in punishment and a fall from Grace. If humans became fully subservient and in compliance with God's laws, then entry back into paradise, where God resides, would be possible. A book of life records all indiscretions or sins. Judgment Day will determine God's reward or punishment, with a destination of heavenly bliss or eternal damnation.

Within this theology came some new understandings for Native people. Eve and all females were cast as temptresses who lead men astray and Earth was often seen as a place where evil existed. Human sexuality was also brought into question. Nakedness,[268] sex and earthly pleasures were attached to a sinful condition. The emotion of guilt was very important in spite of any reconciliatory actions. For Native folks, such teachings seemed to hold a great deal of baggage. It seemed that humanity was saddled with a responsibility to undo what had been done thousands of years ago. Consequently, humans were to feel isolated and obligated to work out their salvation and return to God.

---

[268] From the *Gospel of Thomas* we read: "His disciples said, 'When will you be revealed to us and when shall we see you?' Jesus said, 'When you disrobe without being ashamed and take up your garments and place them under your feet like little children, and tread on them...'" Ian Wilson, *Jesus: The Evidence*, 25.

What was presented was that the purpose of life was to seek the truths that would align one with God's rules and to attempt to earn the love of the Divine through submission and obedience. Not my will but God's will be done! Many denominations claimed to be the holder of the right way back into the presence of God.

Native people understood the concept of consequences for one's actions. Perhaps there was an unwelcomed outcome, but often a life-enhancing lesson would be gleaned from the experience. Punishment didn't seem to fit the Native understanding of the Great Mystery. Reward, for that matter, was not a goal in Native philosophy.

****

The Peace Shield teaches that all life resides within the Spiritual Lodge of the Creator and that nothing exists outside the lodge or the loving arms of the Great Mystery. This is presented as a large blue circle in the Peace Shield drawing. In addition, the Creator is in all life forms and experiences.

In my second book *"Native American Spirituality: A Walk in the Woods,"* I wrote about how the natural world can be viewed as a classroom, but that it is not to be seen as a model of spirituality. A dilemma exists: on the one hand, all things are created with a divine touch; but, on the other hand, each creation had been given its own nature. This includes humans. Tribal Elders, both grandmothers and grandfathers, rounded out the spiritual support system. With this kind of tribal experience each person learned from both males and females, but was free to make their own choices according to their own understanding.

One of the important lessons of nature was Mother Earth's gravity. In the Native way of thinking this force was symbolic of the Great Mystery's connection to *all* life. It also meant that the Creator embraced and loved *all* life forms regardless of their nature, size or gift. Even those creatures that held a harmful nature or had boundaries that were not easily crossed were encircled equally by the Creator's arms; like Mother Earth holding all to her breast. There are various stories of the Creator asking the plants, animals and fish people to be ready to help humans because of their precarious and slow physical development.

The red dot in the center of the Peace Shield drawing represents the idea that the Great Spirit is in the center of all life forms everywhere. Some aspect of the Creator is being reflected to humans at all times, especially as one takes a walk in the natural. So, the Creator is always present and very near in Native philosophy and every lifetime holds the possibility of deepening one's relationship with the Divine. From early in life, there developed a kind of partnership between humans and the Creator. The divine within each person and the divine all around facilitated this partnership. Since there was no distance between humans and the Creator, this meant that the Great Source was within each moment and every experience.

Personal Vision and Group Spirituality

As we have seen, those who crossed the Atlantic Ocean to America represented many spiritual groups looking for an opportunity for religious freedom. Regular worship, usually indoors, provided the container for spiritual development within each denomination. By and large, ministers were men. Dependence upon those with more knowledge or with degrees in divinity reflected the need for external validation. Explicit guidance and teachings provided precise boundaries within which spirituality was to grow. Biblical[269] teachings and the goals of church leaders led to the growth of denominations. Membership and attendance helped churches to grow and each denomination expected loyalty from its members.

The development of a group identity was very important. Congregational life nurtured those who joined up and, of course, there was an expectation of financial support. Commitment to the Church was equated with total submission to God. Religious symbols such as the cross[270] and the fish were incorporated into the design of buildings and the worship services of the various denominations. Along these lines, there was great value placed upon service to others. In some Christian circles it would be seen to be selfish for an individual to claim

---

[269] King James Version of the Holy Bible was written in 1611 AD

[270] Biblical scholar Mark Tully, who has studied the catacombs under Rome, relates another interesting note:*[in the several hundreds of miles of these passages]* We entered a small chamber with pictures painted on the wall and the ceiling. These stucco paintings were the earliest pictures…There was no Crucifixion, no Resurrection, no Jesus in triumph…" opt. cit., 157.

and even honor their personal spiritual gifts. The emphasis is heavily on giving service to others at the expense of one's own desires. I believe that "selfishness" could have a positive connotation. It doesn't need to be viewed as a concern for one's self *alone.* I prefer to use the word humility which doesn't mean groveling, but rather to truly know yourself; both your strengths and your weaknesses.

The family structure mirrored each group's ideology. Predominately, the males were to lead the family and the wife and children were to follow. Some groups preferred to live in close proximity further assuring that peer pressure framed their ethics and life patterns.

* * * * * * * * * * *

In tribal circles, each person generally walked within their own spiritual beliefs. I could use the example of the strength of the chain being only as strong as each link. Each member of the Nation attempted to be responsible for his own life within the tribal traditions and his particular personal ethics. Each child knew their various traditions and customs, but central to Native life was **each person's vision**. One's vision was to be balanced with personal responsibility to the creation, to the community and to the Creator.

Occasionally there were those born with a way of being that was very different than others. In the English language, they would be called contraries, clowns, or in the Lakota language "heyoka." They too had an honored place in village life. They served an important function and role within the tribal system. They presented another choice of how to do things. The sight of someone climbing a ladder upside down, riding a horse backwards, walking sideways, or washing their hands in dirt, demonstrated to Native children another way to approach life. Stories about contrary characters were just as important as any of the stories about traditional ways.

If a Native person's vision was to do ceremony in a different way than was customary, the community understood this. When someone was invited to participate in a ceremony, knowing how to respect another's way of doing things was expected. Also, each person would decide for themselves whether or not to attend. In my last book, *"Native American Spirituality: A Walk In the Woods,"* I give a full description of how to understand and support a person's vision. I also described the vision given to me by the Creator. I will not repeat this information here, but it can be easily accessed in the afore-mentioned book, if you wish.[271] It was only in my early fifties that I finally was able to be in a life situation that enabled me to fully honor the vision given to me many years ago in ceremony.

Even when an individual received a vision, their choice as to if and when they would incorporate it into their life was to be revered. A vision gave a Native person his or her own identity and framed their contribution to village life. One's tribal identity was secondary to their vision or purpose. Clans or defined societies were considered the roots of the community. They were not more important than one's vision, but they provided stabilization and security for the village.

Respecting individual choice within clans and groups was often a delicate balance. For example, if the warrior's clan was asked to defend a village they would meet and deliberate various strategies. If, on the night before the plans were to be carried out one of the warriors had a dream or vision that would be in contradiction to the plans, he was allowed to carry out his vision with honor. He was not viewed as being disloyal to the group. He was given great admiration for honoring the basic foundations of the Native ways—personal vision and choice!

As I have presented before, in the Native philosophy there was little need to judge whether a person was good, spiritual, or better than another. The honorable way was to walk in the vision that was given, to contribute those gifts within the community and to connect with all of life.

Christian Worship and Native Ceremony

Christianity has at its roots, some Jewish concepts. Gatherings and worship services are mostly indoors within places designated as sacred and holy. Much of the focus is centered around altars and worship centers. Coming into church symbolizes the gathering of a community of believers. Worshiping in comfort has come to be important.

It is generally expected that one attend in one's finest apparel, although today, many churches have informal services in which more

---

[271] Eagle. op. cit., 106-115.

casual attire is accepted. "Cleanliness is next to Godliness" is an often repeated injunction, which comes from the Jewish practice of rituals of purification before entering the temple area.[272] Unlike Jewish tradition, no churches that I know of today require a bath before going to church! However, in the Catholic Church there is a small ritual of blessing oneself with "holy water."

Each member is expected to provide regular financial support for the building, maintenance, and beauty of the church home. One's faith is often expressed through spiritual responsibility, duty and attendance. The goal of sharing the gospel with foreign missions depends upon the financial response of members. Specific forms of worship and expectations about appropriate conduct within the church and in one's life are often outlined for the believers. In some denominations specific rituals such as confession become available when one wanders off the path.

Many Christian denominations expect their members to project a moral image to the outer community. The church building itself can add to the member's image and identity. Like Judaism, there is a sense of who is in the right place and who is not. Ministerial guidance and sermons outline the specific theology and there is usually some indication of hierarchy within the leadership model.

* * * * * * * * * * * *

Native ceremony was conducted when there was a specific reason for it. Each day was approached as a ceremony. Most tribes had an early morning ritual to give gratitude for another day to learn about life's lessons and to strengthen their relationship with life and the Creator. A more extensive ceremony would only happen if there was a particular need. So, in most cases, there would not be a ceremony out of some sense of duty or regularity. However, during the year in many traditions certain ceremonies were planned for seasonal events like the

---

[272] The disease that causes body parts to fall off is called "leprosy" in the Bible. Today, it is called Hanson's Disease. Scientists know that Hanson's Disease did not exist in Bible times. Therefore, the leprosy Jesus healed was probably more like a rash, possibly psoriasis. This confusion most likely came about as the result of a mistranslation of the Hebrew word for "impurity" into the Greek word "*leprose.*" History International, *The Naked Archaeologist.*

solstices, full moons, planting, post-harvesting times, etc. These ceremonies were for the purpose of gratitude and being in harmony with the natural cycles and the growing energy of Mother Earth. Often there would be specific rituals for women's cycles and some had spring and fall ceremonies. In most ceremonies there was a call for the participation of a virgin.[273] They represented and actually held the memory and energy of having been fresh from the side of the Creator.

For most Native peoples of long ago, nature was the sanctuary and Mother Earth provided the pews and worship center. Every part of Mother Earth was honorable and sacred. Therefore every place held the presence of the Great Spirit. There was no place where the spirit of the Creator was absent. There were places that held unique energies, but one location was just as important as another. Responsibility to care for the natural world meant conducting oneself as a relative, sometimes even leaving it for awhile and moving to another place in order not to over-stress the environment. Ceremonies were conducted both indoors and outdoors as was appropriate to the ceremony. In all Native ceremonies there was an importance given to connecting with the Earth Mother and there was also the use of various natural elements and herbs. Very few North American tribes utilized substances that would intentionally cause an altered state of mind. The use of fasting, intense preparation, personal focus and a length of time outdoors would instead facilitate desirable states that would ultimately enhance the spiritual experience. Only in the recent 130 years has there been a reach for some mind-altering substances by a few Native groups.

The Human Condition and "Being Natural"

In various forms of Christianity the human condition represented a kind of enemy to oneself. The body and its physical needs were to be viewed as secondary to a person's spirituality, and for some belief systems the body was seen as totally un-spiritual. Many believed that sex was a prohibited pleasure and a sin if it was not for

---

[273] In the Maori traditions, a baby is placed outside for a full night with a deceased person. Only the baby is to be with the body. With a simple roof overhead the baby is to stay near the body outside the person's house. No further explanation for this tradition is given.

procreation. In which case, it led to a fall from the presence and love of God.

All Earth-bound humans would someday change to a divine condition when they finally disengaged from all physical needs and from this earthly condition. Human nature and the natural world were considered evil and obstacles to one's spiritual development. It was a goal to return to a blessed, divine, pre-fallen condition of oneness with God through acceptance and obedience to the churches tenets. Nature was to be viewed as valuable and useful only to the extent that it served humans who were to reign supreme over it and control it.

* * * * * * * * * * * *

In the Native way of thinking each human celebrated being human.[274] As we observed in nature, each creature was happy to be whatever they were born to be. So, humans too were to be happy being a human being. As presented in the movie "Dances with Wolves," Kicking Bird said to his white friend: "...of all the trails in this life there is one that matters most. It is the trail of a true human being."[275]

Ornamental dress was appropriate for certain occasions, but being a natural human meant being aware that the Creator loves each one for who they are rather than how they look. Taking care of one's physical body was just as important as taking care of Mother Earth. So every part of Mother Earth was sacred and every aspect of the human body was sacred as well.

Purification, Cleansing and the Natural Condition

"Impurity as a result of contact with certain substances or because of one's married sexual life is in no sense sinning...it doesn't mean that sexual relations are wrong or forbidden. Impurity is the natural by-product of them in the minds of those people, and all that is required to remove the impurity is bathing afterward."[276]

---

[274] "Perfect" in Aramaic can mean "to be complete." Matthew 5:48 (KJV: "Be ye therefore perfect, even as your Father which is in heaven is perfect.") Douglas-Klotz, *The Hidden Gospel*, 129.
[275] TIG Productions, An ORION Picture Release, 1990.
[276] *Jesus at 2000*. An article written by Alan F. Segal. *Jesus and First-Century Judaism*. Westview Press., 71.

Some form of purification was a part of many of the different religions that came to this land; whether it was before entering into holy places or through baptism. One essential idea was to rid ourselves of an impure condition and to become untainted. Christianity took a lot of cues from the traditions of Judaism including establishing a place or condition of cleanliness of body and spirit in temple worship.

Some of these beliefs about being unclean were projected onto the *menstrual cycle* of women. Many Christian theologies taught that this was a curse or an unfortunate condition that was imposed upon women by God for the indiscretions of Eve in the Garden of Eden story. Some Christian dogma promotes the idea that a curse was placed upon women so that they would suffer labor pains during childbirth as a reminder of their participation in the separation of mankind from God. Biblical scholar, Mark Tully, brings this home to us with the following:

Women were certainly at a disadvantage in Jesus' time, subject to stringent purity laws that excluded them from society. There is a long tradition of Jewish writing in which women are seen as dangerous temptresses.[277]

Let's bring Stephanie into this discussion:

Jewish women, to achieve ritual cleanliness, visit a Mikvah, a ritual bath, upon the conclusion of their menstrual periods and immediately before their weddings. A modern Orthodox Jewish woman will go every month; a Conservative Jewish woman is likely to only ever attend a Mikvah before her marriage. A Reform woman may or may not ever attend one at all.

In Judaism, being "unclean" is a temporary state that comes about as a result of living. You do have to make yourself clean before you can participate in holy acts, but that's easy enough, you just go take a ritual bath and say the appropriate blessings. Being "unclean" is not sinful or evil in any way.[278]

* * * * * * * * * * * *

Native peoples viewed nature as existing in an essentially perfect condition. Everything was constantly striving to be in a harmonious relationship. Of course, animals cleaned themselves and people washed themselves in streams and lakes. But, we did not see any part of nature having a preoccupation with being clean. Each

---

[277] Tully, op. cit., 138.
[278] Stephanie M.

creation was content with how they were created to be. Taking care of one's health and wellbeing was just a part of life. Being in relationship with the Creator and with life was not based upon moving from one clean place to another. Having to release impurities or dirtiness as a pathway toward sacredness was foreign to natural spirituality.

Now I want to open up some discussions of what the Native culture calls women's "moon-time." It is more appropriate for my wife or a grandmother to speak of this, so Mary Rainbow Snake Woman will assist me here. More will be written about this in the future. This natural process in the lives of women was not to be dishonored in any way. The gift for bringing life that the Creator instilled within women included each moon-time and the experience of labor and birth. It was spoken of early in the education of the youth, both boys and girls.

There were ceremonies or coming of age rites for each young person marking their passage from childhood to adulthood. Young girls were especially recognized as integral and highly valued members of the village and tribe. Life could not continue without them. Every moon-time was a welcome reminder of their part in the continuation of traditions and human life. In many tribal customs it was such a time of power that women on their moon had special places to be and were taken care of during their bleeding time because they were seen as being more receptive at that time to receiving divine messages for themselves and the community. In some traditions they did not participate in ceremonies during this time because their enhanced power could change the structure of the ceremony. There was no need to characterize this time as unclean or dirty. It was a time when conception was possible--how could this be impure and shameful?

Mother Earth clearly demonstrates many natural cycles. Some Native teachings included Grandmother Moon in the natural cycles of the oceans and women's "moon time." The Earth is constantly showing natural transitions in her cycles. Some of her cycles are short and some are so long that they often go unrecognized.

The first real example of warrior energy taught to the children was a mother giving birth. The birthing experience demonstrated to all members of the community, time and time again, an intense focus, resolve and trust in the natural plan of the Creator. Great honor was to be given for the process of bringing life into existence.

Male Domination/Women's Guidance

Turtle Island experienced groups who came here with masculine leadership. In this new way of organizing community, males were the primary managers of social, political and spiritual institutions. Women were to remain under male domination. This organizational structure was observed within the family environment and all the way up the institutional hierarchy. Native peoples observed with interest how this worked, because they knew the power of women!

Over time, there developed many decision-making patterns which determined the parameters of how life was to take place. Men set up the structure of the way of life of the community and wrote and enacted the laws. Religious and business circles followed similar patterns. Male leadership, bylaws, constitutions and written guidelines set the standard for behaviors and the consequences for deviating from the prescribed rules and laws. Debate was important, but when voting was part of the decision-making process, a majority opinion won out and the minority was expected to go along with it. Diplomas, certification and degrees identified those having authority. People who lacked a formal education didn't have as much of an opportunity or right to participate in leadership roles. Women were not considered for most social and religious positions of leadership. A hierarchy of leadership developed, based mostly upon accomplishment, ambition and personal influence. The quality of one's life was less important than their résumé!

* * * * * * * * * * * *

Some Native nations before colonization did have various forms of hierarchical leadership. I believe that in more ancient times there was more emphasis upon the development of personal independence rather than the need for being led by strong leaders. Perhaps then tribal life was within smaller groups and more self-reliant. This allowed for less need for authority because each person was directly responsible for their own behavior and vision. Always maintaining an individual's freedom to choose was a primary attribute of the Native way of life. An example of this would be found in the movie, "Dances With Wolves." During a very serious tipi discussion that allowed for all opinions to be expressed, the closing statement by an Elder was: "No man can tell another what to do!"

In Native circles before the Europeans arrived, most individual tribal growth was determined by the feminine energy. Home places, villages and communities were greatly influenced by the roles of women. As I have mentioned in my last book:

In Native American societies women enjoyed high status in many cases. It is clear that women exerted much more influence within Native cultures than did the women who came to Turtle Island.[279]

Women could best provide stability for the foundations of the culture and spirituality. Because feminine energy facilitated the first growing space, the womb, women and grandmothers monitored most aspects of tribal life lovingly and insightfully. Their resolve was *to make sure that the present generation considered the next seven in all present actions and decisions.*

Spiritual understandings were very conveniently housed within physical examples. Often many Elders say, "Everything flows through a woman." Our first nine months of life were very meaningful. The first important spiritual concept is represented by mother's womb. This first experience is essential for life to grow and develop. There is no feeling of disconnection between the mother and the baby. In many Native traditions the mother's mother was to be present during pregnancy to be sure the mother-to-be would carry out certain customs during this time. At birth the child would relocate from the water-world experience into the air-world. In Native life the home was facilitated by the mother. Native traditions would often honor each growing space with ceremony during the pregnancy and at the birth.

In the Okla-Choctaw tradition there would be a naming ceremony after birth and the man's mother-in law would come to occupy the home place. Tradition held that it would be unadvisable for the man and his mother-in-law to ever meet eye-to-eye. If there was to be a lengthy conversation between the two a blanket was hung between them.

The family place of growth was under the total charge of the mother. The only things a father or husband could call his own would be his hunting gear (what was used to provide for the family), his

---

[279] Rainbow Eagle. Op. cit., 41.

eating bowl and his blanket! Everything else in the home-place, the second womb, belonged to the mother. If, on a rare occasion, the man would return some day and see on the front porch his hunting gear, his Choctaw eating bowl and his blanket, he knew that he was now to live outside this growing space!

The village was the third womb. It was under the watchful eyes of the grandmothers. So, the child was very much aware of the influence of females. Most tribal customs taught that every adult was the child's parent, which meant the child felt very cared for. Okla-Choctaw customs allowed the grandmothers of the village to remove a tribal chief if they felt he was not following his vision properly. In the Cherokee tradition, the Beloved Woman was the only person who could declare a war or bring the warrior clan into action to act in defense of the village. I often begin Peace Shield teachings by referring to this belief as "womb-an" education!

To balance this female participation in the life of children, each male brought teachings about what could be experienced in the outer world of nature and other communities outside the village. It was vital to a child's education to get to know experiences outside the womb of the village and encourage an awareness of the unclear boundaries that exist there. Learning how to be in relationship with *all* life forms was often a life-long journey. This would be for both boys and girls to some extent, although in the ancient day's girls were further educated by mothers/grandmothers about what it would take to maintain a healthy growing environment.

In summary, for the first seven years in many traditions all of the children were instructed by the women, so that even the boys could learn the ways of nurturing and the feminine energies. Then, the boys would be taught masculine skills by the men. Women were to focus upon the growing spaces and men were responsible for preparing for journeys involving the unexpected. Tribal traditions attempted to bring balance for members of community by guiding them within safe and nurturing zones as well as making available an education as to how to be in the midst of life outside of the home and village--a walk in the woods.

The Role of Elders

In Christian communities those who place themselves in serving roles are given various ministerial names. Within some denominations there is an assortment of hierarchical positions that reflect different modes of service. Most have attained their roles through training in theological seminaries, while others are considered lay ministers who offer their services voluntarily. It is often assumed that ministers within the church hold a certain authority to teach, preach, baptize and perform other ministerial sacraments due to their ordination and the fact that they have had a more in-depth Christian education than regular church members. Most are given housing as well as a salary for their services.

In most church settings, parishioners are encouraged to come to the ministering person for advice about spiritual matters. It is assumed that the guidance given will reflect the ideology and prescriptions of that particular church institution. Often, there is a prescribed behavior or ritual that is part of the advice given, such as confession in the Roman Catholic Church.

In recent years, ministerial licenses are issued by various governmental agencies which grant the holder the right to conduct and legalize marriages. In some cases there is not a requirement that there be specific training or ordination by a church institution. Some of the independent churches that are springing up now days even offer ministerial positions to people without formal theological training as recognition of their pasturing skills and commitment. Their leadership is welcomed as the result of congregational respect, support and encouragement.

* * * * * * * * * * * *

Village Elders had a special role in Native life. There was no training to be an Elder. One's advice, guidance or authority to conduct a ceremony was sought after and requested because of the respect that the community had for them. They were consulted about decisions, but their wisdom was not to replace the responsibility of each person to decide for himself or herself. Their advice was not based upon an agreed-upon theology or a prescribed spiritual practice, but rather, on their own life experience. The Elders Council was never viewed as the final authority.

The suggestions given by the Elders were to be seen as advice only. If the old ones were too directive, it might diminish the seekers responsibility for their own lives and journeys. Each one who made a request and sat with a Grandfather or Grandmother knew that they were to listen and consider well what was being offered to them. The Elders would never take away the responsibility for each person's choices.[280]

On the other hand, if tobacco was offered and the Elder/teacher accepted a contract to teach certain skills, then the student/apprentice would honor this arrangement. The teacher would outline the apprenticeship and teach according to the learner's readiness. This was often a long journey because every step was reflective of the individual's range of ability and maturity. Having a command of the information and skill was only half of the apprenticeship. Placing them into one's life was the next step. Even when the apprenticeship was complete, whether you were asked by the community to give your gift was dependent upon how people viewed your life patterns.

Right/Wrong, Good/Bad and "Being Related to All"

Those who came to the Western Hemisphere defined life in two ways: that which was described and judged as right, good and American and that which was wrong, bad and un-American. The personal attributes to be developed were loyalty, membership and citizenship.

Various church denominations and institutions developed ethical standards which were role-modeled by ministerial people and upper management leaders within the business world. For the sake of consistency and stability there were written records exemplifying the standards of behavior that were expected and the consequences of non-compliance. Of course the Bible was one such source within the Church. Over time there was an internalization of the various ethical standards into the realms of politics, social life, and individual behavior. Acceptance and the continuation of one's connection to various groups depended upon compliance and outside validation. If a

---

[280] Eagle. Op. cit., 65.

person's behavior, employment skills or ethical patterns did not match the expected standards, a release was given to seek another means of employment, group membership or spiritual expression.

Documentation and periodic evaluation provided the means by which to determine productivity and worth. Each person's self image was housed within the particular peer group, profession or church that they were part of. The parameters for judging what was right and good could often fluctuate from one circle of influence to another. Laws, job-descriptions, productivity records, attendance and titles became the guidelines for determining who was a good worker or a good Christian and who was a bad person or a sinner.

Relationships were framed within various groupings: families, bloodlines, denominations, clubs and organizations. Those who were not determined to be fully within a group or bloodline were sometimes seen as "different" and were not accepted. Being related was more about being selected or deemed worthy of belonging to the group. Nationalism required that everyone be loyal to the ideals of the country and have reverence for the accepted American images of patriotism.

For most Americans being related was limited to a connection with other humans rather than with non-humans. For some, any connection with nature was completely unrelated to their spiritual beliefs. Also, their identity as Americans placed them above people in other lands.

* * * * * * * * * * * * *

In Native philosophies experiences within nature were often reminders of the concept of duality. Physical examples such as calm weather and tornados, sunshine and rain, winter and summer, male and female, comfort and pain, peace and conflict, scarcity and plenty, etc. were natural phenomena that were reflective of the two extremes of life. The Creator surrounded humans with a natural classroom in which spiritual lessons could be learned. There was little need to judge any aspect of the natural to be good or bad, right or wrong.

In nature there are many representations of a variety of life styles, behavior patterns and social systems that humans can understand and appreciate, but we certainly may not want to imitate some of them. It is important to remember that the Great Spirit has created them for us to learn from rather than to directly emulate. Every life form seemed to have specific ways of doing things. Each species conducted themselves within their unique nature. So, Native people could accurately predict and anticipate their actions. Fully understanding their nature allowed for the acceptance and respect of each creation. The predictable classroom of nature, in contrast to the often inconsistent nature of humans, gave clues to the development of one's own true nature. Therefore having an accurate and clear understanding of every aspect of nature led to having a respect for every part of the creation.

This was transferred into the philosophy of dealing with human beings. Knowing the personal vision and the nature of the various tribes was paramount. It might be difficult for people today to understand that this knowledge of nature and people provided the basis for the ancient Native person to develop a respect for all. On the other hand, there were certain people within villages and tribes that presented opportunities to practice respect. There were individual whose behavior could seem to be in direct conflict with the tribe's cultural identity, such as the clowns, tricksters, contraries.[281] They offered many opportunities to consider other ways of doing things.

It was the Native way to encourage and strengthen a person's ability to make personal decisions very early in life. Parents and village members provided a safe place; a perimeter within which each person would exercise their right and freedom to think for themselves. They were able to have a choice and to ask themselves, "Are these examples what I want in my life, or do I choose to keep a respectful distance as I would for the bear, the wolf or the skunk? What have I learned from my own experiences and knowledge of nature?" Applying these same principles to the human experience would obviously prove to be more challenging.

Very meaningful to all Native traditions was the concept of "adoption." If a person demonstrated a heartfelt desire and knowledge of the culture and a willingness to live like other tribal people of a particular Indian nation, that person often had the opportunity to be officially adopted. He or she would be viewed and treated as a full-fledged member of that nation, just as anyone who had been born into the tribe by blood. So, being accepted and allowed to live within a tradition was not a matter of Native blood as it was the choice of the person to live the way of life.

---

[281] Ibid., 51, 54-57, 105.

Concepts of Evil, the Devil and Natural Spirituality

"Every good tree bringeth forth good fruit, but a corrupt tree bringeth forth evil fruit" (Matthew 7:17)

Evil, in many religions, is often contrasted with good and represented as immoral acts or thoughts. It is a real force (an energy/spirit), in some cases personified as an entity such as Satan or the Devil. There is a sense of good versus evil and it is believed that evil cannot exist without good, or good without evil. Religious reformer Martin Luther opens the idea that there is a little evil within good, as he wrote:

Seek out the society of your boon companions, drink, play, talk bawdy, and amuse yourself. One must sometimes commit a sin out of hate and contempt for the Devil, so as not to give him the chance to make one scrupulous over mere nothings...[282]

Some religious groups take a different viewpoint "...that evil is unreal and an illusion...the belief in evil is replaced by the understanding of the universality of good..."[283] Thrown into the mix is the concept of original sin. I will be giving a more extensive discussion to this topic later. For now, original sin is a doctrine promoted as the state of human nature resulting from "The Fall" of man. "Some Christians do not accept the doctrine indicated by the terms 'original sin' or 'ancestral sin,' which are not found in the Bible. The doctrine is not found in other religions, such as Judaism, Hinduism and Islam."[284] Peter Kivy says that one of three main ideas are applied to this issue:

"that there are people who freely and rationally choose to commit pure evil, for its own sake"
"that there are people who freely and rationally choose to commit evil for some other goal"
"...that evil as a concept is a human invention, that doesn't really exist."[285]

---

[282] http://en.wikipedia.org/wiki/Evil.
[283] http://en.wikipedia.org/wiki/Christian_Science.
[284] http://en.wikipedia.org/wiki/Original_sin.
[285] Kivy, Peter. *Melville's Billy and the Secular Problem of Evil: the Worm in the Bud*, in *The Monist* (1980), 63.

As we step into this very involved study, we need to review a previous note. In Aramaic the word for "evil" means "...unripe or not at the right time."[286] As Aramaic scholar Neil Douglas-Klotz further explains:

In Aramaic and in all Semitic languages, the word for "good" primarily means ripe, and the word for "corrupt" or "evil" primarily means unripe...[referring to the about scripture] The tree is not morally bad, but rather unripe: this is not the right time and place for it to bear. The saying gives an example from nature.[287]

Malcolm Godwin in his book Angels: An Endangered Species speaks of early Hebrew attitudes:

The early Hebrews attributed everything which happened everywhere, whether in Heaven or on Earth, to the One God. The evolution of a single separate force for evil which opposed the One Good God only began two hundred years before the birth of Christ. The Old Testament God did not live in such dualistic times.[288]

Generally, in the Old Testament evil is understood to be an opposition to God as well as something unsuitable or inferior.[289] In the New Testament the Greek word *poneros* is used to indicate unsuitable while *kakos* is used to refer to opposition to God in the human realm.[290] French-American theologian Henri Blocher describes evil, when viewed as a theological concept, as an "unjustifiable reality. In common parlance, evil is 'something' that occurs in experience that ought not to be."[291] "Judaism stresses obedience to God's laws as written in the Torah and the laws and rituals laid down in the...Talmud. While some forms of Judaism, do not personify evil in Satan...Satan is viewed as one who tests us for God rather than one who works against God."[292] Rabbi Weinstein explains: "Satan is viewed as one who tests us for God rather than one who works against God." He gives this simple way Jews envision Satan:

---

[286] FN 154.
[287] Douglas-Klotz. *The Hidden Gospel*, 1.
[288] Godwin, Malcolm. *Angels: An Endangered Species*, 79.
[289] Schwarz, Hans. *Evil: A Historical and Theological Perspective*. (Lima, Ohio: Academic Renewal Press, 2001), 42-43.
[290] Ibid., 75.
[291] Blocher, Henri. *Evil and the Cross*. (Downers Grove: InterVarsity Press, 1994), 10.
[292] http://en.wikipedia.org/wiki/Evil.

After death there is like a trial. Satan can be viewed as the "prosecuting attorney" in the heavenly court of judgment. He would remind us of what we might have left out or not mention in our review of life and presents the 'other side' of our dialogue. In our practical day to day experiences, for the modern Jew Satan plays no profound role. We make our choices because of free will and we have the choice to choose evil or not. Satan does not make that choice for us as that would absolve us of any personal responsibility.[293]

    Before moving on I want to re-visit the Cathars of the twelfth century. The Church was teaching about *a* supreme male God whose adversary was the Devil, a fallen angel who was less powerful than God. The Cathars, on the other hand, believed in the good masculine God and in an equally powerful "King of the World," a god of evil. They called him *"Rex Mundi."* An ongoing war was being waged between good and evil. The good one was the god of love, "...entirely disincarnate, a being or principle of pure spirit, unsullied by the taint of matter." In their view, God could not be associated with matter which was seen as the evil creation of *Rex Mundi*. The Church saw this perception as heresy, since in their theology God created the world and Jesus came to save it.[294]

    The Cathars strongly opposed what the Church taught about the Crucifixion and the cross. You see, they not only denied such sacraments as baptism and communion, they "...refused to worship the cross..." The cross to the Cathars "was regarded as an emblem of *Rex Mundi*, lord of the material world."[295]

* * * * * * * * * * * *

    Using the natural creation as a frame of reference, Native Americans, and even other indigenous peoples around the world, did not have a notion of evil.[296] Occurrences that might be seen as unwanted or tragic or that created havoc for individuals were expected. Being knowledgeable of natural law greatly helped indigenous people

---

[293] Rabbi Weinstein. Op. cit.
[294] Baigent, Leigh, and Lincoln. *Holy Blood, Holy Grail*, 53.
[295] Ibid., 54.
[296] In Hawaiian traditions the "kahuna" is one who is known as a "transmitter of the secret." There is "no parallel in Huna to the notion of an evil being." A Ute medicine woman says, "We don't have [concepts] like heaven and hell in our Indian belief." Jackie Yellow Tail, Crow: "I don't think there is a word for 'hell' in our Native language." All of these are cited in my book, *Walk in the Woods*, 285,

to understand many events that would otherwise cause a lot of disruption to village life.

I am not aware of any ancient memories among American Indians that attribute a revengeful response by the Great Mystery in the form of acts of nature in retribution for the actions of humans. In recent dialog with some Native people today, I do hear some expressions about Mother's Earth's anger for what we have done to her, etc. Also, some say that she has been warning human beings about the actions they are responsible for, and calling it a "wake-up call for all humans." Although in the natural creation there would be examples of forces that could cause great change, there was no attempt to label aspects of the creation as inherently bad. There would be beings whose natures demonstrate the opposite way of doing things or what would likely cause an unwanted consequence for some choice by humans. Such examples were an important part of the human experience to observe for the purpose of discerning what behavior to emulate or reject.

Surrender, Suffering, Sacrifice and Participation With All of Life

In order for an animal to be kosher, even if it is an inherently kosher animal, it must be killed in a way in which it feels no pain. This involves severing the head at a particular spot on the neck, which cuts both pipes at once and kills instantly. A giraffe is a kosher animal, but we cannot find the spot on the neck and so can't kill it right, and thus cannot eat giraffe (even if we wanted to). (from Stephanie M.)

A variety of ideas, philosophies and choices came to this land. Within the various church denominations there were concepts of personal sacrifice, religious dedication and even the expectation of suffering. The expectation of total surrender to God and the reward of a return to Paradise[297] prevailed in a variety of church experiences.

Christians were reminded that because of the doctrine of original sin they had an ever-present debt to repay. The forgiveness of sins and the pathway toward salvation involved certain steps that could be taken to become more accepted by God, but this earthly life would

---

[297] "The commentaries in the *Anchor Bible* state that although the word 'paradise' originally meant 'enclosed park or garden' and as such was used to represent the Garden of Eden in Genesis, by the time of Jesus, it had come to mean 'the mystical place or abode of the righteous after death'." Moore, *The Christian Conspiracy*, 191.

fall short of ever being fully blessed with joy and bliss. Gratitude for life here and now was not the most important part of the experience. Eternal life and coming into the complete presence of God is the reward for a life of surrender and sacrifice. If one erred, then another place of punishment was awaiting the sinful.

* * * * * * * * * * * * *

I wrote in "*A Walk in the Woods*" about the place that suffering and sacrifice have in Native American ceremony. My point was that it seemed to me that many of the spiritual themes of Christianity were focused upon the sacrificial images of Jesus on the cross[298] and an emphasis on total surrender to the Creator. Native peoples today have become fully aware of such philosophies, as many have adopted Christianity. However, in ancient times such themes were not part of the Native spiritual thought.

To participate in life everyday was primary. Daily experiences brought additional blessings and gratitude for the Great Mystery. We were fully aware of both the beauty and the reality of the giving and taking of life. When an animal needed to be taken in order to provide food for the community, it was viewed as a "give-away" and that was recognized as part of the process of how life continued. *All* aspects of life were honored as being valuable.

If there was a consistent spiritual characteristic that prevailed in most Native cultures it was the idea of always being ready to give gratitude and appreciation. Early morning, throughout the day, and before sleeping were times to say "thank you" to the Great Mystery for many reasons. It was a way of life in which each person was connected to every moment and aware of life all around. This connection was developed day by day, experience by experience, and lifetime upon lifetime. The Navaho/Dene have a neat expression that goes something like this:

---

[298] "The use of the cross as a symbol was condemned by at least one church father of the third century A.D. because of its pagan origins. The first appearance of a cross in Christian art is on a Vatican sarcophagus from the mid-fifth century. It was a Greek cross with equal-length arms. Jesus' body was not shown. The original cross symbol was in the form of a Tau Cross named because it looked like the letter 'tau,' or our letter T. This cross was a symbol of the Roman god Mithras and the Greek Attis." www.seiyaku.com/customs/crosses/antau.html

I see beauty above me and beauty below me,
I see beauty to my right and beauty to my left,
I see beauty before me and behind me,
Truly, I walk in beauty.

There was a constant realization of the wonder and amazement of life.

Chosen People and Native Identity

Within Christian circles there was an understanding that membership meant being a part of the family of God. All others were not yet within the household of the Divine and were doomed to experience the wrath of God because they did not come into the fold. The term "chosen" is used by many Christian groups to signify becoming a Christian. It was a crucial pathway toward a full relationship with God. Terms such as "saved," "disciple," "follower," etc. designated a position of status and importance within the Church and a special relationship to God.

Having **the** truth and being the **true church of God** precipitated many discussions as to who were the selected and true members of the community of God. Position, status, and authority are often at the core of such discussions. It leads me to ask these questions: Who has the right to speak in behalf of God and voice the teachings of Jesus? Are personal experience and a calling to serve God the standard for ministry or is it more important to have credentials and a seminary degree?

* * * * * * * * * * * *

In classes I have often asked whether the Creator would select a particular species as the most important and tell all the others that they were less valuable. In Native thinking, it would have been difficult to imagine that the Creator would say that everyone was to follow the example of one species over another. Somehow I can't imagine hearing, "I want everyone to be like the eagle because it can fly the highest" or "...be like the buffalo because I have chosen it as the greatest of my creations."

There were two identities to be brought into balance--tribal identity and one's own personal vision. Being a Cherokee for example, was a reflection of one's cultural bloodline and family. Those who were of non-Indian blood were accepted into full participation of the tribe if they personally chose to live the way of life within a tribal community. A personal vision was just as important as one's tribal identity. That life purpose was to be honored and revered as much as any cultural choice. One had the authority or right to be a canoe maker, arrow head maker, handicraft person, hide-tanner, etc. based solely on their vision.

If you have made it this far in the book, you have probably experienced a range of emotions and thoughts. Staying grounded in the midst of new information is not always easy. I find my personal grounding in my understanding of *natural principles* that some refer to as "Native American spirituality."

The Creator is, in some mysterious way, a part of *all* life experiences—fully a participant in everything that happens. I don't believe that the nee Great Mystery needs to test my spirituality. I want to learn the lessons of life without them being a test or a battle and without being a victim. The concepts of submission and yielding to God's intervention are words difficult for me to comprehend. It is a partnership and relationship with the Creator that appeals to me; a sense of companionship (like an elder grandparent), that resides in my heart and nourishes my soul. I would use the words strengthening, nurturing, encouraging, and cultivating to describe this. Just as there are numerous examples of duality in nature and within us, the circle that surrounds everything that exists is the container for both aspects. There are many ways to describe those aspects within the various religious dogmas and spiritual teachings. For me, the most meaningful representation of the dual nature of creation is the "yin-yang" symbol which depicts the truth that some aspect of each polarity can be found in the other. Each person can decide what fits for them. I think many of our beliefs are somehow outside the various religious forms and are, instead, very personal and often private.

The Legend of a Farmer Who Killed the First Roman Catholic Bishop in Finland

In the traditions of most countries there are stories that are told and retold for many generations as a way of passing on national pride and heritage. Sometimes these stories are actual historical events and sometimes they are fictionalized versions of history. I never gave that much thought until I found myself fascinated by the Finnish story of "Lalli" (pronounced "**Lah**-lee"), in the summer of 2009. When Mary and I travel we always have our ears to the ground for something that the ancients of that land are ready to reveal. Our hope is to sense something that reaches way back into older philosophies and reflects a more simple and meaningful way of life.

Finland experienced its first crusade by the Roman Catholic Church in the mid-twelfth century. The Orthodox Catholic Church came into northern Finland from Russia. Today most Finns, about eighty percent, are members of the Evangelical Lutheran Church of Finland.[299] It is a land that has been captured over and over again by the Swedes from the west and the Russians from the east.

After being around Finnish people for a period of time, our good friend Janne had the courage to mention to us that the Finish people typically have great difficulty participating in "small talk." This kind of social, two-way, chit-chat common in America was not customary for the Finns. Over the years we have tried to learn about the various customs of the people we meet. Apparently in Finland it is considered impolite to ask any personal questions about one's family or work! An older man I was staying with reported that once a husband was observing two ladies freely exchanging topics of conversation. They noticed that he was quietly, but obviously, making fun of the situation. One of the ladies, his wife, directed this comment to her husband, "What do you have to say? You are so quiet!" He said, "Men talk when they have something to say!"

Getting back to "Lalli," I spoke to many Finns about this story which is something of a national legend and is told to every child in

---

[299] www.http://en.wikipedia.org/wiki/Finland

school, as a part of Finnish history. It is a story about a farmer who pursued the first Bishop (Henry) of Finland one cold wintery day in January, 1156 and violently killed him with an axe. This English-born bishop had come to Finland with a small armed force from Sweden to help convert Finns to Christianity; but that's another story. Legend has it that this was a justifiable killing and the farmer was never prosecuted. The AllExperts Encyclopedia records that Bishop Henry was "…canonized by Pope Adrian IV and he became the patron saint of Finland."[300]

Here's the short story. One day the bishop paid a visit to a farm, but found that the farmer was not there. His wife provided a nice meal for him in the absence of her husband. It is known that bishop Henry had experienced great difficulty in securing his first conversion after many months of trying to bring religion to the "pagans" in the community! The bishop left to return to his residence and the farmer came home from his travels. There are various versions of the story concerning the ensuing exchange between the farmer and his wife, one being that the bishop came, ate and left. But there are also versions that imply that he took food by force and didn't pay for it. Some say that the wife lied about what took place. Another version was that he took hay for his horse without recompense.[301] Whatever took place, it made the farmer so outraged that he grabbed his axe and killed the bishop on an icy lake some distance from home.

In my conversations with those Finns who came to my classes and with whom I stayed, I can make the following statements at this time. The attitude of the middle-aged folks seems to be that it doesn't matter whether this story is a real happening or a symbolic one. For them the Church's attitude toward the local traditions and the disrespect of the Church toward people in general is what this story addresses. "We didn't ask for the Church to come!" some have stated. What Lalli did was reflective of feelings of resentment for the arrogant attitudes of the Church. Also, there is a long history of the ruling, wealthy people expressing contempt for the rural country folks. Another spoke of the long history of intrusion into Finland by various empires that demanded

---

[300] www.http://en.allexperts.com/e/b/bi/bishop_henry.htm.
[301] Ibid.

the people just follow orders, obey their laws and practice total compliance with their dictates.

The older generation in Finland, who are more skilled in life experiences, tends to focus on what caused this farmer to take such a drastic action. Some point out that the celibate Roman Catholic bishop came a long way, in the middle of a harsh winter. He chose to stay around, waited for food to be prepared, ate and left. What did the farmer's wife say about the visit? What did she not say?" Another said "We know how very stubborn and angry Finns can get!" One Finnish grandmother (obviously selecting what English words she could to apply to the story), spoke about her idea: "I think there was some hanky-panky going on!" I couldn't help but wonder why this story is told to every child in schools and history classes in Finland!

The story is an example of how a significant event is remembered, told and retold, for a variety of reasons. Different age-groups will interpret the various aspects of a legend or en event in light of their own understandings. To me, it represents an attitude of anger toward the Church that persists even today in the minds of the rural people of Finland. Similar feelings can be seen within Native American communities as well, because of the actions of churches in removing children from their homes and placing them in various boarding schools. It also tells something about how the description of historical events and characters changes in the retelling over many generations. Motives and agendas can reshape the original story over time.

Summary of Natural Spirituality and People of the Book

I am including two charts that offer some comparisons of Christian and Natural spirituality at the time of initial contact between the cultures. These charts are not all-inclusive, but provide a way to more easily contrast the two viewpoints.

EARTH-BASED PEOPLE/CULTURES (IDEAS)	CHRISTIANITY (BELIEFS/DOGMA/LAWS)
One great mystery, very close, and within all	One divine father God in Heaven
Learn from the creation and the cosmos	One source for all mysteries (Torah, Bible, *qur'an*)--divinely written by God for the people of the book
Trust in the natural order	
Knowledge means survival	Discipleship and membership
Full awareness of life	Earth is owned and made for humans—having dominion over creation
Can be adopted into the group	
Mother Earth is to be honored, respected and shared	
Live in harmony with all of life	Angelic direction
Elders and spirit guides offer opinions, ideas, and experiences	Laws: right/wrong, good/bad
	Reward and punishment
	Obedience, loyalty and duty
	Sin/repentance/guilt
Encourage personal choice	Seeking the Truth
No mistakes, learn lessons from all experiences and happenings	Group identity
	Submission, surrender, and sacrifice
Personal vision purpose in life	Lost/saved
Important to seek and find balance	Savior/satan/evil
	Male leadership/hierarchy
No death—changing of worlds	Soul can be possessed
No word for evil	Heaven and Hell
Individual sacred space and boundaries	Church, ministers and priests
	Convert the world

Individual responsibility for a relationship with Creator and creation We are all related Interconnection between human, creation and Creator Attitude of reciprocity All of life and humans are sacred Respect for nature and life cycles Belief in many lifetimes Gratitude for life Care for the body and spirit Live within each moment Respect for growing spaces Creator gave natural look at life Sexuality is spiritual Personal right to make a choice Not religion—a way of life Understanding natural order of life and the cosmos Respect for diversity, each ones gift, contribution Every step is a prayer	Organized religion Humans all important Having dominion over creation Humans in a fallen state Sinful, evil human nature One Earthly lifetime End times/final Judgment and then rapture Suffering and victim philosophy Life is a battle—ready to leave this Earth Waiting to be rescued from this Earthly life No respect for spiritual boundaries--conversion--war Pleasure/sex is not spiritual Competition and conversion Becoming chosen by God Identifying an enemy Ambition, seeking success and improvement Concepts of higher, lower, better than

Chapter Four

A Historical Glance at Christianity— After the Ministry of Jesus

"What we call Christianity today has very little indeed to do with the teachings of Jesus and the ideas that he wished to spread...we are led to assume that because things have so long been as they are, they must consequently be correct."[302]

"Emil Brunner has called the Church a misunderstanding. From an appeal, a doctrine was constructed; from free communion, a legal body; from free association, a hierarchical machine. One might say that it became, in all of its elements and as a whole, the exact opposite of what had been intended." "(Jesus)...appeared...bringing a message full of hope, a message of love and goodness, and what did humanity do with it? Turned it into paper, verbiage, power and business!"[303]

"Almighty God! How long will this superstitious sect of Christians, and this upstart invention endure." (Pope Alexander VI)

"It is an act of virtue to deceive and lie, when by such means the interest of the church might be promoted." Bishop Eusibius (260-339).[304]

"Research into the life of Jesus represents a schooling in truthfulness for the Church; and it has been a more painful and belligerent struggle for the truth than has ever before been witnessed."[305]

"...[the Church] it does not know who wrote its Gospels and Epistles, confessing that all 27 New Testament writings began life anonymously: *"It thus appears that the present titles of the Gospels are not traceable to the evangelists themselves...they [the New Testament Collection] are supplied with titles which, however ancient, do not go back to the respective authors of those writings."*[306]

I am fully sensitive to some of the uncomfortable feelings this chapter may produce. In recent years there seems to be more willingness to discuss spiritual ideas. As I have said, there are many

---

[302] Kersten. op. cit., 10.
[303] Ibid.
[304] New Dawn Magazine, No 71, March 2002.
[305] Kersten. op. cit., 22.
[306] *Catholic Encyclopedia*, vol. vi, 655-6.

more media presentations that bear witness to the desire of many to re-examine some of the tenets of spirituality. The contents of this book may certainly appear to be doing the following:

- *Questioning the authenticity of the authors of the New Testament and indirectly attacking the word of God.*
- *Deliberately casting shadows and negatives on the Christian and the Catholic Church (both the Roman and Orthodox).*
- *Taking the glow off various events and happenings of the Judeo-Christian traditions.*
- *Attempting to reduce the importance and beauty of the spiritual contribution of Jesus/Yeshua, perhaps even removing the "divinity" of Christ.*

None of these statements necessarily reflect my intention for this study. I believe that I am a part of a generation of spiritual seekers who want to have more accurate information and who can respect other people's choices and spiritual traditions. I happen to believe that there are many reasons have absolute hope and optimism. In the past forty years I have watched a generation wanting to find more accurate aspects of historical, cultural, and spiritual beliefs.

What is my motivation in seeking the ancient roots of many spiritual paths? In reality I am trying to assemble spiritual guidelines that honor my experience with Christianity as well as Native American spirituality. Both have helped to frame the spiritual philosophy that I embrace today. I want to integrate my present understanding of Native philosophy with a genuine recovery of the most accurate teachings of Jesus. Delving into the research on early Christianity has helped me to feel more optimistic and balanced and has softened the rigidity of some of the Christian concepts I grew up with. Sorting out what I personally want in my life has given me more resolve to fully connect with all aspects of life and with Mother Earth in particular.

Christians make up eighty-three percent of the American population and are divided into more than 600 denominations.[307] Around the world I hear that there are over 20,000 kinds of Christian organizations. Vast differences exist between the beliefs and practices of these groups. While some have modified and softened their viewpoints to be more inclusive of the changing times and personal situations, others are less willing to look beyond ridged theological

---

[307] NBC, *Today show*, 11-14-2006.

stances. Old Native philosophy can teach people to be respectful of all points of view. It is also helpful when there is respect for everyone's choices.

In the last forty years I have observed the emergence of many Christian congregations that welcome a more open expression and personal spiritual exploration. A variety of study materials have now come into existence as well as more lay ministry. Alternative churches are on the increase, which by the way, were common to those who followed Jesus' teachings for hundreds of years. In some church experiences diverse and multi-cultural styles of worship have appeared. Those who have been the trail-blazers for spiritual diversity are to be commended. It is my belief that what touched the lives of the people around the Mediterranean Sea was how the spiritual teachings of Jesus permeated all aspects of life. Jesus' teachings found significance within the many of the cultures that helped shaped his ministry.

Research indicates that religion as a social tradition is the slowest institution to accept change. Businesses change their strategies; sometimes over night. Governments and legislative agendas take longer to change. Educational systems can take twenty years to transform. Social change is long-coming, but changes in religious structures have taken as long as a full century.

Some Conflicting Scenarios

When there has been an extended period of time that people are not given the right to search, to study, to and determine for themselves, traditions are likely to be based upon longevity rather than accuracy. Often spiritual tenets, stances and dogma continue to exist only because they have been around for a long time. Bishop Spong gives us an example of this. Speaking of the Christmas story, he says, "…it is sufficient to say he was born in Nazareth. There were no stars, no angels, no wise men, no shepherds and no manger."[308] Biblical scholar Mark Tully adds:

There is no record of Herod's massacre of little boys in Bethlehem outside Matthew's Gospel. Nor is there any record of a census that would support Luke's

---

[308] Spong. *Jesus for the Non Religious*, 24.

story. There was a census under the emperor Augustus, but it was in A. D. 6 not 4 B. C. ...[309]

Bart Ehrman, of the University of North Carolina religious studies department examines discrepancies in the Holy Book. In his book, *Jesus, Interrupted*, he points out that there are conflicting scenarios regarding Jesus' birthplace in Bethlehem.[310] Had his parents traveled there for a census (Luke's version), or is it where they happened to live (Matthew's version)? Did Jesus speak of himself as God? (Yes, in John; no in Matthew.) Peter, the "one who knew him best," never mentions that the birth of Jesus is special. Only Matthew (A.D. 80-85) and Luke (A.D. 85-92) written a full generation, maybe two,[311] after Jesus lived have full narratives of the birth story.[312]

A simple journey through the gospels reveals another uncomfortable conclusion concerning the birth narratives. Starting with the earliest gospel writer, Paul (A.D. 48-60); he says that Jesus' birth was completely normal; "born [made[313]] of a woman." In Galatians 4:4 Paul uses two terms "made of a woman," and "made under the law" in the same verse. In Jewish law conception would have had to take place within marriage. In fact, Paul clearly states in his letter to the Romans (1:3), that Jesus *"was made of the seed of David according to the flesh."*[314]

The *Gospel of Thomas*, one of the earliest manuscripts (A.D. 50-60), was a list of 114 sayings and prophecies. It was popular in Egypt. The following notes are made about this manuscript:[315]

- *it had no birth story and no miracles stories,*
- *it does not give any rendition of the early life of Jesus or interpretation of his sayings.*

---

[309] Tully. op. cit., 66, 67.
[310] "In the *Gospel of Thomas* (one of earliest manuscripts, 50-60 AD) there are no miracles stories, no unusual birth[310], no account of the crucifixion, no resurrection...Jesus was a wise Teacher and Sage, even a comic at times."
[311] The average life span of Jewish people during Jesus' time was around 45 years.
[312] Erman, Bart. *Jesus, Interrupted*.
[313] King James Version.
[314] Information from the DVD, *Born of a Woman*, Bishop Spong.
[315] I have gathered this information from a number of sources. See Tully, op. cit., 203-204.

- *there is no Crucifixion and no Resurrection,*[316]
- *some communities thought of Jesus as an important spiritual teacher rather than a crucified and risen Lord,*
- *it was understanding and integrating the sayings of Jesus, that led to salvation,*
- *it includes warnings against being wealthy and pursuing a comfortable life,*
- *it emphasizes a personal relationship with God, rather than the outside authority of the church over individuals,*
- *the kingdom of God is present in the here and now.*[317]

Jesus taught that the kingdom[318] of God[319] is present and always available in the present moment within each person. He even mocked the concept of hopes or fears about the end of the world.[320] The kingdom is not some far-off hope for the future, but a present reality for those who know themselves; those who have discovered their *divine nature*. In both the *Gospel of Thomas* and the *Gospel of John*, Jesus again says that the kingdom of God is not just somewhere in the future, but rather, it is a present and continuing spiritual reality.[321] In the *Gospel of Thomas*: Jesus' disciples ask him, "When will the resurrection of the dead come, and when will the new world come?" He replies, "What you look forward to has already come, but you do not recognize it."[322] Historian Ed Sanders, professor of religion at Duke University relates that Jesus was interested in bringing more immediate and lasting change in actual world conditions. The Kingdom was to be available in the here and now:

[Referring to the Lord's Prayer]…The kingdom of God for Jesus and for other Jews who hoped for it did not mean the destruction of the world. It meant its

---

[316] "Gnostics believed…that Jesus' rising from the dead was spiritual, rather than an actual physical event." Kenneth Davis, op. cit., 344.
[317] Tully. op. cit., 203-204.
[318] In the four gospels Jesus uses the word "kingdom" more than a 100 times. Many theologians debate whether the kingdom he had in mind was to be earthly or heavenly.
[319] The word Jesus would have used for God in Aramaic meant "Sacred Unity." The word "God" that we use comes from German, meaning "good."
[320] Jenkins, Philip. *Hidden Gospels*, 10.
[321] Pagels. *Beyond Belief*, 49.
[322] *Gospel of Thomas* 51, in NHL(Nag Hummadi Library), 123.

reordering. God would step in and directly change the world so that [it] would be a better place. I think that is what Jesus longed for.[323]

When there has been a long history of a controlling leadership and a submissive and repressed body of parishioners, personal courage to step beyond defined boundaries is rare or non-existent. Personal reflection is unacceptable. Many in the early history of the Church have stepped away from the rigid institutional rules and dogma only to experience a shortened life!

As history unfolds, spiritual pride takes over and determines which beliefs are the "right" beliefs and those that don't fit the defined dogma. This encasement of viewpoints takes on a life of its own and directly prohibits the likelihood of consideration of conflicting facts that might be forthcoming later. There are a growing number of people whose intuition is telling them that what has been presented as Christianity, especially material about Jesus Christ, is not the whole story. The recent discoveries of old writings give us a chance to become more educated. This means however, we must have a willingness to seek, and even more difficult, have the courage to think for ourselves. I maintain that humankind has for some three thousand years fallen short in the areas of self-direction and personal decision-making.

The question now becomes how to do we get closer to the actual message that Jesus wanted to impart and how can we incorporate his teachings into our lives, if we choose to? Will the truth make us more free or will it turn us away from the journey? Our studies of the Jewish culture in Chapter Five will help to lay the foundation for contemplation. Let me quote from three theologians who appeared on CNN Presents. These statements are very imperative as we move into the next discussions:

In the beginning of Christianity there is diversity. There are different points of view, different interpretations of Jesus, and different ways of understanding God in the world. And in the beginning there is no orthodoxy and heresy. The struggle regarding orthodoxy and heresy never comes to an end. And these battles about truth and inclusion and exclusion are with us to the present.[324]

---

[323] Ibid., 105.
[324] CNN Presents, *After Jesus: the Early Christians*, professor Marvin Meyer, Chapman University.

Sometimes we say if we can just get back to the New Testament Christianity, then the Church would live in unity. But in reality when we look at the pages of the New Testament we find, from the very beginning, diversity characterized their earliest believers whether they were Jewish Christians or Gentile Christians. The Christian message in the Christian Church has always lived in this tension of diversity.[325]

And the Church has gradually and slowly built up a fuller and fuller understanding of what it is be human in the image of God, trying to be honest to the Jesus who walked in Galilee and delivered the Sermon on the Mount.[326]

Then the narrative brings everything into the present time:

Christianity has survived many powerful attempts to kill it off. And today many of the issues that occupied the first Christians are once again causing us to debate, challenge and believe or not, two thousand years after Jesus.[327]

My hope is to come as close as can be understood at this time to what Yeshua (perhaps in Spirit), would really be telling us about how to be fully connected to life, intentionally and optimistically.

The Council of Nicaea and Roman Emperor Constantine

Seventeen hundred years ago, Roman Emperor Constantine formed a council of historians and scholars. Not everyone agreed with Constantine's choice of participants. Indeed, one bishop who disagreed with Constantine's choices was exiled. Later, the gathering came to be known as the Council of Nicaea. The Council of Nicaea was a response not only to the ambitions of Constantine, but represented the growing need to determine what form of spirituality was compatible with the political power of the empire. Teachings and ideas about Jesus and his life had been carried to various areas for over three hundred years. Those who believed in Jesus' teachings were targeted and sent to their deaths.

Many who were torn between their Jewish heritage and the teachings of Jesus had to make personal choices,[328] often in secrecy;

---

[325] Ibid., Professor Claire Plann, University of the Holy Land, Jerusalem.
[326] Ibid.
[327] Ibid.

sometimes even outside of their own Jewish roots. Jesus, to them, represented both a reason to live and a path away from the rigid, logical mind-set of hundreds of years of patriarchal dogma that had evolved into a total dictation of spirituality.

History records that in A.D. 312, after the Battle of Milvian Bridge, the infamous Emperor Constantine issued the Edict of Milan which ended the persecution of Christians. In 325 he called together the Council of Nicaea. Church history says that the council produced a single document in A.D. 325 known today as the Holy Bible. It is part of Church tradition that Constantine is thought of as having *"converted the Roman Empire to Christianity."*[329]

Baigent, Leigh and Lincoln's research indicates that Constantine himself was not even baptized until A.D. 337, on his death bed.[330] I understand that this would not be an unusual practice by rulers of that time since baptism meant being responsible for one's actions afterwards. So it was a convenient decision to wait to be baptized on one's death bed so that it would assure a clean pathway into Heaven. Constantine was not actually a very "Christian" man, you see. Dr. Moore reports:

...it is reported that he [Constantine] personally murdered one of his own sons, had his second wife drowned, had his nephew and brother-in-law killed after he had guaranteed safe passage...[331]

It is clear why most emperors waited until they were on their death bed to get right with the Lord! I had to raise a red flag when I found out that Christianity was not declared the state religion of Rome until A.D. 380.[332] Why there was such a lengthy time-period before Christianity was officially forced upon the populous?

---

[328] "...Christian leaders...transformed many of the Jewish fast days into days of feasting...took the concept of the Sabbath Day—basic to Judaism—and changed it from Saturday to Sunday...declared as obsolete all the dietary laws found in the Bible. By doing this, Christian leaders could put prospective converts to the test: if they really believed in Jesus and wanted to join the Christian community, they could no longer observed Mosaic Law." Sheinkin, op. cit., 17.
[329] Baigent, Leigh and Lincoln. *Holy Blood, Holy Grail*, 366.
[330] Ibid.
[331] Moore. *The Christian Conspiracy*, 58.
[332] "The Church of Christ became a worldwide religion because it was accepted as the state religion of Rome by Theodosius and Gratin in 380 CE." Moore, *The Christian Conspiracy*, 57.

The most important step in making the Christian Church what it is today was the Edict of Milan (313 C.E.). It was proposed by Constantine, the emperor in the west, and by Licinius, emperor in the east, but it originated with Emperor Galerius in 311. This was an edict that encouraged toleration for both Christians and pagans.[333] Put this edict and the fact that Constantine's mother[334] was a Christian together, as well as Constantine's opportunity to grow a bigger empire and we now have a major turn in the road. I would add that years before, when Constantine was just a junior partner in the Roman Empire, then Emperor Diocletian had declared Mithras, the god of a Persian religion, as Protector of the Empire.[335] This deity will be coming up in our study quite often.

Dr. Moore's research indicates that on October 27, 312, Constantine had a dream in which he was shown the Latin words, "*Hoc signo victoreris*," "By this sign you shall be victor." In the vision God promised that Constantine's forces would defeat their foes if they put the sign of the cross on their shields. This occurred right before he was about to enter into a battle with another emperor, Maxentius. Against overwhelming odds Constantine's soldiers were victorious. This battle was later changed to the Battle of Milvian Bridge.[336]

...after the Battle of Milvian Bridge, the Roman Senate erected a triumphal arch in the Colosseum. According to the inscription on this arch, Constantine's victory was won 'through the prompting of the Deity.' But the Deity in question was not Jesus. It was Sol Invictus, the pagan sun god.[337]

Another resource indicates that: "About four years prior to chairing the Council, Constantine had been initiated into the religious order of Sol Invictus,[338] one of two thriving cults that regarded the Sun as the one and Supreme God. The other cult was Mithraism."[339]

---

[333] Ibid., 56.

[334] Tully. op. cit., 65. Constantine's mother (Helena) was responsible for going to the Bible lands and designating and naming all the locations relevant to Jesus' story. Helena decided to build the Church of the Nativity over the site of Jesus' birthplace.

[335] Ibid., 166.

[336] Moore. *The Christian Conspiracy*, 57.

[337] Chadwick. *The Early Church*, 125.

[338] "...the followers of Sol Invictus believed that he was a literal 'Son of God who had been born of a Virgin on December 25'." Moore. *The Christian Conspiracy*, 278.

[339] Bushby, Tom. *The Forged Origins of the New Testament,* Nexus New Times Magazine, vol. 14, Number 4, 54.

Mithraism was a popular ancient religion in Persia during the ninth century B.C.E. It was popular in Rome in the fourth century just before Constantine.[340] "Because of his Sun[341] worship, he instructed Eusebius to convene the first of three settings [of the Council of Nicaea] on the summer solstice, 21 June 325."[342]

What about the sign that Constantine saw in his vision? Christian believers are of the mind that this sign was the sign of the Crucifixion cross. Another resource presents a different story. He saw "...the first two Greek characters of Christ's name, the *Chi rho*."[343] Research indicates that "...There is early evidence of the *Chi Rho* symbol on Christian Rings of the third century."[344] A description of this *Chi Rho* would be two spears crossed like a flat "X" and a large capital "P" place over the crossed spears.

Dr. Richard Watson (1737-1816) offered this opinion: "the clergy at the Council of Nicaea were all under the power of the devil, and the convention was composed of the lowest rabble and patronized the vilest abominations."[345] Some sources relate that Constantine "never acquired a solid theological knowledge" and "depended heavily on his advisers in religious questions."[346] As the reader will note (from the footnotes provided), much of this information is found within Catholic resources!

Let's map out more pieces of the story now. Constantine issued a decree commanding all presbyters and their subordinates to "be mounted on asses, mules and horses belonging to the public, and travel to the city of Nicaea."[347] So, a total of 318 "bishops, priests, deacons, subdeacons, acolytes and exorcists"[348] came to debate whether Jesus was God or man!

---

[340] Moore. *The Christian Conspiracy*, 276.
[341] According to the *Catholic Encyclopedia*, Pope Leo the Great, pontiff from 440 to 461, witnessed the custom of many Christians of his time to stand on the front steps of St. Peter's in Rome "and pay homage to the sun by obeisance and prayers."
[342] *Catholic Encyclopedia*, New Edition, vol. I, 792.
[343] DVD entitled "Helena: First Pilgrim to the Holy Land." Questar, Inc. GD8060.
[344] //en.wikipedia.org/wiki/chi_rho. "It is formed by superimposing the first letters in the Greek spelling of the word Christ..." Also, Google to learn more of this non-cross looking symbol. www.seiyaku.com/customs/crossess/chi-rho.html
[345] *An Apology for Christianity*, 1776, 1796 reprint.
[346] *Catholic Encyclopedia*, New Edition, vol. xii, 576, passim.
[347] *The Catholic Dictionary*, Addis and Arnold, 1917, "Council of Nicaea" entry.
[348] *Life of Constantine*, op. cit.

Let's be reminded that many Roman deities were given the title of "son of god" including Julius Caesar. Most of the common people at the time of the Roman Empire idolized either Julius Caesar or Mithras (the Romanized version of the Persian deity Mithra). It wasn't until after his death (March 15, 44 BC), that Caesar was deified by the Roman Senate and given the name "the Divine Julius." Caesar was later given the title of "Saviour" which literally meant "one who sows the seed." He was hailed as "God made manifest and universal Saviour of human life." Encompassing these titles as well as "Father of the Empire," the Roman people considered him to be "God" for more than 300 years.[349] His successor was Augustus. He was called the "ancestral God and Saviour of the whole human race."[350] So, these types of titles such as "Son of God" were common-place in the Near East. Kings, pharaohs, a great philosopher, or anyone who was seen as capable of super-human acts might be referred to in this way by the people.[351]

The term "son" is used frequently in the Old Testament for the special relationship between God and others. Messengers before God's throne (malakhim in Hebrew, anggeloi in Greek) are called "sons of God" (Genesis 6:2); all Israel is referred to as a divine son (Hosea 11:1)...[352]

Pagan[353] and Roman Influences on Christianity

"The core of Christianity—the worship of a miracle working, walking, talking godman who brings salvation—was also the core of other ancient religions that began at least a thousand years before Jesus."[354]

---

[349] Bushby, op. cit., 55.
[350] Smith, Homer. *Man and his Gods,* Little, Brown & Co., Boston 1952.
[351] Hick, John and Knitter, Paul F., Editors, *The Myth of Christian Uniqueness; Toward a Pluralistic Theology of Religions*, 31. Also in *Introducing the Old Testament* by J. Drane, 88.
[352] Chilton, Bruce. op. cit., 58.
[353] "'Pagan' refers to any religion that is not Christian, Jewish or Islamic. It comes from the Latin word *pagus* which means 'village.' Early Christianity was mostly urban, and so most non-Christians lived in the rural areas. They were therefore called villagers, *i.e.,* pagans." Bramley, op. cit., 48.
[354] www.poem.info/ "Heaven, hell, prophecy, daemon possession, sacrifice, initiation by baptism, communion with God through a holy meal, the Holy Spirit, monotheism, immortality of the soul, and many other "Christian" ideas all belonged to earlier, older Pagan faiths." (quoted from this website)

The cult of Sol Invictus had been introduced to Rome a century before Constantine. In A.D. 321, "Constantine ordered the law courts closed on 'the venerable day of the sun,' and decreed that this day be a day of rest."[355] Before that, Christianity had held Saturday, the Jewish Sabbath, as sacred. One reason that "sun-day" became the sabbath was to help to dissociate Christianity from its Judaic origins.

Until the fourth century, Jesus' birthday had been celebrated on January 6th.[356] For the cult of Sol Invictus, the most important day of the year was December 25th,[357] the festival of Natalis Invictus, the birth (or rebirth), of the sun (solstice).[358] Constantine chose the God of the Christians and simply ignored the Son (Jesus), completely. He felt that Jesus had failed because he was not a warrior leader like David and Solomon. So, Constantine saw himself as following in Jesus' footsteps, yet being more successful.[359]

Constantine died in 337 and his gathering of what now can be viewed as pagan beliefs into a religious system had a great appeal to many pagan worshipers. Later Church writers made Constantine "the great champion of Christianity" which it is said he gave "legal status as the religion of the Roman Empire."[360] Historical records tell a different story. Maybe it was self-interest that inspired him to legitimize Christianity. I believe that he had political reasons for giving a place for Christianity to exist; to increase the size of his empire and to please his mother. She was a Christian and is known to have gathered together Christian artifacts and preserved sacred Christian sites.

---

[355] *Holy Blood, Holy Grail*, 367.

[356] "Originally, the birth of Christ was celebrated twelve days after the solstice on January 6, the day of Epiphany in the Christian calendar…In those days this was also the date of the festival in the Greek Kore, 'the Maiden', identified with the Egyptian Isis…" Anne Baring and Jules Cashford, *The Myth of the Goddess*, 562.

[357] "Many of the Christians were converted from Mithraism. The festival of Mithra's birth was December 25th, the winter solstice, the birthday of Sol Invictus (the invincible sun) and the rebirth of the sun's light. Besides having the same birthday as Christianity's Jesus, Mithras was said to have been born in a manger, among shepherds. The custom of giving gifts on Dec. 25th originated in Mithraism also, hundreds of years before the birth of Christ." www.`/~tandi/tarsus.htm, 2.

[358] *Holy Blood, Holy Grail*, 366-7.

[359] Gardner writes, "…since it was the Emperor who had ensured the Christians' freedom within the Empire then, surely, their true Saviour was not Jesus, but Constantine!" *Bloodline of the Holy Grail*, 139.

[360] *Encyclopedia of the Roman Empire*, Matthew Bunson, Facts on File, New York, 1994, 86.

In summary, Constantine helped ease in Christianity:

- *he brought Mithraic [or Sol Invictus] practices into Christianity,*
- *that led to "many cherished traditions such as worshipping on Sunday,*[361] *celebrating Christmas on December 25,*[362] *and the European tradition of representing the Nativity scene in a cave" (a Mithraic tradition),*
- *he encouraged tolerance for Christians,*
- *he closed "...certain pagan temples which were particularly offensive to Christians, such as those which were dedicated to ritual prostitution."*
- *he was not favorable to public sacrifice.*[363]

"In AD 367 Bishop Athanasius of Alexandria compiled a list of works to be included in the New Testament. This list was ratified by the Church Council of Hippo in 393 and again by the Council of Carthage four years later."[364]

As is obvious by now, in the years of struggle to define itself, Christianity was under considerable influence from the Roman Empire. For the developing Church, it would be simple to reflect the image and organization of the Roman government as a way of spreading its doctrine and building a Church institution. After so many years of having no power and undergoing considerable persecution, becoming part of the Roman Empire must have been a very appealing prospect.

The survival of the selected tenets of the Church was facilitated by them being in the hands of male leadership. I believe there were those who had knowledge of other more feminine teachings. To set the stage for male leadership many texts were selected out by the Council of Nicaea. For the Church or some aspect of it to survive it needed to incorporate the strength of masculine attitudes of power and control.

After his death, Jesus' influence was thinning out within the many small circles of his followers. Often there was discourse and debate between the many factions. Something needed to happen, even if motives were not very "Christian." As we can put together now, the principles of nonviolence and the internalization of the gospels were

---

[361] This day of the week had no particular significance for Jesus or his early followers.
[362] "In Rome, the week preceding the solstice was the Saturnalia, an orgiastic festival that concluded with *gift-giving* and *candle-lighting*." (Hmmmm. Doesn't that sound like a familiar holiday?)(this author's note) Kenneth Davis, op. cit., 351.
[363] Moore, David, Dr. *The Christian Conspiracy*, 58.
[364] Baigent, Leigh & Lincoln. *Holy Blood, Holy Grail*, 318.

beginning to be ignored. Having acquired government backing, Christianity could now act more aggressively and intentionally toward people and also toward Mother Earth. Once Christianity was the only choice of religions the male dictates of those in positions of power began to dominate.

Now the Church took on *Roman* ways of conducting business. With the growth of followers, the Church established doctrines and dogma. Those who opposed were persecuted as heretics. Dr. Moore adds, "Within less than two hundred years of Christianity's being accepted as a state religion, Justinian passed a law which required baptism[365] into Christianity as requisite for citizenship in the Empire."[366] According to Moore, by the end of the first 500 years after Jesus' ministry the Church had:

- 1-defined Christ,
- 2-"required his followers to accept those definitions,
- 3-...defined the follower as being a loyal subject of the supreme Church" because

    a) "...he needed the church..." for salvation,

    b) the Church was as "...meaningful in the life of a Christian as God was..." and

    c) "...followers were defined as those who needed the Sacraments of the Church."

Dr. Moore further writes: "In fact, Jesus taught none of these three important requirements of the Church."[367]

One more point needs to be addressed: The *"Constitutum Constantini."* This document, attributed to Constantine's time, could be called, "the donation of Constantine." It has been viewed as a real happening to this day. This document promoted the belief that the Church had the power and right to select the world's kings and rulers. Also as Ian Ross Vayro reports:

For 600 years they claimed that through this document, Constantine <u>in 315 A.D.</u> had donated half his Empire to the Church and had given the Vatican 'spiritual authority' and 'power over the Kings of the World...No fewer than ten Popes used

---

[365] "The ritual immersion in water originated in India and continues to be practiced daily by the Hindus...the rite of baptism deviates from Jewish tradition altogether..." Kersten, op. cit., 96.
[366] Moore. *The Christian Conspiracy*, 59.
[367] Ibid., 143.

this 'right' to control kings and select dynasties and the document's authenticity was unquestioned until the 15th Century.[368]

Finally, it was determined that this document was put together in about A.D. 760 *Constitutum Constantini* was used by 'Philip the Fair' in 1307, as Vayro writes, "to rob and destroy the Knights Templar...Constantine only founded the City of Constantinople in 324 A.D. ..."[369] where the document was supposedly signed in 315! Someone forgot to check their history. French philosopher Voltaire described it this way: [the above document was] "...the boldest and most magnificent forgery, which deceived the world for centuries."[370]

What was it like to be a Christian believing in Jesus in the sixth century? Dr. L. David Moore summarizes:

...an orthodox Christian on the "true way" had to believe that his leader was completely divine and completely human, with two natures and two wills, even though the belief in the "two wills" would not be officially confirmed for another 130 years. He had to believe that his Lord was divine in a way that no one else could ever be divine, for he had been born of a Virgin. He had to believe that his Lord was the only Son of God, and as such was the only one he could follow...He knew that he had to be "saved" from the original sin" which he inherited from Adam...[371]

In early 2000, the Vatican released a document called *Dominus Jesus* with the approval of the Pope. It was reminiscent of the mentality of the Inquisition. In place of horrible deeds in "the name of God" this document revived an attitude of superiority. In it the Church proclaimed that, "...the Roman Catholic Church is the only true church within Christianity" and the only way to get to God. It went even farther, saying that no other Christian body should be referred to as a 'sister church'."[372]

For additional historical information and a timeline of papal activities go to "Appendix E" in the back of the book.

---

[368] Vayro, *Tears in Heaven*, 166.
[369] Ibid., 167.
[370] Ibid.
[371] Moore. *The Christian Conspiracy*, 211.
[372] Spong. *A New Christianity for a New World*, 225.

Searching for the Ancient Teachings

An Aramaic Study of the Concept of Heaven

"...the word <u>shem-aya</u>, usually translated "heaven." The ending added to <u>shem</u> implies that its effect extends without limits."[373]

In reviewing nearly two hundred books and texts on religion, I was taken aback by the fact that few resources dealt with the subject of Heaven beyond the usual Christian theological descriptions. I would like to offer some ideas that I think can initiate some reflection about this much thought-about subject. It wasn't until the sixth century B.C.E. that the concept of life after death is mentioned in the Old Testament.[374]

As we have the audacity to reevaluate various Christian beliefs, we must pass the concept of Heaven by Aramaic resources. It is helpful for this study to realize that English translations are not wrong; they are simply very limiting. When Jesus was speaking in Aramaic he was touching into life experience in a variety of ways. The Aramaic language allowed for a spectrum of applications—not just one meaning as is truer of English. I like the metaphor that Douglas-Klotz uses: "...[it is] like fruit juice that has been strained through a very fine filter and heated, leaving all of the valuable vitamins, minerals, trace elements, and pulp behind."[375]

I have selected some words and phrases, translated from Aramaic to English, which have the potential of helping our understanding of how a first century person might have heard and internalized them. I believe that Jesus lived in a world where the sacred and the natural worlds were part of each other; not separated. The later ideology of a division between Earth[376] and Heaven[377] is the

---

[373] Douglas-Klotz. *The Hidden Gospel*, 20.
[374] Spong. *Why Christianity Must Change or Die*, 205-6.
[375] Douglas-Klotz. *The Hidden Gospel*, 20.
[376] "...the word 'earth' (*ar'ah*) does not simply mean the ground or the planet Earth, but can simultaneously refer to all of nature and to any being that has individual form—from a planet to a star." Ibid., 100.
[377] Douglas-Klotz gives this interpretation of the Aramaic translation of "*Our Father who art in Heaven*: "We are part of the vibration through which all creation is

result of limiting and inaccurate translation and lack of understanding of the Jewish culture. For example (referring to the above), let's take our words "universe" or "cosmos" which Neil Douglas-Klotz has interpreted as coming from the Hebrew-Aramaic root word *"shem."* When *–aya* is added to the end of *shem*, it indicates that the divine is *"in every particle of existence."*[378]

This presents an interesting discussion. What, if any, are the boundaries here? As Douglas-Klotz explains, "The Aramaic word for 'pass away' can also mean to cross over a boundary or go beyond a limit."[379] If the divine is *in every particle* of the universe, doesn't that mean that the Creator is within every human? In the Aramaic, Hebrew and Greek languages, the words for kingdom (*malkuta, mamlaka and entos* respectively), meant both within and among. All diversity existed within Unity and could not be separated from it. In later Christian theology the kingdom became a far off place where one goes as a reward for a Godly life.

This Sufi saying can help our understanding: *"each person has a unique note in the universal symphony; no one else can strike yours except you."* Therefore there is no separation between Heaven and Earth. As above, so below! Yet, is there a "conductor" of this universal symphony? If so, some might call it "the Law," some feel better with the term Universality. I prefer "Sacred Unity" or "The Great Mystery." The Aramaic language gives us a different look at the word "law." In Matthew 5:18 (KJV) we read: "For verily I say unto you, till heaven and earth pass, one jot or one tittle shall in no wise pass from the law, till all be fulfilled." Again Douglas-Klotz teaches:

The word translated here as "pass" is the same translated as "pass away"..."The word for "law" in Aramaic points by its roots to anything of beauty that helps relieve or take away that which deprives a human being of strength.[380]

According to this interpretation, there will always be beauty that will support our human experience and our strength.

Connected. It means when we pray with the Great Spirit's vibration we are connected to Unity and that experience is 'heaven'. It is not a place—it is here and NOW!!"

[378] Ibid., 70.
[379] Ibid., 101.
[380] Ibid., 102.

Original Sin[381]

"In the Jewish view a sin consists of any departure from God's way, or any transgression of the divine commandments...No sin, according to Jewish tradition, is unforgiveable..."[382]

The Jewish tradition teaches that "most sins are committed because of human weakness or lack of knowledge, not because of inherent wickedness."[383]

"Original sin," a Christian theological idea, is not found in the Bible. It promotes the concept of the universal sinfulness of the human race and is rooted in the first sin committed by Adam. We as humans are all cursed by God, from generation to generation since the time of Adam. Perhaps the Old Testament scripture of how the "sins of the fathers would be visited upon the children to the third and fourth generation" would come close to describing this idea. Actually it was the Christian writer Augustine, the Bishop of Hippo in the fourth century A.D., who expanded the notion of original sin by saying that, "the taint of human sin is transmitted from one generation to the next by the act of procreation."[384] Elaine Pagels argues in her book, *Adam, Eve and the Serpent*, that Augustine effectively transformed much of the teaching of the Christian faith, she says:

Instead of the freedom of the will and humanity's original royal dignity, Augustine emphasizes humanity's enslavement to sin. Humanity is sick, suffering, and helpless, irreparably damaged by the fall, for that "original sin."[385]

Let's step back and push the "pause" button. I grew up being told that our sinful human nature[386] must change. Our human nature was an "enemy to God," because the nature of humans was to be selfish and disobedient. Even this Earth was a place of punishment; a place where the Devil resided; and certainly a place to get out of someday. Remember my earlier Bible School experience about protecting our

---

[381] Developed by Augustine of Hippo during the fifth century C.E. http://en.wikipedia.org/wiki/Original_sin
[382] *Dictionary of the Jewish Religion.*
[383] Ibid.
[384] Davis, Kenneth, op. cit., 362.
[385] Pagels, Elaine. *Adam, Eve and the Serpent*, 99.
[386] "It was Augustine (AD 354-430)…who was the main formulator of the doctrine of original sin." Baring and Cashford. op cit., 534.

heart from being "shot" by the Devil? It seems that our human nature had already been shot down!

Our Native Elders were quick to remind us that a baby was born fresh from the side of the Creator—as pure as the white winter snow! In our old traditions all children hold the energy of innocence until their coming of age ceremony when they step into the vision given to them by the Creator. Each lifetime is a blessing and an opportunity to embrace our humanity, not to fight against it. Our personal spirit is too precious and dear, too connected to the presence of The Divine, to think we are ever apart from it.

Adolphe Franck writes in his book, *The Kabbalah: the Religious Philosophy of the Hebrews*:

The dogma of original sin seems to have been adopted by the modern Kabbalists, principally by Isaac Luria. Believing that all souls were born with Adam, and all formed one and the same soul, he regarded them all as equally guilty of the first act of disobedience.[387]

Moore says, "...neither Jesus nor any of the Apostles[388] use the words, 'eternal damnation' in the scriptures. The closest is 'eternal sin' [Mark 3:29] or 'eternal punishment' [Matt. 25:46], each used only once." Looking at the other side of the story, the term "eternal life" is in the scriptures twenty-nine times!"[389] The *Gospel of Mary* offers this:

...the only sin is that which we create with our sickly imagination. It is this imagination--or rather, impoverishment of imagination--that needs to be healed. We are responsible for the world in which we live, for in a deep sense it is we who create it by interpreting it positively or negatively.[390]

Here is an important note from one of the oldest texts, The *Gospel of Thomas*. It teaches that the soul,[391] far from being corrupt, is eternal: "Happy is the one who came into being before coming into

---

[387] Adolphe Franck, *The Kabbalah: The Religious Philosophy of the Hebrews*, 140.
[388] Bishop Spong: "Even naming the disciples proves to be impossible since as noted earlier the gospels simply do not agree on their identities. We need to be prepared to discover that even the twelve [apostles] are more symbolically real than they are actually real." *Jesus for the Non-Religious*, 38.
[389] Moore. *Christianity and the New Age Religion*, 193.
[390] *Gospel of Mary Magdalene*, 50.
[391] "In an ancient Semitic sense, one does not 'have' or 'posses' a soul: one *is* a soul." *The Hidden Gospel*, 116.

being…" Dr. Kenneth Hanson speaks of ultra-orthodox Judaism and the preexistence of the soul:

The idea of the preexistence of the soul is not foreign to biblical faith. In ultra-orthodox Judaism, for example, there is the concept that all the souls of righteous Israelites were present, mystically, at Mount Sinai, when the Ten Commandments were given, and only later found their place in human form.[392]

Stephanie elaborates:

We know this because we are taught that we were all present at Mount Sinai. This comes up every year during the observance of Passover; we are asked to be thankful for the exodus from Egypt and the giving of the Torah as ones who were present at the time. This can be viewed as preexistence of the soul and mystical presence at the Mount, or as evidence of a Jewish belief in reincarnation.[393]

Sexuality and Spirituality

"Like the Mesopotamians before them, the Egyptians believed spirituality and sexuality went hand in hand. The path to eternal life could just as easily been found in the bedroom as in the Temple. Sexuality and sensuality permeated nearly every aspect of the ancient Egyptian beliefs…"[394]

Throughout history there has always been a cultural and political overlay to the relationship between sexuality and spirituality as well as the position of women within religion. This has led to a polarization of how people think about sexuality. Many who have written about the subject have not focused on the feminine nature of Jesus.

For centuries the Essenes had strict regulations around sexuality. For example, they only engaged in intercourse once a year. Not surprisingly, within the Essene tradition there began to be those who had opinions about how restrictive that was! The Gnostics, as they understood the stories of Jesus, held beliefs that would be closer to far-eastern ideas about sexual intercourse. They felt that Jesus brought some of those concepts into his teachings.

Some early church writers saw sexual intercourse as an invention of the Devil and believed it had no place within Christian life. Some believed that Jesus was celibate by choice. So we see very early the

---

[392] Hanson, Kenneth. *Secrets of the Lost Bible*, 30.
[393] Stephanie M.
[394] History Channel, *"The History of Sex."*

development of a polarity between being human and being spiritual. Attitudes and opinions about the proper place for sexuality in religious experience varied widely and led to considerable debate for centuries after Jesus' lifetime. People gravitated toward groups of like mind and chose their own personal way of resolving the conflict. Over the centuries after Jesus' death the polarity deepened and eventually the need to make Jesus into someone who was not sexual led to the concept that sex had nothing to do with spirituality or that it was outside of the spiritual experience.

In the fourth century The Church began forbidding married priests to have sex with their wives. It was also necessary to add that they were not to father children inside or outside the marriage! Some refused to comply with these laws and faced severe sanctions. Starbird writes that some of these Church-initiated punishments were, "fines, public beatings, imprisonment, dismissal from the priesthood, invalidation of all priestly marriages and papal directives ordering the wives and children of priests to be seized as slaves of the Church."[395] The result of all of these laws was the closeting and denial of the sexual side of life. The spiritual focus was upon service to others, loyalty to the church and obedience to God. I believe those who were the most sexually frustrated were those who placed sexuality out of reach, away from themselves, so they wouldn't have to deal with it. I have found a rather interesting note about the monasteries in Macedonia where there is an ancient library called Mt Athos.[396] Athos takes its name from the Egyptian goddess Athor or Hathor.[397] Yet, author Acharya S reports: "So terrified are those sexually repressed monks of all that is female, they will not allow even *female animals* in proximity of the monasteries.[398]

When sexuality became an abhorrent behavior those who were responsible for distracting men from their spirituality became targets for exclusion as well. Over the next sixteen hundred years women were depicted as temptresses and lesser humans within Christian circles, perhaps in many cultures as well. The goal was to bring celibacy and male domination into spiritual leadership roles, and over

---

[395] Starbird, Margaret. *The Woman with the Alabaster Jar,* p. xiv-xv.
[396] Higgis, Godfrey. *Anacalypsis*, A&B Books, 1995, I, 583.
[397] Ibid.
[398] Acharya S. op. cit., 374.

time this was accomplished. The long-term consequences of this repression of sexual energy and expression are showing up even today within the current generation of celibate priests. The point is made.

Much of the Christian experience since Christ has excluded both sexuality and the contributions and participation of women in spiritual arenas. Other diverse opinions of the time were hidden away as is the case with the *Gospel of Thomas*[399]:

Jesus said to them, "When you make the two One, when you make the inner the outer and the outer the inner, and the above the below, so that you make the male and the female into a single One...then you will enter the kingdom."[400]

Dr. Michael Lerner, in his book, *Jewish Renewal*, recognizes a concept in Judaism which is very similar to the Native American belief that there are masculine and feminine aspects within all human beings.

There is a kabbalistic tradition that when feminine and masculine energies merge and be whole, the repair of the world will take place. Men will embrace the female side that they have previously repressed and women will embrace their male side.[401]

He continues, *"Kabbalists tried to convey this by speaking of God as Shechinah, a divine presence that is the 'bride of God within God, Mother of the world and feminine side of the Divine Self, in no way fully separable from the male Self of God'."*[402]

Just to add to the unfinished story of Jesus and sexuality, the following is attributed to Jesus:

"No (one can) know when (the husband) and the wife have intercourse with one another except the two of them. Indeed marriage in the world is a mystery for those who have taken a wife. If there is a hidden quality to the marriage of defilement, how much more is the undefiled marriage a true mystery! It is not fleshly but pure.

---

[399] "All four of these texts seem to have been written around the 2nd century C.E., the *Secret Book of James* and the *Gospel of Thomas* probably being earlier than the *Book of Thomas* and the *Secret Book of John*. All four preserve older materials, and some of the recorded sayings of the Savior may go back to the historical Jesus." *The Secret Teachings of Jesus,* xvii.
[400] Codex II, pages 37-38. Note: "...the Kingdom that is spoken of in the Gospel of Mary must not be confused with a return to some sort of lost paradise..."p.46.
[401] Lerner. Op. cit., 312.
[402] Ibid. Green, Arthur. "Bride, Spouse, Daughter: Images of the Feminine in Classical Jewish Sources," in *On Being a Jewish Feminist: A Reader*, 255.

It belongs not to desire but to the will. It belongs not to the darkness or the night but to the day and the light..." (Gospel of Philip)[403]

A Grandmother Elder once told me that first the women will heal themselves; then they will help heal the men; and finally, together they will heal the world.

The *Gospel of Mary Magdalene*, originally written in Greek sometime in the second century, contains some interesting discussions:

[regarding the conflict between Peter and Mary Magdalene]"How is it possible that the Teacher talked in this manner with a woman about secrets of which we ourselves are ignorant? Must we change our customs, and listen to this woman? Did he really choose her, and prefer her to us?...At this, Levi spoke up: 'Peter, you have always been hot-tempered, and now we see you repudiating a woman, just as our adversaries do. Yet if the Teacher held her worthy, who are you to reject her? Surely the Teacher knew her very well, for he loved her more than us..."[404]

We close this discussion with some expressions from my Jewish friend, Stephanie. I asked her about the requirement that Jewish husbands and wives have "Sabbath Joy," (sex) every Sabbath. It seems to me to be more of a response to obedience than Joy! Stephanie responded this way:

Ah, but all these laws are designed to trigger certain things in the observer. It is the same idea as having a completely ritualized service with no flexibility or room for improvisation. You spend a lot of time learning the words and going through the motions so that, when you know them, you don't have to think about them. They just flow through you, and true prayer comes out without your having to search for the words. Similarly, there are ways we celebrate the holy days, including the Sabbath. If we are required to have sex on Friday nights, that means that man and wife will make time for it. They have to. It is part of the observance. Otherwise, it might not happen. This tradition guarantees that we remember this particular form of joy one day a week.

When it comes to the Sabbath, there are a whole lot of things we are not allowed to do, and it takes a little while of observing that before you understand why. As a person who did keep that observance for several years, I understand that it changes the whole week – knowing that you cannot write on Saturday means that you do not have to write on Saturday; knowing that you get to really, truly not work on Saturdays means that the rest of the week you procrastinate less, because you have Saturday coming up to relax and defrag and not have to worry.

I got so much more done Sunday through Friday when I knew I could not do anything much on Saturday, and I looked forward to it all week. All those

---

[403] Robinson, James M., general Editor. *The Nag Hammadi Library,* 157-8.
[404] Quoted in *The Gospel of Mary Magdalene*, by Jean-Yves LeLoup, 37-39.

prohibitions – 39 things you may not do – brought me very great joy. It starts off as a matter of observance, but it becomes something beautiful and holy. The Hebrew word for 'holy' really just means 'separate,' after all.[405]

To be in the World, But Not of the World

It was certainly a surprise to me to read that in the eighth century a contest of sorts took place between priests to see who could be the most physically unkempt and dirty. Such actions must have been the result of many years of indoctrination that one's body is not spiritual. The body was connected to the sins of sex and pleasure. Within the same line of thinking was the thought that *being human,* being one's natural self made you an enemy of God. Being human was a condition of separation[406] from God who resided in a faraway place. Because the human condition was historically connected to disobedience to God, it was not to be given a place of respect within spiritual philosophy.

There were various outward displays of religious rites such as fasting and purification within the Jewish culture. It was proper to cleanse before going into the temple areas. Also, there was a designation of where God resided: in the *Holy of Holies.*[407] According to Christian dogma, the Earth was a place of punishment. So not being "of the world" meant not allowing the world to influence or corrupt you. It was best not to be too connected to this world. The Native side of me strongly reacts to this idea. What is wrong with this world? Mother Earth a place of punishment? Our Native American belief is that she is sacred and that all the experiences we have with her are invaluable to our spiritual growth.

---

[405] Stephanie M.

[406] "Orthodox Jews and Christians insist that a chasm separates humanity from its creator: God is wholly other. But some of the Gnostics who wrote these gospels contradict this: self-knowledge is knowledge of God; the self and the divine are identical." Elaine Pagels, *The Gnostic Gospels,* xx.

[407] The most sacred and innermost part of the temple. It symbolized the place where God's presence was most concentrated. It was so sacred that it could be entered by only one person (the Jewish high priest), and on only one day of the year (the Day of Atonement). It was separated from the rest of the temple by a curtain. "Once, this inner sanctum had housed the Ark of the Covenant…But the Temple had been vandalized by an Egyptian expedition five years after Solomon's death (1Kings 14:25-26), and the Holy of Holies [called the *qodesh qodashim*] probably remained empty after that." Chilton, op. cit., 31.

In early Christian beliefs there developed an idea that God was to be found in cathedrals and churches and that He was keeping His distance from humans because they disobeyed Him. There was also the belief that humans must earn the love of God before they can be with God in Heaven again. Humans must graduate and become "chosen" in order to return to paradise where God resides. The residence of God was indoors and the world of nature was where wildness existed, distracting us from our spiritual quest. Some Christian circles inferred that the outdoors or nature was the residence of the Devil. So that which is associated with nature, including the physical body because it was the result of the experience of sex, was bad or evil and not a part of spirituality. It also reinforced the belief that women are inferior beings because of their association with nature and the belief that they tempted men with their sexuality. It was best to distance one's self *from the world*. I can't help but wonder where Christianity in general stands today with these beliefs!

Reincarnation Out...Death In!

Early Christian communities believed in reincarnation until it was declared heretical and forever banned from Christian theology at the Second Council of Constantinople in A.D. 553. There is clear evidence for the belief in the rebirth of the soul into another body in the Old Testament. *Meyer's Konversationslexikon,* a famous German encyclopedia of 1907, speaks of the topic of reincarnation in the Jewish Talmud, "Jews at the time of Christ held the general belief of the transmigration of the soul."[408] Joseph P. Schultz in *Judaism and the Gentile Faiths* writes:

The concept of reincarnation first penetrated Jewish circles in the ninth and tenth centuries, with the eastward expansion of Islam...The earliest kabbalistic work that deals with reincarnation is the <u>Sefer ha-Bahir</u>, *dating from the late twelfth century.*[409]

Today there are volumes of writings being published on the subject of reincarnation. One book, *Reincarnation: A Biblical Doctrine?* by

---

[408] Volume 18, 263.
[409] Schultz, Joseph P. *Judaism and the Gentile Faiths*, 129-130.

Marilyn McDirmit uses more than two hundred scriptures from the Bible to support the belief in reincarnation.[410]

It seems evident that the growing church saw the need to place importance upon the present lifetime in order to make embracing the faith and the tenets of the church more imperative. It's a onetime chance! Having many opportunities for salvation or for joining the community of believers would delay "coming into the fold" and lessen the need for the assistance of the Church.

The doctrine of Purgatory was developed in the sixth century (A.D. 580). This way-station was supposed to house those who did not have an opportunity in their lifetime to join the community of Christians. The Encyclopedia Britannica says:

Purgatory is the condition or process of purification in which the souls of those who die in a state of grace are made ready for Heaven. This is an idea that has ancient roots and is well-attested in early Christian literature, while the conception of purgatory as a geographically situated place is largely the achievement of medieval Christian piety and imagination.

Because of the pressure to come into the Church in one lifetime, the dreaded experience of death became paramount in Christian teachings. Christ's death on the cross[411] was an example of both tragedy and victory. Death meant no more separation from God. However, as I think of the many thousands of Christians who walked to their demise at the hands of various rulers, I wonder if they believed that they were walking into their next lifetime because of their beliefs and their love for the God? I don't believe that they were so convinced that sacrifice would bring them entrance into the Kingdom of God.

---

[410] Two other works, the *Case for Reincarnation, and Reincarnation: A Biblical Doctrine?* also make for compelling reading. Also see the following: by Hans Holzer: *Life Beyond Life*; Joe Fisher, *The Case for Reincarnation.*

[411] Most Christians look to the crucifix as very representative of Christianity in general. "In the catacombs, no figure of a man on a cross can be found for the first six or seven centuries of the era. In fact, the first known figure of a god *on a cross* is a likeness of the sun god Orpheus in the 4th century AD." *Recovering Christianity's Pagan Past*, U.S. News & World Report (special Edition, copyright 2008), 50-51. "...the cross rarely figured in any Christian art of tomb decoration [before the fourth century]." *The Hidden Gospel*, 14. Words attributed to Jesus of "...let him deny himself and take up his cross and follow me" Marcus Borg relates: "Before Jesus death, 'cross' was obviously not yet a Christian symbol but referred to method of execution used by the Romans." Borg, *Jesus: a New Vision*, 112.

Rather, had fear lost its presence in their understanding of Christianity? I don't know for sure, but I know that there were still those at the time who held beliefs in other lifetimes. It was partially the examples of many of the early Christians that I believe caused the Church[412] to bring forth dogma that increased the fear factor and dread of the inevitable death experience. Little or no tolerance was given to anyone who refused to be guided by the Churches dictates.

I recall the words of a Native Elder who was speaking to some seminary students many years ago: "With all the insurance policies paid up, the burial plots arranged and the wills in place, it just seems that the American people are more focused on death than they are on life. It's about becoming a member of this or that. They feel they must join something to become something. Maybe they need to join the human race."[413]

Reincarnation and Karma

"In Buddhism one is reborn a woman because of one's bad karma. Buddhist prayers include: 'I pray that I may be reborn as a male in a future existence. Jewish men are taught, in a book of Jewish prayers, to say, Blessed be the God who has not created me a heathen, a slave or a woman."[414]

This leads us to approach another important discussion about karma. I often dance around discussions of karma because I am not quite able to put into words my concern for the present use of the word. I want to give some room for this idea because it has a relationship to reincarnation. When karma is spoken of in class I have generally learned to have a measured response, in most cases. This concept creates some tension in me because it seems to describe judgment and imprisonment instead of love and freedom. I believe that the earliest

---

[412] "**I don't think hell exists.** I happen to believe in life after death but I don't think it has anything to do with reward and punishment. Religion is always in the control business…It's in the guilt producing control business and if you have heaven as a place where you are rewarded for your goodness and hell as a place where you're punished for your evil then you sort of have control over the population…"(Spong, Dateline NBC,) http://www.msnbc.msn.com/id/14274585/ns/dateline_nbc/)
[413] Muskegon Elder Phillip Deer, at the St. Paul's School of Theology, Kansas City, Mo. (early 1980's).
[414] Spong. *The Sins of Scripture*, 72. In the fourth century, St. Jerome commented: "When a woman wishes to serve God more than the world, then she will cease to be a woman and will be called man.", 87.

definitions of karma might have been different than the understandings that are common today, just as the teachings of Jesus have undergone changes through time. What I reject is the idea that we are somehow bound by our past mistakes to suffer in this lifetime as a kind of punishment for our transgressions. I know that this is only one of the ways karma is presented and that it can also be seen as a way of bringing lessons forward into another life experience. I am addressing the former notion in my remarks here.

My Native side believes that memories, past experiences, and lessons are important. If karma distracts us from being present and fully in each moment today, then the past becomes too dominant an influence. In the Native approach each day was a new day. Every experience was to be viewed with gratitude and fully embraced with both mind and heart. Yes, we have repeat experiences from lifetime to lifetime, just as we have from one day to the next, in order to grow and learn from them. However, every day is another chance to learn and once the lesson is integrated it becomes part of our way of life and being.

The Christian experience often brings with it what I often refer to as "baggage." Humans are plagued with Eve's disobedience and are fallen from the presence of God. Constant reminders are given to each person of their sinful nature and the need to repent and return to God. Some religions even say a new born baby needs to be baptized because they are "born in sin." Consequently, each lifetime falls short of a full embrace by God until the final reward or punishment. That's a lot of baggage for me! Bishop Spong confronts this premise: "Human beings are *emerging* creatures; they are a work in progress. Neither perfect nor fallen, they are simply *incomplete*."[415] A Native person of long ago would quickly say, "Wait a minute here, this means that I am responsible for someone else's actions; that all humans are to carry guilt for not only their own sinful nature, but humanity's disobedience too?"

Karma is a Hindu belief which is also accepted by Buddhists. It is defined as the:

...sum and the consequences of a person's actions during the successive phases of his existence, regarded as determining his destiny...Karma is a law which determines life, for his rebirth is based upon his moral behavior in a previous phase

---

[415] Spong. *A New Christianity for a New World*, 124.

of existence...Thus, this life, which is a burden, must be lived through with no hope of atonement, restitution or experience other than..to enter another cycle of birth-rebirth until all past moral debts have been excised by non-active lives of meditation.[416]

Karma is generally understood as "cause and effect." Every experience in life: eating, sleeping, walking in the natural, etc. has a consequence. Webster offers the following definition: *"Buddhism, Hinduism the totality of one's acts in each state of one's existence."* The totality part appeals to me. The *New Catholic Encyclopedia says:* "Karma, a term that literally means 'action,' came to be used in Hindu doctrine to signify a chain of cause and effect...not only in the physical, but also in moral order." "The goal of every soul is ultimately, by good works...to be set free from karma and to attain liberation." Dr. Moore defines it in another way: "It generally means the sum and consequences of an entity's actions during successive phases of its existence, regarded as determining its destiny."[417]

My *natural* tendency is to reach back into the most ancient frame of reference—if that is possible. In my second book I presented the following ideas from Native philosophy: "It seems that Americans are more prepared to die than they are to live..."[418] The "changing of worlds" is anticipated, even welcomed as a time to honor our lessons and look forward to more experiences in the next lifetime. Each lifetime bring us into a greater relationship with the Creator and with all of our relations.

The Egyptian scholar, Murry Hope, implies a kind of celebration and a positive reflection before entering another lifetime.

...The ancient Egyptians saw this [karma 'as you sow, so shall you reap'] in terms of...the spirit or soul was obliged to say what it <u>had accomplished</u> with kindness and correctness rather than what it had not...If one does not complete that spiritual program, then "the test [the opportunity for accomplishment] has to be retaken in another lifetime."[419]

Another take on karma by researcher Kenneth K. S. Ch'en:

The word karma means deeds. The doctrines of karma and rebirth were already present in India before the Buddha was born...As a result of the deeds performed

---

[416] Ibid., op. cit., 159.
[417] Moore. *The Christian Conspiracy*, 182.
[418] Eagle. op. cit., 49.
[419] Hope, Murry. *Ancient Egypt: The Sirius Connection*, 235-236.

in the past or present, a living being would continue in the cycle of rebirth and assume a different form in each rebirth...He [Buddha] taught...the intention or volition behind the deed is important...[420]

In this instance, an additional concept, "intention" or "cause," was added to a "deed" (action). The Buddhist defined karma as an intention leading to some bodily action (cause and effect). Thus every "thought or act leaves behind some traces which could not be erased."[421]

I think that reincarnation and karma can walk hand-in-hand as a guide for the celebration of life. You might again recognize my bias. We can learn from our achievements as well as what we have done "wrong" and needs to be made "right." Putting the emphasis on *getting it right this time* or *evening the score* seems to me, creates baggage. Karma has value as a natural phenomenon, but it can also be used to foster and instill guilt. In contrast, the Native way of thinking emphasizes the opportunity in each lifetime to more fully understand and tightly embrace the wonders and joys of life rather than an experience of remembering past failings and sins.

This discussion would be incomplete without an ancient understanding from the Hebrew Bible that we have visited earlier. It was so very meaningful for early Hebrew people to experience the Creator's *breath* as being ever-present. The ancient understanding of feeling free and liberated was not necessarily seeking to be "saved" as it was to *breathe freely* as we walk through life each day. Bishop Spong adds:

Nowhere in the gospel do I find the goal of Christian mission to be that of making one religious; rather, that goal is to set one free, to call one to life, to invite one to love..To be spiritual means to be alive. To be filled with the spirit means to be free to live.[422]

Karmic experiences provide spiritual knowledge. In the *Gospel of Thomas* Jesus places knowledge in relationship to salvation: "*If you have this kind of knowledge but still feel that you lack something then you do not have true salvation.*"[423] The Church's idea of salvation is to be saved through adherence to its dogma. Jesus is emphasizing here

---

[420] Ch'en, Kenneth K.S. *Buddhism: The Light of Asia*, 32.
[421] Ibid.
[422] Spong. *This Hebrew Lord: A Bishop's Search for the Authentic Jesus*, 16-17, 21.
[423] Hanson, Kenneth, Ph.D. *Secrets of the Lost Bible*, 36.

the knowledge we gain from personal life experiences is what contributes to true salvation.

Access to God through Jesus and the Church Rather Than a Direct Personal Relationship--The Trinity

"Few Christians are aware that Augustine himself received the Christian doctrine of the Trinity from the pagan philosopher Plotinus (c. A.D. 205-270), who "fed his mind on the attributes of the pagan divinities and was stepped in Hellenistic rational religion and esotericism."[424]

One of the obstacles for the Church that had existed for over three hundred years was that those who embraced Jesus' teachings had little interest in having a "middle man" between them and God. They sent their prayers directly to God. The Hebrew word for confession (*Vidui*) carries the connotation that confession is made directly to God. For many Jews nonstop prayers and direct access to God had been part of their belief system for hundreds of years. Jesus' taught that there was to be direct communication between God and mankind.

In his time, Jesus never suggested that he wanted to be placed on a pedestal, given status and position or be turned into the "Christ" figure. That, I believe, evolved much later. The Church founders of the fourth and fifth centuries systematically fashioned an institutionalized church using the pattern of the Roman government which was hierarchical, privileged, dogmatic and male-dominated. There is also the matter of how various translations of Christian texts have influenced and changed their original meanings. Generally speaking, when the texts were translated into the Greek language there was a shift from *a focus on experience to a focus on belief.*

The One God was placed above all other gods by Moses' Ten Commandments. *Where does Jesus fit in?* After years of political weight being thrown around, history records that in A.D. 540 the doctrine of the Trinity was accepted by the Church. Huston Smith writes this about the Trinity in *The Religions of Man*: "No concept of Christendom has enjoyed a greater reputation for obscurity than this. The Church itself has confessed it to be a mystery; true but beyond the

---

[424] Harpur, op. cit., 47.

reach of mind to fathom completely."[425] In a brief reference to Islamic beliefs Smith continues:

...Islam honors Jesus as a true prophet of God.[426] It even accepts the Christian doctrine of his virgin birth. But at the doctrine of the Incarnation and Trinity[427] it draws the line, seeing these as concessions to man's inclination to seek a compromise between the human and the divine...When Jesus claimed to be the Son of God, He was thinking of God's Fatherhood as embracing all mankind. Every human being was to him a child of God.[428]

Miller offers another Islamic perspective that may be difficult for some Christians to even consider:

...Islam teaches that God has sent to every people a prophet from among their own. In Hinduism, Vishnu is believed to have come to earth in human form many times in response to human need for divine assistance. Some Hindus who admire Jesus understand him to be one of Vishnu's incarnations.[429]

  Jewish Paul would not have even recognized the concept of a "...coequal trinity of Persons in the Godhead..." because in the Jewish mind there was only one sovereign God. It was the Greeks who later developed the idea of the incarnation of God as a reflection of their dualistic theology.[430] The word *Trinity*[431] is not actually in the Bible. The concept of the Trinity evolved over time and was accompanied by a lot of debate within theological circles.[432] If the reader wants to get a

---

[425] Smith, Huston. *The Religions of Man,* 448.
[426] In the Koran Jesus is mentioned more often than any other prophet. "...the Koran affirms Jesus' virgin birth...endorses Jesus' second coming. It credits him as a greater wonder-worker than Muhammud, and it ranks his sanctity above Muhammad's."*Jesus and the World's Religions* by Huston Smith, *Jesus at 2000,* 108.
[427] Gardner, Laurence. *Bloodline of the Holy Grail.* [Isaac Newton (1642-1727)] "Although he [Newton] was a deeply spiritual man, and an authority on early religion, he openly rejected the Trinity dogma and the divinity of Jesus, maintaining that the New Testament had been distorted by the Church before its publication." 274
[428] Smith, H. op. cit., 314.
[429] Miller, Robert J. *The Fourth R.* Literal Incarnation or Universal Love? (May-June 2004), 11.
[430] Spong. *Born of a Woman,* 25.
[431] Thomas Jefferson, writing in his middle forties, wrote that "from a very early part of [his] life" he had experienced the "difficulty of reconciling the idea of Unity and Trinity" in tradition Christian doctrine. (Jefferson to William Short, 31 October 1819, in *Jefferson's Extracts from the Gospels,* ed. Dickinson W. Adams (Princeton: Princeton University Press, 1983), 388.
[432] Moore, L. *Christianity and the New Age Religion,* 182.

sense of the historical development of the Trinity, a short, reasonable and accurate presentation is found in The Encyclopedia Britannica.[433]

The issue of the title "Son of God" placed upon Jesus can be traced by simply reading the King James Version of the Bible. In Paul's writings (A.D. 48-60), Jesus became "Son of God" when Jesus ascended to Heaven[434] and not before. Those writings attributed to Mark (A.D. 65-70), say it was when Jesus was baptized by John the Baptist. Matthew (A.D. 80-85), writes that Jesus became the divine son at birth, and to thoroughly add to the confusion, John (A.D. 95-100), writes that Jesus was *always divine!*[435]

In the entire New Testament Jesus is *called* the "Son of God" or a similar phrase fifty-nine times. Jesus refers to himself as the "Son of God" (or a similar title), only five times in the gospels. Two of these are in the gospels (Matthew 11:27 and Luke 10:22). It is in John that Jesus called himself the title "Son of God" the other three times. Moore believes that even though the author of John and the exact date it was written are not known, it is possible that it was written much later than the others.[436]

The words "only Son" are only used in the gospels three times and *always* in John. There is only one reference in the New Testament outside of the gospels which uses the term "only Son," which is 1 John 4:9. Biblical scholars believe that the Gospel of John and the letters of John were written by the same man, but that this man was not the apostle John.[437]

In contrast, let's look at the use of "Son of Man."[438] This is the most commonly used title for Jesus in the gospels. It shows up **fourteen times** in Mark, and **thirty-one times** in Matthew. Additionally, in Mathew the title "Son of God" is used **only four times**. In the *Gospel of Thomas* when Jesus uses the expression "son of man" he uses it in the context of being fully human or complete.[439]

---

[433] Volume 16, 351-2.
[434] "The ritual of the opening of the heavens…may well derive from Pharaonic Egypt;…" Jean Doresse, *The Secret Books of the Egyptian Gnostics*, 74, 106.
[435] Spong. *Born of a Woman*, 166.
[436] Moore. *Christianity and the New Age Religion*, 168.
[437] Drane, John. *Introducing the New Testament*, 197, 461-3.
[438] "Budda called himself "Son of Man" like Jesus and is likewise called "Prophet," Master" and "Lord." Kersten, opt. cit., 77.
[439] Douglas-Klotz. *The Hidden Gospel*, 164.

Pagels reminds us, that in the Hebrew Bible 'son of man' means "nothing more than 'human being'…The prophet Ezekiel, for example, says that the Lord repeatedly addressed him as "son of man,"[440] often translated 'mortal'…"[441] The only time Jesus clearly admits to being "Christ, the Son of the Blessed," he immediately calls himself something else, "I am; and you will see the Son of man seated at the right hand of Power, and coming with the clouds of heaven."(Mark 14:62) In the *Gospel of Philip* from the Nag Hammadi scrolls Jesus said, "There is the Son of man and there is the son of the Son of man. The Lord is the Son of man, and the son of the Son of man[442] is he who is created through the Son of man."[443]

Just in case you weren't sufficiently confused, let me offer this statement about Jesus as he was on the cross, taken from the Apocalypse of Peter in the Nag Hammadi: Jesus was "glad and laughing on the cross." In the Acts of John, as Jesus is celebrating the Last Supper, he is leading his disciples "as they chant and dance together a mystical hymn, the 'Round Dance of the Cross'."[444]

I close this chapter with an interesting statement by Albert Schweitzer. Early in the twentieth century he said:

What has been passing for Christianity during these nineteen centuries is merely a beginning, full of weaknesses and mistakes, not a full-grown Christianity springing from the spirit of Jesus…I call on Christianity to set itself right in the spirit of sincerity with its past and with thought in order that it may thereby become conscious of its true nature.[445]

---

[440] See, for example, Ezekiel 2:1; 2:8; 3:1; 3:10; 3:17; 3:25; throughout Ezekiel.
[441] Pagels. *Beyond Belief*, 43.
[442] "George Lamsa commented that according to Eastern Christian understanding, 'son of man' simply means 'human being', an ordinary man." *Gospel Light: Comments on the Teachings of Jesus from Aramaic and Unchanged Eastern Customs*, 148-149.
[443] Quoted from *The Other Bible*, 99.
[444] Pagels, Elaine. *Beyond Belief*, 25-26. More discussion is added in chapter four.
[445] Cited in Thomas Kiernan, *A Treasury of Albert Schweitzer*, 123.

Chapter Five

Understanding the Jewish Culture and the Story of Yeshua

"To understand the personality of the historical Jesus…it is necessary to study him against the background of his own day…he was subject to the limitations of knowledge incident to his day; a world-view that…[an]impending catastrophe to the world-process itself…[was] prevalent." (Albert Schweitzer)[446]

"We do not know how to appreciate Jewish books written in a Jewish style and employing Jewish methods."[447]

"In recent years, scholars have put an increasing emphasis on Christianity's Judaic roots, demonstrating that much of Jesus' teaching derived from the Hebrew Bible and rabbinical thought."[448]

"In the first century, a Jewish woman could not legally bear witness in court, and yet, Jesus entrusted to women his most profound revelations."[449]

"…Paul[450] argued that Jesus was not only the Messiah but also the only Son of God, sent to Earth to offer salvation to all of mankind. This doctrine offended and enraged observant Jews, who could not conceive of any man claiming to be the divine substance of YHWH."[451]

"…[It is] absolutely correct in stating that the Greek word *monogenes* was incorrectly translated as 'only begotten.' [One is]…therefore correct when you state that in their original languages, the scriptures do not say that Jesus Christ was the *only* son of God." (Professor of biblical studies in a large mainstream theological seminary)[452]

---

[446] Tully. op. cit. 108.
[447] Spong. *Liberating the Gospels,* 218.
[448] Harpur, Tom. *Recovering Christianity's Pagan Past,* U.S News & World Report (Special Edition, copyright 2008), 47.
[449] Ibid., 15.
[450] Thomas Jefferson wrote his friend William Short that Paul was the "first corrupter of the doctrines of Jesus." Quoted in U. S. News & World Report (Special Edition, *Secrets of the Bible,* copyright 2008), 56.
[451] Isbouts, Jean-Pierre, *The Lost Years,* U.S. News & World Report (Special Edition, copyright 2008), 42.
[452] Moore, Quoted on inside jacket of recommendations for the book, *Christianity and the New Age Religion.*

"He [Jesus] was a Jewish rabbi. He was born a Jew, taught as a Jew, preached as a Jew and died as a Jew." (David Rosen chief rabbi, both in Ireland and in Cape Town, South Africa)[453]

Any attempt to comprehend or even describe ancient cultures through twenty-first century eyes will fall short of a full understanding of the real picture. I am often surprised when I hear those who think they really know all there is to know about world history, American history or the many Native American cultures. How naïve, perhaps even futile, the effort to have the complete picture is. I include myself in this dilemma. Having indigenous drawings (such as the Peace Shield), ancient documents, and archeological evidence can give some meaningful clues but there is much we will never recover because we can't truly place ourselves within the environment, world view or experiences of times long ago.

To add to the dilemma of trying to understand cultures of long ago, there are no examples of any culture or ideology present today which exists in its ancient form. Any cultural circle including democracy, aboriginal cultures, Christianity, Islam and others may say that they are a true manifestation of their roots, but that can only be partially true.

The Nature of Judaism

To give a Jewish perceptive on the forms of Judaism that exist today let's hear Stephanie's expressions:

An **Orthodox Jew** *believes that the religion is housed in the traditions. One cannot ignore the traditions and practices and still be a "real Jew."*
A **Conservative Jew** *believes that the laws and traditions are important and have meaning, but that we, living in the modern world, can flexibly choose what to observe (this results in a wide variety of degrees of observance within Conservative Judaism – some have almost no observance but still have the Conservative mindset, some are observing almost on an Orthodox level but do not consider themselves Orthodox (we call these people* **Conservadox***).*
A **Reform Jew** *believes that there are two kinds of laws/traditions: spiritual and ritual. The spiritual laws are integral to the tradition and must be observed, but the ritual laws are relics of an older time and no longer apply. Thus,*

---

[453] Tully., 82.

an observant Reform Jew will attend religious services, in English,[454] *with instruments, but is very unlikely to keep kosher.*[I refer the reader to Appendix H for more understanding of "kosher **(A Conservative service will be mostly in Hebrew with some English, and an Orthodox service is all in Hebrew, both without instruments and with a lot of ritual chanting instead of songs.)**

Many Jews today will refer to themselves as Reform when they are actually completely secular, and I would like to draw that distinction: there is an actual Reform system of practice. Being Reform does not mean being secular, although it is often understood that way today.

Not getting into delineations within Orthodoxy, the other major group of modern Jews is the **Reconstructionists.** *They cannot really be fit into the spectrum of observance, because being a Reconstructionist is not determined by how much you do but by your view of the text and of G-d. Reconstructionists are kind of the 'new agers' of Judaism, and they allow themselves to change the liturgy in ways that no other branch does. They rewrite things to eliminate all references to gender, and try to get in touch with the Divine as an unknowable spirit rather than as the G-d of Abraham, Isaac, and Jacob, who has a particular personality and a particular way He likes to be worshipped (here the Pagan in me is coming out). Instead of 'Blessed are You, Lord our G-d, King of the Universe, who has sanctified us with Your commandments and commanded us to light the Sabbath candles' (translation of the blessing over the candles), a Reconstructionist is more likely to say something like 'Blessed are You, Divine One, who blesses the world with light.' This is a theoretical example and not an actual Reconstructionist blessing.*

I grew up in a Conservative household with a middling degree of observance; in high school, I became Conservadox and dragged my family some of the way along with me.[455]

If we are able to admit our limitations in being able to accurately step back in time, then we are ready to consider some general guidelines in our study of the Jewish culture during the time of Jesus. Perhaps one immediate frame of reference about the Jewish religion is their claim to be the "chosen people of God." Let's give some attention to this claim. How quickly this position is attacked by anti-Semites and tends to separate humankind. It is no wonder that various denominations and religions are quick to confront this belief. Here's what the *Dictionary of the Jewish Religion* says:

Chosen People. *Deeply rooted Jewish concept that the Jewish people were chosen, in a special relationship to God, to relate his message to mankind. Thus it is*

---

[454] Also my conversation with Rabbi Weinstein indicates that in recent times services are provided with a non-gender specific God and now more Hebrew language is used.
[455] Stephanie M.

interpreted by Jewish thinkers as a mission, rather than an attempt to describe Jews as superior or unique.[456]

Stephanie gives this informative note:

When Jews talk about being the Chosen People, we do not mean we were chosen as G-d's favorites. We were chosen to do His work of healing the world (tikkun olam). The story goes: G-d went first to the Egyptians, and said, "I need a people to lead the world in righteousness and repair the damage that humans are doing. Will you be my people and do my work?" The Egyptians said, "What will be involved?" and G-d said, "Thanks anyway, but I'll look elsewhere." So G-d went next to the Midianites, and said, "I need a people to lead the world in my ways, and work to heal the world of the damage that is being done. Will you be my people and do my work?" The Midianites said, "This sounds great! What would we have to do?" And G-d said, "Never mind." So at last, G-d came to the Jews and He said, "I need a people to be separate from all other peoples of the Earth. You will be isolated and persecuted, but you will be my people, closest to me of all peoples. It will be your task to heal the world of the damage being done to it. Will you be my people and do my work?" The Jews said, "We will do and we will listen." First, we will do, and then we will listen – give us your commandments, we will obey, and then and only then will we ask for your reasons or for what comes next. And for this response were the Jews chosen.

My wife and I had an opportunity to sit in classes offered by a rabbi (teacher), and our memory is the following: God gave the Jewish peoples a pattern, a design, a gift that would be very important to humanity in the future. He actually described it as a map for all of humanity. The Jewish people must survive so that this pattern will be available when it is needed by the world. That map, he said, is the Kabbalah and the teachings of the Tree of Life and the ten *Sefiroth*.

Marcus J. Borg is an internationally renowned Jesus scholar and the author of seven books. The following quote is from the cover of his book, *Jesus A New Vision:*

"In presenting an alternative vision of Jesus and his values, Borg offers a radical criticism of Western culture's interpretation of Christian History...Christians have tended to view culture as having little or no religious significance...But it was not so for Jesus. He sought the transformation of his social world."[457]

---

[456] *Dictionary of the Jewish Religion.*
[457] Borg, Marcus J., *Jesus A New Vision: Spirit, Culture, and The Life of Discipleship*, from cover. "Borg is Hundere Distinguished Professor of Religion and Culture at Oregon State University. He and six internationally known Jesus scholars participated in the first national symposium to commemorate the 2,000th anniversary of the birth of Jesus (Feb, 9-10, 1996)."

My Native heritage leads me to caution against viewing and interpreting any historical event without understanding the cultural setting within which it occurred. To accurately understand Jesus one must study his life, as closely as possible, within the environment of his time and the Jewish culture. It is difficult to see with Hebrew "eyes," of the first century without adding the filter of our current day perspective. As other biblical researchers have concluded, what is missing in many presentations of Jesus is his *Jewishness*. Dr. Bruce Chilton puts it this way: "No one can be assessed apart from one's environment…The 'missing' Jesus is Jesus within Judaism."[458]

Rabbi Lawrence Kushner of San Francisco is a delight to listen to. Information about him can be viewed on the website provided in the footnote.[459] Some years ago, I discovered tapes of some of his lectures in the First Community Church library, in Columbus, Ohio. I really appreciate teachers who are able to provide a clearer understanding of Judaism, especially a gifted one who truly enjoys helping educate non-Jews. Some of his expressions are both challenging and mystical. Rabbi Kushner begins: "Torah does not mean 'law.' Jesus did not read it as law. Torah means 'The Way,' the way of the Universe!" Judaism holds their *sacred texts* in high regard and the reading of them is primary to all Jewish traditions. On the other hand, there is lots of room in Judaism for personal and rabbinical argument.

Rabbi Kushner explains that "Judaism particularly is not dealing with a simple **one way** of reading the sacred text. Judaism thrives on arguing about the meaning of the sacred text." I often hear references to their "sacred deed." Rabbi Kushner explains:

Jews orchestrate their lives by the performance of sacred deed. Jews do not spend much time worrying or thinking about what they believe. Jews don't ask one another what they believe; rabbis don't tell Jews what they should believe. What they do talk about is what they should do and do more of. The way I do organize my religious life is that I try to do as many things as I can that God wants me to do. And sometimes I believe in God and sometimes I don't. But I try to do the sacred deeds whether or not I believe in God.

---

[458]Chilton, Evans, and Neusner. *The Missing Jesus: Rabbinic Judaism and the New Testament*, vii.
[459] "Lawrence Kushner is the Emanu-El Scholar, in residence at the Congregation Emau-El of San Francisco, also a Visiting Prof of Jewish Spirituality at the Graduate Theological University of Berkeley." www.rabbikushner.org

In Judaism there is a tradition that one has the right to argue; even with God. Rabbi Kushner gives a profound perspective on this: "Jews bring themselves into 'being' through arguing about the meaning of sacred texts. The Jewish tradition can handle the hardest question you can throw at it and it can come back for more."[460] In the Jewish culture personal spiritual development is enhanced by the application of argumentation. It seems that Judaism itself is strengthened by its heritage of the right of every Jew to question and hold a personal interpretation of sacred texts. Could I say the same thing about other religions, especially Christianity?

If you have an interest in the Jewish mystical tradition you may want to take a look at "Appendix B" at the end of the book. For an excellent survey of Jesus' role in Jewish culture I would refer you to Jaroslav Pelikan's, *Jesus Through the Centuries*.[461] As we approach the study of first century of Judaism, we can begin with a closer pronunciation of Jesus' Jewish name, "Yeshua." The word *moshia* means "deliverer," one who "makes wide" or "makes sufficient." "One who gives freedom from distress and the ability to pursue one's way." *Moshia* comes from the Hebrew verb *'Yasha'* and Jesus/Yeshua is derived from this same root.[462] According to professors David Flusser and Shmuel Safrai, Orthodox Jews, "*Yeshu*" was how the name "*Yeshua*" was pronounced by Galilean Jews in the first century.[463] That is, instead of saying "Ye-**shoo**-ah" they said "**Yeh**-shoo." "Galileans did not pronounce the Hebrew letter *'ayin'* at the end of a word..."[464]

* * * * * * * * * * * * *

I have planted various Jewish ideas and cultural understandings in my writing up to this point. Let's review:

---

[460] "Reading the Bible through Jewish Eyes," Lecture on March 10, 2001 at First Community Church, Columbus, Ohio.
[461] (New Haven: Yale University Press, 1985; paperback edition published by Harper & Row, 1987).
[462] Website www.hebrew4Christians.net.
[463] Flusser and Safrai. *Jewish Sources in Early Christianity*, 15.
[464] Stern, David H., *Jewish New Testament Commentary*, 1996, 4-5.

- The word *ha-tzelah* meaning the side of Adam[465] seems to imply that Eve was in some way equal to Adam.
- The Hebrew word *teivah* did not mean a boat (or ark) as it meant a box.
- Judaism regards sex as healthy, spiritual, and not sinful.
- There was a written Bible ["law"] and an oral Bible ["law"]: what was taught to everyone and that which was secret and taught only to select individuals.[466]
- Judaism was discussed as one of the major "People of the Book" who brought changes to indigenous life.
- Christianity developed the ideas of worship in a temple (church building) and the symbolism of cleanliness and purity of body and spirit absorbed from Judaism.
- In Judaism, the entity of Satan did not exist in early scripture.
- We learned how the Rabbis were forced to translate the Hebrew into Greek.
- Rabbi means not only teacher, it also means one who is an authority in the practice of Jewish law. In Jewish traditions a Rabbi had to be married, for the Jewish Mishnaic Law that "An unmarried man may not be a teacher." (FN 36)[467]
- Most 1st century Jews believed in the afterlife. "Every Jew desired to earn 'eternity in the World to Come.' The World to Come appears thousands of times in rabbinic literature but, curiously, it is never defined." (FN 247) Marcus J. Borg says that belief in a heaven and hell after death became part of Jewish thought about 500 BCE). (FN 250)
- In Judaism there was an awareness of the importance of individual relationship with God. As an individual would draw closer to God, this would be "independent of the communal covenant." (FN 248)
- Early writers of the Old Testament never mentioned Hell—"for the ancient Jews *Sheol* was a dark and melancholy place for departed souls who wander unhappy, but untormented. Eventually, *Sheol* took on the characteristics of Gehema, Hell in the New Testament, a place of punishment." The Other Bible, glossary. (FN 253) Moore writes, "It is the place of complete inertia that one goes to for reflection when one dies, whether one to be wicked or just, rich or poor. It is a precursor to the Christian idea of purgatory."[468]
- The average life span of Jewish people during the time of Jesus was around forty-five. (FN 311)

---

[465] "The old Hebrew word for human being in Genesis—*adam*—refers to a non-gendered being made up of *dam*—juice, wine, sap, or essence…we as human beings have been given the challenge to hold within ourselves the consciousness of all older life forms, as well as the entire universe, manifest and unmanifest." *The Hidden Gospel*, 36.
[466] Sheinkin. Op. cit, 10.
[467] John's comment: "The rule says that an unmarried man should not be a teacher of children."
[468] Moore. *The Christian Conspiracy*, 324.

- "The Holy of Holies" is the most sacred and innermost part of the temple. It symbolized the place where God's presence was most concentrated. It was so sacred that it could be entered by only one person (the Jewish high priest) and on only one day of the year (the Day of Atonement); and it was separated from the rest of the temple by a curtain. (FN 407)

The following can be added to our study:
- "The Old Testament often mentions heaven; but in Hebrew, the word *samayim*[469] [kingdom of heaven)] is plural though in English it is often translated in the singular." (FN 1063)The word (in Aramaic) for Kingdom is feminine! *"Heaven" in Aramaic present the image of "light and sound shining through all creation."*[470]
- "…Jesus' visit to his hometown is the first instance in recorded history of the custom of *Haftarah*—reading a selection from the Prophets that relates to the weekly Torah portion." (FN 924)
- Rabbi Serzosky says, "Jews have a system of commandments. The medieval scholars often counted up to 613 commandments." (page 251)

In the Preface of the *Dictionary of the Jewish Religion* there are some helpful clues to our study of Judaism. Here is an expression from Rabbi Saul Teplitz:

The Jewish religion is a subtle, challenging, and complex way of life. In the words of the prayer book, it is a "tree of life for those who grasp it." …If we want to discover the treasure of the Jewish faith, we must first find the old roads and dig them. We must examine the bequests of our Jewish past, reverently but critically. It is never either/or—either the past or the present but both in behalf of the future.[471]

With this beginning we will attempt to give a respectful look at the Jewish religion; just as I would hope anyone, if they were interested, would approach an understanding of the Native American "way of life." There are those who don't want to go back and travel the old roads and dig around for ancient information. That's okay for them. I think we can approach learning about any spiritual tradition with honor and respect while, at the same time, realistically and critically questioning the tenets and prescriptions they promote as they

---

[469] Rabbi Weinstein says the word should be spelled, *"shamayim."*
[470] Douglas-Klozt. *Prayers of the Cosmos*, 3. The above italic is directly from Klozt.
[471] Preface, *Dictionary of the Jewish Religion*, vii.

apply to our own spiritual journey. One rabbi is quoted as saying, "Religion is not an escape from life,[472] **it *is* life**."[473]

Early on we must give attention to the longevity of the Jewish religion. What once was a viable force to be dealt with during Roman times later became a visible Jewish nation in the modern world. One thing we know is that Judaism carries the energy of survival! Frederick the Great when asked for the most convincing evidence of the existence of God, declared, "The survival of the Jew."[474] My Jewish sister Stephanie brings this personal reflection:

It seems that the survival of the Jewish people may actually be due to our persecution. Now that it is safe to be a Jew, we don't need to stay so tied to our communities; we intermarry; we bear children who are half Christian or secular; they do not grow up in the religion; they bear children who do not consider themselves Jewish. The fact that it is now safe to be a Jew means that fewer and fewer of us actually are. I think Jews have kind of lost track of that in a lot of branches of the religion.

Observant or well-educated Jews (and here I am talking about a Jewish education, not a secular one) have an understanding of this; that the survival of the Jewish people is important for a reason. The Jews were separated from the other Families of the Earth (mishpachot ha'adamah) *for the purpose of healing the world. But, the rest of the People seem to value survival for its own sake at this point. Why must the Jews survive? Because we have been around for so very long and survived so much.*

Honoring Jewish History

The Nature of Midrash

"…there are such close parallels between the story of the crucifixion and Psalm 22, between the transfiguration of Jesus on the high mountain and the shining face of Moses on Mt. Sinai, between the ascension of Jesus into heaven, and the ascension of Elijah."[475]

"Midrashim are stories told by the rabbis to fill holes in what we know from the Torah. If something is not fully explained (and it is very seldom fully explained), the

---

[472] "The word *hayye*, usually translated 'life,' indicates in both Aramaic and Hebrew the sacred life force, the primal energy that pervades all of nature and the universe." *The Hidden Gospel*, 65.
[473] Preface, *Dictionary of the Jewish Religion*, viii.
[474] Ibid.
[475] Geering, Lloyd. *Is Christianity Going Anywhere?* The Fourth R, (May-June), 3.

rabbis made something up to explain it. Many of those stories are presented to Jewish children as integral to the tradition. There is an idea in some branches of Orthodox Judaism that the writings of the rabbis, including all the midrashim, are all divinely inspired."[476]

Midrash,[477] which is an important part of Jewish thought and writing, is not easy for the Western mentally-dominant mind to quickly understand. Bishop Spong, the well-known author of Bible studies and former Episcopal Bishop of Newark explains for example, the idea that Jesus was in the desert for forty days and forty nights was intended "to illumine events occurring in the present with specific appeals to the people and the events that made up *the sacred past* of the Jews..."[478] It was very important to connect some of the details of the sacred past to experiences being written about in the present time. The purpose was to give validation for the present viewpoint based upon what was written and prophesied in revered historical texts. *Everyone reading the new material understood that this was a commonly used literary technique and was not to necessarily be taken as literal truth.* It was to link past prophesies with the present.

When I heard Stephanie say "the rabbis made something up" I asked her if I heard her right. The rabbis told the children who then believed it?

Yes! Because there is also a tradition that anything the great rabbis said was divinely inspired, so it doesn't really matter whether the story came from the Torah or from the rabbis. It all comes from G-d anyway. We are told, starting at about age 10 or so, when a story is biblical and when it is midrash, but I don't remember there being any sense that the midrashic stories were any less true than the biblical ones. Later on there is a sense that the midrashim may be more allegorical than the biblical stories, when we are old enough to understand that allegory is spiritually true even if it is not literally true.

The *Dictionary of the Jewish Religion* states:

MIDRASH. Discovery of meanings in the Bible other than the literal interpretation. (The word root <u>darash</u> means "to inquire" or "to investigate.") The practice was instituted in order to better understand specific Biblical commands or prohibitions.

---

[476] Stephanie M..
[477] "Midrash or midrashic writing was the Jewish practice of retelling sacred stories of the past to illumine a sacred experience in the present." Spong, *Why Christianity Must Change or Die*, 236.
[478] Spong. *Liberating the Gospels*, 102. (Italics by this author)

There are two ways to view midrash. The above resource relates how the Halachah-oriented midrash sought to extract the laws from the biblical text directly (from the Torah, oral traditions, Rabbinic decrees and laws based on popular custom), while the Aggadah-oriented midrash was concerned with ethical and moral connotations.[479] Their sources consisted of "material unrelated to Jewish law such as homilies based on Bible tales, stories, folklore, aphorisms, and legends...was originally passed on from generation to generation by word of mouth..."[480]

In addition to the above discussion, sometimes prophesies were written in retrospect. You can imagine the debate that has arisen trying to figure out the true history of ancient times! This linkage to previous material simplified the fulfillment of prophecy by connecting the dots. Amy Berstein gives us an example:

...the destruction of Solomon's Temple is foretold in books of prophecy that were first written long after the catastrophe occurred. In this way, time blurs in the Bible. Past events become the stuff of future prophecy, or, put another way, prophecy becomes a foretelling of what is already known to have happened.[481]

Therefore prophecy, in confirming sacred writings, brought an enriched appreciation for Jewish traditions, and also made it possible for Jesus to be seen as fulfilling Jewish law and the old prophesies.

Our journey here is to see parts of the gospels as midrash rather than as literal history. A great deal of difficulty will be experienced if New Testament readers and theologians fail to take into consideration the importance of this Jewish tradition when investigating early Jewish writings. It is often true that people whose perspective is Western-oriented try to interpret Jewish writings without truly understanding Jewish cultural roots. That is why it is important to study the culture that New Testament scriptures come from. Bishop Spong reminds us that:

Midrash represented efforts on the part of the rabbis to probe, tease, and dissect the sacred story looking for hidden meanings, filling in the blanks, and seeking clues to yet-to-be-revealed truth...sacred text was timeless, that it was true in the past, true

---

[479] *Dictionary of the Jewish Religion*, 116.
[480] Ibid., 8.
[481] Bernstein, Amy D., *Courage and Faith*, U.S. News & World Report (Special Edition, copyright 2008), 7.

in the present, and true in the future...was not to be deceitful, misleading, or false...[and when]we develop Jewish eyes with which to read the Gospels, much of that difficulty will fade away.[482]

To add to our understanding of midrash let's look at some more examples. In Mark 1:11 we read "You are my son, the Beloved; with you I am well pleased." This was actually lifted out of the ancient Jewish scriptures taken from Isaiah (42:1) and from Psalms (2:7).

How much of the Judas[483] story can be seen as midrash? The Jewish word for betrayal literally means "to hand over," especially to hand over to a recognized enemy. Looking into the stories of Joseph in the Book of Genesis (37-50) and the Jesus stories we find the following similarities as spoken of by Spong:[484]

--a "handing over"[485] by a group of twelve
--both stories have the betrayal into the hands of gentiles
--death was expected for both Joseph and Jesus
--in both stories God intervened to reverse the outcome (resurrection for Jesus)
--both were imprisoned for a time
--money was given to the traitors(s)
--the betrayer was named Judah or Judas (Gen. 37:26-27)

Another shinning mistranslation with midrashic overtones is the use of "virgin" in the Jesus story. Again, Spong points out:

The word came originally from an Isaiah text, "Behold a virgin shall conceive and bear a son, and his name shall be called Emmanuel" (Matt. 1:23, based roughly on Isaiah 7:14)...the word "virgin" <u>*does not appear in the original Hebrew*[486] *passage in Isaiah!*</u>[487]

Whoever wrote in the name (in Matthew), "has developed an idea

---

[482] Spong. *Liberating the Gospels*, 218.
[483] Bishop John Shelby Spong says: "...I now believe that he [Judas] in fact never existed...that Judas, like Joseph is a manufactured literary character who, as the traitor, was not part of the original story but was first introduced by Mark in the eighth decade of the Common Era." *Jesus for the Non-Religious*, 44.
[484] Spong. *Liberating the Gospels*, 267-8.
[485] Ibid. "...Paul does not seem to be aware that a member of the twelve was the one who "handed him over."
[486] Hebrew as a spoken language ceased to be spoken 300 years before Christ. But it was still used for reading scriptures and for citing information from the Torah.
[487] Spong. *Liberating the Gospels*, 188. (emphasis by this author)

based on a concept that was not present in the original source Matthew was quoting!"[488] It was added later! "The word 'virgin'[489] did not enter the Book of Isaiah **until it was translated into Greek** some five hundred years after Isaiah had written these words and some two hundred years before the birth of Jesus."[490]

Translators selected the Greek word *parthenos* in translating the Hebrew word *almuh*—**meaning a young woman.**[491] "The Hebrew word for virgin is *betulah. Almuh* never means 'virgin' in Hebrew."[492] The substituted Greek word, *parthenos,* meant virgin. The author of Matthew built his whole narrative around this mistranslation. Why didn't he check the original Hebrew?[493] Now we have a mistranslation, a misrepresentation **and** a midrashic treatment of the information in the Greek (or someone's), writing. In summary, the early Christian writers translated the Hebrew word *almuh* ("young woman"), in Isaiah 7:14 into the Greek word *parthenos* ("virgin"), so that the people would recognize their savior as having been born of a virgin. The older Jewish texts said no such thing! This concept of the virginity of Mother Mary was strangely taken to another level with the later assertion that she maintained her virginity throughout the birthing process. As Spong puts it:

> *...it began to be asserted that even when Mary bore Jesus, her virginity had been preserved both during (<u>inpartu</u>) and after (<u>postpartum</u>) the birth of the holy child! Tales actually began to circulate about Jesus being born out of Mary's ear!*[494]

It must be said that the idea of special beings appearing as the result of virgin births had been around a long time before Christianity. Kersten writes this about Buddha: "Like the biblical Christ he [Budda]

---

[488] Ibid.
[489] (virgin birth)"This is tradition in antiquity in general. If you are important you have a special birth. Alexander the Great had a virgin birth. His mother was impregnated by a god." CNN Presents, *The Two Marys*, Prof. Karen I. King, Harvard Divinity School.
[490] Spong. *Liberating the Gospels*, 188. (emphasis by this author)
[491] In other translations it meant a "young woman who has not yet birthed a child." (emphasis by author)
[492] Moore, Dr. L. David. *Christianity and the New Age Religion*, 176. (emphasis by this author)
[493] I refer the reader to an extensive study of "midrash" by Spong in *Liberating the Gospels: Reading the Bible with Jewish Eyes*, Index entry "midrash."
[494] Spong. *The Sins of Scripture*, 84.

is born in a miraculous way. Angels announce him as the savior and predict his mother: 'All joy may come over you, Queen Maya, rejoice and be happy, for this child which thou hast born is holy'!"[495] There were many birth mythologies in the ancient world in which gods come from virgin mothers. These stories would clearly indicate that the child was special in some way. It was sometimes used to designate someone with superhuman qualities or someone who was chosen by the gods. Margaret Starbird gives us a short summary:

In the Greek pantheon, Maia was the virgin Mother of Hermes, while Zeus miraculously gave birth to Athena from his own forehead and impregnated Leda in his guise of a swan. Other gods claimed in mythology to have been born of virgin mothers include Dionysus,[496] Attis, Adonis, and Mithras, all of whom have strong "savior" attributes remarkably similar to those claimed for Jesus Christ.[497]

* * * * * * * * * * * *

"Modern Christianity has to face the possibility that the historicity of Jesus could be revealed at any time." (Albert Schweitzer, 1913)[498]

Most biblical scholars believe that besides the fact that we do not have any of the original copies of the gospels;[499] the names given to the gospels do not necessarily designate the persons who wrote them. Scholars also admit that there are various authors seemingly connected to the same gospel. Because of this there was an opening for later additions and modifications. One example is the final chapter of the Gospel of John (21) which is viewed as a sixth century forgery. It is entirely devoted to describing Jesus' Resurrection[500] to his disciples. The Church admits that "The sole conclusion that can be deduced from

---

[495] Kersten, Holger. op. cit., 75.
[496] "Like Jesus, the Greek god Hermes was also wrapped in swaddling clothing and placed in a manger, as was Dionysus." John Jackson, *Christianity Before Christ*, 206.
[497] Starbird. *The Feminine Face of Christianity*, 17.
[498] Schweitzer, Albert, *Geschichte der Leben-Jesu-Forschung*, 512.
[499] "According to one source, there were hundreds of different versions of Jesus' words, hundreds of 'gospels,' in the first three centuries after his death." See *No Jews or Christians in the Bible*, by Dr. John J. Pilch (1998), 3.
[500] "Resurrection first appears in the Hebrew Bible as a metaphor, symbolizing the rebirth of the nation of Israel," writes Geza Vermes in *A Matter of Faith*, U.S. N & W Report, (Special Edition, *Secrets of the Bible*, copyright 2008), 67.

this is that the twenty-first chapter was afterwards added and is therefore to be regarded as an appendix to the Gospel."[501] As a side note, the gospel of John is void of the story of the last supper. Pagels writes that John says Jesus was arrested on Thursday night and brought to trial the following morning, no mention of the Passover meal.[502]

John also has some differences in its version of the final days of Jesus. Much is written by Mark, Matthew, and Luke about Jesus' actions toward the merchants doing business in the temple. In these versions of the story the turning over of the tables of the money changers is one of the *last* public acts Jesus does before being seized by the Roman authorities. What supposedly led to the arrest of Jesus was this attack on the money changers. Yet, John records this as one of Jesus' *first* acts.[503] Another scriptural discrepancy is that only in John do we find the account of Jesus raising his friend Lazarus from the dead.[504] John implies that this was upsetting enough to the Jewish chief priest that he "planned to put Lazarus to death as well."[505]

Pagels believes that John's gospel differs from Matthew, Mark, and Luke in yet another very noteworthy way: "…John suggests that Jesus is not merely God's human servant but God himself revealed in human form."[506] The *divinity* versus the *humanity*, of Jesus seems to have been debated for centuries.[507] Pagels comments on one of the earliest writings about John by Origen, a third century, Egyptian "father of the church.": "…while the other gospels describe Jesus as *human*,

---

[501] Catholic Encyclopedia, Farley ed., vol. viii, pp. 441-442; New Catholic Encyclopedia (NCE), "Gospel of John", p. 1080; also NCE, vol. xii, p. 407.
[502] Pagels, Elaine. *Beyond Belief*, 23.
[503] Ibid. 35.
[504] Ibid. 36.
[505] John 12:10.
[506] Pagels. *Beyond Belief*, 37.
[507] An interesting note: in A.D. 431 Mother Mary was declared *Mother of God*. Campbell writes: "During the first five Christian centuries the question remained unsettled as to whether Mary had conceived *literally* of God or had normally given birth to a son…It was only in the year AD 431, at the church council held in Ephesus…that the earthly mother, Mary, of the historical Jesus was authoritatively declared to have been literally *Theotokos*, (God bearer, mother of God)." *The Inner Reaches of Outer Space*, 60. *Could this be the beginning of declaring the divinity of Jesus? Yet, what did it mean to be Mother of God?* After the crucifixion, "According to much later tradition Jesus' mother eventually died in exile at Ephesus…" *Holy Blood, Holy Grail*, 343.

'none of them clearly spoke of his *divinity*, as John does'."[508] Further research about Origen reveals that "John does not always tell the truth *literally*, he always tells the truth *spiritually.*"[509] To me this is a red flag that indicates that when all the information from the various gospels is presented as one story, it doesn't represent the whole picture.

I think there has been a rather successful strategy to draw believers away from the real purpose of Jesus' mission—to provide a way to live and to hold onto hope and faith in the Creator. Jesus was all about finding a sense of meaning in life experiences and daily practices.

An eleventh century document called the *Levitikon* has a story to tell. Translated from Latin into Greek, it holds a version of John's gospel that is reminiscent of some of the Gnostic beliefs. It was used for the basis of founding the Neo-Templar Johannite Church in 1828.[510] The members are sometimes called "original Christians." Although dismissed by most researchers such a document, if authentic, would have had to be hidden from the Church in the eleventh century considering what it said. Here are only some of the details as presented by Picknett and Prince in their book, ***The Templar Revelation***:

- Chapters 20 and 21 (of John) are missing.
- "It eliminates all hints of the miraculous from the stories of the turning of the water into wine, the loaves and fishes, and the raising of Lazarus."
- References to St. Peter are not found including the story of Jesus saying "Upon this rock[511] I will build my church."
- (quite interesting is) "Jesus is presented as having been an initiate of the mysteries of Osiris,[512] the major Egyptian god of his day."
- Jesus passed this knowledge and his secret teachings on to his disciple, John 'the Beloved'.

---

[508] Origen, *Commentary on John* 10.4-6. Quoted in *Beyond Belief*, 37.

[509] Ibid. Quoted in Pagels, 118.

[510] Much of the following is provided by Picknett & Prince, op. cit., 144-145.

[511] The Hebrew word for "corner-stone or foundation rock" is *Saphra*.

[512] The Book of the Dead includes a "graphic depiction of how the heart is removed from the body and weighed in the scales by Osiris, lord of the underworld, to determine whether one's good deeds outweigh one's evil deeds." Hanson, Kenneth, Ph.D, *Secrets of the Lost Bible*, 39.

- Nothing is written of the Virgin Birth[513] and it included the fact that Jesus' mother did not know the identity of his father.
- The writings provided an issue of heresy for the Church: "...the elevation of the Feminine Principle, and specifically the acknowledgement of sex as a sacrament."[514]

We leave this discussion with yet another bold statement by John Shelby Spong. In his writings about "midrash" he says, *"I suspect that Joseph, the husband of Mary, never existed."* He believes that he was a product of "midrashic" Jewish use of their sacred scriptures. Joseph as Jesus' earthly father was placed into the story patterned after the Joseph of the book of Genesis and was "symbolized by the fathers of the two major Joshua/Jesus figures of Hebrew history...from the pen of the Jewish/Christian scribe who wrote the book we call Matthew."[515]

I raise another uncomfortable note. Jesus was to be from a linage of Joseph following a genealogical descent from David. Authors Baring and Cashford say, "...the fact that Joseph plays no apparent part in his conception...the Davidic blood would not have been transmitted to Jesus unless Joseph was his father. And if Joseph was his father, what is the relevance of the virgin birth?"[516]

What About Satan?

"...the Jewish scholars considered the very notion of such a figure [Satan], independent of the Divine Presence, incompatible with monotheism."[517]

"...in the Hawaiian traditions, the kahuna is known as one who is known as 'a transmitter of the secret." There is 'no parallel in Huna to the notion of an evil being. It exists as a result of men's ideas about evil. They teach that every human is 'responsible for his own actions and the results of those actions."[518]

Even though the idea of Satan is not in the Hebrew Bible, the development of some evil force or energy was an important belief in

---

[513] Gardner writes the Knights Templars believed that "the Church had misinterpreted both the Virgin Birth and the Resurrection." *Bloodline of the Holy Grail*, 219.
[514] Picknet & Prince, op. cit., 221.
[515] Spong, *Liberating the Gospels*, 216-217.
[516] Baring and Cashford, op. cit., 563.
[517] Hanson, Kenneth, Ph.D. *Secrets of the Lost Bible*, 73.
[518] King, Serge Kahili. *Kahuna Healing*, 9, 53.

Christianity. From where did this concept begin? Dr. Kenneth Hanson writes in *Secrets of the Lost Bible*:

The idea that a satanic, evil force is out there in the universe, in direct competition with God and speaking through the serpent (like a demon possesses a physical body) sounded...like Zoroastrianism... The ancient Zoroastrians theorized two gods, not one: a good deity and an evil counterpart.[519]

The total embodiment of a horrendous male figure known as Satan[520] was completed in the thirteenth century by the Roman Catholic Church. A figure with horns, vicious face, red suit, lengthy tail and a pitch fork served as a reminder of a force that was ever-present in life. It seemed just as powerful as God except when it would be, according to prophesy, corralled for a thousand years when Jesus returns. Douglas-Klotz brings us back to Jewish roots regarding Satan:

...[the] word satan, which come from the Aramaic satana...simply means adversary, or that which causes one to turn aside or go astray. Only later did Christian theology establish the idea of "Satan" as being almost equal to God, and certainly not part of the divine. This notion of an "anti-God" is entirely un-Jewish.[521]

The Devil holds a place in Christian dogma that cannot be overlooked. So let's take courage to take a closer look at this "guy in the red suit." As I related earlier, in my early childhood and Christian experience the Devil was a bad, powerful spirit that required an attitude of protection and fear or else Satan could possess your heart and lead you to the eternal fires of Hell.

Satan had the ability, known as possession, to fully capture one's soul and body. Hell[522] was a place where eternal torment was inflected and experienced. This theology greatly encouraged a person to exemplify behavior that would later lead them into a blessed condition of bliss somewhere in another place known as "Heaven."

---

[519] Hanson. Op. cit., 25.

[520] For the rest of the story of the process by which satan became demonized and identified with the enemy in early Christianity, see Pagels: *The History of Satan*.

[521] Douglas-Klotz. *The Hidden Gospel*, 135. "For instance, the same term in Hebrew (*satan*) is used in Numbers 22:22 to describe the angel of God who blocked the way of Balam's donkey." 187.

[522] In a national survey conducted by *Newsweek* for their edition of March 27, 1989, it was found that seventy-seven percent of the people believe in Heaven and almost all of them thought that they have a good chance of getting there; whereas fifty-eight percent believe in Hell and only six percent believe they will go there.

Christianity was brought into being from the bedrock of Judaism and the Torah.[523] Who was this evil one in the Jewish religion? From the Web we find: "The concept of an evil force in the universe, separate from God is foreign to the Jewish religion. It is clearly expressed in the Torah as well as in First Samuel that there is only God; He does good as well bad acts."[524] In early Judaism there appears to be no separate evil entity opposing God. There is only one God. But what's this note about a God who does both good and bad acts? Let's take a short journey now with the concept of God:

- First God was the "All" (with apparently no concept of an evil force?)
- Next, God[525] had both good and bad actions and deeds
- And finally there were two powerful beings, God and a named evil power, Satan.

The Book of Jubilees,[526] an ancient Jewish writing well known by the rabbis, says the following: Jubilees 17:16 "Then Prince Mastema came and said before God: "Abraham does indeed love his son Isaac and finds him more pleasing than anyone else. Tell him to offer him as a sacrifice on an altar. Then you will see whether he performs this order and will know whether he is faithful in everything through which you test him.""[527]

---

[523] "The idea that the Torah evolved from a combination of various sources is formally known as the 'Documentary Hypothesis'...[as] taught by leading religious schools...Harvard and Yale, the Union Theological Seminary, and both the Jewish Theological Seminary and the Hebrew Union College. The precise identity of who wrote these books is an unsolved—and most likely an unsolvable—mystery..." Kenneth Davis, op. cit., 19-20.

[524] Committee to Disclose the Worlds Greatest Secret.

[525] According to Klotz, the Jewish name for God is *Alaha*—It can mean any of these: Sacred Unity, Oneness, the One without an Opposite. "Even before the Jewish scriptures were composed, some people in the Middle East used a form of this word—*Allat* or *Elat*—to refer to Sacred Unity idealized as the Middle Eastern Great Goddess." *The Hidden Gospel*, 28.

[526] It was written around 150 BCE, yet it is claimed to be authored by Moses. The earliest copies date from the 1500s CE. Hanson, Kenneth, Ph. D, *Secrets of the Lost Bible*, 58. "It is considered *canonical* for the Ethiopian Orthodox Church..." (Wikipedia: Jubilees)

[527] Vayro, Ian Ross, *Tears in Heaven*, 114.

My study of the Abraham and Isaac story as presented in the Bible is that God did test Abraham's faith[528] and willingness to obey. In Hebrew there is another understanding of the word "sacrifice." Some biblical scholars have expressed that it really means *to make sacred*. Rabbi Weinstein helps us with the Hebrew word *korban* that is translated "sacrifice." He says it really means *to draw closer*. In Jewish rites the sacrificial animal was given the opportunity to offer itself as a gift and to be considered sacred. In Judaism there were laws designed to prevent the torture, cruel treatment, and overworking of animals. In their philosophy the injunction of rest on the Sabbath included domestic animals as well as Jews.[529] Stephanie gives this interesting perspective:

Christians tend to refer to this story as "The Sacrifice of Isaac." We call it "Akeidat Yitzchaak," the binding of Isaac. It is not a story of sacrifice. There is also a lot of discussion in modern Conservative Judaism about whether or not Abraham passed the test. What happens to him next? His wife dies. Very next thing. A suitable reward for passing G-d's test? There is a tradition in the Torah of arguing with G-d when He proposes to do things like destroy cities; our righteous patriarchs plead with Him not to. Abraham is prepared to sacrifice his only son for no reason except that G-d has asked it of him. Orthodox Jews, of course, believe that he did pass the test.

But who is this Prince Mastema? Now we have another character from Jewish sources. Researcher Ian Ross Vayro explains the Old Testament idea of God was first "…as a cruel and ruthless warmonger, manifesting deceit, wrath and senseless killing, firmly cementing his position in the minds of the Hebrew scribes as Jehovah-Sabaoth, the Jewish tribal War-God."[530] We can find clues about this perspective of God in earlier passages from Moses: "The Lord is a man of war; YHWH is his name."(Exodus 15:3) "The Spirit of God promotes slaughter." (Numbers 31:17-18, Deuteronomy 20:16-17, Joshua 10: 40-42, Ezekiel 9:4-8) Secondly, Vayro relates that: "Before Satan was added to the Christian Bible at the Council of Nicea in 325 A.D. any unpleasantness in the Godhead was blamed on a 'bad' spirit

---

[528] "Strikingly, the roots of the Latin verb for faith, *credo*, (with which the creeds of the church begin), reflect…[a] connection to the heart. *Credo* comes from two words which together mean, "I give my heart to." See Wilfred Cantwell Smith, *Faith and Belief*, 76-78.
[529] *Dictionary of the Jewish Religion*.
[530] Ibid.

of the Godhead called Mastema…the bad side of God…was given a separate name and identity.[531] The name Mastema actually meant 'the dark, evil or warlike' side of YHWH…"[532]

For this limited discourse we can consult one more writing from the Book of Jubilees. The slaying of the first-born in the land of Egypt was also attributed to the Mastema side of God:

Jubilee 49: "For on this night – the beginning of the festival and the beginning of the joy – ye were eating the Passover in Egypt, when all the powers of Mastema had been let loose to slay all the first-born in the land of Egypt, from the first-born of Pharaoh to the first-born of the captive maid-servant in the mill, and to the cattle."[533] (The same account is also found in Exodus 12:29)

It was a teaching of the Old Testament that man had to fear and submit to being tested or tempted by God. If the test was satisfactorily completed, there was a chance to attain righteousness and favor with God. Our brief study here has shown that in Judaism the entity known as Satan did not exist in early scriptures. By the fourth century, however, Satan was named and fully entrenched within Christian dogma.

The word "Satan" in Aramaic (the language of Jesus' time), simply meant "adversary." Sheinkin, in Path of the Kabbalah, writes that in Judaism he is "… a very loyal servant of God who enables human free will to exist through offering the option of evil."[534] It wasn't until later that Satan was a separate entity working against God and it was later still that somehow Satan was elevated to a powerful god of evil forces. As Vayro explains, "…[Satan] is in no way as sinister as proclaimed by the Church today."[535]

Back to a few biblical scriptures regarding this Jewish-promoted evil side of God:

Exodus 32:14, "And the Lord repented of the evil which he thought to do unto his people."

---

[531] This is in Vayro, *They Lied to Us in Sunday School,* (Joshua Books, 2006), 52.
[532] Vayro. op. cit.
[533] Ibid., 115.
[534] Sheinkin, op. cit, 194.
[535] Vayro. *Tears in Heaven*, 157.

1 Samuel 16:23, "And it came to pass, when the evil spirit from God was upon Saul, that David took an harp, and played with his hands: so Saul was refreshed, and was well, and the evil spirit departed from him."

Isaiah 45:5, 7 "I am the Lord, and there is none else...I form the light, and create the darkness: I make peace and create evil: I the Lord, do all these things."[536]

Finally a very harsh image of God is placed in Amos 4:10: "I have sent among you the pestilence after the manner of Egypt: your young men have I slain with the sword, and have taken away your horses; and I have made the stink of your camps to come up unto your nostrils: yet have ye not returned unto me," saith the Lord.

I have personally been spiritually nurtured by the simple Chinese symbol known as the "yin-yang." This is the law of the I Ching. The law states: "Within the greatest Good is contained the seed of the greatest Evil and within the greatest Evil is contained the seed of the greatest Good." Also, I will add this statement attributed to Socrates in the Crito: "I only wish...that the many could do the greatest evil; for then they would also be capable of the greatest good – and what a fine thing that would be!"[537] In the Gnostic Gospels Jesus is reported to have said:

"Light and darkness, life and death, right and left, are brothers of one another. They are inseparable. Because of this neither are the good, good, nor the evil, evil, nor is life, life, nor death death. For this reason each one will dissolve into its earliest origin...(Gospel of Philip)

For me, this uncomfortable discussion about the possibility of two natures within The Divine brings me to consider the frame of reference of nature and how it might bring us an understanding of life experiences. I do not believe that the Creator has an evil aspect, just as I do not make room for "evil" (as it is understood within most Christian institutions), in nature or in humans. Sometimes this other side of life is spoken of as our "shadow side" or our "soft spots." Even within our strengths lie potential pitfalls and shades of grey.

A severe natural weather happening is not viewed as evil, but just what it is; "a part of nature." We cannot deny that humans sometimes make unfortunate choices out of the personality's

---

[536] Other scriptures to look into regarding the issue of dark and light would be: 1 Kings 8:12, 1 Timothy 6:16, II Chronicles 6:1, Psalm 18:11, 1 John 1:5, 1 Peter 2:9.
[537] Vayro. Op. cit., 424.

unbalanced state of being. There are certainly consequences that result from these choices. Our mental and spiritual limitations can bring about severe and life-affecting experiences for ourselves and others. However, we can also learn from such experiences and we need not see them as an evil part of us caused by Satan. Indeed, in the Native way of life they are not seen as "bad" or "good"--they just are part of life and are dealt with as best we can in the present moment, with the best intention of seeking balance and harmony with the help of the Creator.

A Ute Elder, Annabelle Eagle offers the Native American perspective: "Indians never had a word for evil. That was a force that was not acknowledged, only disharmony. Living in harmony with our fellow men, with nature and with our Creator is the ultimate goal of life on Earth. The word evil and its connotation came with the white man and his religion."[538]

The Essenes and Christianity

Essenes. Early Jewish religious sect that disappeared around the 1st century. Members were extremely uncompromising in observance of religious laws, including dietary, Sabbath, and purity regulations. Considered an ascetic and profoundly pious group (their name is believed to mean, in the Greek version of the Aramaic, "the pious"), they looked forward to an imminent ushering in of the Messianic era. Their principal residence was along the Dead Sea shore; according to Josephus, one part of the sect practiced celibacy. (from the *Dictionary of the Jewish Religion*)

Five hundred years before the birth of Christ, a mysterious group of scholars formed communities to honor an ancient teaching that began before history as we know it. Collectively known as the Essenes, there were various sects that included the Nazarenes and the Ebionites.[539] *Roman and Jewish scholars referred to the Essenes as a 'race by themselves, more remarkable than any other in the world.*[540]

It is my understanding that in the Holy Land of Jesus' time the Essenes were a sect that was as important as the Pharisees and Sadducees. Yet, there is no reference to the Essenes in the Bible. Was this an attempt to distance them from the life of Jesus? According to

---

[538] Pettit, Jan. *Utes: The Mountain People*, Revised Edition, 84.
[539] "Early Christians linked to the conservative Jewish community in Jerusalem who remained loyal to the Torah and the Temple." Margaret Starbird, *Magdalene's Lost Legacy*, 154.
[540] Gregg Braden, *Isaiah Effect*, quoting Edmond Bordeauz Szekely from ed. and trans., *The Essene Gospel of Peace*, Book Three (Matsqui, B.C. Canada, I.B.S. International, 1937), 40.

Baigent, Leigh and Lincoln,[541] the Essenes had many communities throughout the Holy Land and maybe even in other locations dating back to about 150 B.C. They apparently were known to always wear simple white clothing and they honored the Old Testament, as allegory rather than as literal history.[542] [543] Authors of the book *Holy Blood, Holy Grail* comment that "...it is inconceivable that Jesus did not come into contact with them. John the Baptist would seem to have been an Essene."[544]

In chapter one you may remember my previous description of the Essene community as being anti-Roman and anti-establishment. They were focused on retrieving what, in their perception, was the real or lost truth. They thought that the Jewish leadership had strayed considerably from true Jewish beliefs. The Essenes believed that the Messiah[545] was coming any day and they were hopeful that through him they could reclaim the kingship, the land, and the prominence which they felt belonged to them as Jewish people. It was their view that they were the pure remnant of Israel.[546]

Baigent, Leigh and Lincoln are of the opinion that Jesus' connections with the Essenes were probably very real. The famous Dead Sea Scrolls found at Qumran are Essene documents. It seems clear to them that "...Jesus-even if he did not undergo formal Essene training-was well versed in Essene thought. And his aptitude for healing likewise suggests some Essene influence."[547] Gardner writes that, "...the term Essene might well refer to this expertise, for the

---

[541] Baigent, Leigh and Lincoln. *Holy Blood Holy Grail*, 372.

[542] In the writings of Flavius Josephus, he explains that the Essenes received their therapeutic knowledge of roots and stones from the ancients. *The Jewish Wars,* II, ch. 8, 6. John Pratt adds: "Josephus writes, they also take great pains in studing the writings of the ancients, and choose out of them what is most for the advantage of their soul and body; and they inquire after such roots and medicinal stones as may cure their distempers."

[543] Gardner. op. cit., 24.

[544] Baigent, Leigh and Lincoln. *The Messianic Legacy,* 372.

[545] There was disagreement over whether John the Baptist or Jesus was the Messiah that was prophesied of. The Qumran Scrolls suggest that there was an expectation of two Messiahs. One from the priestly caste, called the "Teacher of Righteousness"; and the other from the line of David who would restore the kingdom of his people. For the Qumran notion of the two Messiahs, see John Allegro, *The Dead Sea Scrolls*, ch. 13, 167-72.

[546] Starbird. *The Woman With the Alabaster Jar,* 56.

[547] Baigent, Leigh and Lincoln. *Holy Blood, Holy Grail,* 373.

Aramaic word *asayya* meant physician and corresponded to the Greek word *essenoi.*" There were many interesting similarities between Jesus' teachings and those of the Essenes. Some feel that it is the Essenes who should rightly be given credit for setting the stage for Christianity.[548]

In many of the descriptions of the Essenes and their way of life it is stressed how closely they were aligned with nature. One of their prominent symbols was the Tree of Life. Edmond Szekely says that it "…made it clear to the people how inseparably they are linked to all the forces, cosmic and terrestrial, and it showed them what their relationship is to each."[549] Szekely gives a further discussion of the Essenes. They chose to live in out-lying areas where they grew their own foods, even in the dessert climate and apparently had a vast knowledge of agricultural techniques and weather conditions. They treated themselves as equals, living communally and sharing what they had. Their healthy life-style is said to have allowed them to live for well over one hundred years in robust health and comfort. They were adept at various healing arts, astronomy, and prophesy. They were known to have fasted for long periods of time to facilitate connection with the divine. "They sent out healers and teachers from the brotherhoods, amongst whom were Elijah, John the Baptist, John the Beloved and the great Essene Master, Jesus."[550]

Gardner explains more of the Essenes beliefs:

A fundamental belief of the Essenes was that the universe contained the two cardinal spirits of Light and Darkness. Light represented truth and righteousness, whereas Darkness depicted perversion and evil. The balance of one against the other in the cosmos was settled by celestial movement and people were individually apportioned with degrees of each spirit, as defined by their planetary circumstances of birth...God was held to be the supreme ruler over the two cardinal spirits, but to find the Way to the Light required following a long and arduous path of conflict. Such a path culminated in a final weighing of one force against the other at a Time of Justification, later called the Day of Judgment...But just as the Spirit of Light

---

[548] Kersten. op. cit., 98.
[549] Szekely, Edmond Bordeaux. *The Teachings of the Essenes from Enoch to The Dead Sea Scrolls,* (London, The C. W. Daniel Co. LTD), 27.
[550] Ibid., 6, 12-13.

had its representative on Earth, so too did the Spirit of Darkness.[551]...*A primary responsibility of the designated Prince of Darkness, was to test female initiates within the celibacy, in which capacity he held the Hebrew title of Satan (Accuser).*[552]

I am struck by the obvious similarities between Native American beliefs and those of the Essenes, such as: honoring knowledge, sharing equally and a respect for the natural world and for climate conditions. There are also similarities to some of the later teachings of the Kabbalah,[553] the belief systems of India, and to Buddhism. Kersten writes:

In spite of all attempts to obscure the true origin of the teachings of Jesus and despite the rigorous canonization of the gospels we do still find <u>far more than one hundred passages</u> which give a clear indication that their roots go back to the older Buddhist tradition.[554]

Like most indigenous North American communities, the Essenes had no rich or poor within their communities. Of particular interest to me are their relationship with both the natural world on Earth and their intimate contact with all energies. The Essenes were related, or certainly spiritually connected, to both the concrete world of form and the invisible universe of mystery. They seemed to possess a humble yet firm understanding that the knowledge they protected would be valuable to later generations. We can feel grateful that their writings and philosophies have survived in some form and can still add to our spiritual lives today.

A Hebrew Study of Sin and Repentance

"Repent ye: for the kingdom of heaven is at hand."[555](Matt 3:2 and 4:17, KJV)

---

[551] Whose purpose was seen as providing an oppositional energy within the hierarchical structure. See Barbara Thiering, *Jesus the Man*, ch. 12, 65; Appendix III, 344.
[552] Gardner. *Bloodline of the Holy Grail*, 24-25.
[553] Literally translated, *kabbalah* means "oral tradition," says Rabbi Ohad Ezrah in *Legends of the Star Ancestors* by Nancy Red Star, 17.
[554] Kersten. op. cit., 74.
[555] **Jesus,** *Oxyrhynchus Manuscript.* The word translated "at hand" can mean to touch, arrive, seize, or bring near. "It refers to something happening *now*, in the present, with an almost violent immediacy."

"Rabbi Abraham Isaac Kook…emphasized that it has never been the intention of Judaism to eliminate the religions of the world…Judaism has never been a missionary religion and only accepts converts under special conditions. Rather, she [Judaism] has recognized the value and necessity of all forms of God consciousness even as these very same religions attempted to destroy her."[556]

"By the way, Judaism does not treat converts as inferior in any way. When the Messiah comes, he will be a descendent of King David. David was a descendent of Ruth, our first convert. From this we learn that converts are absolutely as good as and as Jewish as those born into the religion."[557]

As we continue to reach into Aramaic studies we find that the word "repent" can mean, as Neil Douglas-Klotz explains:

…to return, come again, flow back, or ebb… Its roots shows something that turns or returns…as though in a circle or spiral, to its origin or to its original rhythm…In a Hebrew-Aramaic sense, to repent means to unite with something by affinity, because it feels like going home.[558]

Most religious denominations teach about sin and repentance and have certain expectations for their members around these concepts. For most, repentance means: to feel sorry for an error; to feel regret over an action or an intention; or to feel remorse about a past action. It is implied that the offender wished to change their mind and therefore their behavior. Consulting Judaism about "sin" we discover:

Three major categories of sinful behavior are listed: a het, an unknowing sin; an avon, a sin committed with advance knowledge; and a pesha, a rebellious transgression. No sin, according to Jewish tradition, is unforgivable, but to be pardoned the sinner must repent, confess to God, make restitution (where this is applicable), and give charity.[559]

Every action or sin is addressed here, as well as, specific steps for achieving forgiveness[560] and a pardon. Adding to the above, the

---

[556] The first Chief Rabbi of Israel in the beginning of the twentieth century. Quoted in *Kabbalah: An Introduction to Torah Cosmology and Jewish Mysticism*, 8.
[557] From Stephanie M..
[558] Douglas-Klotz. *The Hidden Gospel*, 85.
[559] *Dictionary of the Jewish Religion*.
[560] The Aramaic word for "forgive" could also mean "…something that is restored to its original state, or allowed to return." *The Hidden Gospel*, 125. In Jewish eyes, "The prophetic understanding of 'repent'…As 'turn' or 'return'…which involves a *collective* returning to God. This does not imply that 'saving' individuals is

Dictionary of the Jewish Religion says any deed can be forgiven "…if a person repents and does good deeds thereafter and appeases the injured party."[561] Judaism firmly advocates repentance and it is one of the three concepts stressed in High Holy Day prayers. The other two are prayer and charity.

John Baldock, in his book, *The Alternative Gospel: The Hidden Teachings of* Jesus, says that in most cases the Greek word *metanoia* is "translated by the words 'repentance' or 'conversion'…Because of the close association of these two words with the word 'sin'…"[562] In this study I will attempt to find not only other sources but earlier information. From one source, I find that, "In biblical times, *metanoia* was used in common language for one changing his mind in a non-ethical sense about a variety of things."[563] This means that the word *metanoia* was used in a wide range of experiences in everyday life. Within daily experiences, there would be many opportunities to change one's mind or one's actions, which would not be viewed as an act of disobedience that could be called a "sin." Next, we find that *metanoia* "…literally means beyond the mind…So it's an idea of stretching or pushing beyond the boundaries with which we normally think and *feel*. It means new mindedness, new change of mind and *change of heart* in the Hebrew sense of heart—how you think."[564]

When Hebrew words and concepts were translated into Greek, their meanings often changed. The Greek language was very mental leaving out *the feeling* aspect of living. Therefore, daily experience and feelings got pushed back in favor of a mental response to experiences.

Another look at the idea of 'sin' is very reveling and, I believe, more heartfelt. John Baldock, as well as many others, reminds us that 'sin' means 'missing the mark' a kind of archery perspective. But he adds other meanings such as: "stumbling" and doing the opposite of our *real, true nature and purpose in life*.[565] I like his description of *metanois* as an "…awakening to Reality prompted by the Spirit within

---

unimportant; the point, rather, is that this was not the central concern of the prophets." Borg, *Jesus: A New Vision*, 167.
[561] *Dictionary of the Jewish Religion.*
[562] Baldock, John. *The Alternative Gospel: The Hidden Teaching of Jesus*, 35.
[563] www.Gracelife.org/resources/gracenotes/gracenotes22.pdg 391.
[564] www.Adl.org/main_Interfaith/nostra_aetate.htm?Multi_page_sections=sHeading_2. (italics by author)
[565] Baldock, op. cit., 35.

us... [it] may be sudden, or it may take place over a prolonged period of time."[566]

Chilton reminds us that in the language of Jesus, "Your sins are released," means:

[that] sin was a constraint, a binding of one's natural capacity...and "release" is what the terms in Greek, Hebrew and Aramaic that are traditionally rendered as 'forgive'[567] actually mean...to break open an incapacitating shackle...[the] actual loosing or freeing (aphiemi in Greek, shebaq in Aramaic and Hebrew) of a person from the consequences of his own action by God.[568]

In Webster's New World Dictionary, repentance is represented by the Hebrew word NACHAM and the Greek word *metanoia*. In the Old Testament NACHAM is translated as "repent" over forty times, "yet there are as many as 60 places where it appears as *'comfort'*..."[569] It is further described as "to become re-adjusted in one's feelings." In another website *NACHAM* is explained as "to sigh, breathe strongly, to be sorry in a favorable sense, to console, to ease one's self."[570] Also, another source says *NACHAM* means "to speak to someone in such a way as to calm or console."[571] And finally, *NACHAM* can more closely come within one of these three specific definitions:

- (a) to seek by means of the emotions, a changed attitude in another;
- (b) to have one's feelings changed as to a purpose left unchanged;
- (c) to discard a mental/emotional attitude and adopt a new one, thus to have a change of heart.[572]

Here's another perspective. In Nazareth, it was not uncommon for people to be in debt. Jesus used the metaphor of debt to represent seeking release from the burden of alienation from God. Jews, including Jesus used the Aramaic word *chova* (debt)

---

[566] Ibid., 116, 172.
[567] "'To forgive' can also mean to set free, let go, loosen, leave out, omit, or from the roots, to restore something to its original state." *The Hidden Gospel*, 45.
[568] Chilton, Bruce. op. cit., 110, 49.
[569] www.Web.ukonline.co.uk/geo.morris7list.htm
[570] www.biblos.com
[571] www.makarios-online.org/notes/pdf/comfort.pdf
[572] www.Web.ukonline.co.uk/geo.morris7list.htm

when they wanted to convey the desire to be set free of that separation from God.[573] Those who became servants who had lost their land because of debt "...were technically indentured for only seven years by biblical prescription." "Servants" or "slaves" are interchangeable terms in Aramaic, Hebrew and Greek. If these were Jewish servants they waited a long time to be finally released. Often the servitude was *extended*, "...when the slave was willing to have his ear nailed through with an awl to the master's doorway to demonstrate his voluntary attachment for life (see Exodus 21:2-6)."[574] In the first century a Jew would have understood the metaphor of "debt" as referring to serving two masters. That would be recognized as a "sin" because it indicated mixed allegiance. In Jesus' frame of reference, he was talking about serving Spirit instead of worldly power.

The Jewish Court of Law (*Mishna*)

The dominant historical view is that the Sanhedrin was controlled primarily by the Sadducee associated with the ruling elites, rather than the Pharisees who are better known as a result of the widely-read Christian Bible. The High Priest Caiaphas was a Sadducee appointed by the Roman Governor Valerius Gratus, who was later replaced by Pontius Pilate. Due to the Roman conquest and occupation of Judea in 63 BC, the Roman Empire controlled all officials of the province. Members of the Sanhedrin and the High Priest and other chief priests were subject to the approval of and removal by Rome, and were selected for their expected loyalty to the Roman occupiers. For example, in John 11:48, the chief priests and Pharisees worry that "the Romans will come and take away both our place and our nation."[575]

In my research I have tried to understand the Jewish system of bringing a person accused of some indiscretion against the *Mishna* (the Law) to a Jewish court. In Hebrew the word for "law" is *halachah*. The *Dictionary of the Jewish Religion* helps to clarify this aspect of Judaism with the following:

HALACHAH. Jewish religious law which also encompasses ethical, civil, and criminal matters. Halachah is based first...on Biblical commands...by interpretations of the Torah, oral traditions, Rabbinic decrees issued in specific circumstances, and laws based on popular custom. The Mishnah [Mishna] section

---

[573] Chilton, Bruce. op. cit., 79-80.
[574] Ibid., 81.
[575] (as explained in Wikipedia)http://en.wikipedia.org/wiki/Sanhedrin_Trial_of_Jesus

of the Talmud was the first formal code of Jewish law...Reform Judaism does not consider itself bound by the Halachah.

Since the Temple represented the spiritual center of Judaism, we must review how *Mishna* was carried out within the court. The court of elders and priests that had exclusive jurisdiction in capital crimes was the Sanhedrin. This court consisted of twelve men and its chairman was the high priest.[576] Also there existed, during the time of Yeshua, two other legislative bodies—the "greater" (composed of seventy) and the "lesser" (of twenty-four). Although they had great power, their decisions were not absolute. It was the Sanhedrin that had jurisdiction over the entire Jewish nation and exercised the highest authority of the nation.

Because the Temple was the center of the Jewish faith, it contained the rituals that were crucial to Jewish culture. All Jews were expected to come to the temple for worship at least three times a year. All of the traditions were carried out within the temple and in specific relationship to the *Mishna* (law).[577] Adherence to Jewish law was strict and it was absolutely essential *that proper rituals were done* before a person could be judged, punished, and a human life taken by "stoning."[578]

Here is the form a trial of an accused person took; I will present this lesson in steps:[579]

---

[576] "According to Jewish law, the high priest was to serve for life. However, the Romans took over the right of appointment and replaced high priests whenever they chose...In the fifty-two years from AD 15 to the outbreak of the great war, there were seventeen different priests...Caiaphas's eighteen years being the longest. Presumably he had learned how to work very well with the Romans." Borg, *Jesus: A New Vision*, 188.

[577] "Its central point was the sanctum sanctorium, or holy of holies, which consisted of two rooms...first room was an alter and a table for...showbread...only the priest were allowed to eat...The second room was empty...[where the Jewish God resided]." Tully, *Jesus: A New Vision*, 100-101.

[578] "For even in those limited instances where talmudic law permitted executions, it insisted that the defendant be killed in the quickest manner possible (which is why Jewish law always forbade crucifixion, the goal of which was to prolong and intensify the death agony)." Rabbi Joseph Telushkin, *Jewish Wisdom*, 414.

[579] The information that follows has been greatly facilitated by the book *Archko Volume* and other resources. With later research this may need to be reevaluated but, for now I think it suffices for our study.

1) *When an accused person came before the Sanhedrin, there was a preliminary trial in order to force a plea.*
2) *If they could not get a plea, the accused was sentenced.*
3) *Then they would be sent on to the Roman authority, or governor, to see if he agreed with the sentence.* [580]
4) *The accused was then sent to the high priest for further discussion.*
5) *Next, he went back to the Sanhedrin. He was accompanied by a written version of the charges and the names of any witnesses...*
6) *If the Sanhedrin approved the decision of the high priest, the prisoner was then to be sent back to the high priest for trial.*
7) *The twelve man court of the Sanhedrin was required by the Jewish law to fast and pray for one whole day before any trial could proceed.*
8) *The "urim and thummim" were brought out and placed before the high priest. This could be described as an "oracle" worn by the High Priest that enabled God's will to be known to Israel.*
9) *The high priest wore a veil, representing God doing his work without being seen.*

It was very important in Jewish tradition and *Mechilta* for the accused and those in a place of judgment, as well as the high priest to adhere to the following:

10) *A call was made*[581] *for the lactees (two men, one of whom stood at the door of the court with a red flag, while the other sat on a white horse at a location leading to the place of execution).*
11) *The lactees continually shouted the name of the criminal, his crime, and the list of witnesses, and called for witnesses in his favor to come forward and testify.*
12) *When the testimony was complete the Sanhedrin, accept for the chairman, would vote. Then their decision was shown to the high priest.*
13) *"As he was too holy to act by himself, but only as the mouth piece of God, he went up to a basin or a ewer, as it is called by them, and washed his hands in token of the innocence of the court, thus testifying that the criminal's own action had brought condemnation on himself."*[582]

---

[580] "And Pilate asked him, Art thou the King of the Jews? And He answering said unto him, Thou sayest it."...In the original Greek...it can only be interpreted as "Thou hast spoken correctly." Holy Blood, Holy Grail, 348.

[581] "According to the Talmud (*Sandedrin* 43a), a herald went around forty days before the execution announcing that Yeshu would be stoned to death...persons with anything to say in his defense should come forward. No one did, so Yeshu was hanged [a word sometimes used to mean "crucified"] on the eve of Passover." William Bramley, op. cit., 45.

[582] *Archko Volume*, op. cit., 54-55.

> *14) Soldiers, seeing this (washing of hands) took the criminal to the place of execution, and he would be stoned till he was dead.*[583] *No one "was allowed to speak, not even a whisper, while the execution was going on. Nothing was heard but the pelting of stones and the shrieks of the criminal."*[584]

Stephanie offers this: "A Sanhedrin that executed more than one criminal in a period of seven years[585] (I may have this number wrong, it may have been a much longer time) was considered an evil court."[586]

In the Yeshua story as written in the New Testament, he was taken by the soldiers to be crucified in the manner of Roman law. When Pilate washed his hands the soldiers took him directly to be punished according to Roman law.[587] Well the soldiers, as indicated in the *Archko Volume* and other sources that I have come across, were Jewish soldiers! They were acquainted with the Jewish custom of washing the hands (the thirteenth step in my list). So when they saw Pilate wash his hands they took it for granted that Yeshua was to die. Is it possible that Jewish traditions were circumvented (from steps four through fourteen?)

By Judaic law, the Sanhedrin is forbidden to meet during Passover.[588] Also, they could not meet at night,[589] in private homes, or anywhere but inside the temple. In the gospels Jesus' arrest and trial occur at night. Researcher of Judaism, Mark Tully gives this perspective about the trial details:

> *…it is doubtful whether there was a tradition of releasing a prisoner at the Passover, and it is on this that the Gospel story of Pilate's anxiety to show mercy*

---

[583] "The victim was thrown from a cliff or wall, head first. If that did not kill him, first the witnesses against him and then all Israelites present were to heave large stones on him from above until he died." Bruce Chilton, op. cit., 102.
[584] Ibid., 55.
[585] Rabbi Weinstein says, "some say seventy."
[586] Stephanie M.
[587] Crucifixion was a Roman form of execution, and "it was used for only two categories of people: political rebels and chronically defiant slaves." (Both groups reject established authority). Marcus J. Borg, *The Historical Study of Jesus and Christian Origins,* 140, 170.
[588] Cohn, H., *Trial and Death of Jesus,* 97ff. "There were apparently no women present as would have been customary for the Passover meal…And there is no specific mention of the traditional Passover lamb or customary herbs used in this most sacred of Jewish meals." Davis, Kenneth, op. cit., 403.
[589] Baigent, Leigh, & Lincoln. *Holy Blood, Holy Grail,* 349.

depends...Pilate washing his hands...is probably an interpolation by the Gospel writers to demonstrate that the Romans had no hand in the death of Jesus...It was simply expedient...for the Christians to blame the Jews rather than the Romans...[590]

In the gospels Pilate is depicted in a very positive light, as a decent and even tolerant man who reluctantly approves the Crucifixion.[591] However, my studies of the nature of Pilate in those terrible times for the Jewish people indicate that Pilate didn't need the opinion of the crowd or to appease the Jewish traditions[592] in order to make a decision to put anyone to death. Authors Baigent, Leigh and Lincoln write this about Pontius Pilate (26-36 AD): "...existing records indicate that Pilate was a cruel and corrupt man who not only perpetuated but intensified the abuses of his predecessor."[593] Whether by the direct actions of Pilate or by the hands of the Roman Empire, sources have indicated that there were fifty to even five hundred crucifixions per day.[594] Another researcher Bruce Chilton in his book, *Rabbi Jesus: an Intimate Biography*, concludes that "He [Pilate] did not interrogate Jesus, as the Gospels report...and could not have done so directly for the simple reason he did not speak Aramaic...but only Greek and Latin."[595]

Other discussions open up more "cans of worms." According to Roman law at the time, if a man is crucified he was denied a burial.[596] Roman guards prevented relatives or friends from taking away the bodies. There were four Roman officials who supervised the protocol during all crucifixions.[597] In the Greek version of the Crucifixion story,

---

[590] Tully. op. cit. 114, 117.
[591] Maccoby, H. *Revolution in Judaea*, 57ff., quotes Philo of Alexandria describing Pilate as "cruel by nature."
[592] "There is no extra biblical evidence for the annual custom of releasing a prisoner at Passover." "Also disputed is whether the Barabbas incident and the supposed custom underlying it are historical or the creation of Christian tradition." Raymond Brown, *New Jerome Biblical Commentary*, 627, 1328.
[593] Baigent, Leigh, and Lincoln. *Holy Blood, Holy Grail*, 324.
[594] Presentation *The Complete Story of Jesus*. "The Romans executed hundreds of thousands of people in the Holy Lands in the first century BC/AD." (CNN presents: After Jesus: the First Christians)
[595] Chilton. Op. cit., 268.
[596] Cohn, op. cit., 238.
[597] *The Complete Story of Jesus*.

when Joseph of Arimathea[598] asks for Jesus' body, he uses the word *soma* which is only applied to a living body! Pilate uses the word *ptoma* meaning "corpse" when he gives over the body.[599]

There are many legends about the mysterious figure of Joseph of Arimathea. In the gospels he is described as a wealthy man and possibly a member of the Sanhedrin. He is said to have been an influential person who disagreed with the sentencing of Jesus. John and Mathew say that he was a disciple of Jesus. He had enough power to go to Pilate and ask for the body of Jesus and be granted the right to take it away for burial. It was Joseph who wrapped the body and placed it in a tomb that belonged to him and rolled the stone in front of it.

Jack Mohr writes this about Joseph of Arimathea:

Joseph of Arimathea was reputed to have owned the largest private [naval] fleet in the world. There is further confirmation of this in the Latin Vulgate translation of the Bible where in Mark 15:43, he is referred to as a "Decurio," which was a common Latin term, meaning "A Roman Official in charge of metal mines." In the St. Jerome [Bible] translation, Joseph's official title is given as "Nobiles Decurio," indicating that he was a prominent official.[600]

Elizabeth Clare Prophet, in *Mary Magdalene and the Divine Feminine*, contributes more about Joseph of Arimathea:

Legends from the British Isles say that his great-uncle Joseph of Arimathea, who took care of him after the death of his father, Joseph, was a tin merchant who, with a fleet of ships, regularly sailed to the Isles.[601]

His access to ships, his business contacts and his wealth have invited speculation that he may have facilitated Jesus' ability to travel to other lands, such as India, when he was not accounted for from age twelve to thirty-three. Some tales even place him in India after the Crucifixion.

---

[598] A Dr. Wesley Swift says "It is a matter of historical record that Joseph of Arimathea was a wealthy man who owned the tin mines of Cornwell in Britain. His ships plied the trade of the Mediterranean and on up to the British Isles. He sat in the Sanhedrin because he was a Parisse of great power and renown, but he was also a true Essene..." "Was Jesus Christ a Jew" Sermon #1117, p. 9.
[599] See *The Interlinear Greek-English New Testament*, 214 (Mark 15:45).
[600] Mohr, Jack. *Know Your Enemies*, 129.
[601] Prophet, Elizabeth Clare. *Mary Magdalene and the Divine Feminine*, 29.

In the environment of Constantine's empire, shifting the blame for the Crucifixion[602] of Jesus was a way to add to the need to distance Christianity from Judaism. The Church has taken many antagonistic actions, both historical and theological, toward Jewish peoples to perpetuate the chasm. Here are some examples:

- *Tully relates: "It became an orthodox tenet of Christianity that the scattering of the Jews throughout the world was God's punishment for killing his son..."*[603]
- *"As early as A.D. 306 the Synod of Elvia prohibited marriage or sexual intercourse between Christians and Jews."*[604]
- *"Among later prohibitions were bans on Jews holding public office, employing Christian servants and appearing in court cases as witnesses against Christians."*[605]
- *"The Synod of Geneva in 1078 ordered Jews to pay taxes to support the Church. The Council of Oxford...banned the building of new synagogues."*[606]
- *"In 1267 the Synod of Breslau obliged Jews to live in ghettos".*[607]

It wasn't until the Second Vatican Council in 1965 that the Roman Catholic Church formally absolved the Jews now living of killing Jesus...the Crucifixion should not be charged against all Jews without distinction then alive, nor against the Jews of today.[608]

* * * * * * * * * * * * *

Women biblical scholars today have reached deeply into ancient materials and are now able to provide a different look at the Jewish culture regarding the role of women in early Judaism before the New Testament era.[609] Balancing the perspective of both genders is very

---

[602] "By the third century AD, there were no fewer than 25 versions of Jesus' death and resurrection! Some have him not being put to death at all, some have him revived back to life, and some have Jesus living on to an old age and dying in Egypt." Nicholas Notovich, *The Unknown Life of Jesus Christ*, 6.
[603] Tully. op. cit., 119.
[604] Ibid.
[605] Ibid.
[606] Ibid.
[607] Ibid.
[608] Ibid., 120. "...during the war [WWW II] their numbers declined by about 6 million—two-thirds of the Jewish population in Europe."
[609] Even today an Orthodox Jewish man might include in his morning prayer the words. "Blessed art thou O Lord who has not made me a woman." Tully, op. cit., 138.

relevant to our study of the changing public images of women in Jewish history and society. It would take another book to adequately address the evolution of women's roles specifically in the Old Testament times.

As we know, women have had to make considerable adjustments to the changing times and to the attitudes of a predominately male world view. Clearly, in most cultures on Earth since written history has been recorded, out of balance masculine energy has rather violently left its mark upon societies, cultures and nations. Males have, at times, been very authoritarian and dominant, if not aggressive and intolerant, reflecting an underlying insecurity. The focus has, for a long time, been on short-range accomplishment and there has been a failure to act in light of future consequences. Think about how some of those long-ranging effects are still influencing life today as a result of this reach for power and influence!

These are some generalizations I, a male, put forth here. Is it possible that it takes one to know one? Or is it that many of us, gender inclusive, seek after immediate self-directed goals and gratification rather than having the foresight to consider the outcome of our actions upon the future, way beyond our lifetimes? There are men and women who exhibit a balance of masculine and feminine energy. Maybe what we can strive for is to extend that to the rest of the larger community by example and public policy.

In recent years I have witnessed the rise of feminine energy. Many of us have watched televised reports in November of 2001, showing the women of Kabul throwing off their burkas. There seems to be an "unveiling" of the feminine principle worldwide. Girls of Afghanistan who are going to school know that each day brings the likelihood that they will be ridiculed or threatened by many in their communities. We should note that there are many examples of the heart/feeling side of the masculine emerging as well.

Like Coyote, who shows us focus and perseverance in his pursuit of the Road-Runner, perhaps many of us could benefit from having the courage to retrace our steps. By that I mean can we look again at our circumstances; the paths that we have taken in the past and identify for ourselves repeated impulses, actions, and patterns that have limited our individual growth and happiness and contributed to a lack of harmony in the world?

In ancient Native cultures men (and women) had both feminine and masculine qualities. This was recognized, and balance between the two aspects was sought. Sure, in a given lifetime humans embody more of one aspect than the other. But there were lessons to be learned from self contemplation and from *retracing our steps*. Then, after looking at experiences in light of our spiritual growth and development, women and men could more fully recover their dignity, their honor, their gratitude and their focus upon the relatedness of *all* life, both now and in the future.

As I have mentioned before, it takes real courage to be willing to take another look at life; at what we thought were the facts, but were only glimpses of the complete picture of life. It often seems easier for most females to see what is real, to get everything out onto the table and to be *honest* with themselves. Men are less inclined to look all around at what can bring balance for both themselves and for society in general. Men, I believe, have access to so much more personal dignity and community power when there is an effort to honor personal vision, individual strengths, and spiritual relatedness to oneself and to creation. Many people have yet to learn that honor, respect and regard come from internal sources rather than from outside confirmation and recognition.

Perhaps a brief look at one culture, that of Judaism, will assist both men's reflection and women's resolve to bring clearer understanding as well as balance and harmony once again. Let us begin. I asked Stephanie, to reflect upon the role of women in Judaism in the past and in the present. This is her reply:

Women have their own place in the Jewish tradition. There are specific things that women are expected to do and things that we are not. We are not required to perform any of the commandments that are bound by time – a prayer that must be said at noon, for example – because we care for the children, and if we are feeding the baby at noon, we cannot say the prayer. So we are not bound by those.

This is often seen as sexist – men are the ones who must keep the ritual commandments, so men are the important ones. This is a misunderstanding. There is a blessing that men say every morning, one of a long string of morning blessings: "Blessed are you, Lord our G-d, King of the Universe, who has not made me a woman." Many feminist Jews get very upset about this one. Again, a misunderstanding -- men are grateful to be men because they get to perform all the ritual commandments. Women are grateful to be women, and would have a similar blessing for not being born men, except that the reciting of that blessing is a ritual commandment tied by time, and therefore women do not have to say those blessings.

Of course, there is some sexism in traditional Judaism, because it is men who wrote the liturgy. There is a story of a woman who tried to lead a prayer in an Orthodox synagogue, and was told by the rabbi that "A woman belongs on the bimah (the stage from which Jewish prayers are led) like an orange belongs on the seder plate." The seder plate is used on Passover and has a very specific set of things on it, and an orange is not one of them. Many people now keep an orange on their seder plates as well, to symbolize that we do now permit women on the bimah.

All traditions but Orthodoxy allow women to be rabbis and cantors. In an Orthodox Jewish synagogue, the women pray very quietly, in a separate room from the men, sometimes divided by a partition and sometimes by an actual wall; this is because the sight and sound of women may be distracting to the men. Traditionally, women are not counted in a minyan. There is certainly sexism in modern Orthodox practice. I'm not sure how we got there from ancient times. I am not aware of much sexism in the Torah.

There are many places in Jewish prayer where we invoke "the god of Abraham, Isaac, and Jacob." Reform Jews will now add to that "Sarah, Rebecca, Rachel, and Leah."

Female biblical scholars today have reached deeply into ancient materials and are now able to provide a different look at the Jewish culture regarding the role of women in early Judaism before the New Testament era. Balancing the perspective of both genders is very relevant to our study of the changing public images of women in Jewish history and society. It would take another book to adequately address the evolution of women's roles specifically in the Old Testament times. Here's a short version as provided by Elizabeth Achtemeier and Mary Joan Winn Leith as they contributed their work to *The Oxford Companion to the Bible*. Biblical references are included:

The Role and Status of Women In Judaism

"In the ancient world, women were more highly respected in Egypt than in the Middle East or in the Greek or Roman cultures. An Egyptian woman's legal rights were equal to those of a man of the same social class. Unlike Greek or Jewish women, Egyptian women were permitted to appear in public with their husbands."[610]

"...the anointing of Jesus by a woman—a story so powerful that it appears in all four canonical Gospels!"[611]

---

[610] Prophet. Op. cit., 35.
[611] Starbird. *The Feminine Face of Christianity*, 8.

"...[the]Gnostics prayed to the Divine, Feminine, Virgin Sophia as the 'mystical, eternal Silence', as 'Grace, She who is before all things', as the 'Invisible within the All' and as 'incorruptible Wisdom, or Gnosis.' "[612]

Women, in Jewish culture, had a status and a sense of freedom very much like that of the men. It was certainly an environment of patriarchy, but most Jews believed that women were equal in the eyes of God. After all, the Bible said that women were necessary partners of the man (Genesis 2:18); but they also played an important complimentary and balancing role. Even in Genesis, (1:27) the image of God required both a male and a female component. In the sixth century the subordination of women to men and later the practice of polygamy were viewed as the result of "human sin."[613]

Women served as prophets,[614] judges,[615] and queens[616] before the exile from Egypt recorded in Exodus. Women were included in the worship of God[617] and they were sometimes given status as models of wisdom.[618] They were honored in the Ten Commandments[619] and were protected by certain laws as wives and mothers.[620] Some Jewish women engaged in commercial enterprises, were active teachers of wisdom and served their communities in open and public ways.[621]

Single Israelite females were under the authority of their fathers;[622] but were able to have a say in the selection of a mate. There is no indication that they were ever considered to be merely a piece of property. Sexual practice was seen as a gift from God[623] and marriage was a symbol of the relationship between God and his people.[624] However, that was to change after the Babylonian exile. Achtemeier writes:

---

[612] Pagels, *The Gnostic Gospels,* 628.

[613] Genesis 3, 4:19. Achtemeier in Metzger & Coogan. *The Oxford Companion to the Bible,* 806.

[614] Exodus 15:20; 2 Kings 22:14-20.

[615] Judges 4-5.

[616] 1 Kings 19; 2 Kings 11.

[617] Deuteronomy 16:13-14; 1 Samuel 1-2.

[618] 2 Samuel 14; 20:16-22.

[619] Exodus 20:12; Deuteronomy 5:16.

[620] Genesis 16:5-6; 38.

[621] Proverbs 31:10-31. Achtemeier. Op cit, 806.

[622] Genesis 24:57,67; 29:20.

[623] Genesis 2:23; Song of Solomon.

[624] Jeremiah 2:2; Hosea 2:14-20. Achtemeier. Op cit, 806.

When Israel was carried into Babylonian exile, her priests in exile determined that they would draw up a plan for Israel's life that would ensure that she would never again be judged by God. They therefore collected together and wrote priestly legislation that would ensure Israel's ritual and social purity. At the same time, they emphasized the importance of circumcision as a sign of the covenant.[625] This emphasis brought sexuality into the realm of the cult and related females to the covenant community only through their males.[626]

Men's view of women's menstruation and childbirth began to be seen in a very different light. Women were pushed further away from temple rituals and eventually from the worship of God.

The blood of the sacrifice on the altar became the means of atonement for sin[627] and blood outside of the cult became ritually unclean.[628] Thus, women were excluded from the cult during their menstruation[629] and childbirth.[630] Indeed, women were increasingly segregated in worship and society. They had access to the holy only through their males.[631]

An area designated as a "place for all women" (a women's court away from Temple rituals), was added. By the first century, attitudes toward Jewish women had changed quite a bit. The point of view of the Jewish male developed over long periods of history and other social and ethical practices led to the women of Israel becoming second-class Jews. By now women were not allowed to testify in court, be seen in public, talk to strangers and they were certainly not to teach the Torah. They also were not generally educated. Even in their own homes it was prohibited for them to be taught the teachings of the Torah. *"Their vows to God were no longer considered as valuable as those of males,"[632] and a husband could annul the vow of his wife."* [633]

There was a huge difference in the attitudes toward male and female sexuality. There's only one place in the Bible where male and female sexuality is positive and equal and that is in *The Song of Solomon*. Every bride was expected to be a virgin but her betrothed

---

[625] Genesis 17.
[626] Achtemeier. Op cit, 807.
[627] Leviticus 10:17-18; 16; 17:10-11.
[628] Genesis 9:4.
[629] Leviticus 15:19-31.
[630] Leviticus 12:2-5.
[631] Achtemeier. op cit, 807.
[632] Numbers 27:1-8.
[633] Achtemeier. Op cit, 807.

was not.[634] Husbands had a right to insist on the faithfulness of their wives, while enjoying extra-marital sex themselves. Only men could initiate a divorce.[635] Rabbi Weinstein says, "That, however, changed in the Rabbinic Judaism[636] where a woman could press for a divorce against her husband." In Lev. 12.2-5 of the Bible, "...A woman after the birth of a son was impure seven days, but for fourteen after a daughter's birth."[637]

Mary Joan Winn Leith addresses the different status of women in the lands of Mesopotamia and Egypt:

...Monotheistic Israel differed from Mesopotamia and Egypt, where women served many deities as priestesses and even as high priestesses. The Israelite priesthood consisted of men who inherited the office from their fathers. Some women in Israel, called qedesot (formerly translated as "sacred prostitutes") were apparently consecrated to non-Yahwistic cults (Hos. 4:14; Deut. 23:19-20) but their function is unclear...[638]

It must have seemed quite revolutionary to the Jewish authorities when Jesus taught women[639] and even included them in the traveling groups that followed his teachings.[640] He was seen publically speaking with them often.[641] In addition, it was women who were the first witnesses to the Resurrection.[642]

* * * * * * * * * * *

I present the following very essential ideas, some of which are from Borg, because they hold a foundation that can support our study from here on. From this basis I feel we can reasonably understand the Jesus of the first century. Each of these statements holds the potential for a volume of discussion, and my hope is that this book will stimulate and facilitate that discourse.[643]

---

[634] Deuteronomy 22:13-21.
[635] Deuteronomy 24:1-4.
[636] Rabbinic Judaism refers to First Century Judaism.
[637] Leith in Metzger & Coogan op cit, 809-810.
[638] Ibid., 812.
[639] Luke 10:38-42.
[640] Luke 8:1-3.
[641] John 4:27.
[642] Luke 24:1-11; John 20:18.
[643] Portions of these come from the book *Jesus at 2000*, by Marcus J. Borg, 129-130.

- *Jesus was born and socialized as a Jew*[644] *and was a Jew all of his life.*
- *Jesus never intended to found a new religion, he saw himself as <u>making reforms within the Jewish tradition</u>.*
- *The Bible and the gospels are the <u>products of humans</u>, not direct words from God. The Bible comes from two ancient communities. The Hebrew Bible comes from ancient Israel, the New Testament reflect the views of the early Christian movement. They are to be studied together <u>with</u> other ancient documents <u>and not in isolation</u>. Other individual authors (<u>with personal agendas in mind</u>) were involved, but they were writing for the members of their own communities.*[645]
- *The gospels do contain some historical material but <u>their primary purpose is not historical reporting</u>. They are not biographies but rather they try to express what Jesus had become to individuals and to communities. They were intended to be metaphorical in nature, not journalistic accounts. The gospels preserve some traditions going back to Jesus. They also include <u>symbolic narratives</u> that use the language of myth*[646] *and metaphor.*
- *The gospels of the New Testament were written some 40-70 years after the ministry of Jesus. None of the writers were eyewitness(es)*[647] *to the life of Jesus. The writings and traditions about Jesus <u>continued to expand over time</u>.*
- *Some of the material in the gospels express an <u>apocalyptic mentality</u>; they are voices of those who anticipated the immediate (even within their lifetime) second coming of Jesus.*
- *Jewish writers and rabbis made use of a way to <u>honor sacred texts</u> with what is called <u>Midrash</u>—bringing Old Testament (Torah) events, scripture, and numbers into the writings of the present as part of the story. This honoring of the sacred history and traditions was useful for fulfilling prophecy and bringing the past forward to keep it meaningful. The present writings were never viewed as the actual facts as much as it was a way to tie past traditions with present events.*

---

[644] Underlining is placed by the author for emphasis.
[645] Chilton, Evans, and Neusner. opt. cit., ix. (Refer to page ix for full note)"…the Gospels are…interpretations of Jesus for distinct communities…No one can understand a statement apart from an appreciation of *who is saying, where, and why.*" (emphasis by this author)
[646] "In the early sixteenth century, Pope Leo X[1513-1521] declared: "It has served us well, this myth of Christ." (Baigent, Leigh and Lincoln. *The Messianic Legacy*, 2) This Pope makes another statement: "How well we know what a profitable superstition this fable of Christ has been for us." (New Dawn Magazine. No 71, March 2002)
[647] "…the Gospels…are not the words of eyewitnesses…the virgin birth accounts were not original to Christianity and did not appear in Christian history until the ninth decade." Spong, *Why Christianity Must Change or Die*, 26.

I must add one more reminder. The ancient manuscripts (dating to four or five centuries after Jesus), reflected the particular messages and teachings of Jesus that various writers and communities sought to record and to promote. There was a lot of diversity of ideas at the time. There was just as much variety in the memories and writings during those years after Jesus as there are differing theological ideas within Christianity today. The manuscripts written some two hundred and fifty years after Jesus provide evidence of that diverse theology. As early Christianity moved from a reality of many faiths, cultures, and even many Gods, Christianity began evolving into one unified and promoted message over some 1,100 years time. Then diversity was further expanded during the Reformation.

According to my studies I take the stance that certain "planks" were added and subtracted by various voices throughout history to the "boardwalk" of the Jesus story! The contribution of Christianity to future generations would not have been possible without these influential and politically motivated additions to the scenario. Christianity would not have survived without these growing pains. However, it needs to be discussed that some of the later representations of the wide-ranging beliefs that were circulating within the communities that followed Jesus' teachings *do not accurately reflect the original intentions of those earlier texts*. Here is an example. Jesus Christ never said that he was divine; but three hundred years after the Crucifixion, the men of the Church did. In Greek, the language in which the New Testament was originally written, the scriptures never say that Jesus Christ was the only son of God. Moore says that "In the gospels, there are thirty-five times when Jesus is called some phrase which could be interpreted as 'Son of God'...In most of those references it is quite often God or the author of the gospel [especially in John] who gives him this name. Only rarely could any statement be interpreted as Jesus calling himself by that title."[648]

---

[648] Moore, *The Christian Conspiracy*, 127.

Chapter Six

The Ancient Roots of Christianity: Yeshua and other Traditions

"**I do not believe** that this Jesus founded a church...at the end of his sojourn, returned to God...I do not believe that human beings are born in sin...that women are any less human or less holy than men...that the Bible is the "word of God."(Bishop John Shelby Spong)[649]

"Moses did not write the Torah: Genesis, Exodus, Leviticus, Numbers and Deuteronomy. Moses had been dead for three hundred years before the first verse of the Torah achieved written form. Those books reflect multiple strands of material that were put together over a period of at least five hundred years."[650]

"The Acts of Thomas (c.200 C.E.), probably written in Syraic, claims that Thomas himself evangelized India,[651] and to this day there are Thomas Christians in India who call Thomas the founder of their faith."[652]

Jesus said, "Recognize what is in your sight, and that which is hidden from you will become plain to you. For there is nothing hidden which will not become manifest." (The Gospel of Thomas)

The Gnostic Jesus said to St. Thomas and the disciples: "The Pharisees and the Scribes have taken the keys of Knowledge, and have hidden them. They have not entered, nor have they allowed those who want to enter to do so. As for you, be as shrewd as snakes[653] and as innocent as doves." (Logion 39). The Gospel According to Thomas[654]

---

[649] Spong. *A New Christianity for a New World*, 5-6.
[650] Spong. *The Sins of Scripture*, 19.
[651] For more of "Thomas tradition," see Poirier, "The Writings Ascribed to Thomas."
[652] Pagels. *Beyond Belief*, 39.
[653] Also look in Matthew 10:16, "...be ye therefore wise as serpents, and harmless as doves." Barbara Walker relates: "Early Hebrew adopted the serpent-god all their contemporaries revered, and the Jewish priestly clan of Levites were 'sons of the Great Serpent,' i.e., of Leviathan, "the wriggly one." *The Women's Encyclopedia of Myths and Secrets*, 905.
[654] (Meyer and Bloom), 39.

The Jesus Story and Other Ancient "Saviors"

"Christ wasn't white. Christ was a black man." (*Malcolm X in a 1963 interview*)[655]

"In time all things shall be revealed." At one time, I was seriously thinking of using this statement for the title for this book. These words, attributed to Yeshua, strongly suggest that a greater understanding is to be expected. To me this means that there will be a time when teachings and other information will be hidden and a time when they will be available again. Just know that I am not fault-finding or implying that there has been some organized conspiracy rooted in the past to keep us from the truth. I don't believe there was a futuristic agenda that ultimately produced today's Christian dogma. I believe that the development of Christian tenets and theology by religious leaders was the result of situational conditions reflecting the historical and social environments of the times in which they were written or espoused.

Often, I am told that I hold out some information in my classes, sensing a more appropriate time to open a particular "can of worms." Sometimes I feel that it is necessary to give information in a way that doesn't cause too sharp a disruption in people's spiritual belief systems. There have historically been good reasons for information to be hidden away for a time and brought back into awareness when the environment was more open and receptive to it. That which is revealed today can cause disruptions within many theologies. Unfortunately, it can also mean that some individuals may not be ready for what is to be *revealed*.

CNN Presents makes an interesting statement at the beginning of the presentation, *The Mystery of Jesus*:

...Did he have a real brother? Was Mary really a virgin? How did Jesus live? And why did he have to die? Who was Jesus the man? Why is the greatest story ever told also the greatest mystery never solved?[656]

---

[655] Douglas, Kelly Brown. *The Black Christ*, 1. Note: "More than 450 Black Madonna images are found throughout Europe...Even the Italian Church had depictions of a black infant in his mother's arms...Another theory is that the Black Madonnas are images of the Egyptian goddess Isis and her baby Horus that were brought to Europe by the Knights Templar *c.* 110-1300 and were later wrongly identified as Mary and Jesus." Bramley. op. cit., 163.

Margaret Starbird adds the following statement:

Jesus of Nazareth, whose story is told in the canonical Gospels, was a charismatic, Jewish teacher, but the resurrected Christ found in the New Testament writings has much in common with the Greek gods Apollo and Dionysus, as well as other sacrificed gods—Dumuzi, Tammuz, Osiris, and Ba'al—from even more ancient mythologies in the Near East.[657]

Here's some additional research about thirty to fifty earlier gods in the ancient sacred texts of the world. What might be surprising to most Christians are the details that are parallel to stories told about Jesus. In an article called, *"Recovering Christianity's Pagan Past"* Tom Harpur explains:

The parallels in the birth and life of Lord Krishna,[658] *the Hindu Christ, are now well known. The Persian prophet Zoroaster was born in innocence and of a virgin birth, from a ray of divine reason (Logos). Eventually, he was suspended from wood or "from the tree"—the cross or tree of the later Calvary. There is also the story of Salivahana, a divine child born of a virgin in Ceylon (Sri Lanka). He was the son of Tarshaca, a carpenter.*[659]

Kersey Graves, in his book *The World's Sixteen Crucified Saviors*, quotes a prophecy of the Persian Zoroaster:[660]

A virgin should conceive and bear a son, and a star would appear blazing at midday to signalize the occurrence." Zoroaster told his followers, "When you behold the star, follow it wherever it leads you. Adore the mysterious child, offering him gifts

---

[656] CNN Presents. *The Mystery of Jesus*, 2008. (the bold lettering is the author's).
[657] Starbird, Margaret. *Magdalene's Lost Legacy*, 4.
[658] "Popular god in modern Hinduism, particularily associated with *bhakti* devotional mysticism. A central figure in the *Bhagavad Gita*." Gruber & Kersten, Op. cit., 262.
[659] Harpur, Tom, *Recovering Christianity's Pagan Past,* in *U.S. N & W Report* (special edition, copyright 2008), 48. "…when the Aramaic word for "carpenter" is translated in Jewish commentaries on the law, it means a learned man." Tully, Mark, Op. cit. 76. "He may or may not have been a carpenter; both 'carpenter' and 'carpenter's son' were used metaphorically within Judaism to mean 'scholar' or 'teacher.' " (Borg, *Jesus: a New Vision*, 39)
[660] "According to the Greek writers Exodus, Aristotle and Hermundorius, Zoroaster had lived five thousand years before Moses. He was of royal blood like Moses and was taken from his mother and left exposed…separated the water with the help of his God, so that God's chosen people might cross the sea with dry feet." Kersten, op. cit., 50.

with profound humility. He is indeed the Almighty Word which create the heavens. He is indeed your Lord and everlasting King."[661]

Catholic people would have an awareness of the doctrine of transubstantiation. I have participated in many Christian "communion" services all through my life, but this concept has intrigued me. As found in I Corinthians 10-12, the idea of a miraculous transformation of bread and wine into the actual body and blood of Christ is suggested. Researcher Acharya S notes that "…this sort of magical ritual was practiced around the world before the Christian era"

Imagine my surprise when I learned that even in the Americas there once was the symbolic representation of the body of a god using bread in ceremonies! Amazingly, this was before the coming of the Spaniards!

…the ancient Mexicans, even before the arrival of Christianity, were fully acquainted with the doctrine of transubstantiation and acted upon it in the solemn rites of their religion. They believed that by consecrating bread their priests could turn it into the very body of their god…The doctrine of transubstantiation, or the magical conversion of bread into flesh, was also familiar with the Aryans of ancient India long before the spread and even the rise of Christianity.[662]

In this journey to reach into the ancient understandings, we must visit the *Didache*. In it, "breaking bread" was a form of celebrating that "God had brought people together who were once scattered." As Pagels further explains, "…the *Didache* tells how the initiate…would have learned how sharing in this simple meal of bread and wine links the human family gathered for worship with 'God…and with Jesus…"[663]

Egyptian Stories

Let's briefly step back to look at some notes from ancient Egypt. Researcher Gary Greenberg addresses a Jewish tradition connected to Egypt. Very important to Judaism is the discussion of the twelve tribes of Israel. Greenberg relates:

---

[661] Harpur. Op. cit.
[662] Frazer, Sir James. *The Golden Bough*, 568. Quoted in *The Christ Conspiracy*, 232.
[663] Pagels. *Beyond Belief*, 17.

The Egyptian deities, already transformed from gods to heroic human ancestors, came to look less and less like Egyptians and more and more like Canaanites... [about the twelve tribes?] ...no archaeological evidence demonstrates that this tribal coalition ever existed...The notion of Jacob's twelve sons ruling over twelve territories was derived from the myth of Horus the Elder ruling over the twelve daylight hours. There was also a folk tradition indicating that at one time Egypt was ruled by twelve kings...So, Israel was not created out of a confederation of twelve tribes...And there were no ten lost tribes.[664]

In the well known myth of Osiris and his sister/wife Queen Isis who ruled over the lands later called Egypt,[665] Osiris was tricked into being placed into a box by some conspirators (among them, Seth[666]), and it was shut, sealed, and floated down the Nile. Isis mourns his absence and tracks the box down. She eventually revives him. In one version of the story, Author Murry Hope relates:

...Osiris remained in the box in the tamarisk tree for three days and three nights, but on the third day he rose and ascended into heaven at the time corresponding to the feast of Christmas. The lowest point of the sun at the winter solstice on 22 December was believed to correspond to the death of Osiris, his resurrection or rebirth becoming a reality three days later, on the 25 December. In this version of the tale, Isis is the virgin mother to Horus, the spirit of Osiris[667] *having effected the conception from 'on high.'*[668]

There are some obvious parallels here with the Jesus story. In addition, the story of Osiris' death and revival is representative of the rising and falling energies of creation, as in the waxing and waning

---

[664] Greenberg, Gary. *The Bible Myth*, 19, 273-4.
[665] "A myth tells us that they were divinities from heaven (Star People?) who had descended to Earth to assist in the development of mankind...Osiris was a gentle king, much loved by the people having taught them the arts of civilization and promoted piety, gentleness, good health and well-being amongst them." Murry Hope, op. cit. 63.
[666] "In the Pharaonic religion Seth was the great enemy...of Osiris, of Isis and of Horus...of the later period Seth is identified with the monstrous Greek genie Typon...who has a serpent's body..." Jean Doresse, *The Secret Books of the Egyptian Gnostics*, 104.
[667] "The Osiris myth contains a powerful message of reincarnation, since his son Horus resurrected him using a 'lion grip.' In the third degree of Freemasonry the candidate is raised using a lion grip...Osiris is an important figure for the Freemasons." Michael Bradley, *Secrets of the Freemasons*, 163. Researcher John Pratt says: "Osiris was not resurrected. He became ruler of the undead. He was in the 'next' world."
[668] Hope, Murry., 63-64.

moon, the cycles of fertility and fallowness, and the rise of human creativity and enlightenment.

* * * * * * * * * * * * *

"Time and time again in these long-ignored Gospels we find obvious Egyptian concepts. This is most notable in the <u>Pistis Sophia</u>, the cosmology of which matches that of the Egyptian <u>Book of the Dead</u>. The Gnostic Gospels even employ the same terminology: for example, they use the Egyptian word for 'hell', <u>Amente</u>...The Gnostic Gospels were rejected by the Church Fathers...Not only do those suppressed books tend to stress the importance of Mary Magdalene...they also present a religion that had its roots...in Egyptian theology."[669]

"Often in medieval paintings, Mary Magdalene is robed in green, a color sacred also to Isis and symbolic of fertility and renewal."[670]

Most of you are probably familiar with the pictures and statues of Egyptian gods with animal heads and human bodies. The Egyptians did not worship these gods literally—they worshipped a *principle of "cosmic order"* called Maat[671] that was a sort of Goddess figure. The Egyptian Pharaoh was responsible for maintaining the cosmic order that was symbolized by a feather. Maat was not seen as a real God, but represented that principle. All of the figures and pictures from that time depicted aspects of Maat and the animal figures were seen as representing this. It was meant to be symbolic. In ancient Egypt there was no word that meant "religion" and no word that meant "belief." Therefore, the Egyptians did not have a religion with specified beliefs.

Some similarities between the Isis/Horus story and the story of Buddha[672] are addressed in The Christ Conspiracy:[673]

---

[669] Picknett & Prince. Op. cit., 294.
[670] Starbird, Margaret. *The Feminine Face of Christianity*, 21.
[671] "The goddess Maat and the principle she embodies are perhaps of the essence of Egyptian mythology, binding divine beings and human beings within one universal law, for they all live 'by Maat, in Maat and for Maat'." Lucie Lamy, *Egyptian Mysteries: New Light on Ancient Knowledge*, 17.
[672] "Buddha as well as Jesus never performs miracles in order to create sensations. Thus Buddha says to a yogi who, after twenty-five years...acquired the ability to cross a river without even wetting his feet: 'So you really have been wasting your time on a thing like that, while nothing more than a coin was needed for the ferryman to take you over in his boat.' " Holger Kersten, op. cit., 78.

- "Horus was born of the virgin Isis-*Meri* on December 25th in a cave/manger with his birth being announced by a star in the East and attended by three wise men."
- Buddha was also born on December 25th and his mother was a virgin named Maya. A star announced his birth and wise men and angels sang.
- "At his birth, he [Buddha] was pronounced ruler of the world and presented with 'costly jewels and precious substances.' His life was threatened by a king 'who was advised to destroy the child, as he was liable to overthrow him'."
- Horus's father's name was "Seb" which is "Joseph."
- Both Horus and Buddha had royal ancestors.
- Both Horus and Buddha taught in a temple at age twelve. Horus was baptized in a river at age thirty by "Anup the Baptizer" and he is said to have disappeared for eighteen years. The one who baptized him was said to have been decapitated. The "Spirit of God" or "Holy Ghost" was present at Buddha's baptism.
- Horus had twelve disciples and two of them were named "Anup" and "Aan" which translate to "John."
- "He performed miracles, exorcised demons and raised ElAzarus ("El-Osiris"), from the dead." "Buddha performed miracles and wonders, healed the sick, fed 500 men from a 'small basket of cakes'."
- Horus and Buddha walked on water.
- Horus delivered a "Sermon on the Mount."
- In some traditions, Buddha was crucified. "He was resurrected, as his coverings were unrolled from his body and his tomb was opened by supernatural powers."
- Horus was '...crucified between two thieves, buried for three days in a tomb, and resurrected." Buddha ascended to Nirvana.
- Horus was called "the Fisher" and was identified with "...Fish ("Ichthys"), Lamb and Lion."
- Buddha and Horus came to fulfill the Law. "Buddha was considered the 'Sin Bearer,' 'Good Shepherd,' the 'Carpenter,' the 'Infinite and Everlasting,' and the 'Alpha and Omega'."
- "Horus was called 'the KRST,' or 'Anointed One.'"
- "Like Jesus, 'Horus was supposed to reign one thousand years'."
- Buddha is supposed to return to judge the dead.

---

[673] Quoted section from the book, *The Christ Conspiracy*, 109-110, 115. Please check within this resource for additional footnotes about the information provided.

Zoroastrianism

What about "the end times," Armageddon, and the Judgment Day? To learn more we can look at Zoroastrianism, which was thriving sometime between 1500 and 1200 B.C. in what is now Iran.[674] Researcher Simon Pearson relates that it is commonly believed that this concept came out of Zoroastrianism. It was the religion prominent in early Iranian history. Pearson says that it differed from other ancient belief systems such as paganism, the Vedic traditions and the older religions of the ancient Babylonians, in that they saw the world as continuing into infinity.[675]

Likewise, the concept of endless recurrence would be true of Native American spirituality. The cycles of birth, life, death and rebirth have no "end time." The introduction of Zoroastrianism's *end of the world* belief marked an important moment in the history of the major world religions. Keeping in mind the story in Revelation, here are some of the components of Zoroastrianism:

1) **There is a God *(Ahura Mazda)* and an evil twin *(Angra Mainyu)*. There will be an eventual victory over evil.**
2) **Good deeds, sacrifice and strict observance of purification rites contribute to the good side of creation and lessen the power of the bad. Evil is empowered by bad thoughts, words and deeds.**
3) **Before the end time, if a righteous individual dies, his or her soul goes to a nice place to wait for the Last Judgment when the person's soul re-unites with their body.**
4) **If the soul is judged to be unrighteous it goes to a place of severe punishment and torment.**
5) **God *(Ahura Mazda)* is both a creator and a destroyer. An Armageddon-like struggle between good and evil leads to a final battle. Good will win and the evil *Angra Mainyu* will lose his power and retreat to the "realm of darkness" and molten metal will seal**

---

[674] "Zoroaster was an Aryan...The Zoroaster Bible is called the *Zend-Avesta*, and it speaks of God favoring the Aryan people over all others. After Zoroaster's lifetime, these teachings spread into Persia (now called Iran, which is a derivative of the word 'Aryan')...The term 'Aryan' was first used in its Sanskrit form ('Arya') in the Veda...At that time, Aryans were the lighter-skinned invaders from the west who conquered India...they spoke the Indo-European language of Sanskrit." "Zoroastrianism waned with the rise of Islam..." Bramley, op. cit., 170-171.

[675] Pearson, Simon. *A Brief History of the End of the World*, an over-view written in U.S. News & World Report (Special Edition, copyright 2008), titled, *"Revelation's Pagan Beginnings,"* 50-51.

the door. Similar to Revelations in which Satan is "bound" for a thousand years (Rev 20:2).
6) **There will then be a Second Coming of** *Ahura Mazda* **(God).**[676]

Sounds pretty familiar to me! Since Zoroaster lived around 1500-1200 B.C., these end times themes existed long before the writers of the Book of Revelations. The more optimistic and natural outlook of indigenous philosophies of reoccurring cyclical events were thereby replaced with the establishment of fear and judgment.

Goddess Traditions

Researchers Picknett and Prince even go so far as to say that "the original religion of the Hebrews was, like that of all other ancient cultures, polytheistic – venerating *both gods and goddess.*"[677] They further add that:

The Hungarian-born anthropologist and biblical scholar Raphael Patai, in his major work <u>The Hebrew Goddess</u>*, has conclusively demonstrated that Jews once worshipped a female deity[Asherah]…Solomon's Temple: despite the tradition, it was* <u>not</u> *built to honor Yahweh alone, but also to celebrate the goddess Asherah…the images carved on the Ark of the Covenant actually depict Yahweh and* <u>a female deity</u>*!*[678] (underlined by author)

Prior to 621 B.C.E. the worship of Asherah as the consort of Yahweh was an important part of religious life in Israel.[679] John Pratt says, "Asherah or Ashteroth was also portrayed as a consort of Baal." Rabbi Joseph Telushkin is quoted in the book, *Jewish Wisdom:*

"The greatest in the world refers to King Solomon who…built the Great Temple (Beit Ha-Mikdash) in Jerusalem, the Bible records that he followed the Phoenician goddess Ashoreth and the Ammonite god Milcom, going so far as to build idolatrous shrines 'for all his foreign wives who offered and sacrificed to their gods' (I Kings 11:5, 7-8)."[680]

Stephanie offers this rather thought-provoking addition to the conversation:

---

[676] Ibid. See also Simon Pearson's *The End of the World,* 20-24.
[677] Picknett, Lynn and Prince, Clive. Op. cit., 295.
[678] Ibid.
[679] Patai, Raphael. *The Hebrew Goddess* (3rd ed.), 53.
[680] Rabbi Joseph Telushkin, *Jewish Wisdom*, 334.

Also, in the most basic way, what defines a Jew? We worship only one god. Ultimately, that is what Judaism is about – worshipping only one god. Is it written that way in the Torah? No… But Jews are not taught that. We are taught, "Hear oh Israel, the Lord is our God, the Lord is ONE."

In my interview with Stephanie I needed to ask: "Did I hear this accurately? It's not written in the Torah to worship only one god?"

Oh yes! The First Commandment states "You shall have no other god before me." It does not say "besides me." As Jews, we are taught to pay attention to things like that, to omissions and details and tiny little odd phrasings in the Torah. It does tell us that we should worship HaShem and that HaShem is one – this god we are meant to put before all other gods is only one god. But there are other gods mentioned all over the Torah: Ba'al, Asherat, and so forth. They and their priests are usually written about negatively, but that makes sense when you consider that the writers of the Torah wanted us to worship Adonai and not Ba'al and Asherat.

Modern Jews think that the Torah states that there is only one god, or at the very least that we should only worship one god. It does not say this. It says that we should worship HaShem over all other gods.[681]

Much of this philosophy was carried over to the Greeks. Many Greeks would laugh and even ridicule the various gods because in some of the stories they acted badly, raping each other and eating babies and blatantly setting bad examples for the populous. Making fun of the gods was not to be done publicly, however. Like the Egyptians the Greeks didn't worship the gods either, but they couldn't challenge the gods because they had to preserve the convention of the gods.

Socrates was executed in Athens for impiety and for daring to criticize the Gods.[682] Greek society was based upon these stories of bad acting gods. How much influence did the Greek mythology have upon later philosophies? The Gentiles in the Mediterranean areas who spoke Greek also thought in a particular mindset. In their perception ideas were separated from form and the body.[683] They saw nature and human carnal desires as evil and needing to be controlled, whereas the higher

---

[681] Stephanie M.

[682] Michael Baigent in *The Jesus Papers* discusses this event: "When the Greek philosopher Socrates was condemned to death because he lacked respect for the Athenian gods, he was required to commit suicide by drinking poison.", 201.

[683] "The Semitic language does not divide reality in this way." [mind-body, emotions, psyche, and spirit]["the kingdom is both…"within" and "among"—they are the same word in Aramaic and Hebrew] *The Hidden Gospel*, 18.

aspirations and longings of the soul were to be nurtured as leading to an ultimate "good." This philosophy was conducive to the conception of a God who would incarnate into a human body to do the work of God in the world.[684]

Women in Greek society did not enjoy the same rights as the men. Dr. Jean Bolen writes in her book, *Goddess in Older Women*:

> [In classical Greece] *A woman had no protection under the law except in so far as she was the property of a man. She was not even considered a person under the law and could not go to court. Respectable women were segregated, barred from secular education, forbidden to speak or even appear in public except on special occasions…Many female children were abandoned and exposed soon after birth, or sold. Slave girls were often used as prostitutes, and could be abused, tortured, randomly executed, or sold at any time.*[685]

Riane Eisler believes it can be said that the Greek religion was a dominator religion: "Zeus establishes his supremacy through acts of cruelty and barbarism, including his many rapes of both goddess and mortal women." Male dominance was established and a policy of the ruling Greek elites.[686] Conversely:

> *We know from Aristoxenus the Greek philosopher Pythagoras received most of his ethical lore from a woman, Themisstoclea, a priestess at Delphi. He seemed to have stressed the worship of the feminine principle.*[687] *And Diogenes relates that women studied in the Pythgorean School along with men, as they did later in Plato's Academy.*[688]

To give pause at this point, I appreciate the general insight that Jean Shinoda Bolen offers:

> *Wisdom is a woman, a crone, a goddess, and a feminine archetype. In Greek mythology, she is barely personified Metis, swallowed by Zeus. In the Bible, she is hidden Sophia, the goddess who became an abstract and ungendered concept…Because she is a human archetype, she is not exclusively in the psych of women, but her development is stifled in men and, in general, in patriarchy.*[689]

---

[684] Spong. *Born of a Woman*, p. 208.
[685] Bolen, Jean Shinoda, M.D. *Goddess in Older Women*, 17.
[686] Eisler, Riane. *The Chalice and the Blade*, 117.
[687] Harrison, Jane. *Proleogomena to the Study of Greek Religion* (London: Merlin Press, 1903, 1962), 646.
[688] Ibid., Jacquetta Hawkes. *Dawn of the Gods: Minoan and Mycenaean Origins of Greece* (New York: Random House, 1968), 261.
[689] Bolen. Op. cit., 3.

The shift from the Goddess tradition to a masculine deity was also the result of the migration of cultures and the development of agriculture. The shift from an earth-based feminine goddess to a sky god reflects an ongoing tension that was created when agriculture began to compete with the nomadic way of life. For nomadic people there was a need to seek food and water for herds of animals and people, resulting in the need for a male deity who could control the weather conditions. Nomadic societies developed better weapons which they needed to fight off those who would take their animals.

Spong has a theory about the phallic nature of the weapons males have consistently developed over history beginning with spears and arrows and progressing to long guns. He goes so far as to say, "These weapons served to remind ancient warriors, albeit subconsciously, of their own thrusting male power."[690] I believe, like Spong, that this eventually encouraged the association of women with violence and conquest and led to women historically coming to be thought of as mere property or as an enemy of men. I think that even lovemaking is still viewed by some men today as a conquest and Spong questions whether this is a remnant of the historical association with warfare.[691] Women are still seen as inferior and even as the property of males within some cultures and religions around the world.

Riane Eisler writes in *The Chalice and the Blade*: "Still it can be said that Greek religion was a dominator religion: Zeus establishes his supremacy through acts of cruelty and barbarism, including his many rapes of both goddess and mortal women. Male dominance was established and a policy of the ruling Greek elites."[692]

A final note: The Jews engaged in goddess worship in several areas after Christ. The goddess continued to be the object of worship, under cover, in the personification of Israel as a woman (*Chokmah* in Hebrew) and as "Wisdom" (in Greek). In Jewish tradition, wisdom is always portrayed as feminine, and she was at the side of Yahweh from the beginning.[693]

---

[690] Spong. *The Sins of Scripture*, 73.
[691] Ibid.
[692] Eisler, Riane. *The Chalice and the Blade*, 117.
[693] Ashe, Geoffrey. *The Virgin*, (Arkana, London, 1976), 26-30.

The Aryan Race, the Goddess Tradition and Christianity: From Unity, to Duality, to a Masculine Deity

"God our Father makes no difference between any of his children, all of whom, he loves equally."[694] (attributed to Jesus, *Issa,* found in the Notovitch texts)

It would be impossible to adequately describe the history of humanity's spiritual journey of at least 30,000 years within a few pages. I will attempt to touch on some relevant points, because I have a strong conviction that the history of humanity (or whatever we can call previous beings), has evolved within a cyclical pattern. In 1978 the oldest Hominid footprints ever discovered were found in Tansania, Africa. They were found to be *3.5 million years old.*[695] This discovery has archeologists rethinking how old humanity is. Or, I might say, how many *cycles* have happened before!

Only recently there have been other discoveries of hominid bones that reportedly prove that humans did not evolve from chimpanzees as had been assumed by scientists. Paleontologists found the skeleton of a bipedal hominoid in Ethiopia which is 4.4 million years old. They named it "Ardipithecus." One of the main distinctions about humans is that we are the only mammals that walk upright. Scientists think that bipedality evolved from males using their hands to carry food back to their mates which made them more ideal partners. More recently still, there has been a discovery of bones that are 5.7 million years old. We are not just evolved chimps! Apes and chimpanzees are on a completely different branch of the evolutionary tree from us. The search goes on for the common ancestor of humans and apes which will be much farther down the tree.[696]

---

[694] Attributed to Issa of the Notovitch texts. "Issa…opposes the abuses of the caste system, which rob the lower castes of their basic rights…" Kersten, op. cit., 17.
[695] http://record.wustl.edu/archive/1996/02-15-96/2767.html.
[696] Discovery Channel, *Discovering Ardi,* Nov. 12, 2009.

My motivation to include this discussion is to suggest that a journey to the most remote and distance past can be a meaningful spiritual reflection, especially if what is happening now has happened before. What are some of the spiritual roots that existed at the beginning of human cycles? Could those concepts reflect something closer to universal and cosmic spirituality? What changes and alterations has been part of the human journey? And, for this Native American, "What can bring us and the cosmos back into relationship?"

I believe that there has been a progression in the way humans have perceived divine energy. To begin this discussion I will reflect on some of the information that has been included in the footnotes of this book in various chapters. My discourse will be built upon research that I have selected in order to provide a foundation to support the story. I have identified what I believe are five phases.

Phase one began a very long time ago in the early stages of the development of human consciousness. From the very beginning, people have attempted to understand how the universe works, specifically what brings about and animates life. In this phase, it was a universal energy that held all life together in relationship. Originally it probably had no name. It was "…binding divine beings and human beings within one universal law."[697] One rabbi in my acquaintance speaks of the divine principle this way: "There is no other one, no other *thing*, no 'otherness'—period. All that can be said to literally exist in the unqualifiable and ineffable Divine Oneness…It negates even the possibility of 'otherness'."[698]

Later, as I mentioned, in Egyptian mythology this energy or principle was embodied in the goddess Maat. This essence (*goddess* or *Great Mother* for lack of a universal name) would check the *balance* of those who had finished their earthly journey. Using a "single ostrich feather, which was put in the balance beside the heart"[699] this goddess

---

[697] Lamy, Lucie. *Egyptian Mysteries: New Light on Ancient Knowledge*, "The goddess Maat and the principle she embodies are perhaps of the essence of Egyptian mythology, binding divine beings and human beings within one universal law, for they all live 'by Maat, in Maat and for Maat'." 17.
[698] Rabbi Joel has asked that I not use his full name.
[699] Baring and Cashford. op. cit., "The goddess wore upon her head a single ostrich feather, which was put in the balance beside the heart of the deceased…often pictured giving the breath of life to the pharaohs by holding the *ankh* to the nose…she breathes

would determine the degree of spiritual balance that had been achieved in an individual's lifetime. "...Often pictured giving the breath of life to the pharaohs...she *breathes life* into the beginning of everything."[700] Most interesting is that "...she was 'there' in the beginning as the one who brings the heart of the Supreme Being alive."[701] This means that within the one Great Mystery there was a second feminine aspect that existed in the beginning to activate the heart.

It is possible that there are other philosophies, such as the Gnostic beliefs, that would have been similar to the Egyptians. Like the concept of the activation of the heart by Maat, the Gnostic gospels were concerned with "how to awaken the soul to awareness of its divine nature...from a state of 'sleep' to one of 'wakefulness.'"[702] A "cosmic order" or essence was breathed into all (the *sacred* in Native American terms), awakening humanity out of a deep sleep to their *divine nature*.[703] I think this happens in repeating cycles.

In most earth-based cultures at the dawn of human consciousness, people attempted to explain how life came about and how nature worked in its mysterious way. Since they lived primarily in nature, it made sense that their cosmology would mirror what they saw in the natural world. To them, everything happened in cycles. It was the feminine that birthed all life. So, of course the divine creative power must be feminine, or at least be a co-creator of the world. At that time, everything was within this divine feminine power. Ipupiara (Epu), a Brazilian Elder from the Amazon whom I have sat with, gives this description in his culture of the time of drastic change called

---

life into the beginning of everything...Like Sophia, she was 'there' in the beginning as the one who brings the heart of the supreme being alive." 260. "A lower manifestation of Sophia brings forth God, the biblical Creator...Sophia is then literally the mother of God..." *The Other Bible*, 735.

[700] Ibid.
[701] Ibid.
[702] Ibid. "The Gnostic Gospels show that their deepest concern was with how to awaken the soul to awareness of its divine nature and its innate potential for the growth of insight and understanding; how to transform consciousness from a state of 'sleep' to one of 'wakefulness'. Their record of the teaching of Jesus shows him to be connected *not with beliefs and worship* but with the act of *metanoia*, or 'turning around' to face the inner world of the soul." (bold emphasis by the author) 618-619.
[703] "My spiritual work is to awaken the divine nature that is within." Quoted in Kenneth Hanson, Ph.D, *Secrets of the Lost Bible*, 73.

"pachacuti". He told me that among other meanings, pachacuti means "*to return to our divine origins.*"[704]

Phase two can be described as bringing duality into the human understanding of God. In the Aramaic language we discover that the word "adam" means: "to carry the essence of the cosmos."[705] Our previous study of Judaism revealed that "adam" is the container (human being), on earth that holds divine Essence or Unity. That is our true nature. In other words, humans are the container that carries and holds the cosmic divine essence. Jewish Stephanie remarks: "Literally, 'adam' means 'earth,' 'man,' and 'red.' I was never taught anything about it having any other meaning."

Unlike in phase one where there is Unity and no other, *adam* (in Aramaic), "contains both masculine and feminine created at the same time." Remember, in the Hebrew *Chokmah*, or in Greek *Sophia* (Wisdom), "wisdom is portrayed as female, and as having *co-existed* with Yahweh from the beginning."[706] This phase introduced a kind of "two in one" deity.

Now the Great Principle has a second aspect or reflection. Looking in the glossary for the term Sophia we find: *Holy Wisdom, the Greek personification of the Holy Spirit, the "consort" or "mirror" of God.* Biblical scholar Raphael Patai says "that Jews once worshipped a female deity [Asherah]…[and]concerning Solomon's Temple:**…**[it]was *not* built to honor Yahweh alone, but also to celebrate the goddess Asherah."[707] Patai explains in his book, *The Hebrew Goddess*: "…the worship of Asherah as the consort of Yahweh…was an integral element of religious life in ancient Israel prior to the reforms introduced by King Josiah in 621 BCE."[708]

Many traditions around Europe and the Far East had gods and goddesses. Researchers Picknett and Prince have written that King

---

[704] "The prophecies say it is a time of opportunity [pachacuti] rather than a punishment or a time of doom and gloom." Rainbow Eagle, op. cit., 195.
[705] See Glossary.
[706] As Geoffrey Ashe in *The Virgin* explains, "the goddess survived 'under cover' in two forms. One is the personification of Israel as a woman; the other, the figure of Wisdom--in Hebrew *Chokmah*, or in Greek *Sophia*." "…it is clear that *Chokman* has another meaning: wisdom is portrayed as female, and as having co-existed with Yahweh from the beginning." 26-30. (as quoted in Picknett & Prince, op. cit., 296.)
[707] Quotes taken from Picknett, Lynn and Prince, Clive, op. cit., 295.
[708] Patai, Raphael. *The Hebrew Goddess*, 53.

David himself had been a goddess worshipper, as had King Solomon.[709] They also place the Hebrew tradition within this ideology saying:

The original religion of the Hebrews was, like that of all other ancient cultures, polytheistic—venerating both gods and goddesses. Only later did Yahweh emerge as the pre-eminent deity, and the priests effectively rewrote their history to erase…the earlier worship of goddesses.[710] *…goddess-worshiping Jews continued to thrive in several areas, notably Egypt.*[711]

Well into the second and third century A.D., many Jews who embraced the ministry of Jesus were located in Egypt. Some were called Coptics and others were known as Gnostics. We find that the reason the Gnostic traditions were so attractive was because they recognized "that God is male and God is female. There are gods and there are goddesses, there are male and there are female manifestations of the Divine. And this gives a power and inclusiveness to Gnostics theology."[712] The Gnostics were most active in the second and third centuries, and their ideas are prominent in the Nag Hammadi[713] writings found in northern Egypt. They believed in equality; they practiced equal participation within their spiritual communities and equal access to knowledge. They even cast lots to determine who would lead a particular ceremony. There are known Gnostic writings and gospels attributed to Mary Magdalene, Peter, and others.

We have studied in early Judaism the movement from an "only one God" (the All), to a God with both good and bad actions. The Great Goddess was seen at the source of all life, and held everything within her. Then the Great Divine contained duality. The next step was to recognize two powerful beings—God and Satan.

Phase three led to a systematic and devastating impact upon the ancient traditions specifically those of Europe and the Far East. The cultural philosophies of "the old country" were about to experience a change that would turn cosmic principles upside down. Many nomadic peoples began to migrate from the northern areas of Europe

---

[709] Picknett, Lynn and Prince, Clive. Op. cit., 296-297.
[710] Picknett & Prince, op. cit., 295.
[711] Ashe, Geoffrey. *The Virgin*, 26, (quoted in *The Templar Revelation*, 296).
[712] CNN Presents, professor Marvin Meyer, Chapman University.
[713] "Scholars such as Jean Doresse—in his study of the Nag Hammadi documents—acknowledge the pervasive influence of Egyptian theology on the Gnostic writings." Picknett and Prince, op. cit., 294.

into Mesopotamia and the Far East. They held fundamentally different ideas of the nature of the Divine Energy.

About seven thousand years ago, a pattern of disruption of the old Neolithic cultures in the Near East occurred.[714] Riane Eisler gives this description:

There is evidence of invasions, natural catastrophes, and sometimes both, causing large-scale destruction and dislocation. In many areas the old painted pottery traditions disappear...development of civilization come to a standstill.[715]

The invaders from the north and east are called the Kurgans who were Aryan-language-speaking stock. They are also referred to as the Northern Invaders or the Indo-Europeans. We first learn of them from 15,000 to 8000 B.C.. Researchers say they were not the original Europeans, others say their ancestors were from Scotland, Estonia and the Netherlands. The Aryans were "idealized by Nietzsche and then Hitler[716] as the only pure European race."[717] Simon Pearson writes that during the time, in Gerany, "If the Jews were the equivalent of the Antichrist, then the Aryan was the savior-figure of humanity."[718] They had no written language as they were hunters and very primitive farmers. Eisler describes the nomadic peoples as:

Ruled by powerful priests and warriors, they brought with them their male gods of war and mountains. And as Aryans in India, Hittites and Mittani in the Fertile Crescent, Luwians in Greece, Kurgans in eastern Europe, Achaeans and later Dorians in Greece, <u>they gradually imposed their ideologies and ways of life on the lands and peoples they conquered.</u>[719]

---

[714] Mellaart. *The Neolithic of the Middle East*, 280.

[715] Eisler, Riane. Op. cit., 43-44.

[716] "...Hitler himself was raised a Roman Catholic...All during his regime, Hitler worked closely with the Catholic Church, quashing thousands of lawsuits against it and exchanging large sums of money with it." Acharya S, op. cit., 3. John Pratt adds, "Hitler was at odds with all organized religion and especially Catholics. Reinhard Heydrich (leader of the SS) told his subordinates in late spring 1943: "We should not forget that in the long run the Pope in Rome is a greater enemy of National Socialism than Churchill or Roosevelt." See the papal encyclical *MIT BRENNENDER SORGE* which speaks against the attitude of German Government towards Catholics. It also speaks against racism."

[717] Eisler. Op. cit., 44.

[718] Pearson, Simon. *The End of the World: From Revelation to Eco-Disaster*, 179.

[719] Ibid., see Cyrus Gordon, *Common Background of Greek and Hebrew Civilization*; Merlin Stone, *When God was a Woman*.

Other nomadic invaders were conquering other lands. One of them was the Semitic people we later call the Hebrews. They were a "warring people ruled by a *caste* of warrior-priests (the Levite tribe of Moses, Aaron and Joshua)…they too brought with them a fierce and angry god of war and mountains (Jehovah or Yahweh)."[720]

Where did the caste system come from in India? Not from Buddhism. My research has led me to think that some of the Northern Invaders brought the concept. Buddhist scholar Kenneth Ch'en writes:

Some [scholars] have contended that the Aryans originated the system [caste system] to protect themselves from absorption by the indigenous people whom they faced after invading India. Others have surmised that it was created by the priestly Brahmans in order to preserve the purity of the Aryans.[721]

"Sometime during the millennium 3000-2000 B.C. …the Aryans began pouring into India…After they settled in India, they produced the Vedic literature…that furnish us with a considerable amount of information about the life and beliefs of the early Aryans before and after they arrived and settled in India."[722]

Huston Smith describes the appearance of the Aryans who came to India: "…during the second millennium B.C. a host of Aryans possessing a different language, culture, and physiognomy (tall, fair-skinned, blue-eyed, straight-haired) migrated into India."[723] Karen Armstrong in *A History of God* writes:

In the seventeenth century BCE, Aryans from what is now Iran had invaded the Indus Valley and subdued the indigenous population. They opposed their religious ideas, which we find expressed in the collection of odes known as the Rig-Veda.[724]

Elizabeth Clare Prophet promotes the theory that Jesus traveled to the Far East. She believes that when he left the Himalayas, between the ages of twenty-seven and twenty-nine, he passed through Kabul in Afghanistan and Persia where Jesus confronted the "false priesthood of Zoroastrianism even as he rebuked the false priesthood of Hindusim."[725]

Of the Aryan/Iranian invaders, Larson says:

---

[720] Eisler., op. cit., 44.
[721] Ch'en, Kenneth K. S. *Buddhism: The Light of Asia*, 10.
[722] Ibid., 1.
[723] Smith, Huston. *The World's Religions*, 55.
[724] Armstrong, Karen. *A History of God*, 28.
[725] Prophet, Elizabeth Clare. Op. cit., 34.

These Iranians did more than drive the Semitic race into permanent eclipse: themselves descended from older Sumerians, they were the pre-historic conquerors of Egypt and India as well as the progenitors of the Greeks, the Romans, and the Teuton: in short, they have ruled most of the civilized world for two and a half millenniums.[726]

Robert Graves gives us a brief look at the impact of the nomadic invaders upon ancient Europe:

"...judging from surviving artifacts and myths, ancient Europe had no gods before the nomadic invaders came from the distant North and East. Until then the concept of fatherhood had not been introduced into religious thought...When the invaders came, they viewed themselves as superior...subjugated the people of the goddess...The once Great Goddess was fragmented into many lesser goddesses and...became subservient consorts or daughters of gods.[727]

The events that led to change were clearly impactful and long-lasting. However, research indicates that it was a gradual change *with an agenda* to conquer and in some cases to amalgamate masculine gods and local goddesses.[728] According to some researchers, there was an introduction of "power over" systems which replaced "power with" systems.[729] Finally, slowly but surely, masculine deities replaced feminine representations of the divine energy. All feminine symbolism and goddess principles in both women and men were pushed into humanity's unconscious. As generation begat generation, the feminine aspects of society became more distant and the new social order began to place a higher value on "the power that takes, rather than gives, life."[730] In summary, the majority of these roving invaders (including the Aryans) could be characterized as:

- **Male dominant and violent; introduced the concept of "fatherhood"**
- **Authoritarian and subjugated the people; social structure was generally hierarchical**

---

[726] Larson, Martin A. *The Story of Christian Origins*, 83. (quoted in *The Christ Conspiracy*, 383)
[727] Bolen. Op cit. (information attributed to Graves' introduction to *The Greek Myths*), 15-16.
[728] Baring and Cashford. op. cit. "The impact of Aryan Gods on the goddess culture was in some respects catastrophic, but, in others, where the culture was able to some extent to assimilate them, it became intensely creative, and especially where the new gods married the older goddess, as happened in Greece.", 294.
[729] Eisler, Riane. Op. cit.,69, 145.
[730] Baring and Cashford. op. cit, 48.

- **Acquiring material wealth through effective technologies of destruction; use the horse; they acquired the ability to make metal weapons (of iron, copper and bronze) from peoples they conquered and used the skills to wage fierce warfare. They actually worshipped the BLADE AS POWER.** [731]
- **They believed in dark/light, good/evil duality.**
- **They disliked dark skinned people,** [732]
- **Power was attained and held through force and wealth.**
- **They worshipped a male Deity who was a STORM GOD of the mountains with components of fire, thunder and lightning.**
- **After death one went to the realm of Eternal Light.**

These concepts exemplified a new phase in the development of human consciousness. Humanity was looking outside itself to a nature of divinity that directly represented the human psyche. Humans were in a struggle to manage their own voices of duality within. Each person fought with their two sides—a choice to pursue individual spiritual growth and contribute to the Whole, or to open to the other side, and participate in the limiting or destruction of the growing energy of life, both within and in the outer collective world. That is the essence of what we call "morality" in our social and spiritual discussions.

My research into the Aryan phenomena convinces me that two strong tenets of racial pride are evident: one is the importance of linage, bloodline, and race; the second is the idea of a "chosen people of God." Each of these concepts has become embedded within many of the ideologies common today. Some examples would be: Hebrew kingship, Jews as the "chosen people," Jesus' bloodline in Southern France, the royal bloodline of Europe, in some indigenous tribal traditions, Freemasonry, etc.

So that we do not wonder to far from this story I will now give a few descriptions of twenty-first century beliefs rooted in Aryan-based

---

[731] Gimbuttas, Marija. Beginning of the Bronze Age, 202-203.
[732] Those who aligned themselves with the Aryan bloodline today are called "Christian Identity," "because its converts claim they have finally realized their identification as descendents of the lost tribes of 'white' Israel…" Quarles, Chester L., *Christian Identity: The Aryan American Bloodline* Religion, 7.

systems. These are generalized, but have relevance to our discussion of the great changes that took place in ideologies. Some of those ideas held today are:

- *"...race, not grace" determines whether a person inherits eternal life..."*[733]
- *"Only Adamic man[Caucasians] has the potential for eternal life. All races have a type of salvation but not eternal life."*[734]
- *Those who claim this bloodline are "descendants of the lost tribes of 'white' Israel..."*[735] *"...and thus, are the true chosen people of God.*[736]
- *God's family, "the race of Yahweh," the true Israelites, are Caucasian.*[737]
- *"The Tribes of Israel...these [ten] tribes were white...as Abraham and David were white, and as Jesus Christ was a white Aryan, as well."*[738]

Our study has now taken us though the transition from a principle of All in One, to the god/goddess concept, and finally to a male god theology. Religions (people of the book), finally end up with a Father God ("a consortless god"), who is the supreme and sole creator of life. As explained by Baring and Jules: "...god becomes the *maker* of heaven and earth whereas the goddess *was* heaven and earth."[739]

The environment of Jesus' time is **phase four.** The first century was certainly dominated by two controlling systems: the Roman Empire and the Judaic upper class religious leaders. How much presence the goddess culture had in the first century is yet to be clarified. However, goddess temples continued to exist through the fifth century.

It can be said that, for the most part, Jesus and most of his followers worked outside both of the systems that were dominate at the time. Two controlling extremes existed: the ego-driven, rigid, male

---

[733] Quarles, Chester L. *Christian Identity: The Aryan American Bloodline Religion.*, 8.
[734] Bushart, Craig and Barnes. *Soldiers of God*, 35.
[735] Griffin, Robert S. *The Fame of a Dead Man's Deeds,* 14.
[736] Quarles. op. cit., 9.
[737] Udvary. *Identity Bible Reference Manual*, vol. 1, B-1.
[738] Quarles, op. cit., 23.
[739] Baring and Jules. Op. cit. "Now a father god establishes a position of supremacy in relation to a mother goddess, and he is gradually transformed into the *consortless* god of the three patriarchal religions know to us today: Judaism, Christianity and Islam. The god is then the sole primal creator, where before the goddess had been the only source of life. But the god becomes the *maker* of heaven and earth whereas the goddess *was* heaven and earth." 274.

Jewish leadership, and the uncompromising dictates of the Roman officials. Also, the Jewish culture was a mixture of uncompromising practices and customs. By now the concept of a masculine deity was full entrenched within the Roman Empire.

The Jewish hierarchy watched for and targeted rebels and anyone who might be disrespecting the strict practices of Judaism. Many contending voices were expressed within the Jewish culture. Various Jewish factions had existed for centuries and there was resentment toward those who were working with the Romans. The various Jewish communities felt beaten down and under the control of the ruling powers on many fronts. The Roman leadership was fully aware of the growing numbers of Jewish people, their allegiances to culture, and their propensity to publically express themselves if Jewish practices were interfered with. Many Jews were praying for a savior to relieve the social and governmental tensions and to bring change that would be a Godly kingdom free from everyday oppression.

Phase five encompasses the years after Jesus' time to the fourth century. Even though the predominant theology during Roman times venerated a masculine God, there were those groups whose ideology still reached back to the earlier philosophies that we have discussed. Even some of the Goddess temples existed until well into the fifth century. The Egyptian Coptic Christians were attempting to carry forward the teachings of Jesus. Researcher Leonard Shlain writes of the direct contribution of the Coptic writing had upon ancient Egypt: "Almost overnight, the cumbersome hieroglyphics and hieratic script disappeared..." He says "...it is doubtful that Christianity could have ever gained a footing in Egypt if the Gospels had been written in hieroglyphics."[740] Shlain offers this perspective of the Coptic/Egyptian history:

Coptic is so intertwined with Christianity that today the term "Coptic" has two specific meanings: one refers to the Egyptian alphabet, the other to Egyptian Christians.[741] *In Egypt, where women had enjoyed the greatest equality, Clement of Alexandria vowed to destroy their rights...he claimed that Jesus had warned, "I have come to destroy the works of the female"*[742,743]

---

[740] Shlain, Leonard. *The Alphabet Verses the Goddess*, 259.
[741] Ibid.
[742] Stone, Merlin. *When God Was a Woman*, 194.

Elaine Pagels speaks of the Gnostics of this phase who were very prominent at this time:

...[the]Gnostics prayed to the Divine, Feminine, Virgin Sophia as the 'mystical, eternal Silence', as 'Grace, She who is before all things', as the 'Invisible within the All' and as 'incorruptible Wisdom, or Gnosis.'[744]

Baring and Cashford adds this about the Gnostic Christians:

The Gnostic Christian image of the deity was androgynous, both male and female, Mother and Father...the explanation may lie in a break in transmission between the gender distinctions intrinsic to the Hebrew and Greek languages and those of Latin and later European languages. The aspect of the godhead as Holy Spirit—as Hokhmah and Sophia—was feminine in Hebrew and Greek until it became assimilated to the masculine concept of Logos, and then to the Latin <u>Spiritus Sanctus</u>, which also had a masculine gender.[745]

    Here's another reference to the continued story of Judaism. As Geoffrey Ashe explains, (with the goddess-worshiping Jews in several areas after Christ), "...the goddess survived 'under cover' in two forms. One is the personification of Israel as a woman; the other, the figure of Wisdom..."[746] Stephanie offers this insight: "Let's not forget the Shechinah! All little Jewish children are taught about the Shechinah; the feminine aspect of G-d. We are not taught that She is a protectoress and that we have other Goddesses for other feminine attributes, but we are taught that there is a Divine Feminine."[747]

    As Elaine Pagels summarizes: "By the time the process of sorting the various writings ended—probably as late as the year 200—virtually all the feminine imagery for God had disappeared from orthodox Christian tradition."[748] She adds: "[the]...absence of feminine symbolism in the image of God...is to mark Judaism, Christianity and Islam in striking contrast to the world's other religious traditions.[749]

    The memories and influence of Yeshua carried well into the fourth century. However, the early development of Christian theology

---

[743] Shlain, op. cit., 259.
[744] Pagels. *The Gnostic Gospels,* 628.
[745] Baring and Cashford., op. cit., 627-28.
[746] Ashe, Geoffrey. Op. cit., 26-30. Look at FN 706.
[747] Stephanie M.
[748] Elaine Pagels. *The Gnostic Gospels,* 57.
[749] Pagels, Elaine, 'The Suppressed Gnostic Feminism', *The New York Review*, 26, no. 18, November 22, 1979, 42.

was a way of life rather that an established religion. It is my hope that you have been able to glimpse a more realistic version of the early Christianity of the first few centuries after Jesus than is often presented in the more glorified version that is promoted in Christian theology today.

It is my opinion that Jesus himself would not recognize the real heart and soul of his ministry. I am bold enough to believe that he would most likely take actions once again to bring authenticity, life and hope back into our human experience. Maybe he would lead us toward a more universal and cosmic way of being. Jesus would often speak of the wonder and beauty of everyday living. He was often described as sitting in the wild places and connecting with nature, singing his words both aloud and silently.

"...Rather, the Kingdom is inside of you, and it is outside of you. When you come to know yourselves, then you will be known, and you will realize that you are the sons of the living Father..."

"It will not come by waiting for it. It will not be a matter of saying 'Here it is' or 'There it is.' Rather, the Kingdom of the Father is spread out upon the earth, and men do not see it."[750]

How and Why—Reasons for Changes in the Jesus Story

In the Introduction I offered a story about the log cabin down the lane from our place in the country. That metaphor can facilitate our consideration of the historical conditions that surrounded the "construction" and "additions" to the Jesus story as it extended into later centuries. Something spiritually revitalizing can come from the original and ancient languages that were the foundation of Jesus' teachings. If we are able and willing to honor the older research (the "log cabin"), without fault-finding or applying a victim philosophy, it can lead us to a healthier spiritual perspective.

I would like to suggest that during Jesus' lifetime there might have been a more balanced understanding of Jesus' teachings, or better

---

[750] *Gospel of Thomas*, 32.19-33.5 in Nag Hammadi Library 118. 42.7-51.18, NHL 123-130.

said, his "ideas." After his death, there began to be divergent groups of people who gathered to carry on the philosophy and practices that they found to be valuable. Even early on there were disagreements about who Yeshua was and what he taught. Over time, the Church and the tide of history continued to add to and take away from Jesus' message and the events surrounding his life. I would encourage us to try to see this as the result of historical environments and not necessarily only the ambition or agendas of the Church.

Some will be bothered by the over-simplification of this discourse. History always holds volumes of information that helps to shape the complete picture. However, what I want to accomplish here is to stimulate enough contemplation to get past the tendency to blame Church officials for intentionally causing the message to change. Many believe that somehow the Church wanted to make the Jesus story different; they engaged in a cover up, and then eliminated or confiscated all conflicting writings that weren't hidden away. Yes, all of these things have occurred to some degree, but within the context of historical events that shaped those actions.

The first reason for the changes has been suggested throughout this book—the actual meanings of Hebrew and Aramaic words were often lost or distorted in the various translations that later occurred. As manuscripts were being written in other languages, word choices were made that reflected the opinions of translators. Also, there is the difficulty of translating accurately. When memories, experiences and expressions are housed within the Greek language, there's more of a reach for mental concepts.

Secondly, Jesus' story, his life and his messages were going to be heard outside of the Jewish culture. His ministry was quickly being disseminated to Gentiles. In between the Jewish mindset and the others, were those Jews who sought polarized groups to celebrate and review the newness of Jesus' words. One such group was called the Coptics of northern Egypt. Other Jews escaped to Persia, an enemy of Rome who welcomed the Jewish Christians. Yet another was in Southern France. These "in-between" Jews wrote their own versions of Jesus' words and the events of his life.

The third contributing factor in the changes that happened was that as some Gentiles embraced Jesus' ideology they housed it within various cultural hero stories in an effort to understand and internalize the meaning of his life within their own cultural context. This third reason for change came slowly as persons and groups processed the attributes of the Jesus' story.

A fourth reason for the tendency to "remodel" the story was the personality, the idiosyncrasies, and the personal spiritual struggles of various church writers and leaders. It is obvious to me that there are glowing indications of personal bias and sexual hang-ups. We must remember that it is the nature of the Jewish thought process to debate personal ideas and political philosophies.

Now let's look at two other major causes for change that span hundreds of years. There needs to be more focus on each one of these. The important thing to look at is how the people related to, and spoke about, God and Jesus in the early Christian circles, and how that gradually changed. Generally speaking, it can be said that during the first 500 years there were many varying philosophies and practices within the many Christian communities. Even though the Church was trying to promote a universal Catholic dogma, for all their efforts no single theology existed.

The followers of Jesus for 500 years were willing to face and accept death because of their very personal connection with Jesus. Death only meant a reunion with him. It wasn't dogma that inspired them, but their personal love for his humanness. He walked among the people without judgment. They remembered the Jesus who was open to all peoples; who was approachable by children and sinners alike; who encouraged forgiveness, loved even those who were deemed unlovable and spoke of the need to embrace one's enemies

Having said that, there was a time of tremendous change *within* the Church from around A.D. 500 to the 1400's that could be discussed. This topic is not even approached by Christians today, because the Church wanted to present a consistent, unchanged philosophy from the first century on. That was not the reality at the time.

During this period, I believe the Christian (Catholic), Church was not as focused on the teachings of Jesus as believers were before. This was due primarily to *historical considerations.* It wasn't a conspiracy to change things from the way they were in earlier times as much as it was the result of what was occurring historically in that time-frame.

The Dark Ages

I came across an audio tape of Father Thomas Doyle in which he gives a description of two historical influences upon the Catholic Church during the Dark Ages. First, there was the Barbarian Invasion. In the sixth century very large groups of invaders (perhaps from the Northeast, we are not really sure), conquered and took over the Western (Catholic), Church in northern Africa, Spain, Italy, and Southern France. Their intentions were to exterminate and replace any regional cultures and religions. He says that before coming, these invaders had incorporated some Christian beliefs into their own belief system as they migrated. Their form of religion is known as "Arian" (not to be confused with the earlier Aryan Invaders), or at least "Semi-Arian."[751] This form of Christianity was considered heretical by the Catholic Church.

According to Father Doyle, this radical group of "Christians" was very forceful in their belief that "Christ was not God." To them Jesus was someone who had superior human qualities, but he was certainly not DIVINE. Earlier believers saw Jesus as both **truly** human and **truly** divine—essentially two natures in one. The persecution of these local believers by the invading group led to them speaking less of Jesus' humanness and more of Jesus' divinity, minimizing more and more over time his dual nature. The influence of the barbarians who were saying of Jesus, "He's not God, he's only man" was severe.

The local believers couldn't speak of Jesus' humanity very much now because that philosophy was being promoted by the invaders, and the locals didn't want to be identified with the Barbarians. They began to emphasize the divine aspect of Jesus as a way of distancing themselves from the invaders. They began to speak less of his humanity and more often of Jesus as the true "Son of God,"

---

[751] Rev. Thomas Doyle. Cassette tape #3 "Barbarian Invasion and the Dark Ages" January 23, 1979. He is "the whistle-blower priest and former Vatican canon lawyer who, twenty-five years ago, warned Catholic bishops about the looming clergy sex abuse nightmare." Thislittlelight-thebook.blogspot.com/2009/06/review-of-rev-thomas-doyle.htmlFather Doyle. Also The New York Times wrote an article "Catholic Priest Who Aids Church Sexual Abuse Victims Loses Job. April 29, 2004. *Copyright 2004 - The New York Times.*

eventually adopting the stance that "Christ *is* God." Jesus' humanness and the first century memories that touched believers so personally, began to be left out with the new emphasis on his divinity. By the sixth century, the shift from the blessedness of Jesus' exceptional humanness to the recognition of Jesus' holiness and divinity was firmly entrenched. After many decades the message became that Jesus had always been divine. By the end of the Dark Ages, the majority of Christians believed that Jesus was exclusively divine. Instead of "both/and" (human and divine), it was an either/or (one or the other), position. Jesus now held a place equal to God. I don't believe this was planned. It was not the result of someone's agenda for the future. It just came to be over time.

In review: During the first century and for a time beyond, the view of Jesus was more of an appreciation of his compassion and openness to people and their everyday life situations. They wanted to follow his example, expressing in their own lives the love that he demonstrated and the message he brought. They had a deep personal relationship with Yeshua. They wanted to be like him. Then, over time, Jesus became God; set apart from the people and worshiped. All aspects of the understanding and sensitive Yeshua and the memories of his everyday *way of being* were lost. It is helpful to remember that Jesus, himself, had not changed. It was these later conditions that brought about change. Jesus became a more distant being. As Father Thomas Doyle says, "Christ became the object of worship and not the subject."

Because of this, the understanding of the Mass, that is the Eucharist, was becoming very confusing to the people.[752] In simple terms, worshipers began to have difficulty keeping the identity of Jesus and God's identity separate. Jesus had always been one who made sacrifices *to* the Father. Now, it seemed that the sacrifices were being made to *him*. How can he be a separate person who gives himself to "the will of his father" and also **be** that father? Father Doyle relates that the fear and the distant relationship that Jewish believers had with God was now transferred to Jesus. The motivation for paying attention

---

[752] Ibid. I draw from Father Thomas Doyle's tape in the following paragraphs. I feel that this information is valuable for our study of the atmosphere that existed during Jesus' ministry.

to Jesus shifted from gratitude for his love and care to fear that if one doesn't respond—they would be judged and go to Hell!

The early followers of Jesus called themselves "saints." They felt a calling or they wanted to be like Jesus and quickly identified themselves as "acting Christ-like." They had no fear of death and were ready to die; for that meant that they would come back into the presence of God and Jesus. Heaven was a home—a reunion of believers and saints. There was no fear of judgment and of death as many saints were thrown into the lion's den. Going forward, we find that the images of God/Jesus were no longer loving and caring. There began to be a fear of death because it meant there would be a judgment. By association, they also began to fear Jesus.

The second historical happening was the rise of the Roman Catholic Church as a political and social entity. There was a second invasion by the Barbarians in the eighth century after which the Church received considerable land and holdings in the resulting treaties. Seventy cities in north central Italy were given to the Pope. Europe at the time consisted of mostly small, relatively weak states. As these papal states developed, it became tempting for Church leaders to become more secular and seek after more economic power and influence. Whereas before, the purpose of the Church was to serve; now *it* was to *be* served. As Father Doyle puts it, the Church, "…became an institution with power, wealth and sway." All of this in the face of the fact that Jesus had warned against the pursuit of political and economical power by spiritual leaders.

* * * * * * * * * * * *

It is not my purpose to present theological arguments about any of the following statements. I will accept them based on my own and others' research, and because they open for me a more personal relationship with Jesus. These ideas, rather than most of the theological stances that I have encountered, help me to focus more on what Jesus meant to those who knew and loved him and remembered his teachings.

- *"In the fourth and fifth century CE, Jesus Christ got defined in a way that was vastly different from the way he defined himself."*
- *"He did not present himself as being God incarnate…"*

- *"...nor...as the one who was going to establish a new religion; for a new religion was not needed if the kingdom of God[753] were to come as soon as he taught."*
- *"He was a Teacher who showed the authority and a presence of God as he taught; and*
- *he did admit to being son of God which in his time and space meant he was close to God, was in the spirit of God, and was a servant or instrument of God."*[754]

By the end of the sixth century the Church had successfully taken a stance **between** the people and their God, as well as, between them and Jesus. For all intents and purposes, the Church decided *how* Jesus should be viewed and dictated the proper behavior of a follower and loyal subject of the supreme Church. Followers were told that they *needed* the Church and its sacraments ("There is no salvation outside the Church"), just as much as they needed God. It was not enough to merely believe—one must *submit* to the sacraments of the Church or else be condemned. In fact, as Dr. Moore concludes, "Jesus taught none of these..." ideas.[755]

To the earlier Christians of the first through the fifth centuries, the Eucharist was an expression of their joyful devotion to the Father. They gathered together with the priest in celebration of God's love and sacrifice. Even the structure of the services was conducive to the equality of all present. People came *to* the Sacraments out of love. With the new perspective of the Church, the Sacraments became confusing to the people. Father Doyle points out that the relationship between God/Christ and the people was now one of awe and adoration rather than a feeling of closeness and familiarity. The Sacraments began to be brought by the priests who were, by the sixteenth century, ordained through the institution of the Church. That made them Holy while the people were deemed "unworthy."

Even the architecture of the churches had changed by the eighth and ninth centuries. Due to influences originating in Constantinople, their construction began to mimic the court of the Emperor. The people

---

[753] "[Albert] Schweitzer believed that Jesus thought the Kingdom of God would come immediately, even in his lifetime..." Tully, op. cit., 107.

[754] Moore, *The Christian Conspiracy*, 145. "The ancient Hebrew kings were often called a son of God when they lived as a servant ...of God. It is relatively innocent language, and easily understood in the context of the ancient Near East." Ibid.

[755] Ibid., 143.

were placed farther away from the altar and the Eucharist. All of the action took place on a raised level *above* the unworthy common people. The holier, ordained bishops went to God *for* the people. An altar rail separated the "unholy" from God. As Father Doyle puts it, "Take and eat is gradually switched to stand back and adore!"

The end result of all of these changes was that the people became detached from the Mass. Many of them were uneducated and could not understand Latin. They didn't quite get the relationship between God and Jesus. The feeling of having a personal relationship with God/Christ, was replaced with a formal ritual, led by an authority figure who related to God *for* you. The Eucharist itself became a symbol of God's sacrifice and the proper response was to be in awe of Him and to feel unworthy in His presence. Even the host underwent a change from bread to a wafer that seemed, as Father Doyle comments, "otherworldly and divine." Meaning was lost in the process. By the twelfth century, few were going to Mass; so in 1215 the Church made it mandatory to go once a year!

Before we step into the next chapter, this statement by Albert Schweitzer is worthy of contemplation:

"The historical Jesus will be to our time a stranger and an enigma."[756] *"We can find no designation which expresses what He is for us. He comes to us as One unknown, without a name, as of old, by the lakeside, He came to those who knew Him not."*[757]

---

[756] Schweitzer, Albert. *The Quest of the Historical Jesus*, 397.
[757] Ibid. 401.

Chapter Seven

Sifting Out the "Actual" Teachings of Yeshua

"What we call Christianity today has very little indeed to do with the teachings of Jesus and the ideas that he wished to speak...The truth about Jesus and what he actually wanted is a thousand times more fascinating than all the stories that have been invented about him."[758]

"I will give you what no one has seen, what no one has heard, what no one has touched and what no one has even thought of." (Gospel of Thomas) quoted in[759]

"Things I was asked in times past, which I never told you then, I now want to tell you, only you never inquire about them." (*Gospel of Thomas* quoted in)[760]

"One is overwhelmed by how little of the accounts about Jesus in the New Testament can be called authentic...The historical figure of Jesus is only traceable in a few words of the Sermon on the Mount, the conflict with Pharisaism, a number of parables and some further narratives."[761]

"...except for the words of the institution of the Lord's [Last] Supper themselves, Paul does not in any of his epistles quote the exact words of any of the sayings of Jesus as we now have them in the Gospels. Nor does he mention a single event in the life of Jesus—between his birth and his death on the cross. From the writings of Paul we would not be able to know that Jesus ever taught in parables and proverbs or that he performed miracles or that he was born of a virgin."[762]

This chapter will represent an incomplete and in many ways impossible voyage. As we attempt to find more of the original story of Christianity and Jesus' teachings in particular, we must face the fact that the story will always be somewhat incomplete and fractured and

---

[758] Kersten, Holger, opt. cit., 10, 31.
[759] Ibid.
[760] Ibid.
[761] Der Spiegel Nr. 14, 1966, A specialist on the New Testament in Tubingen, Ernst Kasemann, summarized the results of research on the life of Christ. Kersten, op. cit. 27.
[762] Pelikan, Jaroslav. *Jesus Through the Centuries: His Place in the History of Culture*, 10.

will remain the subject of much discussion and interpretation. There are those who will disagree with what is presented here because they argue that a particular religious form of Christianity represents the true facts reaching back to Jesus' time. I hope that I can provide enough lights in the passageways to make this journey pertinent to our reach for ancient wisdom.

In my last book, *"Native American Spirituality: A Walk in the Woods"* I wrote:

My intuition tells me that the real impact of Jesus upon the lives of people is important to bring to light. For me personally, the image of Jesus with the young people and his loving,[763] *personal manner touches me in a meaningful way. In my older and more mature years, I am drawn toward beliefs that support a daily relationship with Jesus, rather than to ideas of power, protection, submission and graduation into heaven.*[764]

This was a clue that I would someday seek more knowledge about my Christian heritage. Like my father's journey to seek out his Choctaw "roots," I found myself being pulled toward both my ancient Native roots as well as the real meaningful roots of Christianity from my mother's side. The farther I got into the research and writings about early Christianity, the more I realized that it was going to take courage and a certain boldness to share with others what I had discovered. Writing this book has taken me over twelve years, and I try to be careful that what I share in classes honors where people are and is presented as respectfully as I can.

So far in this study, we have explored Judaism because that *is* the tradition that Yeshua lived and taught within. Also, we realize that Judaism was viciously and powerfully victimized by the Roman Empire. I believe that Yeshua's ideas and teachings were offered with the intention of supporting everyday life, and I have a guarded confidence that they can be sifted out from all of the misinformation that has essentially obscured them for a long time. In the *Gospel of Thomas* saying 77 it says, *"I am the Light that is above everything, I am*

---

[763] Natural Spirituality teaches that the Great Mystery accepts us where we are, each one of us is where we are suppose to be, and the Creator knows that we are always in process of growing. "Come unto me and I will give you rest." (Rest is the capacity to accept ourselves in every stage of life. Spong, *This Hebrew Lord: A Bishop's Search for the Authentic Jesus*, 125)

[764] Eagle, Rainbow, op. cit., 15.

all....Split the wood and I am there. Lift up the stone and you will find me there."[765] Having an understanding of the Jewish way of life, however distant we are from first century Jewish culture, and our study of Hebrew and Aramaic terms has hopefully brought us closer to a sense of who Jesus was. We are now prepared to look *through* some of the dogmatic theology that has evolved in the centuries since he walked the Earth. I use the term "through" in order to emphasis that it is possible to see *past* the current characterizations of "Christianity" to a different way of perceiving and experiencing the teachings of Yeshua. Without judging any particular form of worship, I hope there can be a choice to embrace the "way of living" that Yeshua demonstrated so profoundly throughout his lifetime.

What I have written here and taught in my classes about the Native American ideology will assist us too, I am sure. Placing Native ideas alongside ancient Christian teachings and writings will hopefully help me to guide you toward a consideration of the gifts of 1st-century Christianity. My personal relationship with Yeshua both excites and challenges me. I feel personally supported and guided by what I understand to be the teachings and the living example of this great Master. At the same time, I feel a responsibility and a challenge to represent what I believe Yeshua wanted to offer to those who listened to him during his lifetime and to those who have "ears to hear" today.

In this chapter I will bring together some of the ideas that I have presented earlier. Our study of various Greek words has shown us some of the issues involved in translation. I remind you that, **for me**, it is the life-supporting teachings, and guidance, rather than the events or even the miracles attributed to Jesus that sustains me. Salvation is not a far-distant goal to be achieved or earned, but a way of life that I can walk with daily. As theologian Lloyd Geering says, "Jesus, being a Jew, was more concerned with how people acted than with what they believed." This is the pathway I want to lay out. Geering continues: "So Jesus talked much more about how to live wisely and act righteously than he did about what to believe about God."[766]

For me, Jesus was not in favor of the invention of more laws. He said "for where there is no law, there is no sin." New York Rabbi Serzosky says, "Jews have a system of commandments. The medieval

---

[765] Written in Jenkin's book, op. cit., 70.
[766] Geering, op. cit., (July-August Issue), 4.

scholars often counted up 613 commandments. A pretty large corpus of do's and don'ts."[767] In his gospel, Paul said, "For without the law, sin *was* dead"[768]

This discussion will be void of any advice or evangelism about "what to believe." I will focus rather on having an active and alive experience in everyday life; a "way of life" that I personally can revere. In ancient times the Elders offered their ideas, opinions and guidance with no expectation that the receiver accept it. Relying on some of the recovered Christian teachings, my Native American heritage and other philosophies, I will attempt to bring together **my** selection of spiritual guidance for you to consider and take what fits for you.

* * * * * * * * * * * *

Some years ago, I was beginning to be aware of people who came to my teachings saying that they often spoke of themselves as *not religious but wanting to be spiritual.* Further discussions made me aware that perhaps many are distancing themselves from the usual need to belong to or participate in organized religions. They related such reasons as: no longer believing the church dogma, feeling that sin and guilt were no longer motivating or supporting their spiritual lives, being disappointed that their spiritual needs weren't being met in other ways and even that their own personal study of Christianity had led them away from the organized church. My immediate reflection was that whatever meaning Christianity, or even Jesus, had for them had somehow changed. They were disillusioned and felt they were no longer being spiritually fed.

I think it is important to speak about the role of the Church. Many hold tightly to their particular traditional forms of spirituality, while others explore more contemporary models. Over the years, I have seen the development of many alternative churches which address this need for a more open and liberal interpretation of Christian teachings and experience. People seem to be interested in developing a relationship with an infinite presence within rather than an external divine power that is far away. They are becoming less willing to accept indoctrination. They long for a community and a spiritual practice that

---

[767] Sunday Today CBS 1-11-2009. Also see *The Genesis Factor*, 46-47.
[768] Romans 7:8.

puts them in touch with the infinite center of *being* and helps them discover their true purpose and potential.

In most cases many of the people I have met still have an important connection with Jesus, but the churches they have experienced no longer meet their personal spiritual needs. It can sometimes be a difficult and often lonely journey to find spiritual meaning and a relationship with a spiritual community that fits.

My own journey with Christianity certainly held intense and even hurtful experiences at times, but I wasn't ready to "throw the baby out with the bath water!" It was my hunger to reach for the ancient roots of Christianity that lingered after I decided to walk away from regular church attendance and membership.

I speak of myself as a "Christian." But it's a different kind of Christian; more of my own interpretation. I would not call myself a "believer" in the more traditional sense of belief in Jesus as a Savior who died to save me from my sins, but I do hold an intention to live by what I understand to be the real teachings of Yeshua. This chapter is my first attempt to articulate the pathways I have discovered, which I feel connect my Native heritage and my heart to the early teachings of Jesus.

I begin with some statements to consider:
- It is important to me to know or to find out what Yeshua really taught.
- It is the ageless, life-supporting, spiritually uplifting and hopeful concepts that I want to recover.
- I do not think that the present-day theologies and dogma of mainline Christianity are representative of the real gifts and contributions of Yeshua.

Getting to know Yeshua

My wife and I enjoyed the movie "New in Town" which is about a young corporate executive (Renee Zellweger) who comes to a small town from the big city to close their local factory. She is picked up at the airport by an elderly local woman who is obviously quite religious. As they ride along, without hesitation this God-fearing Christian lady asks, "Have you found Jesus?" Clearly, this is an important question for this community with a long history of faithfulness to Christianity. The stunned big-town executive spontaneously replies, "*I didn't know he was lost?*" As flippant as this reply is, it is a metaphor for us as we are challenging ourselves to honestly seek for a better understanding of who Yeshua was and what he taught. Without trying to be critical, it seems that Christianity asks its followers to *believe in* Yeshua rather than to *listen* to his teachings.

The Peace Shield teaches that we need to have respect for all divine teachers. To be spiritual, or to lead a spirit-filled life, is an ambition in almost every religious tradition around the world. To this point we have explored hundreds of ideas, opinions and beliefs. As in old Native village life, we have visited many Elders-of-sorts. Now, the next step is to decide where we go from here; what to take or leave behind. What will our choices be? What ideas will we decide are important to us? Are we free to follow through on our choices? Who will be with us? How will this point of view change us and our relationships? Let's walk forward in relationship with the Great Creator as the pathways open before us. William Langewiesche says: "Flight's greatest gift is to let us look around, and when we do we discover that the world is larger than we have been told and that our wings have helped make it so."[769]

As we open our discussion of this chapter, I am presenting some of the concepts that I believe were prominent at the time Jesus was teaching:[770]

- "...the very earliest followers of Jesus were people who believed in him enough that they wanted to tell others about him."(Matt 4:19,20)
- They were eager to be taught by someone who inspired them and taught with authority, "not as the scribes." (Matt 7:28, 29)
- Jesus accepted his followers regardless of their social position. (Matt 9:10-13)
- He was compassionate toward the needs of His followers and their hunger to be led. (Matt 9:36)
- They brought themselves and their loved ones to Him to be healed.
- They had established a personal relationship with Jesus, beyond dogma and ritual. Their relationship meant so much to them that they sometimes faced persecution and even death to follow His teachings.
- He continued to teach even though He knew the dangers of challenging Roman and Jewish authority.
- He encouraged the development of personal power and told His followers that they had the capacity to do what He did, and even more.

---

[769] Langewiesche, William. *Inside the Sky*, 240.
[770] The first six entries are from *The Christian Conspiracy* by Moore, 139-140. The rest are my own conclusions.

- He taught in parables to allow people to find their own meaning in the teachings. The Aramaic language lent itself to open interpretation.
- He gave guidance that was applicable to daily life.
- He taught women and included them in His inner circle, even though it was not customary in His culture.

See "Appendix A" for more information about the Jewish religion in the first century.

One of the biblical scholars who formed the "Jesus Seminars" gives us twenty-first century folks something to ponder:

Instead of focusing on concepts such as sin and judgment, redemption and otherworldly salvation, early Jesus followers were seekers after mystical illumination, of heavenly Wisdom. Neither hierarchical nor liturgical, the movement was individualistic, ...and diverse. Based on The Gospel of Thomas, it is claimed that Jesus' message is strongly counter-cultural: he shuns materialism and directs the reader toward the simple life, a spiritual existence...Jesus here is not a messiah but a social radical, telling listeners to reject society's phony piety and the hollow values of the business world.[771]

So, this chapter will focus on finding and hearing those words that come closer to the actual words of Yeshua. The beginning of the Jesus story and even the ending events are important discussions, but for me, it is what can be found in-between, in the every-day teachings, that I want to know more about.

In the years after his death it was the memories of what Yeshua taught and the embracing of his life philosophy that was revered. I think the ideas and titles that were attributed to him later were not present in the testimonies of those who originally chose to follow him. They held Yeshua in their hearts and loved his way of life; his way of *being in life*! We can still do that today if we choose to. Once again I lift up the words of Bishop Spong:

"So look at him! Look not at his divinity; but look, rather, at his freedom. Look not at the exaggerated tales of his power; but look, rather, at his infinite capacity to give himself away. ...look, rather, at his courage to be, his ability to live, the contagious quality of his love."
"For Jesus, to be Messiah meant that he must bring love to the unloved, freedom to the bound, wholeness to the distorted, peace to the insecure...love was the deepest meaning of Jesus' life."[772]

---

[771] Funk, Robert. *The Five Gospels.*
[772] Spong. *This Hebrew Lord*, 159, 172.

What did Yeshua really say about himself? The *Gospel of Thomas* records a different version of "...Who do men say that I am?...You are the Christ," from Mark 8:27-29. Compare this to:

Jesus said to his followers, "Compare me to someone and tell me who I am like." Simon Peter said to him, "You are like a just messenger," Matthew said to him, You are like a wise philosopher." Thomas said to him, "Teacher, my mouth is utterly unable to say what you are like." Jesus said, "I am not your teacher. Because you have drunk, you have become intoxicated from the bubbling spring that I have tended."[773]

To continue this theme, the *Gospel of Thomas* also records that Jesus refuses to validate the meaning of an *experience* that the disciples must discover for themselves: "They said to him, 'Tell us who you are so that we may believe in you.' He said to them, 'You read the face of the sky and of the earth, but you have not recognized the one who is before you, and *you do not know how to read this moment*'."[774]

Here is one of the rear examples of a physical description of Yeshua allegedly written by Gamaliel found in the St. Sophia Mosque at Constantinople in the Talmuds of the Jews, A.D. 27:

He is a picture of his mother, only he has not her smooth, round face...He is not a great talker, unless there is something brought up about heaven and divine things, when his tongue moves glibly and his eyes light up with a peculiar brilliancy; though there is this peculiarity about Jesus, he never argues a question; he never disputes...he takes no pride in confuting his opponents, but always seems to be sorry for them.[775]

As presented in the introduction of *Profiles of Jesus* by Roy W. Hoover, the following refers to a twelve year period of a systematic study of all the words and acts of Jesus in the ancient texts. This examination was conducted by the fellows of the Jesus Seminar. Also I believe most biblical scholars of the last thirty years would agree to the following statements:

- "...Jesus did not refer to himself as the Messiah..."[776], Son of God,[777]

---

[773] *Gospel of Thomas,* Saying 13.
[774] Ibid., 48.20-25, in NHL 128.
[775] *Archko Volume,* op. cit., 92.
[776] Hoover, Roy W. *Profiles of Jesus,* 3.

- "...nor did he claim to be a divine being who descended to Earth from Heaven in order to die as a sacrifice[778] for the sins of the world. These are claims that some people in the early Church made about Jesus, *not claims he made about himself.*"[779]
- Jesus had brothers[780] and his family was a significant part of the community in Jerusalem.
- At the heart of Jesus' teachings and actions was "a vision of life under the reign of God."[781] This could be characterized as a "...vision of what life in this world could be; not a vision of life in a future world..."[782] It was one of the most important tenets of his ministry.
- "...God's generosity and goodness[783] is regarded as the model and measure of human life; everyone is accepted[784] as a child of God..."[785]
- Jesus did not hold, "...an apocalyptic view of the reign (or kingdom) of God—that by direct intervention God was about to bring history to an end[786] and bring a new, perfect order of life into being by a miraculous act of God."[787]

---

[777] Ibid. "[Jesus] never indisputably uses of himself the title 'Son of God'" From Charles W. Hedrick's article, *A Profile Under Construction*, (Also see Brown, *New Testament Christology*, 89; cf. 71-89. But compare Matt 26:63-64; Luke 22:67-69.)

[778] "Matthew, Mark and Luke are certainly mistaken in describing a Sanhedrin trial and Jesus' execution during Pesach [Passover]." From Mahlon Smith's article, *Israel's Prodigal Son*, 108-109. Note: "The Seminar overwhelming endorsed this unequivocal conclusion: It is not just the content of the trial but the fact of a trial that lacks historical foundation." (Fall '95; cf. Funk et al, *Acts of Jesus*, 147f.)"...an earlier vote (Spring, '94) overwhelmingly rejected the thesis of the synoptic gospels that Jesus' last supper was a Passover meal."

[779] Hoover. Op. cit., 3.

[780] "...all the brothers and sisters of Jesus became 'cousins' or children by Joseph's previous marriage or something equally as farfetched."Spong, *This Hebrew Lord*, 39.

[781] Hoover. Op. cit., 3.

[782] Ibid., 4. "A problem with this view of Jesus [setting up an empire of God] is that it runs counter to the assumption that he is the founder of a new religion." From Bernard Brandon Scott's article, *The Reappearance of Parables*, 39.

[783] "Indeed people should trust God to know what they need even before they ask. This utopian vision was the core of what Jesus had to say." From James M. Robinson's article, *What Jesus Had to Say*, 15.

[784] From Robert W. Funk's article, *Jesus: a Voice Print*, "He would not have said, "All human beings have sinned and fallen short of the glory of God." 10-11.

[785] Hoover. Op. cit. , 3, "...in Greek *agapao*, the verb used throughout the New Testament to characterized God's love for humankind...it is grounded in God's unlimited goodness...The love of God is a generosity that transcends all differences between people and peoples." From Hoover op. cit., *The Jesus in History*, 56.

[786] "Not the imminent last judgment and end of the world, but the attraction of the ideal is what motivated and empowered him [Jesus]." From Hoover op. cit., 50.

[787] Ibid., 4.

- "...taking Jesus' social world into account[788] and locating him in it is crucial to..."[789] fully understanding his teachings.

All of the contributors to the work of the Jesus Seminar conclude:

[these profiles of Jesus are]...views about Jesus as a figure of history...views of a noteworthy young man of first-century Palestine rather than the icon of myth and creed; and in so far as the truth about the Jesus of history is relevant to the credibility of Christian faith, these profiles will have their uses for faith as well as for history.[790]

Jesus was not a "Messiah" to his followers. In the New Testament we find the Hebrew or Aramaic word "Messiah" and the Greek equivalent "Christ." They both mean "the anointed one." In Mark there are only three times when Jesus is referred to as being the Christ or Messiah [Mark 8:29; 9:14; and 14:61-2]. So, in the time of Jesus, he was only rarely said to be "the anointed one."[791] Bishop Spong reminds us that the concept of the divine rescuer was a Greek idea. He says this about Jesus and the Hebrew tradition of the Messiah: "The image of a crucified messiah,[792] hanging limp and dead from a wooden cross, violated Hebrew messianic expectations...His closest friends certainly did not understand him as a messiah. One of them betrayed him, another denied him, and all forsook him and fled."[793]

It is certainly accepted that Jesus taught by example. Jesus would have understood the Jewish concept that the one doing the teaching was to exemplify what was being taught. The Hebrew word *lamod* means "to teach," but it also implies teaching by example.[794] I

---

[788] Ibid., "Jesus always talked about God's domain in everyday, mundane terms—dinner parties, travelers being mugged, truant sons, the hungry and tearful, toll collectors and prostitutes, a cache of coins." 10.

[789] Ibid., 5.

[790] Ibid., 7.

[791] "The title 'Christ' or 'Anointed' (*Mashiah*) was in reality held by all kings of Israel..." Acharya S, op. cit., 47.

[792] "In the Philippines today, some men have themselves crucified like Jesus as part of an annual religious celebration. Although this is extremely painful and damaging to the body, the men survive it." Bramley. op. cit., 247.

[793] Spong. *Born of a Woman,* 37.

[794] McIntosh & Twyman. *The Archko Volume,* Records of the Jerusalem Sanhedrin, by Eliezer Hyran, B. 24. Taken in Constantinople, October 16, 1883. *The Achko Volume: or the Archeological Writings of the Sanhedrim & Talmuds of the Jews.*

think we can all visualize what it means to teach by example.⁷⁹⁵ It is written that Yeshua often taught leaning against a tree, "calmly addressing the multitude."⁷⁹⁶ He spent most of his ministry with small groups of people and, I believe, tried to plant seeds with his teachings among those who continued to come around. One devout Catholic is quoted as saying, "Jesus himself would have suffered and died at the hands of the Pope's inquisitors, for he talked with heretics and sinners and he dined with publicans and prostitutes."⁷⁹⁷ It is spoken of him:

*"that he and their brother [Lazarus, Mary and Martha's brother] would go upon the house-top and stay half the night, and sometimes all night, talking and arguing points of interest to them both. Mary said she had often gone near, so she could listen to them..."*⁷⁹⁸

Jesus often walked in the woods. I especially appreciate knowing this! He demonstrated his relationship with the animals, and his teaching metaphors were full of references to nature.

*"...when they were out in the mountains, as they are most all the time, Jesus can tell him all about the flowers, trees, and rocks, can tell him everything in the world, and none of the wild animals are afraid of him...Their brother thinks he is perfectly safe if Jesus is with him. He says often the stag and the wolf will come and stand for Jesus to stroke their mane, and seem almost loath to go away from him."*⁷⁹⁹

*Another plan he has of setting man right with the laws of nature: he turns nature into a great law book of illustrations...He makes all nature preach the doctrine of trust in the divine Fatherhood.*⁸⁰⁰

Judaism considered everything which God created to be good and they gave thanks for it. His Jewish culture taught him that there was no separation between the world of spirit and the natural world. As Dr. Moore says:

---

[795] The Hebrew word *lamod* signifies "to teach," and to "teach by example."
[796] Arcko Volume., 131.
[797] De Rosa. *Vicars of Christ, The Dark Side of the Papacy*, 180.
[798] Arcko Volume., 94.
[799] Ibid., 92.
[800] Ibid., 88. "...there was no word for 'nature' in the Hebrew language...For them, reverence for God meant reverence for nature, that is, learning to accept the way the world works and responding to it appropriately." Geering, op. cit., The Fourth R, (July-Aug Issue) 2004, 3.

This included everything: wheat, trees, knee joints, sex organs, giraffes, monkeys, mountains -- everything. Therefore, all dualistic religions which proposed the evilness of material things could not fit within the Judeo-Christian movement of the early centuries.[801]

As has been mentioned, the temple was not only the visible center of Judaism; it was the container of "holiness, ritual and scripture." These statements are attributed to a report by Caiaphas, a main leader of the Sanhedrin, who Pilot sent Jesus to be interviewed by at the time of the Crucifixion story:

Jesus completely ignores this [God's holy] temple; says the priests have made it a den of thieves; and sets up a sneer, and even scoffs at its sacred ordinances...says it shall be destroyed...But what would be the condition of our people if this temple was removed?[802] *He has introduced common bread and wine [of the customary supper given to Moses, unleavened bread], which are not only forbidden, but are well qualified to excite men's passions and make them forget God...*[803]

The supposed writings of Caiaphas give two of his ideas about why Jesus was able to deceive the common people and lead them to ignore the laws of the temple and the expected ways of being saved:

First, the people[804] *to whom he preached were an ignorant set...a restless sort of men, who are always finding fault and wanting something new, and never associate with the more enlightened part of the community in order to learn. Another reason of his having many followers*[805] *is, his doctrines are congenial to unsanctified flesh. They are so suited to human nature and they require no sacrifices; they need not go to the temple to worship God...pay no tithes...every man can be his own priest and worship God as he chooses.*[806]

I particularly relate to the following statement about Yeshua. There are those who have endured my classes for years who make similar remarks!! "Many of his statements were like a sealed letter—not to be

---

[801] Moore. *The Christian Conspiracy*, 53.
[802] Records of the Jerusalem Sanhedrin, by Eliezer Hyran, B. 24. Taken in Constantinople, October 16, 1883. *Archko Volume*, 101.
[803] Ibid., 115.
[804] "...he ate with unclean sinners, ... and lepers, and permitted harlots to touch him, while his disciples went so far as to eat their meals without washing themselves." Ibid., 108.
[805] "He travelled mostly on foot in the company of his disciples and some suspicious women, and lived on the charity of his friends." Ibid., 109.
[806] Ibid., 104.

opened but by time. A grain of mustard was to result in a tree. All of his ideas refer to the future…"[807]

I hope that whatever can be discovered about Yeshua's teachings will be useful in the present moment and help assure that the future will continue to contain relevant spiritual ideas. Even if the above statements and sources are controversial, or are merely "impressions" of what was remembered, they represent for me a closer look at first century Christian history.

The Hebrew Meaning of "Soul" and "Spirit"

My goal in this discussion is to explore, as much as possible, the Hebrew/Jewish traditions and spiritual concepts that were prevalent during Yeshua's time. The understanding of the nature of the human soul, to a Kabbalists, is that:

…every living thing has a soul. There is a vegetable soul. There is also an animal soul, which has feelings, intelligence, imagination, and memory. Divine soul binds us to the highest spiritual levels. Each human has all three souls.[808]

Dr. Michael Lerner, in his book ***Jewish Renewal***, says:

…Adonai (YHVH) refers to the aspect of God that embodies the capacity for freedom and transcendence, while Elheynu refers to the aspect of God which is the God of nature, the God who created the universe…it calls upon us to witness that the God of nature is the God of freedom…[809]

How would a Hebrew describe spirituality? Yeshua's words originally were spoken in the context of his Hebrew heritage and later were translated into Greek. The Greek word *psyche* means "mind" "or spirit." The English words *soul* and *spirit* are an effort to translate the Greek word *psyche* into English. Predating the Greek word are two Hebrew words, *nephesh* and *ruach*.[810] By focusing on the nonphysical and leaving out the physical aspect of life, the Greek translation takes away part of the original Hebrew meaning.

---

[807] Ibid., 90-91.
[808] Sheinkin. Op. cit., 189.
[809] Lerner. Op. cit., 67.
[810] Spong. *This Hebrew Lord*, 18.

Nephesh can be translated as breath; like the breath of God; and r*uach* means the wind of God. As Bishop Spong expressively writes:

The primary purpose of breath and wind was to animate, to make vital, to bring alive the whole person, body and mind...God who created a human body by molding it out of the dust of the earth... [then] breathed nephesh into it...The function of spirit was to bring life.[811]

Dr. Moore offers additional insight. "...the Old Testament uses the Hebrew word *nepes (*or *nefesh)* which comes from the verb 'to breath as their closest approach to the concept of soul." *Nepes* means that breath sustains life but, "...*nepes* does not make a differentiation between 'life' and 'soul.'" So, "...when God 'breathed into his [Adam's] nostrils the breath of life'" [Genesis 2:7] it is close to saying that "...the soul (or life) of man comes from God."[812] All this means is that in any of the sayings of Jesus which have been translated as "soul," the word "life" can be used. Now, since that is so, in Hebrew thought at the time of Jesus there was no immortal soul! Dr. Moore explains that without its Greek influence, the Hebrew concept is that, "...the soul and the body are together, that soul and life are interchangeable and that the soul is immortal only as 'the breath of life from God' is immortal."[813]

In Native American terms, the "sacred breath of all our relations" as symbolized in the smoke that comes from the prayer pipe also honors the breath or life force within *all* of creation. Native American people walk with the awareness that the Creator surrounds us and is within us. Sometimes the sacred breath is placed upon our body, implying that the breath of the Holy is giving attention or a blessing where there is a need for healing.

Spirituality, in the understanding of both Native philosophy and Hebrew, the spirit or breath of God enters the physical body and animates it and gives it life. To be filled with the spirit meant to be powerfully alive and functioning in the world. It meant to be so inspired by the indwelling spirit of God that one is moved to fully give their gifts in real life. Every breath was a reminder of the constant presence of the Divine.

---

[811] Ibid., 19.

[812] Moore. *The Christian Conspiracy*, 160.

[813] Ibid., 161. Dr. Moore makes this unique statement, "Man does not *have* a soul: he *is one",* 165.

The Greek Philosophy of Separation of Spirit and Matter

As Hebrew words and ideas began to be described and written in Greek the concept of experiencing a full connection with life changed. The shift toward a mental perspective left out the physical dimension of having a spiritual experience. The Greek perception of reality separated the spiritual and the physical. Where at one time God and His creation were one, they had now become separate from each other. One could better experience God if the focus was on improving the soul and forgetting the body. It was best to retreat from nature and the more mundane parts of life. Eventually, the physical world came to be considered a mere distraction from spiritual pursuits and therefore evil.

For indigenous peoples the cyclical nature of the physical world contributes to an attitude of trust. There is no beginning or ending to life. That is a mystery which cannot be explained, but it means that life was not something to be escaped. It was important to enjoy life and to be grateful for it. Death was not to be feared because the circle of life does not end; it goes on within a new cycle.

Here are some words from the *Gospel of Thomas* (Saying 18):

The disciples said to Jesus: Tell us how our end will be. Jesus said: "Have you then discovered the beginning so that you inquire about the end? For where the beginning is, there shall the end be also. Blessed is he who shall stand at the beginning, and he shall know the end, and he shall not taste death."[814]

I believe that the beauty and wonder of Yeshua's teachings were compromised as later attitudes of suffering, seeking a "higher realm," and escaping from life gained prominence. All things physical, including nature, as well as pleasure and sex, were no longer a part of spirituality. To become spiritual meant escaping the "burden of the flesh." Spong uses a physical metaphor in his description of the dualistic Greek philosophy concerning life experience. He says that the body could be seen as divided somewhere in the region of the diaphragm! Anything below was identified with physical passions and instinctual drives which needed to be reined in. The mind, intellectual

---

[814] Saying 1.

thought and the heart were the centers above the diaphragm and were associated with higher passions such as love, creativity, truth and spirituality.

The ultimate Greek influence was when the Blessed Virgin Mary[815] became perpetually a virgin.[816] Jesus could not have been involved with the human body and its functions, especially sexuality, because it became evil. Perpetual virginity meant that all of the brothers and sisters of Jesus spoken of in earlier texts had to become "cousins" or children by Joseph's previous marriage in order for Jesus to be untainted![817]

Many Christians may be surprised to know that the lives of Jesus and Mary are written about in the Koran [*qur'an*]. Like the Bible, the Koran [*qur'an*] claims that Jesus was born miraculously to the Virgin Mary. Similarly, an angel tells Mary she is pregnant despite being a virgin, but the story changes quite a bit after that. In the *qur'an*'s version there is no stable, no manger, and no mention of Joseph! In the Bible Mary has a passive role as the mother of Jesus. The *qur'an* gives a much more detailed account of her ancestry, her birth, her childhood, her connection to the Temple of Solomon and her role as the mother of Jesus. Many Muslims are not aware that there is a whole chapter about Mary in the *qur'an* and that she is the only woman mentioned by name.[818]

---

[815] The gospels only mention Mary, or intimate her presence, 13 times and not always by name. "There's actually more about Mary in the Koran than there is in the New Testament, word for word. The story of her in the Koran is wonderful. The chapter on Mary in the Koran shows her pregnant, having to leave her village, going out into the desert and giving birth to Jesus under a palm tree under the protection of the angel Gabriel." CNN Presents, The Two Marys, Lesley Hazleton, Author of "Mary: A Flesh and Blood Biography of the Virgin Mary.

[816] Looking down the road we find that Pope Pius XII pronounced on November 1, 1950 the doctrine of the bodily assumption of the Blessed Virgin into heaven. Spong says, "She was systematically desexed, becoming first a virgin mother, then a permanent virgin and finally a postpartum virgin...The Blessed Virgin thus escaped both the trauma of a real birth into humanity and the trauma of a real death by her translation into heaven." Bishop Spong, *The Sins of Scripture*, 85.

[817] "Joseph's first marriage has been recognized from the fourth century, by a theologian and historian named Epiphanius..." see Richard Bauckham, "The Brothers and Sisters of Jesus: An Epiphanian Response to John P. Meier," *Catholic Biblical Quarterly* 56 (1994), 686-700.

[818] *The Hidden Story of Jesus*, Juniper Productions, YouTube, Executive Producer: Samir Shah.

What Does it Mean to Have Faith?

"To have faith, for the Hebrew, was to have the courage to enter life, for that is where God is to be found, always calling us into tomorrow."[819]

"In Aramaic, the word for faith is *haimanuta*—which can also mean one's confidence, firmness, or integrity of being in Sacred Unity...a sense of certainty or rootedness, a 'staying within' that allows one to be unshaken by phenomena outside oneself."[820]

I want to address how this spiritual idea is spoken of from three perspectives: Christianity, Native philosophy and Jewish/Hebrew. For over fifteen hundred years, the judgment of Church officials and their interpretations of biblical injunctions have largely determined whether a person is considered "spiritual" or not. So, spirituality is decided from outside one's self, by institutional dogma, the decisions of authority figures, and peer pressure from religious communities. Becoming spiritual is accomplished through having knowledge of the rules and the expected behaviors that the religion dictates and accepting and complying with them. Believers are enticed to be faithful by the offer of an eternal reward in Heaven, and they are threatened with the consequences of non-adherence to the Churches dictates-Hell.

Having faith also can involve being a member of a particular denomination. Often there is an expectation of loyalty to the beliefs of the group and a lack of tolerance for questioning or doubt. I think of the injunction, "You just have to have faith." What we don't understand or cannot get answers for we must accept on faith. This reminds me of some of the expressions I have heard parents use with children to encourage blind obedience. "You don't have to know why, just do it." "Just trust me; you don't have to know the reasons." Having faith means believing in something even when one's belief cannot be substantiated by facts. There is no room for doubt. Consequently, within most Christian churches having faith means we are not encouraged to question. The Hebrews made room for spiritual doubt. You might be familiar with the biblical saying from Mark (9:24), "Lord, I believe, help thou my unbelief." It has been interesting for me to learn that even Mother Theresa wrote in her journals that she

---

[819] Spong. *This Hebrew Lord: A Bishop's Search for the Authentic Jesus*, 33.
[820] *The Hidden Gospel*, 33-34.

was plagued with doubts about her faith. Apparently, she sometimes questioned the reality of a personal God, maybe because she saw so much suffering up close over such a long period of time. To the Hebrews, faith was not of the mind and the intellect, but of the heart. As in the Native American perspective, it wasn't about what you believed as much as it was a way of living life every day with the courage to face whatever came along.

So, this dialog about faith is not at all about a declaration of belief. In Native life an awareness of the processes and cycles of life and nature helped to balance the inevitable turns in the road. Individual experiences were placed in relationship with natural law and design. There was a kind of trust in the larger pattern that underlies and guides life experiences. Life was seen as unfolding within certain consistent perimeters and boundaries governed by predictable natural laws.

Each Native person was assisted in knowing the particular gift/vision that was theirs to give to the community, and to life. It was the opportunity of each lifetime to just *be* and to walk within each moment, holding a gratitude for life. There would be a sense of trust in both the grand design of creation as well as a knowing that every being was important and present through divine intention. Unexplained mysteries were held in trust. Later experiences and reflections offered the opportunity for deeper understanding to those mysteries. Life was so near at hand that every moment held wonder and mystery. A full embrace of the spirit of life was developed from childhood through eldership.

Looking backward from English to Greek to Hebrew we can expect some issues of translation and perhaps some revelations. We find that in Hebrew the word for faith was *enunah* which meant "the capacity to trust, the courage to act, the willingness to commit…It dealt with *being* far more than it dealt with *doing*."[821] A statement attributed to Gandhi is, "You must be the change you want to see in the world." This is a powerful statement worth contemplating, especially in our current climate where complaining and blaming have become predominant. Found in the Koran [*qur'an*] is the human responsibility to look within: "Verily, God does not change men's condition unless they change their inner selves."[822]

---

[821] Spong. *This Hebrew Lord*, 22-23.
[822] Quoted in *A History of God* by Karen Armstrong, 163.

Within Hebrew life we find faith was not a matter of belief; rather, it was an attitude toward life. Faith came closer to being an approach to life, a way of holding life as meaningful and adventurous. They, like the ancient Natives, believed that God works through his creation and is present in every aspect and moment of life. As beliefs were exported across the waters to the Western World, two different ways of viewing the relationship between God, humanity, and nature developed. The Western Christian Church began to emphasize faith in Jesus as the way to salvation and excluded nature in this process. Nature and wilderness became defined as arenas to conquer and exploit rather than to embrace. In the eastern Church, however, nature remained a support for the spiritual life and a participant in "salvation."[823]

The Hebrew word for faith, as I have said, was *enunah.* It was translated into the Greek word *pistis* (a function of the mind). The Greek culture had a mental orientation, and that made it easier to associate faith with following the dogma and proper behavior that was required of the "faithful." Faith now moves from trust, an attitude of *beingness,* to a mental description of what faith looks like, *an action.* There is now an opening for the church to dictate how faith should be exemplified and to what degree there is compliance to the doctrines. That which once was more heartfelt is now defined by mental creeds.

The Meaning of Salvation

"...salvation means the fullness of living now as well as eternally. Eternity had little reality for the Hebrew, except insofar as it was received in the *now* of their lives."[824]

For indigenous people, Mother Earth represented a gift given by the Creator, designed to facilitate our spiritual growth. Cherishing the lessons and applying them to life was blessedly anticipated. The introduction of the idea of needing to be lifted out of earthly life was very strange and unwelcome. For Native people it was very important to be fully aware, related, and personally connected to life in all forms. Every individual walked their own path, offering their gifts. This was

---

[823] Gratitude to the early work on spiritual ecology of Sufi scholar Seyyed Hossain Nasr. *Man and Nature: The Spiritual Crisis in Modern Man,* 99-100.
[824] Spong. *This Hebrew Lord,* 29.

what led to a fulfilling, spiritually uplifting and physically healthy condition. Every aspect of life was to be understood, experienced and celebrated. Each experience and every lifetime helped to bring one into full relationship with the Creator the rest of creation.

In the Exodus story, Moses saved the Israelites from their captivity and became the first role model of a savior for the people. The Hebrew word "...*moshia* (a participle form of the verb *yasha*, to deliver or to save), **does not occur with any great frequency in the scriptures** (it appears nearly half the time in the latter part of the book of Isaiah)."[825] We could question why this significant concept appears so scarcely in the scriptures. I found an interesting quote about that. "In the Jewish mindset, the concept of salvation is more national (corporate), than personal (as modern Christianity tends to view it). The salvation of the individual Jew is directly bound up with the salvation of the entire people..."[826]

The Christian term "to be saved" is a most important idea. It typically represents being in the select community of believers who will be lifted to Heaven to be with God at the end times. Yet, as we have seen, in Hebrew "to be saved" is translated as to "breathe freely."[827] Neil Douglas-Klotz[828] writes that there is little indication in the earliest texts like Q and the *Gospel of Thomas* that Jesus wanted people to believe in him in order to be saved. He was more interested in people changing their lives and acquiring spiritual wisdom.[829]

The English word salvation was translated from the Greek word *soteria* meaning both "health" and "wholeness." I have found a Gnostic text called *Gospel of Truth* in which Jean Doresse relates: "*Salvation is represented here as the response to a Call coming from*

---

[825] www.hebrew4Christians.com.
[826] Ibid.
[827] Jean-Yves Leloup. *The Gospel of Mary Magdalene*, 52.
[828] "We do not have any Gospel manuscripts in Palestinian Aramaic...the translation Douglas- Klotz used is the Bible of the Eastern Christians, called the Peshitta, which is written in Western Aramaic, often called Syriac by Western scholars...The Peshitia is the most Semitic—the most Jewish if you will—of all the early versions of the New Testament...Peshitta means simple, straight, and true." *The Hidden Gospel*, 6, 16.
[829] Ibid., 64. "The Old Testament of the Peshitta was translated from the Hebrew, probably in the second century. The New Testament of the Peshitta, which originally excluded certain disputed books, had become the standard by the early 5th century, replacing two early Syriac versions of the gospels."
(http://en.wikipedia.org/wiki/Peshitta)

below, like an awakening out of deep sleep..."[830] I'm not sure how "salvation" as we know it today evolved from this. The end of life in Christian terms means escaping life; being taken somewhere beyond this earthly world to a "better" place. Salvation became seen as deliverance **from** the world and being saved and rewarded with a place in Heaven where one would be returned to a previous blessed life with God.

The Gnostic[831] Gospels [Nag Hammadi], offered a personal way to salvation. The Gnostics believed in direct contact with the divine and their practices were focused on developing inner wisdom through knowledge. Well known biblical scholar and theologian Elaine Pagels said:

If Jesus said something like if you bring forth what is within you, what you bring forth will save you. It doesn't suggest that you need a church or a priest or you don't maybe need to be baptized. So it's about seeking, a very different kind of path and it was different from the one that the leaders and bishops of the church found useful for organizing the Christian communities.[832]

In my own discussions with a particular rabbi I learned that one way to determine whether a rabbi was "worth his salt" was whether or not he was willing to discuss religious matters with intense discourse and conviction. Judaism thrives on intellectual and spiritual argument about the meaning of the texts. He told me that in Jewish thought there were twenty-two versions of what happened on Mount Sinai. In the synagogues it was important that each rabbi stand up and verbally, with feeling and passion, defend his selection of one of the versions. He did so, not at all with the intent of debating facts and reason, but rather to speak of his personal conviction; his personal heartfelt connection to the experience that a given version touched deep within him. I'm reminded of Rabbi Lawrence Kushner's comment about, Jews bringing themselves into *being* through arguing about the meaning of sacred texts. He tells the story of a much older rabbi who came over to his

---

[830] Doresse, Jean. *The Secret Books of the Egyptian Gnostics*, 240.

[831] "One of the features of Gnostic thought that made the Gnostics so attractive is the fact that the Gnostic were clear in acknowledging that God is male and God is female. There are gods and there are goddesses, there are male and there are female manifestations of the Divine. And this gives a power and inclusiveness to Gnostics theology." CNN Presents, Prof. Marvin Meyer, Chapman University.

[832] CNN Presents. *The Two Marys*.

study table where many Jewish books were stacked. He said, "Do you believe in God?" Rabbi Kushner said, "Yes, of course!" Then the old rabbi quickly said, "I don't! Now let's argue!" As Stephanie relates, "The book of Jewish law-thought-discussion that Jews study today, the Talmud, is actually a volumes-long transcript of debates between ancient rabbis. This is central to what Judaism *is*." It was his life experience that aligned him to a particular interpretation of ancient writings and teachings and made them emotionally and individually meaningful in the present moment. In other words the rabbi was expected to speak about a text, compare and contrast it with earlier interpretations and then make the text relevant to the hearers.

The Hebrew/Jewish attitude toward life was being willing to stand within one's own experience so that the sacred texts might be heartfelt. Active dialog was not about whether it was true or not. Our Western mentality is to vigorously seek THE truth and nothing *but the truth*.[833] Speaking one's mind was not that unusual in the culture in which Yeshua was delivering his teachings, even if the message was against the Roman Empire or the Council of Elders—the Sanhedrin. The Hebrew culture allowed room for discussion. However, we must also recognize that in the time of Jesus, Judaism was certainly heading toward institutionalizing practices that had to be obeyed.

For the Hebrew's, salvation meant living fully in the here and now. They didn't relate to the concept of waiting for a future eternity. For them, salvation was received in their present lives.[834] The Hebrews had a reverence for life in all of its forms. They trusted that if God created the world then it must be full of goodness and they were free to enjoy all of its blessings and experiences. They saw no separation between body, mind, and spirit. Like Native Americans, the Hebrews knew that the creation was a reflection of the God who created it. God was to be found and engaged in everyday life; in the present moment.

I have waited a long time to hear that other cultures had a reverence for life and a love for Mother Earth. I was heartened to learn that the early Jews embraced the now, honored being fully human and rejected the idea that we have an inherent evil nature. On this side of

---

[833] "The word *sherara*, translated as 'truth,' has several meanings in Aramaic and Hebrew: that which liberates and opens possibilities, that which is strong and vigorous, and that which acts in keeping with universal harmony." *The Hidden Gospel*, 43.
[834] Spong. *This Hebrew Lord*, 29.

the world, I was both blessed and thrilled to hear the following words by a white minister who grew up, like me, in the Bible Belt:

Our problem is not that we are born in sin, our problem is that we do not yet know how to achieve being fully human. The function of The Christ is not to rescue the sinners but to empower you and call us to be more deeply and fully human...maybe salvation needs to be conveyed in terms of enhancing your humanity rather than rescuing from it.[835]

Seeking out and studying what can be recovered of ancient knowledge can lead us to self-empowerment, and toward being fully human. The Creator loves each one of us so much that before us are many paths, many lifetimes to achieve being fully ourselves.

Ancient Clues to Help Sift Out the Teachings of Yeshua

I have presented some cracks in the modern foundation of Christian thought. In the past 170 years, the ground has literally opened up and many publications and media productions are courageously focusing on pre-Christian history. To me, these are "signs of the times" that are forcing modern Christian institutions to face the fact that people are searching for their own spiritual truth. The Christian history that has been repeated for centuries is currently experiencing a period of re-evaluation and reinterpretation. As nature and creation demonstrate, in order to achieve harmony, diversity and inter-connectedness, all aspects of creation and human life must once again be honored and integrated into social and spiritual structures and cultural circles around the world.

I believe that if the first followers of Jesus[836] actually had written about their time with Yeshua it would have been, in some form, a gathering of Jesus' sayings. Jesus was originally first remembered

---

[835] Bishop Spong, Dateline NBC.
[836] Thomas Jefferson writes about Jesus: "a man, of illegitimate birth, of a benevolent heart, [and an] enthusiastic mind, who set out without pretensions of divinity, ended in believing them, and was punished capitally for sedition by being gibbeted according to the Roman law." Jefferson to William Short, 31 October 1819, in *Jefferson's Extracts from the Gospels*, ed. Dickinson W. Adams (Princeton: Princeton University Press, 1983) 388.

for his wisdom and compassion. Various researchers are giving just such a focus—upon the alleged sayings of Jesus.

Early manuscripts of well-known writings have assisted in this process. There are two that have been especially helpful in reconstructing the words of Jesus. The *Epistle of Barnabas* was discovered at St. Catherine's at Mt. Sinai in 1859 (written in Alexandria in A.D. 130, which we will look at later), and the Didache, also known as the "Teaching" of the Twelve Apostles. It was found in 1875 in the patriarchal library of Constantinople.[837] Other writings such as the *Gospel of Thomas*, the *Gospel of Phillip*, Coptic[838] Gnostic writings, and more recently the *Gospel of Judas*,[839] and The *Gospel of Mary Magdalene* have been frequently used resources for those who would study the roots of early Christianity. Most biblical scholars are aware of another possible source known as the *Gospel of Q* which I have already spoken of in chapter one.

The Oldest Bible in the World—The Sinaiticus (Sinai) Bible

In the thousands of classes that I have brought to people, my guess is that less than one percent would have any awareness of this Bible. I myself was not familiar with it until the last three years. As I consulted some fifty recently published theological books, I found only two that made any reference to this Bible. The Sinai Bible can be found displayed along with the world's second oldest known Bible, the Alexandrian (or Alexandrinus) Bible, in the British Library in London.

I have selected this study because it can help direct our journey toward Yeshua's teachings rather than to the events surrounding him or even the miraculous stories about him. For example, it is *what is not in*

---

[837] Mack, Burton. Op. cit., 15.
[838] "The writing of the ancient Egyptian language in slightly modified Greek letters was called *Coptic*. The French scholar, Fabre d'Oliver, in 1815 wrote a book, '*The Hebraic Tongue Restored*', in which he argued that the Hebrew language was derived entirely from ancient Egyptian." Vayro, op. cit., 237-238.
[839] In this gospel Judas is selected by Jesus to participate in a mission that Jesus had helped plan. Judas is portrayed as a disciple who was more special than the other apostles. "Muslims have always contended...that Jesus was never crucified, that a disciple took his place, or that Judas was crucified instead." Harvey Cox, *Jesus and Generation X*, from the book *Jesus at 2000*, 96.

this old Bible that could be embarrassing for the Church. Even the earliest gospels like Paul do not contain stories of the miraculous birth of a Savior. Modern Bibles are five translations from early editions. Today, there are several other Bibles which were written in various languages during the fifth and sixth centuries.[840]

I enjoyed researching the story of how this Sinai Bible was found. It was discovered by Dr. Constaintin von Tischendorf (1815-1874), a German biblical scholar who devoted his life to the study of the New Testament. On February 4th, 1859, 346 leaves of this ancient codex were discovered in the furnace room at St Catherine's monastery at Mt Sinai (a remote Egyptian monastery). Written in Greek on donkey skins, it contains both the Old and New Testaments. The donkey skins were later dated by archaeologists to around the year 380. Tischendorf has studied the Alexandrian as well as the Vaticanus and the Vatican Bible which is believed to be the third oldest Bible dating to the mid-sixth century.[841]

The Church predictably made attempts to invalidate this material and even denied that it existed. Witness this excerpt from an article that was published in the *London Quarterly Review* in 1883 that was dramatically in opposition to the story of Jesus Christ presented in the Sinaiticus Bible:

...without a particle of hesitation, the Sinaiticus is scandalously corrupt...exhibiting the most shamefully mutilated texts which are anywhere to be met with; they have become, by whatever process, the depositories of the largest amount of fabricated readings, ancient blunders and intentional perversions of the truth which are discoverable in any known copies of the word of God.[842]

Of course, by criticizing the contents the writer indirectly validated its existence! The British Museum in London purchased the Sinai Bible in1933 from the Soviet government. Before that it was displayed for many years in the Imperial Library in St Petersburg,

---

[840] The Syriacus, the Cantabrigienis (Bezae), the Sarravianus and the Marchalianus. Bushby, op. cit. 56.
[841] *The Various Versions of the Bible,* Dr Constantin von Tischendorf, 1874, available in the British Library. It was locked up in the Vatican's library. When a guard took breaks, he wrote notes on the palm of his hands and even on his fingernails! ("Are Our Gospels Genuine or Not?" Tischendorf lecture, 1869.) Also see Busby. Op. cit., 56.
[842] John W. Burgon, Dean of Chichester.

Russia where "few scholars had set eyes on it."[843] When compared to the New Testament of modern texts, some 14,800 editorial alterations can be found.[844] What about this is important for our consideration? I quote here from Bushby:

...the Gospel of Mark in the Sinai Bible carries the 'first' story of Jesus Christ in history, one completely different to what is in modern Bibles. It starts with Jesus 'at about the age of thirty' (Mark 1:9), and doesn't know of Mary, a virgin birth or mass murders of baby boys by Herod. Words describing Jesus Christ as 'the son of God' do not appear in the opening narrative...and the modern-day family tree tracing a 'messianic bloodline' back to King David is non-existent in all ancient Bibles (51 in total)...The Sinai Bible carries a conflicting version of events surrounding the 'raising of Lazarus", and reveals...omissions...[of] the resurrection appearances of Jesus Christ and his ascension into Heaven. No supernatural appearance of a resurrected Jesus Christ is recorded in...Mark. (but a description of over 500 words now appears in modern Bibles (Mark 16:9-20)[845]

Historian and scholar John Pratt adds: "The end of Mark at paragraph 16 verse 8 ends with an empty tomb? The women are told that Jesus is raised. In A.D. 180 there was the long version that is in most bibles. In the fifth century there were four endings to the book of Mark." Catholic Encyclopedia adds the following:

...no supernatural appearance of a resurrected Jesus Christ is recorded in any of the earliest Gospels of Mark[846] *available. The resurrection verses in today's Gospels of Mark are universally acknowledged as forgeries and the Church agrees, saying 'the conclusion of Mark is admittedly not genuine...almost the entire section is a later compilation'.*[847]

There are other texts in which there are missing pieces compared to the King James version of the Bible. Resurrection

---

[843] *The Daily Telegraph and Morning Post*, (January 11, 1938), 3.
[844] Bushby, op. cit., 57.
[845] Ibid.
[846] "The oldest manuscripts of the scriptures, including the *Codex Vaticanus* and the *Codex Sinaiticus*, do not have the present ending in Mark. In both of them Mark's Gospel finishes at 16:8." Baigent, Leigh, and Lincoln, *Holy Blood, Holy Grail*, 472.
[847] Encyclopaedia Biblica, vol. ii, p. 1880, vol. iii, pp. 1767, 1781; also, Catholic Encyclopedia, vol. iii, under the heading "The Evidence of its Spuriousness;" Catholic Encyclopedia, Farley ed., vol. iii, pp. 274-9 under heading "Canons."

appearances[848] are also missing in the Alexandrian Bible, the Vatican Bible, the Bezae Bible and an ancient Latin manuscript of Mark.[849]

A Church or a Gathering of "God's People"?
Christianity Came to a "Y" in the Road!

Why did the church decide certain texts were heretical? Why was the Gospel of John selected while the *Gospel of Thomas* was not? These are important questions that must be addressed before the next chapter. Biblical scholar Pagels has researched what I call the "turn in the road" for the followers of Jesus before the formulation of the Roman Catholic Church and the Nicene Creed in the early fourth century. Much of my selection of important teachings of Yeshua will be found in The *Gospel of Thomas*. Many notable biblical scholars have also focused in this direction. It was declared heretical by the Church; but why?

I believe that the followers of Christianity had set a pattern of worship and fellowship before the fourth century. Our study of the nature of two gospels with two different philosophies will demonstrate a change in the intent of Christian believers as found in the Gospel of John and the *Gospel of Thomas*. One led to organized religion and dogma which developed into a Church and the other brought heartfelt camaraderie and supported individual spirituality. Let me explain.

One might have thought that this book was about determining some earlier version of "First Century Christianity." This discussion is not necessarily aimed at finding the most pure, the simplest, or the earliest form of Christianity, but *more about how each believer experienced Jesus personally*. The concept of a formal church was formed by the Council of Nicaea, but for nearly three hundred years most Christians came together in *gatherings* rather than defined,

---

[848] "Pentecost, which literally means 'fifty days after Passover,' was originally a Canaanite holy day marking the early when harvest. The Jews had taken it over and given it new and specifically Jewish content." Spong, *A New Christianity for a New World*, 99.
[849] "...code-named 'K' by analysts. They are also lacking in the oldest Armenian version of the New Testament, in sixth-century manuscripts of the Ethiopic version and ninth-century Anglo-Saxon Bibles." Bushby. Op cit., 58.

organized groups. What were the informal gatherings like after Jesus? Some descriptions might help in understanding this split in the Christian focus.

Tertullian, a Christian spokesman of the second century, gives some wonderful comments about those who gathered in the name of Jesus. He calls them the *"peculiar Christian society"* and comments, "look how they love one another!"[850] "What marks us in the eyes of our enemies [he says], is our practice of lovingkindness..." According to Pagels, Tertullian says that outsiders ridiculed the Christians because they viewed themselves as "members of God's family" and believed that all humans were interrelated. Thus Tertullian said, "we call each other brother and sister...we are your brothers and sisters as well, by the law of our common mother, nature..."[851] I would love to understand more about this reference to a "common mother, nature." Another early writer, Justin, traveled from Asia Minor to Rome (c. 150 C.E.), and participated in various second-century Christian groups. He writes about what he observed:

All those who live in the city or the country gather together in one place on the day of the sun, and the members of the apostles or the writings of the prophets are read...Then we all rise together and pray, and then...bread and wine and water are brought...[852]

My point here is that those who we can call "Christians" gathered in groups, prayed, related their memories of Yeshua's words, and then shared in a simple meal together. Many considered themselves to be *God's people*. It was known that baptism was also practiced. As Pagels relates that, "When members of this group baptized newcomers, they understood baptism as their fellow Jews did then, and still today: as a 'bath' that purifies outsiders—that is Gentiles..."[853] This was done to prepare them to come into the fold of God's people; not necessarily into membership in a church.

Christians today need to understand that when early Christians joined God's family, they had to go through a ritual "death" that symbolized becoming a "new person." Baptism meant not only a

---

[850] Tertullian, *Apology 39*, quoted in Pagels, *Beyond Belief*, 10.
[851] Quoted in *Beyond Belief*, 10. The Tertullian reference is from his *Defense of the Christians*.
[852] Justin, I *Apology* 67.
[853] Pagels., *Beyond Belief*, 17.

separation from one's former self, but also a drastic severing of all ties with family and friends. Unlike most baptisms today, this caused a lot of controversy at that time. Non-Christian families found this hard to understand and they often rejected the followers of what they saw as an "illicit sect."[854] According to the writings of Tertullian:

The husband...casts the wife out of his house; the father...disinherits the son; the master commands the slave to depart from his presence: it is a huge offence for anyone to be reformed by this hated name [Christian].[855]

    For many years I have found myself being "out of the box" with those who were once very good friends and close family. Even today when my wife and I look ahead to various gatherings of family and friends, we have to emotionally prepare ourselves to remain connected. Often we are viewed as being very different, especially in terms of religious beliefs. To the credit of our families and our close long-time friends, they are able to hold a kind of heart connection that goes beyond ideology. Our Native American circles and gatherings, whether for ceremony or not, are wonderful times to just enjoy being together, discussing freely what is often difficult to speak about in other settings. Then we share a "pot luck" meal. It continues to amaze us how much food appears seemingly out of nowhere at feast time! In a similar vein, Pagels gives us a picture of the early gatherings of Christians after Jesus: "And by 'breaking bread' together, his people celebrate the way God has brought together people who once were scattered, and has joined them as one."[856]

    Now we need to study the two gospels that led to two different paths: a defined, named "Church" and a series of "gatherings" that celebrated a relationship with the spirit of Yeshua. One clue about the later is that those who gathered really believed that their God loved the human race and wanted love in return. When the concept of "the kingdom" was discussed, it was understood that it was already present within. There was no organization or entity required to lead people to the kingdom. The focus was on living and dealing with the present moment rather than a program of salvation resulting in a future reward when one finally entered the kingdom. These concepts were

---

[854] Ibid., 10.
[855] Tertullian, *Apology* 3.
[856] Pagels, *Beyond Belief*, 17.

predictably in conflict. There were many early writings that led to this turn about. Symbolically, we will discuss two gospels that can represent the philosophical divide that led to one path surviving and the other seemingly becoming lost in time. I believe the recovery of ancient writings has provided another choice that can keep Jesus' ministry alive today; perhaps even in some form of *gatherings* similar to those of the first century followers of Yeshua.

If I were to recommend one ancient source that I believe is a genuine path to many of the actual teachings of Yeshua, it would be the *Gospel of Thomas*. Here are the facts:

Thomas has forty-seven parallels to Mark, forty parallels to Q, seventeen to Matthew, four to Luke, and five to John...About sixty-five sayings or parts of sayings are unique to Thomas. (...so that the total number of individual items in Thomas exceeds one hundred and fourteen.)[857]

No one knows who actually wrote either the Gospel of John or the *Gospel of Thomas*. Without a lengthy dissertation, I will present the basic ideas that led to the "Y" in the road.[858] I am excited that there are notable Biblical scholars who have approached the topic with the courage of their convictions. This writings will only present a sampling of the extensive study that is now available on this subject. Quotes in the following indicate Elaine Pagel's research:

*1) John opposed the Gospel of Thomas teaching: "that **God's light shines** not only in Jesus but, potentially at least, **in everyone**."*

> This directly implies that *every* person can walk with God's light as Jesus did. There are no chosen, selected, or elite people.

*2) John requires that people must **believe in Jesus**; Thomas's gospel encourages the hearer "to seek to know God through **one's own, divinely given capacity**..."*

> Every human has the capacity, as they become 'ripe'; as they step into their potential, to access their personal, divinely given ability know and to come into relationship with God. The

---

[857] Funk, Hoover, and The Jesus Seminar. *The Five Gospels*, 15.
[858] An excellent study can be reviewed in Elaine Pagels book "*Beyond Belief*" chapter Two: Gospels in Conflict: John and Thomas.

writers of the Gospel of John want defined beliefs. There was an expectation of obedience to those beliefs and an insistence upon church membership leading to God.

*3) "For Christians in later generations, the gospel of John helped provide a foundation for a unified church, which Thomas, with its **emphasis on each person's search for God**, did not."*

Having a personal relationship with God and the honoring of people's right to search for God was Thomas's emphasis.

*4) "John says that we can experience God only through the divine light embodied in Jesus...[and in Thomas's gospel]...**the divine light Jesus embodied is shared by humanity**, since we are made 'in the image of God'...the image of God is hidden within everyone..."*[859]

God's presence and spirit are shared with all of humanity; not exclusively through Jesus.

*5) "In one of the earliest commentaries on John (9c. 240 C.E.), Origen makes a point of saying that, while the **other gospels describe Jesus as human**, "none of them clearly spoke of his divinity, as John does.""*[860]

The *Gospel of Thomas* emphasized a person's capacity to experience the Divine and John's gospel stressed beliefs. Since the Church had developed tremendous social and political power, Christian-minded followers were faced with a fork in the road: on the one hand, aligning with a church empire and on the other participating in forbidden gatherings. Also, any writings outside the canons could be judged as heresy. Most students of Church history are well aware of the intentional collection and destruction of any writings that varied from the Church's dogma and teachings. What has been destroyed or hidden away in the fifty miles of shelves in the Vatican Library is yet to be determined. Yet, I am confident there are enough early writings, including the *Gospel of Thomas,* which can be examined and made available for individual consideration and study. The previous discussions are now pointing to some of my personal preferences for spiritual truths or ideas.

---

[859] Ibid., 34, 40-41.
[860] Origen, *Commentary on John* 1.6. Quoted in *Beyond Belief, 37.*

Albert Schweitzer courageously spoke out about his view of the spiritual Christ who he believed was still capable of conversing with mortal men. His statements are remembered for the impact they have had on twentieth-century theology:[861]

"He comes to us as One unknown, without a name, as of old, by the lake-side, He came to those men who knew Him not. He speaks to us the same word: "Follow thou me" and sets us to the tasks which He has to fulfill for our time."

"He commands. And those who obey Him, whether they be wise or simple, He will reveal Himself in the toils, the conflicts, the sufferings which they shall pass through in His fellowship, and, as an ineffable mystery, they shall learn in their own experience Who He is."[862]

---

[861] The words have even been set to music and used in Christian worship services!

[862] Schweitzer, Albert. *The Quest of the Historical Jesus*, 403. "For Schweitzer, the living Christ called him to Africa, even though Schweitzer's understanding of the historical Jesus as one who was profoundly misled by the eschatological beliefs of his day left Jesus firmly anchored in his own time. No wonder Schweitzer wrote that Jesus is 'a stranger to our time' (*Quest*, 401)." Borg, *Jesus: A New Vision*, 19.

Chapter Eight

And Yeshua Said:

Jesus said, "Look, the sower went out, took a handful (of seeds), and scattered (them). Some fell on the road, and the birds came and pecked them up. Others fell on rock, and they did not take root in the soil and did not produce heads of grain. Others fell on thorns, and they choked the seeds and worms devoured them. And others fell on good soil, and it produced a good crop..."[863]

"I was taught growing up that Jews believe in an afterlife but we do not talk much about it. We are to focus on *this* life, not the World to Come. We know we do not believe in a Hell, exactly, but reincarnation? Heaven? Some kind of limbo state? Judaism does not explain. We are not supposed to worry about it too much. Our purpose is to make *this* world better, not fixate on the next one."[864]

When you know yourself, you will never know what it is to die, spiritually. The *Gospel of Thomas* says it well: "**Whoever discovers the true meaning of the sayings will never die**."[865]

The Master Jesus says: [if your leaders tell you,] "Look, the kingdom is up in the sky," know that the birds will get there before you. If they tell you, "It is in the sea," then the fish will get there before you. But know that the kingdom is within you and without you. When you finally know yourselves, you will become known. You will understand at last that you are the living Father's children. However, if you do not know yourselves, you will live in poverty, and you will be that poverty."[866]

There have been at least five events in my life that have justified my Mother's comment about us twins: "The Lord's guardian angel had to work overtime with you two!" And we know that mothers are only aware of **some** of their children's experiences! Without going into great detail, I was rushed to the hospital at age five for an emergency appendectomy. I remember making a decision at that time to return to my life experience.

Another time, in our teenage years, my twin brother and I were exploring a cave when we found ourselves clinging to a rock wall

---

[863] *Gospel of Thomas*, Saying 9.
[864] Stephanie M.
[865] Hanson, Kenneth, Ph.D, *Secrets of the Lost Bible*, 31.
[866] Ibid., 32.

eighty feet above an Oklahoma river. We were having a great deal of trouble trying to locate the next hand and foot hold. I didn't know if we would be able to make it down alive, but somehow we did.

When I was thirty-three years old, (the age of Jesus' when he died, as implied in the Bible), I took my first journey on an airplane. It was to New York City. As I temporarily struggled to find my balance with this new experience, I remember saying to myself, "I will trust the skills of the makers of this airplane, the pilot, and the Creator and stay in this joyful and present life." At that time, I decided what my "transition song" would be. I had learned of this old tradition from the Native Elders I had visited. I still carry this song to this day.

Around my fortieth year, I remember climbing a sandy red stone cliff in Arizona to get to an ancient cliff-dwelling in Canyon de Chelly. Yes, it was an illegal journey, but I wanted to feel the ancient energy there. I found myself locating the place where I would land if I fell! For perhaps the first time, doubts about my physical prowess came to mind!

I was sixty-two years young when my wife and I decided to experience our first scuba diving adventure. She had done snorkeling before, but never dove. I had never experienced either. Once signing the release forms and learning of every possible calamity that might befall us, we boarded our small boat and made our way off the coast of Mexico, out into the Gulf. We were part of a group of experienced divers who patiently waited for us to get our training. In shoulder deep waters, we were given instructions and about ten minutes of practice with our equipment before we re-boarded the boat and headed out to deeper water. Our guide instructed us as to what we were to do every ten feet of our dissent, which was fifty feet! One instruction was that we were not to come up suddenly, for fear of injury. The other divers enthusiastically jumped in with their own equipment, holding underwater cameras in hand. My wife and I were both guided to follow.

About twenty feet down I realized that my face mask was leaking. I went into full concentration mood. Mary noticed my "large eyes" as we swam around. What she didn't know was that I had already come to an interesting conclusion. If this was the time for me to transition, I would become at one with the natural! It was such a strange experience to be seeing such beauty in the life around me and accepting that it might be my last sight in this lifetime! However, I had decided that I would accept whatever the Creator had in mind for me, and I became willing at that moment to become *totally one with all of life*.

I can step into that moment even today. What an interesting place to be. That memory brings me to the ancient ways of walking into the next life. As the Elders would say, "There is no death. It's only a changing of worlds!" After what seemed like hours, we began to head upwards. All the while, I continued drinking the little bit of salt water that was leaking into my face mask. I know now, after talking to more seasoned divers, that this experience bordered on scuba malpractice on the part of the instructors. In any case, I sure was glad to be breathing Mother Earth's air again!

I was sitting in a waiting area one day, and to pass the time, I reached for a book that was on a near-by table and began casually leafing through it. To my surprise, it was *Planet of the Apes*! Strangely, I opened the book right to this wonderfully insightful quote, which reflects how I felt in those near-death experiences.

> *...[he] felt no fear at all. Instead, a sudden rush of freedom filled him and lifted his spirit, the freedom that comes to a man when his life moves beyond everything that has come before, moves beyond even himself, and rests at last in something greater. Death may wait in that place, but fear is forever banished.*[867]

When I discovered some of the hidden sayings of Yeshua, I came across one that I really related to: "Whoever discovers the true meaning of the sayings will never die!" I have had other near death experiences. All of them have helped me know that I have a purpose for being here at this time, and each one has allowed me to let go of the fear of death and learn to embrace life in every moment.

* * * * * * * * * * * *

I think we *have* lost Jesus![868] At least the loving and constant companion that many first century followers knew. Over time the real mission and identity of the Master Jesus has been reconstructed. It is

---

[867] From the Book "Planet of the Apes," by William T. Quick, William Broyles, Jr., and Lawrence Konner & Mary D. Rosenthal, 122.

[868] Dr. Bruce Chilton puts it this way: "No one can be assessed apart from one's environment...The 'missing' Jesus is Jesus within Judaism." Chilton, Evans, and Neusner. *The Missing Jesus: Rabbinic Judaism and the New Testament*, vii.

no longer the "log cabin" that once housed the followers who came to see and experience life differently as they walked with Yeshua, and later as they carried his words and ideas forward. After Jesus' ministry the followers who wrote many of the ancient manuscripts harbored a love for him and, I believe, recorded their memories in order to preserve their relationship with him. My prayer is for my brother Jesus to be the revered teacher and life sojourner again.

Throughout this book I hope I have been a "**sower of seeds**." Some of the information is thrown out for only momentary contemplation, while other seeds are sown very intentionally. Whether or not you receive the information is totally up to you. For me, this has been a process of seeking out the ancient roots of Christianity and recognizing the aspects of Jesus' teachings that nourish my spiritual life. Is this a selection of spiritual "truths?" For the word "truth," we can use substitute one of meanings of the Hebrew word "*sherara*," which can mean, "that which liberates and open possibilities."[869] The formation of your truths and mine will free us and open each of us to other ways of looking at life. So, if the seeds that I have planted bear fruit, **I offer it for you to taste**.

As I have researched the materials available and read many of the authors who have contributed to the study of early Christianity, I have tried to remain rooted within my Native American beliefs, while honoring my relationship with Yeshua. So, in many ways, it could be said that I have **passed the teachings of Yeshua** that can be called "First Century Christianity," **through a Native American philosophical filter.** In this closing section I am sifting out some of the most meaningful ideas that have accompanied me on my daily walks with Yeshua. I can almost hear him saying to those near him centuries ago: "Things I was asked in times past, which I never told you then, I now want to tell you, only you never inquire about them."[870] It reminds me of my many journeys to visit with Native Elders who waited so long for someone to come and ask them to share their knowledge. They were so happy when I arrived that someone was interested enough to come and listen.

As I have presented at the beginning of this book, "A Christian is any person who reveres Christ and tries to follow his teachings as

---

[869] Douglas-Klotz, *The Hidden Gospel*, 43.
[870] Ibid., Saying 92.

that person understands them."[871] What I will present is **my selection** of Jesus' teachings. I value the words and wisdom of many Native American Elders, rather than any titles or positions they may hold. Similarly, for me it is the teachings of Yeshua that I am particularly drawn to; not the titles given to him, nor the events attributed to him; or even the miraculous stories told of him. Others may think differently as they decide what is important to them. It is **the life-supporting teachings** that provide me with optimism and hope. When I visited Native Elders, I gave each one room for their particular take on things. I did not see any of them as having *the* truth or *the* right guidance. I accepted each ones gift for what it offered to me.

* * * * * * * * * * * *

One must keep in mind that, in light of the various texts that have surfaced, **there existed many different communities of believers** after the ministry of Jesus. Among them there were a variety of ideas about Jesus and his teachings. Each community selected what teachings were most meaningful to them and what they would walk with and share. Later, as the groups faced persecution, it became important to write down what they remembered and in some cases to hide the writings so that they would not be destroyed and could be recovered in the future. Little did they realize that it would be hundreds of generations before the time would be right for them to re-surface. They would come to people who could once again select what had meaning for them, in the present time, and what could bring a sense of **nearness to the Master**.

In the old days, Jesus was close to his followers. He planted his teachings with those he loved, both in person and from a distance. He said, "I am the light that is over all things. I am all…Split a piece of wood; I am there. Lift up the stone, and you will find me there."[872] Even when Jesus was no longer available, his followers felt Jesus' love and support: "For it is within you that the Son of Man dwells."[873] [Jesus tells his disciples] "Let no one lead you astray, saying, 'Lo, here!' or 'Lo, there!' For the Son of Man is within you, Follow after

---

[871] Davis, Lola A. *Toward a World Religion for the New Age*, 122. (italics are mine)
[872] *Gospel of Thomas*, Saying 77.
[873] *Gospel of Thomas*, Luke 17:21.

him!"[874] I believe **the strongest message that Yeshua planted was his love**. He said, "Love your brother like your soul, protect that person like the pupil of your eye."[875]

He also said, "Fortunate is one who came into being before coming into being." "If you become my followers and listen to my sayings, these stones will serve you."[876] It is so important for this generation of spiritual gatherers to have the **willingness to embrace mystery and even to have a sense of humor and divine comedy.** The *Gospel of Thomas* says: "Jesus was a Wise Teacher and Sage—even a comic at times." In Native cultures there was a developed capacity to be open to and to manage the mysterious aspects of life. Every culture had individuals who were a source of laughter and invoked contemplation. Being comfortable with mystery requires a personal relationship with the divine, and an understanding of the natural environment as well as one's own experiences. Then it is possible to carry unresolved and mysterious experiences until they can be better understood.

Indigenous people were able to deal with present experiences as well as future ones, because they felt confident that all things would be revealed in time. One ancient text quotes Jesus as saying that many of his statements were like a sealed letter—not to be opened, but in time.[877] Sometimes, once something is opened it can be troubling. Yet, there is a promise connected to such an experience. As one moves through the mystery to a more enlightened perspective, wisdom can be gained. Yeshua addresses this journey: "Let one who seeks not stop seeking until one finds. When one finds, *one will be troubled*, one will marvel and will rule over all."[878]

As I have mentioned, now that so much information is accessible to us, humanity must learn to activate an aspect of human behavior that has been somewhat dormant for nearly five thousand years—*the ability to think for ourselves!* We have heard many times that knowledge is power, but historically, knowledge and power have been used to manage and control people. Often, such power has been in the hands of ambitious, usually male, leadership. According to the

---

[874] (*Gospel of Mary* 8:15-20)
[875] *Gospel of Thomas*, Saying 25.
[876] Ibid., Saying 19.
[877] *Archko Volume*, 90-91.
[878] *Gospel of Thomas*, Saying 2.

ancient meaning of the term apocalyptic times, we *are* living in a time of "an unveiling of hidden truth, hidden knowledge... [and] lifting the veil."[879] "Jesus said: "Know what is in front of your face and what is hidden from you will be disclosed to you. For there is nothing hidden that will not be revealed![880] This certainly can apply to spiritual information, but also to personal information. "The Kingdom of Heaven is within you and whoever knows himself shall find it. Know your Self."[881] All spiritual traditions suggest that it is important to "know thyself." Jesus really opened the door to the coming of spiritual teachings when he said, "I will give you what no one has seen, what no one has heard, what no one has touched and what *no one has even thought of.*"[882] That is most intriguing to me, because I know this journey is far from being over.

I have previously addressed the idea that the gathering of **truth is partially based upon the accessibility of information.** Then it is inner discernment that validates the truth for each individual. For so long information has been doled out to the common people and promoted as truth with the expectation that it must be accepted based on the authority of those in power. Today many are dissatisfied with a list of spiritual "do's and don'ts." It is critical that truth be viewed from many angles. We are blessedly living in times when there is a variety of spiritual ideas being offered to us. Truly we see a "**spiritual smorgasbord**" of life-supporting beliefs and concepts that await our selection.

Knowledge is power, but only if it is accompanied by action and guided by wisdom. Spiritual seekers can act like "heretics"; valuing the right to make choices and to decide for themselves. Yeshua gives this comment: "I have thrown fire upon the world, and look, I am watching it until it blazes."[883] Taking the action to decide for oneself is often like building a fire; and then having a big wind come up! Jesus, as quoted in the *Gospel of Thomas*, places **knowledge in relationship to salvation**: "If you have this kind of knowledge but still feel that you lack something then you do not have **true salvation**."[884]

---

[879] Starbird, Margaret. *Magdalene's Lost Legacy*, 85.
[880] *Gospel of Thomas*, Saying 5.
[881] Jesus, *Oxyrhynchus Manuscript.*
[882] *Gospel of Thomas*, Saying 92.
[883] *Gospel of Thomas*, saying 10.
[884] Hanson, Kenneth, Ph.D. *Secrets of the Lost Bible*, 36.

Our research has yielded the Hebrew meaning of being "saved." As you might remember, it is "to breathe freely." For me, and I believe for first century followers of Yeshua, I reject the central doctrine of Christianity: the original sin of disobedience. I do not believe that it is passed on to humankind through the act of conception. Nor do I believe the literal story that the sacrifice of Yeshua on the cross was necessary to absolve us of our sins.

For the Native of long ago, and for some today, each moment we are able to fully embrace life and breathe in the breath of spirit creates an experience of freedom. **Salvation means living in the fullness of life now**, in the future and in every lifetime--eternally. Therefore, salvation is within our grasp; but we must accept it. Jesus said, "If you bring forth what is inside you, **what you bring forth will save you**. If you do not bring forth what is within you, what you do not bring forth will destroy you."[885] This statement certainly does not tell you what to believe, but on the other hand, it challenges us to be responsible for what is *within*—our gifts and our purpose.

Remember, an Aramaic interpretation for "have faith in God" is to *"Remain within yourselves—live in a place of rooted confidence in Sacred Unity."*[886] Also, this pushes us to dig deeply in order to discover what lies hidden within ourselves that could joyfully contribute to our "breathing freely." On the other hand, it also calls for us to know our growing points as well as our strengths. It means that we must face the darker parts of our own psyches so that we do not project them onto others or onto the world at large.

I remember a Native elder saying, "Search for your true identity with the Great Spirit and your past. Otherwise you are like a canoe, drifting in a stream. Search your legends and teachings." Our study here has been **to recover the dignity of being human;** to learn from each lifetime what can bring us into a more complete relationship with all of life and with the Creator. All humans are not inherently evil. I believe that they are just trying to step more completely into their full purpose. I like the feeling of speaking of our human journey as "recovering our *authentic* humanness." Mary Magdalene is reported to have said, Jesus "…is calling upon us to become fully human."[887] In

---

[885] *Gospel of Thomas*, Saying 70.
[886] Douglas-Klotz, *The Hidden Gospel*, 27.
[887] Leloup, op. cit., 29.

the Greek language *anthropos* is translated as "human." As Leloup explains: "We are this Anthropos—both 'already' [human] and 'not yet' [human]—just as the acorn is both already and not yet the oak tree in all its splendor."[888] This is a neat concept that reaches again into Native spirituality.

As I was growing up with Christian beliefs, I never quite understood what was meant by "be ye perfect." The *Didache* offers a more balanced meaning than the one found in Matthew, which creates an expectation of perfection. It seems to have a softer approach. First, it advises "bearing the whole yoke of the Lord" or "obeying the whole law." Then, it offers a more balanced concept, "If you cannot [be perfect], ***do what you can***."[889] This is a more loving suggestion rather than the more rigid emphasis in Christianity upon the believer's obedience.

Every lifetime we walk within a particular "vision" or purpose in life. After many lifetimes we become more of who we really are and more authentically human. Now we can add another saying of Jesus, "See, I have been guiding her [Mary Magdalene] so as to make her into a human [Anthropos]…Any woman who becomes a human will enter the Kingdom of God.[890] The idea here is "to become whole, a human being must integrate in herself or himself the complementary gender."[891] In Native philosophy this means to **balance both aspects of our spirit/nature: the masculine and the feminine,** that reside within each of us. Yeshua brings this very close to home when he said, "The Kingdom of Heaven is within you and whoever knows himself shall find it. Know your Self."[892]

Our true identity is found by continued searching and learning. Each human spirit or soul finds their true Self, through many lifetimes of experiences and lessons. By doing so, hidden mysterious wonders can be found. Saying twenty-six of the *Gospel of Thomas* points us to **honest self-examination**: "Jesus said, 'You see the speck that is in your brother's eye, but you do not see the beam that is in your own eye. When you take the beam out of your own eye, then you will see clearly to take the speck out of your brother's eye."

---

[888] Ibid., 102.
[889] Pagels. *Beyond Belief*, 16.
[890] *Gospel of Thomas*, Saying 114.
[891] Meyers, op. cit., 103.
[892] Jesus, *Oxyrhynchus Manuscript*.

Remember Rabbi Akiba who said, "**Love thy neighbor; now go study?**" These suggestions point to the importance of personal journeys and individual study. I have had many wonderful experiences with people who are seeking information that they did not get in regular school or through their Christian education. Those who wrote the ancient Gnostic texts regarded the attainment of knowledge as, "the key to a salvation that emphasized the mystical awakening of the self, the god within."[893]

These are some of the concepts that I embrace:

1- Honoring and respecting nature and Mother Earth is spiritual.
2- It's important to embrace life here with Mother Earth;to live in the present moment.
3- There's no need for the concepts of a future heaven and hell.
4- Spirituality and sexuality are complimentary.
5- Human nature is not inherently evil.
6- The Kingdom already exists on Earth and within each human.
7- Life is cyclical; there is no end to life.
8- Everything is about relationship.
9- It is Jesus' ministry of love and his teachings that are important, not his miracles or his death on the cross.

The Aramaic language stresses "coming into rhythm or timing with nature as an expression of Unity."[894] In the *Gospel of Mary Magdalene* we read: "What is matter? Will it last forever? The teacher answered: 'All that is born, all that is created, all the elements of nature are interwoven and united with each other. All that is composed shall be decomposed; everything returns to its roots; matter returns to the origins of matter."[895] In Native spirituality nothing exists totally independent of the rest of creation; for all life is interconnected and interwoven. This is also true of the nature of the physical body. No one part is separate from the whole body, even though a part may have a specific and unique purpose. Here's another reference about **Jesus' connection with nature** that stresses the Hebrew view that nature and

---

[893] Meyers. Op. cit., 12.
[894] Douglas-Koltz. *The Hidden Gospel*, 132.
[895] LeLoup. *The Gospel of Mary Magdalene*, 25.

God are synonymous: "Another plan he has of setting man right with the laws of nature: he turns nature into a great law book of illustrations..."[896] I like this next quote that emphasizes how important it is to be responsible for our Mother Earth. From the *Gospel of Mary* we read: "...We are responsible for the world in which we live, for in a deep sense it is we who create it by interpreting it positively or negatively."[897] It is my belief that the Great Creator is very present within all life. The sacred spirit or energy force that is attributed to the Creator's prevails everywhere. It is not just located in a particular place or within any one theology. Our study of ancient language has revealed that the "...word *hayye*, usually translated 'life,' indicates in both Aramaic and Hebrew **the sacred life force, the primal energy that pervades all of nature and the universe**."[898]

    As Bishop Spong reminds us, "The Hebrews were life-centered, not life-denying people...**Their passion was for life**." What a wonderful attitude to be so enthusiastic and involved in everyday life experiences! Jesus gives a useful perceptive for honoring Mother Earth's lessons of duality in the *Gospel of Philip*: "Light and darkness, life and death, right and left, are brothers of one another. They are inseparable...for this reason each one will dissolve into its earliest origin..." I wonder what the "earliest origin" means. Does that support the idea of a cyclical history? The Aramaic word for "forgive" means, "...something that is **restored to its original state**, or allowed to return."[899] To me this has something to do with accessing the *still available* dimension that can be called "the Garden."

    In Judaism and in Ancient Native American spirituality, there is not a fully developed concept of a future in which humanity will be rewarded or punished. For Jews there was a place for the departed souls to wander unhappily, but not necessarily to be tormented. During Jesus' time the greatest threat to Jews was the Roman Empire itself. In very recent times, I wonder how many people are aware that even Pope John Paul II has said: "Hell is not a place, but a state of being." **For**

---

[896] McIntosh & Twyman. *The Archko Volume*, 88. "...there was no word for 'nature' in the Hebrew language...For them, reverence for God meant reverence for nature, that is, learning to accept the way the world works and responding to it appropriately." Geering, op. cit., The Fourth R, (July-Aug Issue) 2004, 3.
[897] *Gospel of Mary Magdalene*, 50.
[898] *The Hidden Gospel*, 65.
[899] Douglas-Koltz. *The Hidden Gospel*, 125

both ancient Judaism and Native American spirituality there's never been a Devil or a concept of Hell. Today Native Americans and others can determine for themselves whether or not to accept these ideas and beliefs.

There is no end to life, no apocalyptic end-time. As we find in the *Gospel of Thomas*, "Jesus…performs no physical miracles, reveals no fulfillment of prophecy, announces no apocalyptic kingdom about to disrupt the world order."[900] In saying 51, "His followers said to him, 'When will the rest for the dead take place, and when will the new world come?' He said to them, 'What you look for has come, but you do not know it." A part of saying 113 tells more about Yeshua's position on the future: "It will not come by watching for it…" "the father's kingdom is spread out upon the earth…"

As I have shown, Judaism has an open attitude toward sex, and demonstrates an awareness of the fact that the sexual drive is part of the human experience. **Sex is not sinful or shameful by nature**. So I would expect that Jesus would have understood these attitudes. We discovered the following attributed to Jesus:

"No (one can) know when (the husband) and the wife have intercourse with one another except the two of them. Indeed marriage in the world is a mystery for those who have taken a wife. If there is a hidden quality to the marriage of defilement, how much more is the undefiled marriage a true mystery! It is not fleshly but pure. It belongs not to desire but to the will. It belongs not to the darkness or the night but to the day and the light…" (Gospel of Philip)[901]

The discussion of sexuality and spirituality is important. In Judaism we have discovered that human beings are not to be considered flawed or intrinsically evil. It is human innocence and the inability to sustain good intentions and not evilness that causes most sins.[902] Another translation of the word "sin" is "to miss the mark." It's a miss-calculation. Let's remember that one meaning of the word "evil" in Hebrew is *"to be unripe"* or to just not be ready to give ones true gift. Opposite the "unripe" are "those who soften what is rigid, inside and out; they shall be open to receive strength and power—their natural inheritance—from nature."

---

[900] Meyers, op. cit., 10.
[901] Robinson, James M., general Editor. *The Nag Hammadi Library*, 157-8.
[902] *Dictionary of the Jewish Religion*.

Jesus' did speak about "Thy Kingdom Come..." but the Aramaic language brings an interesting understanding. Rather than a futuristic goal, **"...the Father's kingdom is spread out upon the earth, and the people do not see it**."[903] Whatever is meant by the "kingdom," is very present and available here on Mother Earth. In Appendix B, I have included a study of Jewish Mysticism that suggests that the Garden of Eden is still very present in the here and now. It is only in a collapsed condition, so that it is not apparent to us. I think that Yeshua wasn't speaking of a spiritual goal in the future nor a place called Heaven when he said, "Repent ye: for the kingdom of *heaven is at hand*."[904](Matt 3:2 and 4:17, KJV)

There's more to discuss about the Aramaic understanding of "thy kingdom come." Klozt offers this interpretation: "Come into the bedroom of our hearts, prepare us for the marriage of power and beauty." In Judaism "confession...[was] made directly to God." Jesus would not place himself between the people and God for any reason. This certainly touches into the Native American perspective that the presence of **the Divine is very near;** even within the sacred place of our being. How does one enter the kingdom? Jesus says this: "When you make the two one, when you make the inner the outer and the outer the inner, and the above the below, so that you make the male and the female into a single One...then you will enter the Kingdom."[905] But the strongest statement, to my thinking, is **"...the kingdom is inside you**[906] **and it is outside you."**[907] It's already present! Let's add this interesting statement in the *Gospel of Mary Magdalene*: "This is why the Good has come into your midst."

Jesus challenges us to discover for ourselves what we must through personal experience rather than merely following someone's direction; even if there is a great regard for one's teacher. The apostles would not believe Jesus unless he explained who he was. He directs,

---

[903] *Gospel of Thomas*, Saying 113.
[904] Jesus, *Oxyrhynchus Manuscript.* The word translated "at hand" can mean to touch, arrive, seize, or bring near. "It refers to something happening *now*, in the present, with an almost violent immediacy."
[905] Codex II, pages 37-38.
[906] Luke 17:20-21.
[907] *Gospel of Thomas*, Saying 3. "the kingdom is both..."within" and "among"—they are the same word in Aramaic and Hebrew] *The Hidden Gospel*, 18.

even scolds, them and instructs them to learn to embrace each moment. From the *Gospel of Thomas*:

They said to him, "Tell us who you are so that we may believe in you." He said to them, "You read the face of the sky and of the earth, but you have not recognized the one who is before you, and <u>you do not know how to read this moment.</u>"[908]

How important it is to hold each moment for the beauty and wonder it can offer. Often those who have been handed a medical diagnosis with a fearful prognosis learn to value every minute of life.

Another aspect of the **teachings of Yeshua is that they are both cyclical and mystical in nature**. My hope for this book has been to bring an understanding of the earlier spiritual philosophies of Christianity and Native American spirituality and to cycle through to the more current understandings of their precepts. Somewhere on that journey I hope I have shed some light on what transpired during the space in between! Native teachings are all about circles. As the cycle comes to completeness we stand again at the beginning of another cycle of learning.

In Native American terms: **"Everything is about a relationship!"** This means a direct relationship with one's self, with others, with nature and with the Creator. Those who stood their ground and maintained their resolve in the years after Jesus did so because of their special relationship with Yeshua and their selection of his teachings.

Everything in nature and in the cosmos is important. Each life form; every spirit and energy; either known at this time, or yet to be introduced, has some contribution to my life. Often, I truly walk with all my relations; sharing the "sacred breath" and a purpose for my existence. Some life forms and energies are easy to be around, others declare their boundaries. All and have a unique nature that often reflects back to me some aspect of what's really also inside of me. I feel the presence of the Divine in myself and, not often enough, I am able to sense the Divine in *all* life, including humans and plastic! I do not choose to include the ideas of guilt, heaven or hell, ambition, fear or unquestioned obedience to a judging God in my daily walk. Like the scorpions, the tarantulas, and the copper head snakes I grew up with, I want to distance myself from certain ideas and concepts while

---

[908] *Gospel of Thomas*, 48.20-25, in NHL 128.

respecting that they have their own validity and right to exist. I want to honor the "growing spaces" of all life forms and I hope that my choices will also be given respect.

* * * * * * * * * * * *

We are entering a time of integration in which we have the opportunity to select from a variety of spiritual concepts. We are creating a new, personal, spirituality, based upon the truths that resonate with our own experiences of the Divine. Neil Freer, author of *God Games*, addresses what he describes as the characteristics that mark the new human, which are:

...an unassailable personal integrity...profound compassion, robust depth of informational data, understanding of the universe in terms of a full unified field, broad-spectrum competence...facility in dimensional shifting...a profound ability to enjoy...an expanded capacity to literally have great fun creating new realities, with the primary focus on the multi-dimensional.[909]

Does this give us insights into the nature of the human existence in the not-so-distant future? If so, how can our spirituality be in harmony with these coming realities? Freer gives this reply:

...unless we know who we are and how and where we came from we will remain at odds with each other over the definitions we give as to what we are--and therefore, what we are about.[910]

The late Gershom Scholem, professor of Jewish mysticism at the Hebrew University of Jerusalem explains: [the path of *kabbalah* is to seek to know God] "not through dogmatic theology but through living experience and intuition."[911]

* * * * * * * * * * * *

---

[909] Freer, Neil. *God Games: What do you do Forever?* 13.
[910] Ibid.
[911] Quoted in *Beyond Belief* by Pagels, 94.

"The soul answered: 'That which oppressed me has been slain; that which encircled me has vanished; my craving has faded, and **I am freed from my ignorance**." (*Gospel of Mary Magdalene*)

"Be in harmony…" If you are out of balance, take inspiration from manifestations of your true nature. Those who have ears, let them hear." After saying this, the Beloved One greeted them all, saying: "Peace be with you—may my Peace arise and be fulfilled within you!" (*Gospel of Mary Magdalene*)

"Faith is our **earth**, in which we take root; hope is the **water** through which we are nourished; love is the **air** through which we grow; *gnosis* [knowledge] is the light through which we become fully grown." (*Gosple of Philip*)

* * * * * * * * * * * *

I have a fantasy that one day there might be a discovery that would, once and for all, tell me who Jesus was and how he was able to inspire so many people to follow him during his lifetime and for so many centuries thereafter. That may never happen. I think, in the end, that we must be comfortable embracing the mystery. In Native American spirituality, we experience life moment by moment; content with the knowledge we have gathered, but always searching for additional wisdom.

What have we learned about who Jesus was? First, and very relevantly, he was a Jew. He was born and socialized within the Jewish culture and understood Jewish Law, even though he often spoke in opposition to some of the applications of various laws. He knew the Hebrew Scriptures and he referred to them often in his teachings. The purpose of his activism was to transform the social, religious and political environment *within* Judaism. He was proposing an alternative social vision with compassion as its core value.

The Temple was the one place where God was accessible and present to the people. But, it was in Jerusalem and most people had to travel long distances to get there. So they did not feel that they could personally connect with Him on a regular basis. Jesus taught that anyone could have a relationship with God in their every-day life. He prophesied that God would destroy the Temple as part of the bringing of a re-ordering of society which, in turn, would eventually bring about a better world.

Bishop Spong has a theory that Jesus was influenced by a part of the Hebrew tradition that was not dominant in Israel, but was favored by some of the smaller groups like the Essenes. A text was written around 540 B.C.E. The writer was, "…a prophet of the exile whose writings were attached to the back of the scroll of the prophet Isaiah; hence, this writer is called The Second Isaiah."[912] It presents the image of the "suffering servant of the Lord," who would embody, "…a higher, grander, more noble destiny for Israel than any Hebrew before him had ever envisioned." The powerless people of Judah would serve God and bring about freedom and blessings for the world.

Second Isaiah also allows that this vision might be fulfilled by a single person. He describes the qualities that would be necessary for that servant figure. He would be meek, gentle, humble and staunchly dedicated to his purpose. However, he would eventually be "overwhelmed" (Isa. 53.8), and "…be slain as a criminal" (Isa. 53.9). Spong goes on to say that, "Nevertheless, God would reverse the sentence of death, and he would go on uninterrupted until he accomplished his task of bringing all people into unity with God, with each other, and with themselves (Isa. 5-10ff.)"[913] Was Jesus influenced by this scripture? Spong believes that he was, or at the very least, that later midrashic treatment incorporated the ideas in Second Isaiah into the story of Jesus.

Jesus was a spiritual teacher. He warned against seeking freedom and happiness through wealth and comfort. He stood against the accumulation of wealth, by individuals or by the Jewish hierarchy. Only by pondering his words and parables and searching for Spirit within could one find the "kingdom of God," and it was *always* in the here and now in the mind of Jesus. He was interested in what the world could be *now*, not in the far-distant future. He used the social climate of the times to get his points across. Debt was a big problem in Galilee at the time, and Jesus used the concept of debt often as a metaphor to help people see that real poverty was the absence of a relationship with Spirit.

---

[912] Spong. *This Hebrew Lord*, 98.
[913] Ibid., 102-3.

Jesus was generally against the patriarchal structure. He had a remarkably enlightened view toward women for his time, including them in his inner circle. Most scholars today believe that Mary Magdalene was the closest and most influential of the apostles. He was often seen socially embracing, and even physically touching, the "unclean," which was a prohibition within his culture.

One question that continues to spark heated debate within scholarly circles is: What accounts for the growth of the Church after Jesus' death? His followers essentially ran away and hid in fear of the Roman authorities after the Crucifixion. There is little evidence that they were particularly courageous or that they had unusual leadership skills during his lifetime, but some took courage to step into those leadership roles after his death. Why didn't they stay underground? Something very impressive must have happened for the movement to have spread so quickly all around the Mediterranean and for it to have been so feared by Roman authorities. Within twenty years, there were those who believed that Jesus was divine, even though that was not a common belief during his lifetime, and he himself made no such claims. One explanation, which many scholars support, is that several groups of his followers believed in the Resurrection and *that* belief accounts for their revived courage and passion.

Mark Tully approaches this discussion in his book, *Four Faces: A Journey in Search of Jesus the Divine, the Jew, the Rebel, the Sage*. He points out that the gospel accounts of the appearances of Jesus after the Crucifixion are incompatible. "According to Paul, the Resurrection body was not of flesh and blood. It was transformed, in the same way that Paul thought believers' bodies would be transformed."[914] The apostles didn't have an adequate vocabulary or the philosophical context from which to make sense of what they experienced. Tully writes that Paul's way of expressing it was that he saw a "spiritual body." There were groups who did not focus on the Crucifixion or the Resurrection. Tully relates that they were more interested in continuing Jesus' cause to reform and renew Israel. For them, it was more about living out the mission of the martyred prophet: to be the spiritual servants of God.

What was the Resurrection? Were the apparitions of Jesus after the Crucifixion mystical, metaphorical, or physical? Did the disciples

---

[914] Tully. *A New Vision*, 144-45.

"see" him inside themselves or in the external world? There are no definitive answers. It is a matter of personal discernment today, as it was in the first century. What is clear is that something extraordinary happened that fueled the growth of the Christian movement and allowed it to flourish throughout history. What is also clear, according to many Biblical researchers, was that the Jews were expecting some form of divine intervention to come to Israel. They were impressed by Jesus' entry into Jerusalem on a donkey and by his actions against the Temple, which convinced some of the people at the time that he had come to deliver them from oppression as the prophesies had foreshadowed. The Resurrection, whatever it was, ended up being the "icing on the cake."

Many people today are leaving organized religion and institutionalized churches because they can no longer believe what is required of them to call themselves Christians, which is: that they believe Jesus was God in human form who died to save us from our sins and rose from the dead. Further, that he will return to judge everyone and reward the faithful, while eternally punishing the unbelievers. Many are struggling to believe the doctrines of their church, because in the light of modern understandings, they just don't make sense! Jesus himself was not a Christian. There was no such thing during his lifetime. It was not even a movement yet. Christianity was not an organized religion until Constantine's time. As we have seen, the belief that he was divine came after his death, mainly due to belief in the Resurrection.

The gospels were written for particular audiences by writers with specific goals in mind. None of them were written by actual eyewitnesses to the events of Jesus' life. Modern scientific analysis of the texts has shown them to be shaped by the opinions and beliefs and motives of the writers.

Also, the advent of the field of psychology has opened up a whole new perspective on the early writings as metaphor and/or personal interpretation leading to a different definition of "truth." We now recognize the validity of symbolic as well as literal truth. However, in our society today, we do not always honor a relationship with Spirit as a valid experience. I believe that there are many ways to know God; not just one. I don't believe that the Bible has to be taken literally in order to discover personal truth within it. Jesus most certainly had the ability to commune with Spirit. He spent time in nature in what Native Americans might call a "vision quest." He spent many hours in meditation and was familiar with the Hebrew stories of the prophets having had experiences of alternate realities.

Jesus was one who reflected the qualities of the Divine: freedom, courage, joy, wisdom, gentle power, humility and certainly compassion in his teachings and in his manner. He was also human; he walked his talk! He was a model for what we all can become through our own reflection of Spirit. This is as true today as it ever was. I see Jesus as both a real man and a container for the spirit of "the Christ." He urged people to follow him, but the true sense of that was to be like him; to embody those qualities that he lived; individually as well as collectively. It was intended that community was to support that process. Jesus was a revelation of God in the world. In the Peace Shield teachings from the Ojibwe, the orange circle represents all of the reflections of the Creator. We can witness God through extraordinary people, circumstances, experiences, and indeed, through each and every aspect of His creation.

Freedom, as Jesus understood it, was freedom from the "boxes" that entrap humanity. Marcus Borg says it this way:

As the movement to a life grounded in the Spirit of God, it is a movement away from the many securities offered by culture, whether goods, status, identity, nation, success, or righteousness. Life in Spirit however, does not simply draw one away from culture. Not an individualistic vision, it creates a new community, an alternative community or alternative culture.[915]

To be "in the world but not of the world" was not meant to be against earthly life, and certainly not against nature, but it meant not being attached to the superficial in life. When he spoke of the "son of God," he meant that he was close to God or under the influence of Spirit. He did not see spirit and culture as separate. I am convinced that he didn't even see religion and politics as being separate. The U. S. Constitution notwithstanding, do we ever **really** exclude our spiritual beliefs from our political discourse; or **should** we? That is a subject for another time and place!

Today we long for connection and inspiration; for some greater purpose to believe in. Many churches have fallen into imitating the predominant cultural values. They are focused on recruiting new

---

[915] Borg. A New Vision, 194.

members, raising money to maintain or expand their property and influence. In some denominations religion is more like a corporation than a spiritual community. How would Jesus view a society today in which we must continually consume more and churn out exponential economic growth in order to maintain our power and status in the world economy? Technology keeps us craving the newest and shiniest gadget. We foul our nest with the discarded remnants of "progress," all the time denying the consequences.

A popular Christian fad a few years ago was to wear a bracelet that read, "WWJD," signifying, "What would Jesus do?" If Jesus were among us today, he would probably not align himself with the dominant cultural values we prize: power, wealth, fame, success, nationalism, pride, and consumerism. He would likely advise against looking there for happiness. He would be more likely to speak out compassionately for the disadvantaged rather than for those who seek to maintain economic power and superiority. Jesus would care for the natural world; not just to preserve the economic benefits to humans, but to teach us how to learn from the reflections of the Creator that the natural world makes available to all.

The kingdom he spoke of is not ruled by an earthly king, but by the Spirit of God within each person. It was "The Way": the way of life of a spirit-filled person and the beauty and harmony that resulted from living a life from which the love of God flowed to the world. It is freely available to all in the present time. All of our actions in our outer life are to be examined with the values of Spirit in mind. In Native terms, we are to think of the consequences of our actions on the seventh generation that follows us. We are to strive to live out our beliefs and values every day, in all of the choices we make. My hope is that as we become re-acquainted with Yeshua, we can once again "follow him" and fulfill his dream of creating a New Kingdom by transforming ourselves and the world through emulating his life.

What a wonderful feeling to know that "the sun is always shining," as my father always said, and that the Creator is ever-present. In those times when I have felt encircled by all life around me, with my sacred spirit in the center, I have experienced deep gratitude for my relationship with The *Great Hushtale*. There is no end to life. Life is really all about being connected and related. **"Religion is not an escape from life, it *is* life."**

Appendix A

Jewish Religion in the First Century

First century Jews believed in one God. They were not supposed to have any physical representations of the divine or worship any other gods. Wylen reports:

"Early in the Second Temple period Jews began the custom, universally observed from then until now, of reciting twice a day [every morning and every evening] the verse from Deuteronomy, chapter 6: 'Hear, O Israel, Adonai is our God, Adonai is One." Jews acknowledged this recitation as the essential doxology (faith statement) of Judaism."[916]

Stephanie comments:

Yes, but! While we say it, we make the shape of the letter Shin on our forehead and eyes with our right hand. Shin stands for "Shaddai," the name for our nurturing Goddess! Polytheism strikes again![917]

Since Judaism at this time was becoming more ritualistic, I feel it is important to give a more complete description of the Jewish worship protocol and ideology. It is my understanding that in the First Temple era there was no regular prayer service. Prayer was a part of sacrifice and was entered into when there were particular occasions of gratitude or great trouble.

"The biblical term for prayer was 'lifting up the hands'...The sages called prayer 'Tefilah'...This word comes from a root meaning 'to make an account of oneself"...There were no books of daily prayer in Jesus' time...Every blessing began with these (six) words (in Hebrew): "Blessed are You, Adonai our God, ruler of the universe..."[918]

Strphanie comments:

They still do. The service of God was called Avodah...[which] means to do divine labor, to be literally a servant of God. This was accomplished through the sacrifices[by priests] that were offered in the Jerusalem Temple...[the priests] did not work the land for a living; they ate the sacrificial offerings of the Jewish people...Inside the Temple they tended the incense altar, the table of show-bread, and the menorah—the seven branched oil lamp. The inner room of the Temple, the

---

[916] Wylen, Stephen M., *The Jews in the Times of Jesus: An Introduction*, 82.
[917] Stephanie M.
[918] Wylen. Op cit., 86, 87.

Holy of Holies, was empty. It was the place where the invisible God of Israel resided on earth.[919]

The true name of G-d, what gentiles read today as Yaweh, is a four-letter name for which the pronunciation has been lost. In the times of the Temple, it was known only by the High Priest. Once a year, on Yom Kippur, he would go into the Holy of Holies and pronounce the Name. This was considered such a powerful magic, the true Name of G-d that he would go into the room with a rope tied around his waist so that if he fainted after uttering the Name, his fellow priests, who were not allowed inside the Holy of Holies, could pull him out.

"In the Second Temple Judaism there was a growing awareness of the importance of individual relationship with God...Relationship with God required more than the public performance of the rites which identified one with the Jewish community (sacrifice, Sabbath rest, purity immersion). It also required an inner turning to God, a devotion that was not visible to the community but made the worshiper known before God."[920]

"To Pharisees...the inner turning of the heart is of utmost importance. Performance of the law was necessary, but for many laws the mere observance did not fulfill the divine will. The law had to be fulfilled with kavannah—"intention," "directedness," "will."...Kavannah means fulfilling the law with all of one's will, without divided thoughts."[921]

"The High Priest, the ruler of the Jewish people, performed the most important sacred functions himself...A lower sacred caste, the Levites, performed secondary service like singing in the Temple choir and maintaining a guard at the gates....Jews believed that the God of Israel needed no food...The daily offerings confirmed the constancy of the relationship between God and God's people, Israel...Sacrifice was universal, but first century Jews were unique in the establishment of daily liturgical[repetitive] prayer."[922]

The synagogue was not spoken of in the early Old Testament. Yet, after the Jewish revolt there were over one hundred in Jerusalem.[923] They largely served as places of prayer, meetings and education; they even sometimes served as hostels. In the first century the synagogues were mostly for people to come and hear scholars read and interpret the scriptures. The Sabbath was very sacred to the Jews,

---

[919] In the First Temple the Ark of the Covenant was in the Holy of Holies, accompanied by the two cherubim. In the Second Temple the Holy of Holies stood alone.
[920] Wylen, Stephen M., *The Jews in the Times of Jesus: An Introduction*, 93.
[921] Ibid., 94.
[922] Ibid., 84-5.
[923] Jerusalem has been conquered over eighty times and destroyed eighteen separate times. DVD entitled "The Gates of Jerusalem" distributed by Questar, Inc.(QD3403)

but it took time for these readings of the scriptures to become a regular scheduled part of worship on that day.[924]

Stephen Wylen says:

Jews were extremely proud of their Sabbath...refrained from all work...from sundown Friday until sundown Saturday...did not travel about, carry items abroad, or light fires...did not buy or sell...The Essenes did not defecate on the Sabbath!...Sabbath was a day for joy. People ate their finest meal of the week and socialized with one another. Sabbath morning was spent in the synagogue, learning scripture.[925]

There is a Rabbinic list of 39 things it is forbidden to do on the Sabbath. We think that this list is actually a list of the things that were necessary for the building of the Arc of the Covenant, which was the work that people would have been doing at the time that the law to observe the Sabbath was given. So it includes things like tying knots, untying knots, separating threads, skinning a dear, etc. Interestingly, you are allowed to tie one knot/write one letter/etc – you are given an extra moment to remember that it is forbidden. When modern Jews do not use electricity or drive their cars on the Sabbath, what they are actually doing is not lighting fires; when you start your engine or flip a switch, you make a spark.[926]

The English words "clean" and "unclean" (referring to physical cleanliness), fall short in describing the Jewish practice of "ritual purity." Actually, "pure" and "impure" are also inappropriate terms. "A person or thing which was *tahor*—'ritually pure'—was suitable to enter the sacred precincts of the Temple, to approach the divine. A person or thing which was *tah-may*—'ritually impure,' could not come near to God and so could not enter the Temple precinct...Since everything touches everything ultimately, the attempt to remain in a state of ritual purity was a constant battle."[927] The word *tahor* was later replaced with the concept of something being *kosher*. In order to remove impurity it was necessary to undergo *mikvah*, a ritual bath using "living" water which was free flowing. Afterward, the person also washed his clothes and waited until evening when they would be

---

[924] "...Jesus' visit to his hometown is the first instance in recorded history of the custom of *Haftarah*—reading a selection from the Prophets that relates to the weekly Torah portion." Wylen, Stephen M., 87. Rabbi Weinstein says, "Some hold that this was instituted during the period of the Macabees because reading of the Torah was prohibited, consequently, a text from the prophets that paralleled the ideas in the Torah was read."
[925] Wylen, Stephen M. op cit., 88.
[926] Stephanie M.
[927] Wylen. Op cit., 88, 89.

considered pure or tahor. If the impurity involved death special rituals were required and this could mean a full week of purification rites.[928]

One well known practice in Judaism is the rite of circumcision. Bishop Spong makes this interesting speculation:

Women could lose their blood and not die; they could also produce a new life and, in the process, stop the menstrual flow. Men envied this power...men suffer from menstruation envy. Through the ages men have yearned to capture that female life power that enables women to bleed from their genitals and not die. That is, I believe, how circumcision entered the human and religious arena.[929]

Jewish men wore *tzitzit*, on the four corners of their skirts; but later the tzitzit were changed to the tallit, which is a kind of shawl that is to be worn only during worship. Also, they wore a headband called a *tefilin* which had four compartments for scriptures and there was also a matching armband. It is said that Jesus criticized some Jews who wore their *tefilin* all day in order to show off how pious they were.[930]

Stephanie adds:

Modern Orthodox Jewish men still wear the tzitzit at all times. However, we cannot fully observe that commandment, because we are commanded to dye one thread in each corner blue using a specific process that is lost to us.[931]

Every Jew voluntarily donated a half-shekel to the Temple each year. Farmers brought many offerings including "first-fruits, firstborn animals, a tithe (one tenth) of all produce, and a second tithe to be given to the poor or consumed in Jerusalem on a rotating schedule."[932]

How would Yeshua be viewed by first century Jews? Jewish scholar Bruce Chilton spculates:

Few in Nazareth could read, but everyone knew what Scripture said in their local targum: "No mamzer shall enter the congregation of the Lord" (Deuteronomy 23:3). A mamzer [a child of doubtful fatherhood] was, in effect, an untouchable—a status that continued for ten generations...[933]

Because Mary could not prove that she became pregnant by a known father, it was assumed that her pregnancy was the result of sexual

---

[928] Ibid., 88-9.
[929] Spong. *The Sins of Scripture*, 98.
[930] Wylen. Op cit. 91.
[931] Stephanie M.
[932] Wylen. Op cit., 91.
[933] Chilton, Bruce. op. cit., 14.

relations with someone forbidden. This could have been an incestuous relationship or even a union with someone outside the community. This term *mamzer,* as applied to Yeshua, is not exactly illegitimate as we might define it today (a child born out of wedlock); because Joseph publically accepted him and treated him as a son.[934] Chilton writes:

The term mamzer refers specifically to a child born of a prohibited sexual union, such as incest. The fundamental issue was not sex before marriage (which was broadly tolerated) but sex with the wrong person...Jesus was considered a mamzer, what the Mishnah at a slightly later period calls a shetuqi, or "silenced one", without a voice in the public congregations that regulated the social, political, and religious life of Israel (Deuteronomy 23:2).[935]

Appendix B

Jewish Mysticism

Webster's New World Dictionary gives us this definition of mysticism: "...belief in the possibility of attaining direct communion with God or knowledge of spiritual truths."

The Hebrew word for confession (*Vidui*) in Jewish thought is made directly to God... (*Dictionary of the Jewish Religion*)

With regard to the special and meaningful times we live in, Kabbalist, R. Shlomo Eliyashiv offers this description of the increased accessibility of Jewish mystical teachings:

What was forbidden to investigate and expound upon just yesterday becomes permissible today. Numerous matters whose awesome nature repelled one from even approaching in previous generations, behold, they are easily grasped today. This is because the gates of human understanding below have been opened up as a result of the steadily increasing flow of Divine revelations above."[936]

---

[934] Ibid., 13.
[935] Ibid.
[936] R. Shlomo Eliyashiv Leshem Sh'vo V'Achlamah, Chelek HaBi'urim, 21d. (my underline for emphasis)

He cites the following, coming from an unexpected yet highly authoritative source, R. Yisrael Salanter (1810-1883), the leader of the Musser Movement. He is said to have commented: "Prior to 1840 the study of the Kabbalah was a closed book to all but the initiated." He further adds:

> *Thus, from 1840 forwards, permission has been granted for those who truly desire to enter within. The Kabbalah is no <u>longer the private domain of the initiated masters</u>.*[937]

As I reflect on the words of the rabbi I am reminded of the ancient Peace Shield drawing that has been entrusted to me. Like the Peace Shield, the Torah has both the obvious information (which most Jews are familiar with from childhood), and also holds a more covert wisdom as well. The Torah (the Pentateuch, the Prophets and the Writings), and the Kabbalah, which is the mystical portion of Judaism, each exist side by side. Mystery is honored in Native life as well. Native Elders often suggested that if there was something in life that was not fully understood in the moment, it could be tucked away in a "mystery bag." The experience could be revisited at a later time when further knowledge might help one more fully understand.

As was explained earlier, Judaism preceded Christianity and Islam and was the soil in which both religions were rooted. It is predicted in the Kabbalah[938] that in the future Jerusalem will be "as a lantern onto the Nations of the World," and "Nations shall walk in your light'(Isaiah 60:3)." For Jews one of the purposes of the Nation of Israel is to be a *container* for all scientific and religious belief as well as the schools of mysticism. The Peace Shield is also a container of sorts. The Peace Shield Teacher often told me that in the Seventh Fire all spiritual truths are invited into the Peace Shield.

Some general comments about the study of Jewish Mysticism are necessary before we jump feet first into what can be a very unclear and mysterious aspect of Judaism.
- Orthodox Jewish mysticism is inseparably married to the outer form of Jewish practices. I have heard this external form of Judaism expressed as

---

[937] Leshem Sh'vo VeAchlamah, Sefer De'ah 1:5:4 (p. 76). (underline for emphasis)
[938] "In the Jewish mystical tradition of Kabbalah, the spiritual practice of interpretation called *midrash* begins with a study of the Hebrew letters themselves, which symbolize cosmic or universal patterns of energy." *The Hidden Gospel*, 35.

her[939] rituals, *her* prayer/meditations and *her* emphasis on the attainment of knowledge.[940]
- Using a physical analogy (physics), and applying it to the mystical, a living cell or a soul is really part of a greater whole; the body or the cosmos respectively. In Jewish theology, change that takes place within each man, woman and child is a process that is projected to spread to the world.
- The word Torah is of the female gender. The Torah is viewed to not only contain the design of all creation (including the past, present, and future), but also includes *her* verses, words, and even the letters. All of these are viewed by Jewish rabbis as the lens through which all reality is evolving—a sort of "womb" within all reality.
- The teachings of the Torah are meant to be seen in organic terms. Some parts were to be revealed only in "seed" form: not intended to sprout until conditions were right.
- Rabbinic discourse and opinions are to be realized in the context of heartfelt and even emotional exchanges. To discuss ones belief was both very personal as well as historical.
- One's past (and heritage), is to be honored and present within one's present state of being. Unlike the tendency within the spiritual traditions of the modern Western Hemisphere to debate what is the "ultimate" truth, Jewish traditions stressed seeking one's own interpretation of theology.
- Professor Kenneth Hanson, Ph. D. relates this about Jewish mystics:

The Jewish mystics organized their understanding of the workings of the universe into Four Worlds: The World of Knowing (Briyah), the World of Being (Atzilut), the World of Feeling (Yetzirah), and the World of Doing (Asiyah)…When we harmonize the four life forces—Knowing, Being, Feeling, and Doing—we get in touch not only with ourselves, but also with the marrow of the universe.[941]

Using a mechanical metaphor, this study is more about understanding what it means to keep a car motor running (gas, oil, water, etc.), or to drive it, than it is about having the expertise to examine each intricate part of the car. When working with myths and stories it is important to allow for feelings and intuition and not be overly analytical. Using a Jewish approach, I would like to present only a small sample of some of the Jewish mystical ideas as I presently understand them. Open your heart and really *feel* the story. Try not to *think* too much!

---

[939] I rather like the emphasis upon the feminine in Judaism, so I am utilizing the word "her."
[940] Stephanie M.
[941] Hanson, Kenneth, Ph.D. *Secrets from the Lost Bible*, ix, 5.

The Garden of Eden Story

This discussion is not intended to be a definitive study of the Jewish mystical teachings of the Garden of Eden story. I am however, confident that some spiritually significant information can be learned from our study. The following is my own interpretation of what has been shared with me by my Jewish sources.

The Garden of Eden in Jewish mystical tradition is considered to be both "real" and metaphorical—a reality within a realm of reality. It is spoken of as being like an allegory and is not to be taken literally. However, it contains subtle truths that can only be fully understood as one commits to an in-depth study. Be prepared for more puzzling statements in this multi-dimensional, mystical journey! I will tell the story within the context of Jewish mysticism from a layman's point of view. I anticipate that there may be dissenting opinions which may come later and add to my current knowledge. My own spiritual journey has been richly enhanced with even the most meager understandings that have come to me thus far. I trust the reader will be blessed as well.

We will begin with some descriptions of God or *Ain Sof*. All that exists; all that has been created; all that is; everything literally exists within the Divine Oneness. To the Absolute, this totality never changes; but for those in a specific reality this perception of reality is most difficult. For *Ain Sof*, there is no "otherness" period! Just as there is no "other", there is no "end." This is a non-dualistic reality that includes all realities. As it states in the Zohar,[942] at the heart of Jewish mystical teaching, "there is no place devoid of Him." There is nothing that intervenes and separates Oneness from Itself. Since God is all inclusive and all powerful, then Ain Sof doesn't have needs. If He has needs then Ain Sof isn't God. I will use "He" in some places to denote God because this is the reference commonly used in the resources I have studied. However, in reality all aspects of masculine and feminine are contained within Ain Sof.

Adam and Eve are also part of the God consciousness, not separate from it. In Jewish mysticism the name for Eve is "Chava."

---

[942] "Sefer Ha-Zohar (The Book of Radiance). Attributed to the Spanish Kabbalist Moses de Leon who died in 1305. Its source is ancient Midrashic works of the first centuries AD, written in Aramaic. Much of it is a mystical commentary on the Torah." *The Other Bible*, 736.

Adam and Chava are one. In this All-reality, they were not human as we are today. They were forms of divine, god-like consciousness acting within a very different framework of existence. Speaking of Adam, the Jewish mystics would say that everything was inside Adam: the minerals, plants, animals; all were within him. In addition, all of these are all still within us too. As a Native person I fully understand this perceptive. We speak of being connected and related to all—as if everything is a part of us personally. A Native Elder once commented to me that, "We are the universe." Within *Ain Sof* and this all inclusive dimension, all animals had the ability to speak on the level of humans today. Each part of the whole was in full communication with each other specifically and with the Absolute Oneness in particular. One must understand that this study assumes the awareness that there are multiple dimensions which are all part of *Ain Sof's* all-inclusive reality. So, the dimension that existed in the Garden was a completely different reality, which was not bound by our present laws of physics and logic.

What is spoken of as mankind's "fall from grace" (the fall of man), can be described in Jewish mystical terms as a *"collapse"* of realities. The dimensions (which include ALL), collapsed. Before this happened, all realities were united within the Great Unity. Using a cardboard box as a teaching tool, if we folded (or collapsed), the box it would appear to us as a line if we were viewing it from the side. It would be the **collapse** of a dimension, not necessarily the **disappearance** of that dimension. It is said that this collapse happened slowly, over eons of time.

Now, after this cave in, all reality has become fractured and this causes us to perceive it as separateness. The *Ain Sof*, in the Absolute mode is always in a state of perfection and cannot go beyond itself. But, the Absolute creates (brings from Itself), an opposing, and at the same time complementary, polarity; or we might say a duality. All that appears as separate is really one. It's two different aspects of the one *Ain Sof*—two parts of the same thing. Since Adam, first man/woman consciousness, is forever united with the Absolute consciousness, that means that an aspect of Divinity exists within part of a lower and more physical dimension. In Isaiah 63:9 we read: *"I* (God) *Am with him* (man) *in his affliction."* We can keep in mind that all knowledge, both the spiritual and the material, existed together within the Unity of the higher dimension.

Since the collapse, Oneness has chosen to appear in two different states—the "Divine perspective" and "our perspective." Jewish mysticism relates that with the appearance of another dimension, the database of all knowledge has split itself into "spiritual" and "material" planes of existence. This has led us into the experience of a historical conflict between religion and science.

Observing the Sefiroth (ten representations or reflections of God), we can see how all of the information contained in the whole is also in each piece; like a hologram. In other words, each one of the Sefiroth contains both its part and also the whole. Each Sefiroth has a virtue or ethical attribute. All the pieces are needed and necessary. In the Garden of Eden all knowledge was unified before reality got split into fractured pieces.

The Kabbalah teaches a step-down system, " that ten spheres of energy called *Sefiroth* emanate from *Ain Sof* [God] down to our realm...only seven *Sefiroth* are to be accessible to humans; three are inaccessible. Above these higher three *Sefiroth* are a number of steps leading to *Ain Sof.*"[943] It is the same with us. We are a part within the whole of God: always have been and always will be. Bringing the pieces together into an un-splintered perspective is the task of humanity. Adam and Eve were all part of the God consciousness, not separate. Adam and Eve are one. Since everything was within Adam, Eve, (or Chava), was the female part within Adam. Chava was drawn out to exist in this dimension and in all realities to be a separate being.

In the Garden of Eden story it is spoken that God set up Adam to be gone when Eve was speaking to the serpent, *Nachash.*[944] This snake and everything that crawls upon the Earth has meaning, because Torah is code; all important; every detail. Nahash was king over all animals, and was between Adam and other animals. He became envious of Adam and Chava and desired the woman.

The Tree of Knowledge and the Tree of Life are the same tree. There are three stages involved in the eating of the fruit of the tree. Each one corresponds to parts of the physical body. First is *Keter* (thought), the second is *Daht* (throat), and the third is *Gasot/mahoat* (sexuality). In Native terms, everything that is in the physical realm also has a corresponding presence in the spiritual realm. So, when the

---

[943] Sheinkin. Op. cit., 39-40, 54.
[944] "...often translated as 'serpent'..." Sheinkin, op. cit., 193.

fruit is "eaten," in our physical experience we first have the thought of it and then we take it into our mouth and throat and finally we have pleasure from the experience. In fact, in both Hebrew (*hokman*) and Latin (*sapere, sapientia*) the word for wisdom means "to taste!"[945] "Taste and see the Lord is good," says the Psalmist (34:8). Physical experiences also have a correlation with our spiritual experience.

When I sat with one of the rabbis who explained this to me, he told me that the Torah was not intended only to be read. It is more like the telling of historical events, a collection of stories and poetry. The Torah is a map of how things were before the collapse as well as how it will be when the original plan is restored. He said there is a "cosmic code" that brings meaning to what is experienced in this dimension, including understanding the Torah. Each word and each letter within the word has a numerical relevance that is part of this code and brings deeper spiritual information when understood. The word "naked," when viewed this way really means *transparent*.

There is no sin in Judaism. It is more accurate to say that sin is "miscalculation." What took place in the Garden with both Adam and Chava was that they responded to a thought, passed what was eaten from the tree through them and experienced the pleasure of it; all in metaphoric terms. In Jewish mysticism food and knowledge can be synonyms for each other. To "eat" means to "know." There is a process involved in the consuming of information as it is passed through ourselves which can lead to knowledge and eventually to wisdom. However, the process has a particular order to it that must be followed if the results are to be maximized. The "miscalculation" of Adam and Chava was to shortcut the order of the process. As I understand the Garden of Eden story, there was no sinful action, but only a choice that was made. In some of their actions in the Garden, the humans were out of harmony with the natural order that governs the integration of knowledge. In Native spirituality there is a similar concept that the Creator has a plan and there is an overall process to the unfolding of creation. The Peace Shield, like the Kabbalah, contains the process in which to digest the concepts that are offered in the teachings. As you take in the information I present in this material, you too will be involved in a process of digesting it and taking what nourishes your soul. You can then determine if it brings knowledge.

---

[945]Fox, Matthew. *The Coming of the Cosmic Christ*, 26.

As you integrate your understanding of it into your life, it can become wisdom for you.

Back to the Jewish mystical perspective--God is NOT an authoritarian! The Absolute Oneness is giving advice here. He was warning Adam of the consequences of disregarding the process (the eating), of knowledge. You will "*die*," and "Don't do it!" are some of the expressions made. There is a structure (as represented in the Kabbalah, and in the Creator's Plan in Native American understandings), that must be respected here. Since there are no mistakes (sin), a choice was made that would bring about a consequence. As was articulated by the rabbi, "Adam couldn't wait! He tried to hurry up the process!" A part of the modus operandi of the three stages of the eating of the fruit is *Gasot/mahoat*, or the sexual component. It could also be seen as the passion or pleasure derived from the process. There is not the angst and guilt in Judaism that is found in many Christian traditions around the subject of sexuality. In the Jewish mystical teachings there is a respect and reverence for the experience of sexuality as a reflection of our relationship with the Divine, and our relationships with the human reflections of the Divine.[946] In Hebrew teachings the body is not evil. It is mixed up with evil in some way, but separate. Like a virus, evil needs a "host" to do anything. If that host chooses not to make an opening for evil then that host can't be called "evil" because it is *a part of* the Divine.

As Absolute Oneness spoke, "death" (whatever that means), was brought from within All Realty to this lower dimension. What happens after death? Some Jewish mystics would say that the body goes into the ground and 99.9 % of the soul goes back to *Ain Sof*. The other .01 % remains as a holographic fractal. Vapors of the bone stay until resurrection when all will be reconstructed. These "vapors" will become meaningful later as we touch on holography.

In the *Gospel of Philip* it is written: "Light and darkness, life and death, right and left, are brothers of one another. They are inseparable. Because of this neither is the good, good; nor the evil,

---

[946] Stephanie gives this response: "Christians read the creation story as saying that Adam and Eve did not have sex until after they had been kicked out of the Garden. This is a mistranslation due to a poor understanding of Biblical Hebrew grammar. It does not read "and Adam knew Eve," but rather, "and Adam *had known* Eve," an unusual construction at that point in the story. From this we learn that Eve conceived Cain while still in the Garden."

evil; nor is life, life; nor death, death. For this reason each one will dissolve into its earliest origin..." Death only exists in duality. Perhaps its earliest origin has something to do with the Totality. Since everything is within the ALL, what can be called "death" can only be properly described in this present reality or dimension.

There are similar views about death among the many teachers of Jewish mysticism. One opinion is reflected in the words of an observer after attending a funeral conducted by one of America's most prominent Conservative rabbis:

At the grave site, the rabbi commented, "Judaism does not believe in a life after death. Rather, we live on in the good works we do and in the memories of those we leave behind.[947]

Remember the example of the "collapsed box." The dimensions that collapsed are *still present*. We see the collapsed dimensions as a simple line, like a dime flat on a table. If seen in all three dimensions, it has horizontal and vertical properties as well as depth. In the collapsed condition (which still exists), we experience it as a line, if we perceive it or experience it at all. These Jewish teachings say that our former existence in the Garden (in another dimension), still exists! Once we have seen the dime in all of its dimensionality, we are able to know what it is like, even if we are seeing it from the side, lying on the table or if we are no longer looking at it. We remember what its reality is. Similarly, there are rare spiritual occasions when we actually are able to glimpse that previous intact Totality today. Through meditation, having a "mountain-top experience," or some other experience that transcends this reality, we are sometimes aware of our existence within the One Reality. Most of us are not conscience of its existence while going about our everyday life. Even most Native people have lost the ability to perceive it. But, once we have had such an experience, we know that it is real and we no longer doubt its existence. At times, we are able to recall how that felt.

In summary, Adam, first Man/Woman, made a miscalculated choice to rush the process of "eating" knowledge. This caused the collapse of dimensions. *Ain Sof* brought forth another aspect of Itself to allow the digestion of Life (knowledge), to occur. Before the collapse all was within the One. It still is, but we perceive it not to be so. Humanity can experience, on rare occasions, being present within the

---

[947] Prager, Denns. *Is This Life All There Is? Ultimate Issues*, Spring 1987, 2.

Oneness. The Garden of Eden dimension is always very near and present. Our journey here in this reality is to perceive what is called "death." Everything we do in life is part of *reconnecting* with the Oneness that already exists. Another way to speak of this as our spiritual journey is to go deeper inside Self. We are within God.

From the Native perspective we don't just go into God as one mashed together entity! Within nature, even though everything is part of the natural creation, each entity is revered and holds an individual sacredness. In mystical philosophy, it is always a multitude of fractal parts that make up the whole. Each individual spirit, like each Sefiroth, holds the essence of the whole and also maintains its' individual *part* of the whole. What was experienced as separate never was separate. When the Tree of Life is mended, that which made us feel separate from the Whole will no longer exist. What will be missing is what separates us now. Whew! You made it through!

* * * * * * * * * * * * *

Let's take a breath and look at the experience of "Exodus" within the context of Jewish mysticism. According to the tradition, those Israelites who were brought out of Egypt by Moses collectively experienced the "death" of their former condition of slavery and were "resurrected" into a new condition of greater understanding of the cosmic code.

From Stephanie:

> *...we are taught that we were all present at Mount Sinai. This comes up every year during the observance of Passover; we are asked to be thankful for the exodus from Egypt and the giving of the Torah as ones who were present at the time. This can be viewed as preexistence of the soul and mystical presence at the Mount, or as evidence of a Jewish belief in reincarnation.*

Religious historian Geza Vermes says that "Resurrection first appears in the Hebrew Bible as a metaphor, symbolizing the rebirth of the nation of Israel."[948] Jewish mystical tradition teaches that the genetic bloodline of each soul was *altered*, permanently changing this nomadic

---

[948] Vermes, Geza, *A Matter of Faith*, U.S. News & World Report, (Special Edition, *Secrets of the Bible*, copyright 2008), 67.

community into a singular and collective archetype—the newly born Nation of Israel.[949]

The Torah is a map of how it was before and after the collapse. Israel is said to be "chosen" to carry the knowledge of how to reverse the process. Rabbis have been keeping the maps throughout time and trying to repair The Fall (collapse). Abraham, Noah, Jacob, and Isaac all had maps. King David also had maps. However, he made miscalculations with these maps, so to speak, in his arrogance.

Referring to the notes I took during my visits with several rabbis, the idea of a chosen people is just a projection of the Christian, hierarchal, Western mind. What it really means to be chosen is *to carry the map*. The map helps us to make sense of reality; to bring together all people and to bring all of the individual parts of reality back into Unity. This is called "resurrection." Another way of interpreting being chosen is being the *background* of the puzzle; to make sense of the process and to bring together all pieces into the whole.

The Jewish nation is to help direct the return, or resurrection, from the contraction that has occurred. All peoples, plants, and energies are represented in the map. We are part of the larger reality, but are only aware of it infrequently. You are where you *think* you are. If you think you are separate, you are. If you think you are part of the Whole, then that's the reality you find yourself in.

The Role of Technology and Judaism

In the thirteenth century, a revelation was recorded in the Zohar[950] which predicts that in the year 1840 the gates of wisdom from above and the wellspring of wisdom from below will open up and usher in the next stage of evolution. Wisdom from above (the Kabbalah), and wisdom from below (technology/science), together will empower messianic consciousness and give us greater understanding. Jewish prophecy foretold of a time when technology would help us understand how to reconnect the parts of the whole. Let's take a look at the technology of the hologram. A hologram is an optical storage

---

[949] Stephanie M.
[950] *Zohar: The Book of Enlightenment*, translated by Daniel Chanan Matt.

system.[951] This modern-day technology is a method of recording, and then reproducing, a complete image of a three-dimensional object. The theory was developed by a Hungarian Jew, Dennis Gabor in 1948, for which he was awarded a Nobel Prize. Amazingly, if you take a holographic photograph of a small animal and cut one section out of it, say the foot, and then enlarge that section to the original size, you get not only a large foot, but a picture of the whole animal! The part (in Hebrew, the *prat*) is in the whole (the *klal*), and the whole is in each part.

Earlier, we mentioned that the "vapors of the bones stay until resurrection." Now we have some understanding that the part of the body that is in the ground will be reconstructed or reunited with the soul at resurrection. The process of this coming together will be speeding up and at some point it will have a life of its own. This dimension will take on not only three dimensional properties, but it will also reconstruct itself to reveal its' totality. We are causing this to happen right now. Chaos will be part of the experience as we get closer to the birthing time.

I have learned that, for the Kabbalist, every act, word and thought is for the purpose of reconnecting the severed pieces within human consciousness. All are part of the redemption process. *Mitzvah,* used more as a verb, means the act of making it possible to reconnect the Absolute Oneness with His own displaced Self. All thoughts and experiences are part of the redemption process. We can delay the process or even make another choice with our miscalculations. Therefore, we need a map from outside—the Torah. Jewish born Stephanie speaks of "mending the vessel":

The Kabbalists talk of healing the world as "mending the vessel." This vessel was a mystical glass container in which all the good (or possibly evil, I don't remember which) of the world was housed. It was broken at some point, and every time a Jew performs a mitzvah (meaning fulfills a commandment, not does a good deed), another piece of the vessel is mystically made whole with the rest. So when Kabbalists fulfill commandments, they see themselves as mending the vessel.

When the tools of technology and science are reconnected with spirituality, they can help us redirect their application from destructive

---

[951] The following comes from my understanding of explanations given by a rabbi whom I interviewed.

uses toward facilitating our interconnection with all of the creation. This new wisdom is to be shared with all.

Appendix C
The Jesus Seminars

The Fellows of the Jesus Seminar are Biblical scholars who have been trained in the best universities in North America and Europe. They came together to inventory all of the surviving ancient texts, searching for words that could accurately be attributed to Jesus. They then examined all of those words in the several ancient languages in which they have been preserved. William Bramley comments on the process:

...the Gospel of Thomas was rejected even though modern scholarship [i.e. the Jesus Seminar] attributes as many authentic sayings of Jesus to this Gospel as to any of the four Gospels which were chosen as canon.[952]

He continues:

The sayings of Jesus from the Gospel of Thomas have been highly rated by the Jesus Seminar...The work of this Seminar, the methodology they use and the difficulty which they have had in communicating their results to the public is documented in Mack's book,[953] *starting on page 193.*[954]

"They produced a translation of all the gospels, known as the **Scholars Version.** And finally, they studied, debated, and voted on each of the more than 1,500 sayings of Jesus in the inventory...a six-year process."[955] Each saying attributed to Jesus is color-coded and presented in a completely new translation of the Greek and Coptic texts. In the judgment of the Jesus Seminar:

---

[952] Bramley. op. cit., 81.
[953] Mack. *The Lost Gospel: The Book of Q & Christian Origins.*
[954] Bramley. op. cit., 327.
[955] *The Five Gospels: The Search for the Authentic Words of Jesus*, ix.

- *"only those sayings that appear in RED type are considered by the Seminar to be close to what Jesus said"*;
- *" the words in pink less certainly originated with Jesus..."* or were more likely to have been modified in transmission;
- *"The words in gray are not his, though they contain ideas that are close to his own"*;
- *The sayings in BLACK "...have been embellished or created by his followers, or borrowed from common lore", words that were given to Jesus to speak by his admirers (or, in a few cases, by his enemies), and are therefore inauthentic words of Jesus.*[956]

The Book that came out of the work of the Jesus Seminar is entitled: <u>The Five Gospels: The Search for the Authentic Words of Jesus</u>. It should be remembered that those who first encountered the gospels did so as "listeners" rather than as readers. "The Scholars Version is based on the ancient languages, in which the gospels were written or into which they were translated at an early date: Greek, Coptic, Latin, and other exotic tongues...The Scholars Version is free of ecclesiastical and religious control...not bound by the dictates of church councils, its contents and organization vary from Traditional bibles...The Gospel of Thomas has survived in full form only in Coptic, though its original language was Greek..."[957]

The Five Gospels contains the *Gospel of Thomas* in addition to the four canonical gospels. Because scholars believe the Gospel of Mark was written first, they have placed it first among the five. The Scholars Version is authorized by world renowned scholars. According to the Seminar, of the "...more than 1500 sayings attributed to him...**no more than 20 percent of the sayings attributed to Jesus were uttered by him.**"[958] Remarkably, there are no red-flagged sayings in the whole of St. John's gospel!

Let's list some of the **"red lettered" sayings** from the four gospels that are suggested by the Jesus Seminar scholars. Remember, these are selected[959] because of being most likely spoken by Jesus; all others are not as likely to have been what Jesus said:

---

[956] Ibid. ,from the dust jacket.
[957] Ibid. *xviii*.
[958] Ibid. (From the dust jacket).
[959] Taken from *The Scholars Version* in The Five Gospels: The Search for the Authentic Words of Jesus.

Matthew 5:39-41 "...Don't react violently against the one who is evil: when someone slaps you on the right cheek, turn the other as well. When someone wants to sue you for your shirt, let that person have your coat along with it. Further, when anyone conscripts you for one mile, go an extra mile. Give to one who begs from you; and don't turn away the one who tries to borrow from you."

Matthew 5:43 "Love your enemies."

Matthew 13:33 "...Heaven's imperial rule is like leaven which a woman took and concealed in fifty pounds of flour until it was all leavened."

Matthew 20:1-15, The story of the "vineyard laborers"

Luke 6:20-21,, "...Congratulations, you poor! God's domain belongs to you. Congratulations, you hungry! You will have a feast. Congratulations, you who weep now! You will laugh.

Luke 10:30-35, The story of the "good Samaritan"

Luke 16:1-8, The story of the "shrewd manager"

Luke 20:25 "...Then pay the emperor what belongs to the emperor, and God what belongs to God."

This represents all of the sayings of Jesus in all of the four gospels! Some of these sayings were repeated in other gospels. The Jesus Seminar is as project of the Westar Institute. To learn more about the Westar Institute, please contact:

The Westar Institute
POBox 6144
Santa Rosa, CA
707-523-1323

Appendix D

Recent Events: Writings, Movies and Resources to Consider

In this section I want to touch upon some of the vast cache of published materials and media presentations that have been available to the general public recently. I have to believe that there might be, if you will, some divine intervention here! These stirrings remind me of what I often refer to as, "the ancient Elders and Mother Earth speaking to us from the dust of the land." That which has been pushed away from spiritual consideration will ultimately make its way back. The wisdom of the past will come back in a powerful way, serving even more people than it served originally.

Let's walk through some of the information that has peaked the interest of many who are exploring the Christian journey. Keep in mind that some of these offerings will represent extreme positions. Yet, I believe they could potentially hold pieces of an enormous puzzle that could take years to complete. The March/April, 2000 issue of the Biblical Archaeology Review, contains an article entitled "The Search for History in the Bible," which reports on a conference of mainstream academics in the field of biblical archeological research. The focus of the conference was to discuss the historical origins of Jewish history. The article states that, "No one at the conference argued that he had any archaeological evidence of an Israelite presence in Egypt. Nor did anyone argue that he had archaeological evidence of an Israelite Exodus from Egypt." Today there is heated debate between "minimalists" and "maximalists" about how much history the Bible contains.[960] Another researcher, Kenneth Davis, writes about this supposed event:

***Elaborate court records survive of many of the Pharaohs before and after the presumed time of Joseph. But none of them mentions a Semite slave becoming a high official who had translated the Pharaoh's dreams and helped save Egypt in a time of extraordinary famine.*[961]**

In the last few years I have begun to mention some of these various texts, opinions, findings, etc. in my classes. I have found that few people I encounter have had any awareness of some of the information that I was presenting until recently. It is controversial to be sure, but I believe the information has enough elements of truth that it warrants attention and further exploration.

There have been many authors who have approached the subject of the changes that have occurred in the original understandings of the teachings of Jesus.

---

[960] Davies, Philip. *What Separates a Minimalist from a Maximalist? Not Much.* An article from Biblical Archaeology, March/April 2000, Vol. 26, No.2. 22-27.
[961] Davis, Kenneth. Op. cit., 91.

This is meant to be a brief sampling of what is available in the literature of today concerning how the representation of Jesus' life and teachings has evolved from the time when he lived to the present day. I give my gratitude for the authors I will refer to for having made a valiant attempt to bring this information to the general public. Until recently, the effort has not grown many roots. Now, however, it is becoming a topic of much interest in many quarters.

In this study we find at the top of the list of "outside the box" published materials, a publication entitled *The Unknown Life of Christ*. Political writer and traveler Nicolas Notovitch published the book in 1894 in France. Notovitch claims to have seen very old writings about Issa[962] (a name given to Jesus in the Far East), in ancient "Buddhist volumes located at the Hemis monastery in the Ladakh region of the Himalayas."[963] These records were not originals but "...compilations of older writings that had been penned only three or four years after Christ's cucifixion by Indian merchants who were returning to India from Palestine..."[964]

Elizabeth Clare Prophet has written about what the Buddhist texts record of Jesus in the Far East, specifically that he spent six years at Juggernaut,[965] India. He came into a conflict with "the Brahmins and Kshatriyas (the priestly and warrior castes), for teaching the Holy Scriptures to the lower castes. His enemies plotted to kill him. He left Juggernaut by night and went to the foothills of the Himalayas..."[966] To view more about Issa and to hear from some of the debunkers of this information, check out her book (see the footnote provided).[967] A strong verification came in 1922 when Swami Abhedananda of India made his own journey to view the Jesus passages. He became interested after reading about "St. Issa" in one of Notovitch's books. He, in turn wrote his own book, *Journey Into Kashmir and Tibet* and his translations are nearly identical to Notovitch's.

The following book review is from authors Baigent, Leigh and Lincoln:

"...in 1863 the French writer Ernest Benan caused a major international controversy with his celebrated bestseller The Life of Jesus. This work, which sought to strip Christianity of its supernatural trappings and present Jesus as 'an incomparable man', was perhaps the single most talked-about book of its age. Its impact on the public was enormous; and among the figures it most deeply influenced was Albert Schweitzer... [A] generation of Modernists... had begun to appear in the last quarter of the nineteenth century... And the majority of Modernists...were working within the framework of the church--until, that is, they were officially condemned by Pope Pius X in 1907 and an anti-Modernist oath was introduced in 1910...both German biblical scholarship and the Roman Catholic

---

[962] "Issa" is apparently based on either the Greek name for Jesus ("Iesous") or the Roman variation ("Iesus")." Bramley. op. cit., 135.
[963] Ibid.
[964] Ibid.
[965] John Pratt, "I would use the word Puri, India."
[966] Prophet, Elizabeth Clare. *Mary Magdalene and the Divine Feminine,* 33.
[967] Ibid., 136-141.

Modernists had begun to find their way into the arts. Thus, in 1916, the Anglo-Irish novelist George Moore published his own fictionalized account of Jesus in The Brook Kerith...depicting Jesus as surviving the Crucifixion[968] and being nursed back to health by Joseph of Arimathea."[969]

Biblical experts still disagree about what the real words spoken by Jesus are. Church historian Joachim Jeremias courageously wrote *The Unknown Words of Jesus* (*Unbekannte Jesus-Worte*) in 1957. In his work he claims to have identified only a mere twenty-one quotations which can definitely be attributed to Jesus. Another theologian, Rudolf Bultman, wrote, "The character of Jesus, the clear picture of his personality and life, have faded beyond recognition."[970]

Other fictionalized accounts of the gospel stories have been published. In 1946, Robert Graves published *King Jesus,* in which Jesus again survives the Cross. And in 1954, Nikos Kazantzakis the Noble Prize-winning Greek author, caused an international rumpus with *The Last Temptation*. In contrast to Moore and Graves, Jesus does die on the Cross. Kazantzakis writes:

But before he does so, however, he has a vision of what his life should and would have been like had he not voluntarily submitted himself to his final sacrifice. In this vision--a kind of "flash forward" in fantasy--Jesus sees himself married[971] to the Magdalene (for whom he has lusted all through the book) and fathering a family upon her.[972]

Gardner writes of the information from the Nag Hammadi scrolls: "they describe a world in which Jesus gives his own account of the Crucifixion,[973] and in which his relationship with Mary Magdalene reaches enlightening new proportions."[974] From *The Messianic Legacy* we read:

---

[968] In Gnostic literature (*Acts of John*) "...the Christ reveals to...Apostle that it was only in appearance that he had undergone the Crucifixion;..." Doresse, op. cit., 95.

[969] Baigent, Leigh and Lincoln. *The Messianic Legacy,* 3.

[970] Kersten. Op. cit., 27.

[971] See Luke 10:38-42. Martha asks Jesus to order her sister, Mary [Magdalene], to assist her with kitchen chores. "Martha understood that in Jewish society a woman's husband had the power to command and the wife had the duty to obey...This passage suggests that Jesus had a wife, a fact that apparently was once acknowledged! This is a hint that did not get repressed by biblical redactors." Spong, *The Sins of Scripture*, 106.

[972] Baigent, Leigh and Lincoln. *The Messianic Legacy*, 3,4.

[973] "The Islamic Koran (chapter 4, entitled Women) specifies that Jesus did not die on the cross, stating: 'Yet they slew him not, neither crucified him, but he was represented by one in his likeness...They did not really kill him'." Gardner, op. cit., 68.

[974] Gardner, 19. Also, an early Coptic tractate called *The Second Treatise of the Great Seth*, claimed that, "...there was a substitution made for at least one of the three victims of the Crucifixion." "Jesus is himself quoted as saying after the event, 'As for

The Passover Plot (1963) by Dr. Hugh Schonfield argued that Jesus staged his own mock crucifixion and did not die on the Cross; the book became an international bestseller, with more than three million copies now in print. More recently, controversy was provoked by Jesus the Magician, in which Dr. Morton Smith depicts his protagonist as a typical wonder-worker of the age...[975] *...On a theological level, a number of Anglican clerics provoked considerable controversy by questioning Jesus' divinity in a collection of essays, The Myth of God Incarnate.*[976]

The image of Jesus choosing Mary Magdalene as his especially beloved disciple runs through a large Gnostic work called the *Pistis Sophia,* which was available in a popular English translation as far back as 1896.[977] Another important book, *The Gnostic Gospels* by Elaine Pagels, came out in 1979. It has had a wide readership and has attracted quite a bit of attention among biblical scholars and the public alike. It is a study of the Nag Hammadi Scrolls, discovered in Egypt in 1945. The discovery of this material has opened up new research and has led to some radical new interpretations of Christian teachings and traditions.[978]

As you probably are aware, a number of movies have attempted to add to the growing discourse surrounding Jesus' life. *The Last Temptation of Christ, Jesus Christ: Super Star,* and the very graphic but perhaps telling movie *Stigmata* are just a few presentations that suggest that there is more to the story than we had thought. The authors of *The Messianic Legacy* list some of the new books have appeared since 1982. "In 1983, *Illusionist,* a novel by Anita Mason, offered a controversial, but historically valid perspective on the coalescence of the early Church. In 1985, Anthony Burgess…explored much the same territory in *The Kingdom of the Wicked."* Michele Roberts wrote a novel entitled, *The Wild Girl* which uses evidence in the Nag Hammadi Scrolls and "…depicts Mary Magdalene as Jesus' lover and as the mother of his child."[979] I would add another movie called *The Body* to the list. Set in present-day Bible lands, this well-produced movie depicts the dramatic reactions of the Palestinians, the Israelis, and the Catholic Church when the actual bones of Jesus are discovered in a lower chamber of a merchants shop in the Bible lands. In recent years the history channel has aired many presentations with differing views surrounding the events and the biblical facts of Jesus' life. Often controversial points of view as well as the accepted biblical story are presented side by side for people to consider.

The latest movie "*The Passion of Christ*" presents a very graphic depiction of the final days of Jesus. Given an "R" rating for its graphic violence, it contains

---

my death—which was real enough to them—it was real to them because of their own incomprehension and blindness'." Gardner, 68.

[975] Ibid., 4.
[976] Ibid., 20.
[977] Mead, G.R.S., ed. *Pistis Sophia: A Gnostic Miscellany* (1896; London: J. M. Watkins, 1921).
[978] Ibid., 5.
[979] Ibid., 21.

added scenes that are not recorded in the gospels, even though it claims to be a very conservative and accurate account of the gospel stories. Dan Brown's book "the Di Vinci Code" has created some polarizing within the Christian community. Like those I have already mentioned, it is the fictional story of secret societies that purported have hidden the knowledge that Jesus and Mary Magdalene[980] were married and had children. It claims that the great artist Di Vinci embedded a code into his famous painting of "The Last Supper" that reveals his belief in this controversial theme.

    I am aware that there were unmarried rabbis in Jewish traditions around Jesus' time. Any writings that a rabbi produced would have had to be signed in such a way as to indicate that they were unmarried. It was normal in the society at the time for a male of his age to be married. Since it was not mentioned in the scriptures that Jesus was **not** married (as it is mentioned of Paul), then he could have been married.[981] At the time of Jesus, the Pharisees, one of the major groups within Judaism in the first century A.D., insisted that "it was a man's unconditional duty to marry."[982]

    None of this discussion affects my admiration and gratitude for the teachings of Jesus. Reflecting upon Native American philosophy, this would mean an even greater appreciation of Jesus for being able to walk a balanced life within his vision of bringing a new form of spirituality to the people. He walked upstream against the current of the prevailing social and religious laws, knowing how his teachings and actions could put his life in jeopardy. Yet, he remained true to his vision and that is most honorable in my view.

    The most famous source of ancient texts known by most Christian believers is, of course, the Dead Sea Scrolls, discovered in 1947 in the ruins of the Essene community of Qumran. My research indicates that most seminary students who prepare for the ministry today will learn at least something of the Dead Sea Scrolls, the Nag Hammadi Scrolls and the controversial theological scholarship reflecting the history and evolution of New Testament studies. In my conversations with seminary students twenty years ago, I became aware that many of the issues I just discussed were typical and accepted discourse around the dinner table, even back then. At that time I was seriously appalled, and could not imagine these things to be true. Recalling the Bible lessons from my childhood and my adult Christian education, I simply had no room for this information. It did, however peak my curiosity! My question is now, why has there been little or no dissemination of this new knowledge related to the story of Christ and Christianity within church settings such as Bible classes and sermons from the pulpit? If this knowledge was an important part of the curriculum of seminary students why has it not been passed on to the public?
Let's look at some of these widely distributed magazines:

--*Time*, ran a recent cover story on Heaven, entitled Does Heaven Exist? "...a question our ancient Forebearers would never have raised." March 24, 1997.

---

[980] Martin Luther thought that Jesus and Mary Magdalene may have been a couple. CNN Presents, *The Two Marys*.
[981] "Martin Luther believed that Jesus and Magdalene were married, as did Mormon patriarch Brigham Young." *Time* magazine, August 11, 2003.
[982] Ranke-Heinemann. *Eunuchs for the Kingdom of Heaven*, 40.

--*Newsweek,* March 29, 1999, pp. 52-65, Kenneth L. Woodward, "2000 Years of Jesus."
--*Atlantic Monthly,* Dec. 1992, pp. 51-68, Charlotte Allen, "The Search for a No-Frills Jesus."
--*GQ,* June 1994, pp.116-23, Russel Shorto, "Cross Fire."
--*Atlantic Monthly,* Aug. 1993, pp. 39-64, Cullen Murphy, "Women and the Bible."
--*U.S. News & World Report,* Nov. 8, 1993, pp. 75, Jeffery L. Sheler, "Cutting Loose the Holy Canon[983]."
--*Time,* Aug. 15, 1988, pp. 37-42, R. N. Ostling, "Who Was Jesus?"
--A U.S. News poll shows that more Americans believe in hell today than did in the 1950s or even 10 years ago. But like the Pope, most now think of hell as "an anguished state of existence" rather than as a real place. A full front cover display entitled: Hell: A new version of the netherworld.[984]

--"Is the Bible True?" The front cover of U. S. News & World Report, October 25, 1999. "As early as the fifth century, the great Christian theologian Augustine warned against taking the six days of Genesis[985] literally; these were not successive days, he said. Most biblical scholars consider the story of the Flood[986] a myth; archaeologists have found no direct evidence to corroborate the dramatic story of the Exodus. Inscriptions from ancient Egypt contain no mention of Hebrew slaves, of the plagues, or of the destruction of the pharaoh's army during the Israelites' miraculous crossing of the Red Sea.[987] There is not even any indication, outside of the Bible, that Moses existed."[988]

--*Newsweek,* February 11, 2002. "The Bible and the Qur'an: Searching the Holy Books for Roots of Conflict & Seeds of Reconciliation." "Both the Qur'an and the Bible tell the story of Adam and Eve[989] in the Garden of Eden.[990] But for Muslims,

---

[983]"...[from the Greek *kanon,* literally meaning 'cane used as a measuring rod' or loosely translated as a 'rule' or a 'standard]."' Moore, *The Christian Conspiracy,* 34.
[984] U. S. News & World Report, January 31, 2000, 46.
[985] Dr. Errico, in his book *The Mysteries Of Creation: The Genesis Story* writes: "...the term beginning, to the Eastern author, puts emphasis on God's creative acts. It does not connote a beginning as we might attempt to understand it. Nor to the Semitic writer depicting God as First Cause. To him the universe was not caused, but created, by God. The universe is a constant happening—continual, endless creating. It is like a tree perpetually bearing fruit because of God's creative act.", 81.
[986] "...the Hebrew word for "earth" in Gen. 6:17 also means "land" or "country," which would suggest a much more limited flood." Kenneth Davis, op. cit., 62.
[987] Ibid. "There is plenty of evidence, even within the Bible, that many of the 'Children of Israel' were already well established in the 'Promise Land' before the Exodus from Egypt under Moses (see Exodus).", 85.
[988] U. S. News & World Report, October 25, 1999, 50-59.
[989] Adolphe Franck, in *The Kabbalah: The Religious Philosophy of the Hebrews,* relates: "Before they were beguiled by the subtleness of the serpent, Adam and Eve were not only exempt from the need of a body, but did not even have a body—that is to say, they were not of the earth." 130.

and for Jews, their 'original sin' of disobedience is not passed on to humankind, so they don't require salvation through the sacrifice of Jesus on the cross—a central doctrine of Christianity."[990]

--"In an episode of the TV show *The X-Files*, a forger produces a bogus '*Gospel of Mary Magdalen*,' which records a sexual relationship between Jesus and Mary. Convinced of the document's authenticity, a cardinal who is considered a likely candidate for the papacy purchases the supposed gospel in order to suppress it. Ultimately, the cardinal murders the forger."[992]

--January 31, 2000 U. S. News & World Report. "In an editorial in *La Civilta Cattolica*, an influential Jesuit magazine with close ties to the Vatican: **Hell 'is not a place but a state of being'** in which a person suffers from the deprivation of God. A few days later, Pope John Paul II told an audience at the Vatican that 'rather than a place, hell indicated the state of those who freely and definitively separate themselves from God.' The pontiff said, the Bible "uses a symbolical language" that "figuratively portrays in a 'pool of fire' those who exclude themselves from the book of life, thus meeting a second death."

--Another recent media presentation about the growing interest in Jesus research was *The Search of Jesus*, a prime-time ABC documentary hosted by Peter Jennings in 2000.

--**Time**, August 11, 2003, "Mary Magdalene: Saint or Sinner? A new wave of literature is cleaning up her reputation. How a woman of substance was 'harlotized.'"[993]

--December 8, 2003, **Newsweek**, Cover title: "Women of the Bible: How Their Stories Speak to Us Today, Mary Magdalene: Decoding 'The Di Vinci Code'."

--U.S. News & World Report (Special Edition) Feb 3, 2004. *Mysteries of Faith*.

Episcopal bishop of Newark, N.J., John Shelby Spong, advocates taking another look at scriptures in his book, *Why Christianity Must Change or Die*. He points out that we tend to romanticize the gospel accounts and many people are unaware that none of the gospels were written by eyewitnesses to the events.

Most believers, for example, have never been told that there are no camels in the biblical story of the wise men and no stable or stable animals in the story of

---

[990] "Much of what we know as the Old Testament (the Hebrew Bible) was first written down in Babylon. It is hardly surprising that Sumerian and Mesopotamian stories were grafted onto the early Jewish cultural tradition—including accounts of the Garden of Eden, the Flood, and the Tower of Babel...the fact remains that stories such as that of Adam and Eve were by no means restricted to Hebrew tradition." (Gardner, *Bloodline of the Holy Grail*, 15.

[991] *Newsweek*, February 11, 2002, 53.

[992] *Hidden Gospels*, 18-19.

[993] Note: "Three decades ago [1969], the Roman Catholic Church quietly admitted what critics had been saying for centuries: *Magdalene's standard image as a reformed prostitute is not supported by the text of the Bible*." 52. (date and bold lettering by author)

Jesus…They do not learn in church that the virgin birth accounts were not original to Christianity and did not appear in Christian history until the ninth decade.[994]

What we know today as the Bible is a translation of a translation of a translation. The Coptic[995] scrolls were hidden at Nag Hammadi in about A.D. 400 during a period in which the Orthodox Christian Church (having been declared the official church of the Roman Empire by the Emperor Theodsius), began persecuting and destroying the documents of sects it deemed heretical. The Coptic scrolls, many of which are second and third century parchments, predate any of the developed gospels by centuries! And, miraculously they survived the purge of the early Church, just as the Dead Sea scrolls of the Qumran community survived destruction by the Roman legions during the Jewish revolt of A.D. 66-74 when the Nation of Israel was virtually destroyed and the Christian community of Jerusalem was wiped out.[996]

We close this section with one more note about Jesus. Jesus' childhood and adolescence were scarcely mentioned at all in the known gospels. What we know today is that a person's early experiences are so important to understand their later life and legacy, yet we are given very little to go on. Writers and historians of his time and shortly thereafter seem to have no awareness of Jesus or they don't consider him worth mentioning.[997] In A.D. 66, Flavius Josephus, a foremost historian of the era, places Jesus "…firmly within the historical fabric of the time, but without any mention of his divinity…"[998]

Appendix E

Historical Notes and the Catholic Popes

Of course, it is mainly those who are Roman Catholic who look to the Pope as their spiritual figure, but I believe that the Pope's role over the history of Christianity reveals some data that would be of interest to Christians in general, and even to non Christians who revere Jesus and his teachings. I have had dreams of being visited by the Pope, even though I have never been a Catholic! This has aroused my curiosity about papal traditions. There seems to be a fair number of people who come to Native American classes who refer to themselves as "recovering Catholics." I am always pleased that they are interested, and I am often curious as to why they are looking to other spiritual circles to bring meaning to their lives.

---

[994] Spong. *Why Christianity Must Change or Die*, 72-73.
[995] "Coptic is a vernacular form of the Egyptian language, no longer written in hieroglyphs but by means of the Greek alphabet…Making us of this writing…the Christians of the Nile Valley produced an abundant literature." *The Secret Books of the Egyptian Gnostics*, 64.
[996] Starbird, Margaret. *The Woman with the Alabaster Jar*, 54.
[997] Kersten. op. cit., 22.
[998] Gardner. op. cit., 130.

I want to draw attention to some notes that I have come across as I have researched papal history. I have found some of the information to be interesting and somewhat mysterious. There's a variety of historical antidotes that, although sometimes disconnected, might be thought-provoking. Some of the actions of various popes have had a significant impact upon the times in which they reigned. This is certainly true of the Inquisition, the Crusades, the issuing of the Doctrine of Discovery (1452), and the Church's edicts over members of the clergy. However, I believe that most papal utterances throughout the history of the church have had little to do with the individual members of the Catholic faith. Like the train caboose attendant trying to steer the train, the stance of the Pope was often viewed with mixed degrees of importance. The same can be said today with regard to how the Pope's influence affects some Catholics.

There is a degree of mystery surrounding some papacies. Often, historical information about them surfaces little by little, over time. There has been extensive research done by other writers on the subject and I will not attempt to summarize it all here. I will merely present some of the information that has captured my own imagination and let you add more information from the sources that I list in the footnotes and the bibliography.

Pope John Paul II offered more apologies than any pope in history. In the *Chicago Tribune* (June 5, 1995), an article appeared declaring that Pope John Paul II had urged the Roman Catholic Church to take advantage of the "particularly propitious occasion of the new millennium to recognize the dark side of its history." In a 1994 confidential letter to cardinals which was later leaked to the Italian press, he asked:

***How can one remain silent about the many forms of violence perpetrated in the name of the faith—wars of religion, tribunals of the Inquisition and other forms of violations of the rights of persons?*[999]**

Are the apologies for previous historical actions attempts to admit that injustices and errors have been made in the name of the Church? I think so. What lies beneath the surface that prompts the need to apologize for past actions? Is there growing concern that some of the old writings and documents that have become widely available might lessen the influence and control of the Church and its place in peoples' hearts? How far can the strings of authority be stretched? Pope John Paul II visited places in the world that no other pope would consider going. For example he attended a Muslim Mosque for the first time. Why would that be historically meaningful?

I hold dear my memories of a couple of elderly women in Sweden who smiled as they proudly referred to themselves as "cafeteria Catholics." Similar experiences have convinced me that a lot of people within the major Christian denominations are starting to think for themselves. Within some of the elaborate worship centers the pews are often noticeably empty. I meet people nearly every day who are reaching for alternative ideas and practices in order to meet their spiritual needs. To my surprise, they have freely offered some of the information that I have gathered for this section of my book.

---

[999] Peggy Polk, Papal State, Chicago Tribune, June 5, 1995, Temp, 2.

I visited a Catholic Church in the late 1970's on a Native reservation that had built a hogan structure complete with a dirt floor inside the building! This was done for the benefit of the Navaho attendees who were used to a worship environment in which there were no corners, and to facilitate their connection with Mother Earth. I do not know whether it still exists today, but this was an attempt to provide the local indigenous people with some connection to their heritage. In my journeys within the United States I have seen Native American sweatlodges, sweetgrass and other cultural elements being included in worship services within otherwise traditional Christian settings; even convents. All of this appears to represent some openness on the part of a few denominations to some changes in their usually strict mode of worship.

Now let's begin to look at a brief summary and timeline of some of the information that I have gathered. I continue to look for more research and welcome input from others who have information and insights to share. I would not have decided to write this book if I had not gotten considerable encouragement from concerned and conscientious Christians over the years.

Historic Dates and Notations:

--(374-419) Saint Jerome translated the scriptures into Latin.

--The Third Ecumenical Council (431) proclaimed Mother Mary as the Mother of God.

--850 A.D. Holy water was introduced into the Roman Catholic Church.

--In 879 A.D. the Pope (Rome) and the Patriarch (Constantinople) excommunicate each other.

--In 1022 the first trial for witchcraft occurred in Orleans, France.

--In 1074 A.D. all married priests were excommunicated.

--In 1095 Pope Urban II called for a crusade at the Council of Clermont and "...promised [crusaders] full forgiveness of all their sins if they made the crusade to liberate the Holy City..."[1000]

--The Church ruled that all priests must be celibate[1001] which became a law in 1139 A.D.

--"In 1184, the Waldenses and the Cathars were declared heretical by Pope Lucius III and were excommunicated by the Church. Later a similar group, the Humiliati of northern Italy, was also excommunicated, primarily because

---

[1000] Starbird, *The Feminine Face of Christianity*, 62.

[1001] In 1139 the Roman Catholic Church forbade both marriage and sex for priests. Corinthians 9:5 lends credence to the idea that The Apostle Peter, the supposed founder of the Catholic Church and first Pope, "was certainly married and traveled about with his wife." Baigent, Michael, *The Jesus Papers*, 106-7. "St. Peter's walking on the water, was first achieved by a follower of Buddha. And in the same way as Peter begins to sink, as soon as his belief starts wavering." Kersten, op. cit., 77.

this group held religious meetings in their homes rather than attending church."[1002]

--The Eleventh Ecumenical Council in 1179 C.E. and the Twelfth [1215] issued proclamations that condemned the Jews for killing Jesus.

--1215 Pope Innocent III set a policy known as *"Nulla salus extra ecclesium"* (Outside the Church there is no salvation).

--In 1229 the Inquisition in Toulouse forbids Bible-reading by laymen.

--Pope Gregory IX brought the first Catholic Inquisition in 1231 A.D. and the Church condemned the "Grail lore."[1003] In 1233 he also established a permanent institution to suppress heresy.

-- During the Inquisition, the church burnt 12,000 volumes of the Talmud in an attempt to completely wipe out any Rabbinic information about Jesus.[1004]

--The powers of the pope's (Innocent IV) inquisitors were increased in 1252 A.D.[1005] in the form of a papal bull which permitted the use of torture in order to get a confession of heresy.

--In 1255 Pope Innocent IV gave the Inquisition the authority to declare all witches were practicing heretics.

--In 1302 A.D. a papal bull called "Unam sanctum" declared that the pope is supreme—"when he speaks *ex cathedra*, that is when in exercise of his office…he is infallible, i.e. he can make no mistake."[1006]

--Pope Innocent II created the Council of Basel (1431-49), basically calling for book burning.

--1452 .D. the "Doctrine of Discovery.

--In 1492 A.D. the Jews and Moors in Spain are ordered to convert, or be burned.

--In 1501 A.D. a Papal bull orders any book that questions the authority of the Church be burned.

--(The Reformation 1517 to present) Martin Luther posted "his memorable 'Ninety-five Theses' on the door of the castle church in Wittenburg."[1007]

--1542 A.D. Pope Paul III's Roman Inquisition against Protestants began.[1008]

--1554 Solomon Romano burnt thousands of Hebrew scrolls,

--1559 All Hebrew books in the city of Prague are confiscated.

[1002] Moore. *The Christian Conspiracy*, 103.

[1003] Gardner, op. cit., 204.

[1004] New Dawn Magazine. No 71, March 2002.

[1005] Ibid., 206.

[1006] De Rosa, Peter, *Vicars of Christ, The Dark Side of the Papacy*, 250.

[1007] Moore. *The Christian Conspiracy*, 115. Moore adds: "Through the Inquisition, through the system of Indulgences, and through a series of debilitating church taxes…the continually bankrupt Church had become corrupt. Through moral laxity such as clerical simony, nepotism, absenteeism and concubinage, the Church was becoming an open eyesore to the increasingly educated and literate laity…the Church simply had to be reformed."

[1008] Gardner. op. cit., 206.

--"Gian Pietro Caraffa, Bishop of Chieti who became Pope Paul IV in 1555...equipped his own home as a torture chamber at his own expense...established the Index of Forbidden Books...forbidden to be read by any Christian...until Pope Paul VI discontinued it in 1966.[1009]

--In 1569 the Inquisition arrived in both Mexico[1010] and Peru. Between 1519 and 1605 Indian population in Mexico declined from about twenty million to less than one million.[1011] "...in all of Latin America, fully 90% of the population, more than fifty million Native Americans, lost their lives during the first century following the introduction of the 'one true God'."[1012]

--On July 21, 1773 Pope Clement XIV "forever annulled and extinguished the Jesuit Order." Pope Pius VII in Aug. 1814 reinstated the Jesuits to all of their former rights and privileges.[1013]

--"Papal Infallibility" was proclaimed at the First Vatican Council in 1870 and stated, "The Pope is incapable of error when defining matters of Church teaching and morality from his throne!"[1014]

Vatican I council declared that since the Pope is supreme, "when he speaks *ex cathedra*, (when in exercise of his office) he is infallible and can make no mistakes."[1015]

--1854 The doctrine of the Immaculate Conception by Pope Pius IX decreed that Mary, the mother of Jesus, was conceived without Original Sin.

--1950s Pius XII defines Mary's Assumption into Heaven.[1016]

--The Twenty-First Ecumenical Council (1962-1965) often called Vatican II, Dr. Moore says, "has changed the Roman Catholic Church to such an extent that it will never again be uniform in its worldwide practices."...[it] repealed *xtra ecclesiam nulla salus* (no salvation outside of the Church) to "*All must be converted to Christ as He is made known by the Church's preaching.*"[1017]

-- 1963 In its *Nostra Aetate* document on the Jews, The Catholic Church noted that no one should be condemned for Jesus' death.[1018]

--1964 Pope Paul VI proclaims Mother Mary as Mother of the Church.

--In 1968 Pope Paul VI prohibits artificial contraception.

--In 1970 Pope Paul VI reaffirms the rule of priestly celibacy as a fundamental principle of the Roman Catholic Church.

--The late Pope John Paul II, in his encyclical *Redemptoris Mater*, ruled that Virgin Mary's hymen remained intact.[1019]

[1009] Moore. *The Christian Conspiracy*, 105.
[1010] "...the pyramid at Cuicuilco, Mexico, is evidently at least 2,500 years older than the earliest known Sumerian finds..." Acharya S, op. cit., 399.
[1011] *Encyclopedia Britannica*.
[1012] Moor. *The Christian Conspiracy*, 111.
[1013] Cooper, M. W., 91.
[1014] Ibid., 180.
[1015] Dowely, Tim, Editor. *The History of Christianity, A Lion Handbook*, 250.
[1016] Ibid., 179.
[1017] Moore. *The Christian Conspiracy*, 60, 117.
[1018] Wylen, Stephen M. op. cit., 124.

Appendix F

What's this about the Free Masons?

In my review of Roman Catholic history I have noticed some changing attitudes toward the Free Masons over time. You can decide for yourself whether to delve further into the research or not. It's important to get some background about the Freemason society. According to researcher William Bramley, Freemasonry (a.k.a. "Masonry") is often referred to as a "secret society," even though it has become less secret over time. It started out as a guild for construction workers and stone masons thousands of years ago, possibly even dating to the time of the building of Solomon's Temple. They differed from the unions of today in that they conducted mystical rites. Today, it is not usual for a large number of the members to be in the building trades. They still have metaphysical teachings and special initiation rites that are done in secret, but it is mostly a fraternal organization that supports the members' spiritual and philosophical growth. Members participate in social and charitable work. I have been very surprised at the number of documentaries that have come out about them in the last fifteen years.

Most Masons consider themselves to be Christians and believe in a Supreme Being that is referred to as "The Great Architect of the Universe." Bramley continues:

Essenes and Mandaeans had similarities to a mystical practice called Freemason. For example, today's Mandaeans use a special ritualistic handshake, initiations, and teachings that resemble Freemasonry. Josephus reveals that ancient Essenes gave their new candidates an apron as part of the acceptance process. Ritual aprons and step-by-step initiations are integral to Freemasonry.[1020]

The origins of Freemasonry are not clear, but it is commonly agreed upon that its roots go back to a period before ancient Egypt. The Masons themselves claim to have participated in the building of the Tower of Babel and Solomon's Temple. Jim Marrs writes that part this confusion over Freemasonry's origins was caused by the split between the Roman Catholic Church and the Protestant Church of England. Many records and Masonic libraries were destroyed during the associated wars and revolutions.[1021] Marrs further relates, "Freemasonry, the oldest and most powerful secret society in the history of the world, had planted firm roots in early-day America..."[1022] The writers of *Holy Blood, Holy Grail* write that the Merovingians, "...claimed descent from Noah, whom they regarded, even more than Moses, as the

---

[1019] *Eunuchs for the Kingdom of Heaven*, 347.
[1020] Bramley. op. cit., 101.
[1021] Jim Marrs. *Rule by Secrecy*, 244-245.
[1022] Ibid., 217.

source of all biblical wisdom...which surfaced again a thousand years later in European Freemasonry."[1023]

In the late Middle Ages one of the only organized groups that could travel widely in Europe was the guild of stone masons who had established "lodges" in the major cities. Other opponents of the Holy Roman (Catholic), Church were not allowed to openly meet. The Masons themselves believe that their secret knowledge of architecture, stone work and construction date back to Egypt[1024] and even farther. What we know is that their expertise was essential to the building of a vast number of churches and cathedrals in Europe.[1025] For example, the All-Seeing Eye symbol in Masonry is similar to the Eye of Horus found in Egypt and the symbolic apron that is part of their ceremonies can be seen in some of the ancient drawings of Egyptian gods.[1026]

As written in *"Holy Blood, Holy Grail,"* "In 1738 Pope Clement XII issued a papal bull condemning and excommunicating all Freemasons, whom he pronounced to be 'enemies of the Roman Church'."[1027] Any Catholic who becomes a Mason would be excommunicated.[1028] A letter published for the first time in 1962 and purported to be written by Pope Clement declares that Masonic philosophy is based on an older heresy: the denial of Jesus' divinity. The Pope goes on to assert that the same founders of Free Masonry also were responsible for inciting the Lutheran Reformation.[1029] I wonder what information the Masons were aware of that would bring them to speak against the divinity of Jesus?

In 1884 Pope Leo XIII issued a proclamation stating that Masonry was one of the secret societies that was attempting to, "revive the manners and customs of the pagans" and "establish Satan's Kingdom on Earth."[1030] What were these charges based on? The Masons are accused of promoting Satan's Kingdom! My intuition tells me that something is amiss here. My experiences with the Masons I know today would certainly contradict such accusations. Will we ever know the reasons for these statements?

During the short term of Pope John XXIII (1958-63) there was a revision in the Church's position on Freemasonry. It became permissible for a Catholic to be a Freemason. Then in November 27, 1983, Pope John Paul II retracted all of the papal bulls against Freemasonry and allowed Catholics to again become members of secret

---

[1023] Baigent, Leigh, and Lincoln. *Holy Blood, Holy Grail*, 238.

[1024] "...Alexandria...was one of ongoing intellectual and philosophical fusion, and the collection of the library, which fueled the process, is known to have exceeded 400,000 papyrus scrolls." Fideler, David, *Jesus Christ: Sun of God*, 5.

[1025] Marrs, op. cit., 242-243.

[1026] Bramley. op. cit., 101.

[1027] Baigent, Leigh, and Lincoln. *Holy Blood, Holy Grail*, 185.

[1028] Cooper, Milton William, *Behold a Pale Horse,* Light technology Publishing, Flagstaff, AZ, 87.

[1029] Peyrefitte, *La Letgtre Secrete, p.* 197ff. -attached to the papal bull on April 28, 1938.

[1030] Cooper, M. W. op. cit., 87.

societies without fear of excommunication.[1031] Why the change of heart? Why is it now okay for a Catholic to hold membership in secret organizations?

In recent years information about Freemasonry has become more available. Perhaps it is the explanation given by 33rd degree Mason Manly P. Hall that places "allegiance" in question. He says in *The Lost Keys of Freemasonry*:

The true Mason is not creed-bound. He realizes with the divine illumination of his lodge that as a Mason his religion must be universal: Christ, Buddha or Mohammed, the name means little, for he recognizes only the light and not the bearer...The Masonic order is not a mere social organization, but is composed of all those who have banded themselves together to learn and apply the principles of mysticism and the occult rites.[1032]

Jim Marrs gives this final note about the Freemasonry organization:

The secrets of the origins of Freemasonary have been tightly held despite the publication of numerous books and literature on the subject. Walter Leslie Wimsburst, a ranking Mason and author of The Meaning of Masonry, *wrote, "The true, inner history of Masonry has never yet been given forth even to the Craft itself." Many researchers believe that even most Masons themselves have lost sight of the organization's true origin and purpose. "The overall picture is one of an organization that has forgotten its original meaning," wrote the authors of* The Templar Revelation.[1033]

Like many examples throughout history, what used to be the original intent of Freemasonry is now lost or unrecognizable in its present form. However, the real reasons for the formation of the organization are still important to me. I think that the earliest beginnings of this secret organization are significant for the information we might learn. I want to have a more complete look at the real intent of the groups and why it became necessary to keep it secret from powers that existed at the time. What were the motives for hiding information that shaped the lives of thousands of people?

I have only briefly touched on the history and actions of the Catholic Church and its position regarding the Freemasons.[1034] I am positive that there is much more

---

[1031] Ibid.
[1032] Bradley, Michael. *The Secrets of the Freemasons*, 78.
[1033] Jim Marrs, op. cit., 245.
[1034] I add two notes at this point: 1) "...there is evidence that the ritual ascribed to the Templars—trampling and spitting on the cross—was in the air at least half a century before 1307...it is mentioned in connection with the Sixth Crusade, which occurred in 1249." Baigent, Leigh, and Lincoln. *Holy Blood, Holy Grail*, 85. 2) "A least one group of Crusaders brought back more than just heretical hearsay—they reportedly returned to Europe with hard evidence of error and duplicity in church dogma. These Crusaders over time became known as heretics and blasphemers and an attempt was made by the church to exterminate them. They were the Knights Templar, whose

to be understood and revealed. I feel that the inconsistent attitudes of the Church and the decrees that were issued around this secretive organization, without much explanation, suggest that there might be some hidden details that are not being revealed. Maybe someone will want to pursue this subject further. I believe the resources are available for more research to happen.

Appendix G
The Original Transcript of the Interview With Stephanie M.:

Rainbow Eagle: "Please share with me some of your background growing up as a Jewish person":
"I grew up a Conservative Jew, studied Judaism extensively through high school, lived in Israel for a time, speak some Hebrew. Both parents were born Jewish, we celebrated all the holidays in our household; my brother and I attended Hebrew school three days a week from age 5 until we each took our Bar or Bat Mitzvah. I continued to a Jewish high school for more intensive study. Now, I am a practicing Wiccan but refuse to give up all Jewish practice – I still keep kosher and observe a number of the holidays."[1035]

"How do other Jews react to you leaving the Jewish religion":
"It's *bad*. It's a betrayal of our people, particularly because I am an educated Jew and kept such a strong practice for so long. It is not important for my sake, but rather for the sake of my children. If I am now a Pagan (which is a term with serious stigma attached), surely my children will not continue our religion and traditions. Because I have such a solid Jewish education, this is a major waste – my parents and teachers invested a lot of time in me, thinking that I would carry on the religion very strongly. Our survival and continuity as a people is tremendously important to the Jews."
(Jewish saying) *"It is a betrayal of our murdered ancestors to abandon the tradition now."*

"Becoming Wiccan means a betrayal of this most basic principle. I have actually not told my extended family about my Wiccan practice, because I have cousins with young children, and I love them and enjoy playing with them. There is a very real

---

traditions live on today within Freemasonry." Quoted in *Secrets of the Freemasons*, by Michael Bradley, 95.
[1035] Stephanie M. from California has personally written her comments and has given permission for them to be included in this book. July 30-August 1st, 2009. I will present her expressions as closely as possible to her original writings.

possibility that, when my cousins learn that I am now Pagan, I will no longer be allowed to associate with their children."

"I grew up in a Conservative household with a middling degree of observance; in high school, I became Conservadox[to be explained later] and dragged my family some of the way along with me."

"Would you explain how you 'dragged your family' into the traditions?"

"Well, if you're 16 and still living at home and suddenly you're keeping kosher, and your mother is willing to encourage and accommodate your increasing observance, she might begin to cook kosher food more and more often. It makes life easier on you, and hey, the whole family really should be keeping kosher anyway, right? This is what happened in my household. I wanted to be going to synagogue more often, and I didn't have a driver's license yet. That means someone has to go with me. I was at a Jewish high school, and coming home and talking about what I was learning – studying Judaism is a big part of Jewish observance, we are very big on study, so just me coming home and talking about what I was learning brought my parents farther into the tradition."

"I started observing the Sabbath – not working or writing or using electricity, etc. My parents did not ever join me in this, but they were aware for the first time of what it actually meant to observe the Sabbath (called being *shomrei Shabbos*) and why a person would want to. It was part of their awareness of the week, the difference between Shabbos and all the other days, for the first time. That sort of thing."

"There is a Rabbinic list of 39 things it is forbidden to do on the Sabbath. We think that this list is actually a list of the things that were necessary for the building of the Arc of the Covenant, which was the work that people would have been doing at the time that the law to observe the Sabbath was given. So it includes things like tying knots, untying knots, separating threads, skinning a dear, etc. Interestingly, you are allowed to tie one knot/write one letter/etc – you are given an extra moment to remember that it is forbidden. When modern Jews do not use electricity or drive their cars on the Sabbath, what they are actually doing is not lighting fires; when you start your engine or flip a switch, you make a spark."

A Side note: a man once asked Rabbi Akibah, one of our greatest rabbis, if he could summarize the Torah while standing on one foot. Rabbi Akibah said, "Love thy neighbor; now go study."

"What are the various sub-groupings of Jews today?"

"An **Orthodox Jew** believes that the religion is housed in the traditions. One cannot ignore the traditions and practices and still be a 'real Jew.'

"A ***Conservative Jew*** believes that the laws and traditions are important and have meaning, but that we, living in the modern world, can flexibly choose what to observe (this results in a wide variety of degrees of observance within Conservative Judaism – some have almost no observance but still have the Conservative mindset, some are observing almost on an Orthodox level but do not consider themselves Orthodox (we call these people ***Conservadox***)."

"A ***Reform Jew*** believes that there are two kinds of laws/traditions: spiritual and ritual. The spiritual laws are integral to the tradition and must be observed, but the ritual laws are relics of an older time and no longer apply. Thus, an observant Reform Jew will attend religious services, in English, with instruments, but is very unlikely to keep kosher. (A Conservative service will be mostly in Hebrew with some English, an Orthodox service all in Hebrew, both without instruments and with a lot of ritual chanting instead of songs.)

"Many Jews today will refer to themselves as ***Reform*** when they are actually completely secular, and I would like to draw that distinction: there is an actual Reform system of practice. Being Reform does not mean being secular, although it is often understood that way today."

"Not getting into delineations within Orthodoxy, the other major group of modern Jews is the ***Reconstructionists***. They cannot really be fit into the spectrum of observance, because being a Reconstructionist is not determined by how much you do but by your view of the text and of G-d. Reconstructionists are kind of the 'new agers' of Judaism, and they allow themselves to change the liturgy in ways that no other branch does. They rewrite things to eliminate all references to gender, and try to get in touch with the Divine as an unknowable spirit rather than as the G-d of Abraham, Isaac, and Jacob, who has a particular personality and a particular way He likes to be worshipped (here the Pagan in me is coming out). Instead of 'Blessed are You, Lord our G-d, King of the Universe, who has sanctified us with Your commandments and commanded us to light the Sabbath candles' (translation of the blessing over the candles), a Reconstructionist is more likely to say something like 'Blessed are You, Divine One, who blesses the world with light.' This is a theoretical example and not an actual Reconstructionist blessing.

The Bar/Bat Mitzvah—"Coming of Age" Ritual

"The Bar Mitzvah is the Jewish coming-of-age ceremony. In modern America, it has kind of gotten lost under the celebration that accompanies it. In a traditional Bar Mitzvah, the young adult leads the service, reads from the Torah, reads from the Haftorah, and gives a sermon – basically carries the responsibility of conducting the whole service. Jews are very big on the letter of the law, as I've said before – it is very important that things are chanted accurately. We actually have a guy standing next to the guy reading from the Torah and correcting him if he messes up, because if the congregation does not hear the words correctly, the mitzvah of reading that week's Torah portion has not been fulfilled. (When you consider that almost no one in the congregation is likely to understand more than the occasional word of the Torah portion (called the *parsha*), you see what an extreme thing this is to do.)

"So giving a 13-year-old the responsibility over all this is a huge thing, and that is our coming-of-age ritual. Of course, the child has the actual leaders of the congregation standing up there with him and helping him along, and in most modern ceremonies the kid doesn't actually do *everything*…at my Bat Mitzvah, I lead about 2/3 of the service, with help; read one section of the *parsha;* read the whole of the Haftorah portion (this is the weekly reading from other books of the Bible that are not the 5 Books of Moses – the Torah is only the 5 Books of Moses); and made a sermon. So you see that I did not lead everything. Most of the people I grew up with did not do even so much as I did at theirs (most of them grew up less religious than I)."

"The Bar/Bat Mitzvah is important because the celebrant is now an adult and as such has the rights and responsibilities of an adult. He can now be counted as part of a *minyan,* the group of 10 adults required to hold a service. He can lead sections of the service, and indeed he has been trained to do so. He must perform the ritual commandments, such as wearing the tefillin and giving tzedakah (charity, but not exactly, because it is required of us and not simply encouraged – the word actually just means "righteousness"). Also, he is now responsible for his own transgressions. A child does not have his own metaphorical plasterboard (back to what I wrote before about sin and repentance in Judaism); his sins are pinned into his parents'. Once you become Bar Mitzvah, you are responsible for your own actions."

"An interesting side-note: a child becomes Bar or Bat Mitzvah whether or not s/he ever celebrates it. A boy becomes Bar Mitzvah the day after his 13th birthday, and a girl the day after her 12th, whether or not they ever think about it at all. The service and the celebration are in honor of the event. They do not cause the event."

"What is being taught about the afterlife, Heaven and hell?"

"I was taught growing up that Jews believe in an afterlife but we do not talk much about it. We are to focus on *this* life, not the World to Come. We know we do not believe in a Hell, exactly, but reincarnation? Heaven? Some kind of limbo state? Judaism does not explain. We are not supposed to worry about it too much. Our purpose is to make *this* world better, not fixate on the next one."

"Can you explain more about 'keeping kosher'?"

"Kashrut is the Jewish dietary laws. Keeping kosher means following them. They are set down in basic form in the Torah: a land creature must have cloven hoofs and chew its cud, a sea creature must have fins and scales, you may not simmer a kid in its mother's milk (commonly interpreted as a dietary law: don't mix milk and meat), and there is a list of forbidden birds that basically comes down to don't eat scavengers or hunters (vegetarian birds only). So, no shell fish, no reptiles, no rodents, no humans, no insects (except locusts, because sometimes there were swarms and you couldn't help it, so an exception is made for locusts), no pig, no catfish, no cat, etc. All these animals are *traif,* meaning inherently unkosher."

"After those basic laws, there are also rules about how an animal must be killed and cleaned. We are not allowed to eat blood, so there is a very thorough cleaning process involving lots of salt. The animal must be executed humanely. I've talked about this elsewhere. An animal that is not *traif* must still be killed and cleaned right in order to be kosher. And then you have all the fences around the law of milk and meat. You wind up with people with separate sets of dishes, for example.

"Also, a 'kid' expands to include beef, and also chicken, because in poor lighting and with a person who is not paying attention beef could be mistaken for chicken, so you might mix beef and milk thinking you were mixing chicken and milk, so we'd better just not mix chicken and milk either. Interestingly, to a Jew, fish and eggs are not considered meat. They are in the same category as fruits, vegetables, and grains – they are *parve,* meaning they are neither milk nor meat. Often, if you buy food at the grocery store, you will see a little K written on the package, or a U in a circle; these are called hekshers, and they mean that the food is officially kosher. Sometimes, near the heksher, will be the letter P – that means it is parve."

"What defines a Jew"?
"Also, in the most basic way, what defines a Jew? We worship only one god. Ultimately, that is what Judaism is about – **worshipping only one god.** Is it written that way in the Torah? No... **But Jews are not taught that.** We are taught, "Hear oh Israel, the Lord is our God, the Lord is ONE."

"Did I hear this accurately? It's not written in the Torah to worship only one God"?
"Oh yes! The First Commandment states "You shall have no other god *before me.*" It does not say "besides me." As Jews, we are taught to pay attention to things like that, to omissions and details and tiny little odd phrasings in the Torah. It does tell us that we should worship HaShem and that HaShem is one – this god we are meant to put before all other gods is only one god. But there are other gods mentioned all over the Torah: Ba'al, Asherat, and so forth. They and their priests are usually written about negatively, but that makes sense when you consider that the writers of the Torah wanted us to worship Adonai and not Ba'al and Asherat."

"Modern Jews think that the Torah states that there is only one god, or at the very least that we should only worship one god. It does not say this. It says that we should worship HaShem *over* all other gods."

"I understand that 'Yom Kippur' is the most solemn day of the Jewish religious year. Can you explain"?
"The true name of G-d, what gentiles read today as Yaweh, is a four-letter name for which the pronunciation has been lost. In the times of the Temple, it was known only by the High Priest. Once a year, on Yom Kippur, he would go into the Holy of Holies and pronounce the Name. This was considered such a powerful magic, the true Name of G-d, that he would go into the room with a rope tied around his waist so that if he fainted after uttering the Name, his fellow priests, who were not allowed inside the Holy of Holies, could pull him out."

"Jews do "confession" once a year, in a big way, on Yom Kippur. The idea goes like this: G-d sits in judgment upon all people at the new year, Rosh HaShanah. He has before him the Book of Life, in which all people will be inscribed for a good life or a bad life for the year to come. On Rosh HaShanah, He reviews your behavior for the previous year, and inscribes you for good or bad. You then have ten days to change his mind."

"The liturgy says, "On Rosh HaShanah it is written, and on Yom Kippur it is sealed: who shall live and who shall die, who in the fullness of years and who before, who by fire and who by flood, who by sword and who by stoning, etc..." At the end of that passage, it says, "But repentance, charity, and acts of kindness can remove the severity of the decree."

"In the Ten Days of Awe, the time between Rosh HaShanah and Yom Kippur, we go to everyone we have wronged over the past year and apologize, and we make our apologies to G-d, we perform *t'shuvah*. On Yom Kippur, we fast, we pray all day, we wear white to symbolize that we are now as pure as the angels, having been absolved of our sins from the past year. This is the nearest thing to confession that we have in Judaism."

"It does not go through a priest. The cantor, the person who leads the prayer chants for the congregation, does have a special prayer in the High Holiday services (Rosh HaShanah and Yom Kippur) in which s/he asks G-d to accept his/her prayers on behalf of the whole community even though s/he is unworthy…that's the nearest thing to confession via priest."

People say that there are two kinds of Jewish holidays: "They tried to kill us, we won, let's eat!" and "They tried to kill us, we lost, let's fast!" This is, of course, an oversimplification, but also basically accurate. There is a huge element of martyrdom in the Jewish tradition (we see it most clearly at Yom Kippur, when there is a whole service devoted to the Martyrs). Most of our stories involve the fact that the Jews have been strangers in every land and persecuted everywhere we go (even now, we have our own land, and still we are under attack there!). Passover is "we won, let's eat!"

"We have a holiday commemorating the destruction of the Temple (both temples were actually destroyed on the same date in the Jewish calendar), and we do a full fast, which in Judaism means no food and no water for 25 hours. We have various half-fasts commemorating other massacres."

"Hannukah? We won, let's eat! Purim, we won, let's eat. The list goes on. You ask why this idea is promoted – I think it's to reinforce in modern Jews the idea that, even though we feel safe now in the Diaspora, holocausts have happened to us before (more than once) and can happen to us again at any time. We are actively taught this as small children: yes, the Nazis are no longer ruling Germany, and we live in America, but do not be fooled! At any time, we can be scapegoated for the ills of the world and massacred again."

"In Judaism what is the place for women, in the past and now"?

"Women have their own place in the Jewish tradition. There are specific things that women are expected to do and things that we are not. We are not required to perform any of the commandments that are bound by time – a prayer that must be said at noon, for example – because we care for the children, and if we are feeding the baby at noon, we cannot say the prayer. So we are not bound by those."

"This is often seen as sexist – men are the ones who must keep the ritual commandments, so men are the important ones. This is a misunderstanding. There is a blessing that men say every morning, one of a long string of morning blessings: 'Blessed are you, Lord our G-d, King of the Universe, who has not made me a woman.' Many feminist Jews get very upset about this one. Again, a misunderstanding -- men are grateful to be men because they get to perform all the ritual commandments. Women are grateful to be women, and would have a similar blessing for not being born men, except that the reciting of that blessing is a ritual commandment tied by time, and therefore women do not have to say those blessings."

"Of course, there is some sexism in traditional Judaism, because it is men who wrote the liturgy. There is a story of a woman who tried to lead a prayer in an Orthodox synagogue, and was told by the rabbi that 'A woman belongs on the bimah (the stage from which Jewish prayers are led) like an orange belongs on the seder plate.' The seder plate is used on Passover and has a very specific set of things on it, and an orange is not one of them. Many people now keep an orange on their seder plates as well, to symbolize that we do now permit women on the bimah."

"All traditions but Orthodoxy allow women to be rabbis and cantors. In an Orthodox Jewish synagogue, the women pray very quietly, in a separate room from the men, sometimes divided by partition and sometimes by an actual wall; this is because the sight and sound of women may be distracting to the men. Traditionally, women are not counted in a *minyan*. There is certainly sexism in modern Orthodox practice. I'm not sure how we got there from ancient times. I am not aware of much sexism in the Torah."

"There are many places in Jewish prayer where we invoke 'the god of Abraham, Isaac, and Jacob.' Reform Jews will now add to that 'Sarah, Rebecca, Rachel, and Leah.' "

"Jewish women, to achieve ritual cleanliness, visit a Mikvah, a ritual bath, upon the conclusion of their menstrual periods and immediately before their weddings. A modern Orthodox Jewish woman will go every month; a Conservative Jewish woman is likely to only ever attend a Mikvah before her marriage. A "Reform" woman may or may not ever attend one at all.

In Judaism, being "unclean" is a temporary state that comes about as a result of living. You do have to make yourself clean before you can participate in holy acts, but that's easy enough, you just go take a ritual bath and say the appropriate blessings. Being "unclean" is not sinful or evil in any way."

"You mentioned 'mending the vessel'; can you explain?"

The Kabbalists talk of healing the world as "mending the vessel." This vessel was a mystical glass container in which all the good (or possibly evil, I don't remember which) of the world was housed. It was broken at some point, and every time a Jew performs a mitzvah (meaning fulfills a commandment, not does a good deed), another piece of the vessel is mystically made whole with the rest. So when Kabbalists fulfill commandments, they see themselves as mending the vessel.

"What can you tell me about the movements that accompany prayers?"

When a Jew prays, he tends to bend rhythmically at the waist more or less constantly throughout the service. This is similar to ritual dance that you see in other traditions, and in some Jewish traditions, particularly Chassidut (the Chassidim are a sect of Orthodox Jews), it becomes an actual circle dance like what you see in the energy raising of Pagan traditions. The bending at the waist is called shukkling, and it just sort of happens when you're very involved in the prayer. It is how Jewish prayer fits into the body and moves through you. If you watch the Voodoun dance, it is a particular type of motion that comes out of the rhythms of their drumming, a different movement than you see in other traditions. The shukkle is just what comes out of the rhythm of Jewish prayer. We also have various places in the prayers where we pray (bend at the knees, bend at the waist, rise back up – "kneel, bow, then stand straight before your god," I was taught), and those are usually timed to lines that begin with "Blessed are You," the phrase that begins the first and last lines of many paragraphs of Jewish prayer. There are occasional other things that we do – there's one place where we say "holy, holy, holy," and rise on our toes with each iteration, to bring us closer to G-d. Jews only actually kneel on the floor once a year, and Americans seldom even do that – you see it more often in England. There is a place in the service where we bow for two full lines (the sentence begins with "We bow..."), and on Yom Kippur we prostrate ourselves fully there. That is the only time and place that we do that, because that is the posture that Pagans adopt when they bow to their idols, and we do not bow to idols. There are only three Jewish laws that we are expected to die before breaking: killing someone else, some forms of sexual licentiousness (I was never told which), and bowing before idols. We are meant to allow people to kill us rather than bow to an idol.

"What is meant by 'building fences around the Law'"?

This reminds me of the Jewish custom of "building fences around the law." There is this sense in Judaism that the letter of the law is very important and must be strictly upheld – the letter of the law often *over* the spirit of the law. For example, it is forbidden to write on the Sabbath. So, observant Jews will actually put all their pens and pencils in a locked drawer for that day, so that they are not tempted/do not forget and start writing by accident. Jews do not play musical instruments on the Sabbath, not because it is in itself forbidden, but because, if it breaks, we will be tempted to fix it, and that will probably require actions that are forbidden (ie tying knots). This translation of the Torah was accurate and complete, but because the name of G-d was written in gold ink, it was not holy and basically *didn't count.* (Side note: writing down the name of G-d is a bad idea, because if you ever want to get rid of the piece of paper or whatever, it has to be buried with ceremony in a special part of a Jewish cemetery. Even though the English word "God" is not the true name of the Deity and therefore does not have to be disposed of this way, modern Jews will often honor the Name by writing the word as "G-d" instead.)
True, but interestingly, most traditional Jewish sects require a *minyan,* a group of ten adults (some groups say, ten adult men), to hold services.
The book of Jewish law/thought/discussion that Jews study today, the Talmud, is actually a volumes-long transcript of debates between ancient rabbis. This is central to what Judaism *is.*
Literally, "adam" means "earth," "man," and "red." I was never taught anything about it having any other meaning.

"What about the idea that Jews are the 'Chosen People'?"

When Jews talk about being the Chosen People, we do not mean we were chosen as G-d's favorites. We were chosen to do His work of healing the world (*tikkun olam*). The story goes: G-d went first to the Egyptians, and said, "I need a people to lead the world in righteousness and repair the damage that humans are doing. Will you be my people and do my work?" And the Egyptians said, "What will be involved?" And G-d said, "Thanks anyway, but I'll look elsewhere." So G-d went next to the Midianites, and said, "I need a people to lead the world in my ways, and work to heal the world of the damage that is being done. Will you be my people and do my work?" And the Midianites said, "This sounds great! What would we have to do?" And G-d said, "Never mind." So at last, G-d came to the Jews. And He said, "I need a people to be separate from all other peoples of the Earth. You will be isolated and persecuted, but you will be my people, closest to me of all peoples. It will be your task to heal the world of the damage being done to it. Will you be my people and do my work?" And the Jews said, "We will do and we will listen." First, we will *do,* and then we will listen – give us your commandments, we will obey, and then and only then will we ask for your reasons or for what comes next. And for this response were the Jews chosen.

"Modern Orthodox Jewish men still wear the tzitzit at all times. However, we cannot fully observe that commandment, because we are commanded to dye one thread in each corner blue using a specific process that is lost to us."

"I understand there are some requirements for Jews who 'handle the energies of the Kabbalah'."

"No one knows about this! But it's true. You had to be married, male, and over 40 to study Kabbalah. There's a myth about a young man who resorts to Kabbalistic magic to try to win back his fiancée after her father decides to marry her to someone else. He is not grounded enough to handle the forces, and so he dies; his spirit possesses the girl for a while; eventually she dies too and they're reunited in the World to Come. We know this story as the play "The Dybbuk."

"How have the Jews survived throughout history"?

"It seems that the survival of the Jewish people may actually be due to our persecution. Now that it is safe to be a Jew, we need to stay so tied to our communities; we intermarry; we bear children who are half Christian or secular; they do not grow up in the religion; they bear children who do not consider themselves Jewish. The fact that it is now safe to be a Jew means that fewer and fewer of us actually are. I think Jews have kind of lost track of that in a lot of branches of the religion.

Observant or well-educated Jews (and here I am talking about a Jewish education, not a secular one) have an understanding of this, that the survival of the Jewish people is important for a reason; the Jews were separated from the other Families of the Earth (*mishpachot ha'adamah*) for the purpose of healing the world. But the rest of the People seem to value survival for its own sake at this point. Why must the Jews survive? Because we have been around for so very long, and survived so much."

"I understand that married couples are actually expected to have sex on the Sabbath, as part of honoring it and keeping it holy. It is part of 'the Sabbath Joy'."

So, observant Jews will actually put all their pens and pencils in a locked drawer for that day, so that they are **not tempted/do not forget** and start writing by accident.

Fear of breaking the 'laws' seems to be a spiritual neuroses here? How is the idea of being 'tempted' seen into Judaism"?

The Jewish idea of being tempted is very different from the Christian idea. It has nothing do to with a Devil or evil spirits. Jews recognize that within ourselves we have both a Good Impulse (*yetzer ha'tov*) and an Evil Impulse (*yetzer ha'rah*). The tempter is built in to humans. The idea of being tempted does not need to be "instilled" into Judaism; it's just part of us. If you are not allowed to write, and you want to, it's harder to resist writing with a pen in front of you than without one. It's just like a person on a diet not keeping cake in the house.

Yes, I would agree that there may be a "spiritual neurosis" about breaking the laws. I hadn't ever thought about it that way – it's just part of what being traditionally Jewish is about – but you may be right.

Being "unclean" is not sinful or evil in any way.

"Could you explain more of how this addresses and negative energies"?

I don't know all that much about ritual uncleanness in Judaism. I remember learning that a person is unclean after touching a dead body and therefore the priestly caste (back when there was one) did not. But it's just part of life, particularly for women. That's why we have a way (and a fairly simple way!) to become ritually clean again. Being unclean isn't really a positive or a negative thing; it's more like it's just not a big deal.

Christians tend to refer to this story as "The Sacrifice of Isaac." We call it "Akeidat Yitzchaak," the binding of Isaac. It is not a story of sacrifice. There is also a lot of discussion in modern Conservative Judaism about whether or not Abraham passed the test. What happens to him next? His wife dies. Very next thing. A suitable reward for passing G-d's test? There is a tradition in the Torah of arguing with G-d when He proposes to do things like destroy cities; our righteous patriarchs plead with Him not to. Abraham is prepared to sacrifice his only son for no reason except that G-d has asked it of him. Orthodox Jews, of course, believe that he did pass the test.

Also note: Christians read the creation story as saying that Adam and Eve did not have sex until after they had been kicked out of the Garden. This is a mistranslation due to a poor understanding of Biblical Hebrew grammar. It does not read "and Adam knew Eve," but rather, "and Adam *had known* Eve," an unusual construction at that point in the story. From this we learn that Eve conceived Cain while still in the Garden.

By the way, Judaism does not treat converts as inferior in any way. When the Messiah comes, he will be a descendent of King David. David was a descendent of Ruth, our first convert. From this we learn that converts are absolutely as good as and as Jewish as those born into the religion.

"Is there a Jewish bloodline? What is taught about how the Jewish tradition came about? The Mt Sinai experience brought many groups (bloodlines) together to 'follow the Law', right?"

Surely there is a Jewish bloodline. This is not metaphorical at all, it is literal fact. There are genetic diseases that only Jews get, due to what is ultimately inbreeding on a very large scale. We are not taught anything about different bloodlines coming together at Mount Sinai – we know who was there, because there are paragraphs of "so-and-so begot so-and-so" in Genesis and Exodus, and we can watch the children of Israel increase in number. The people at Mount Sinai were the Hebrew slaves. You were born into slavery in Egypt the same way you were born into slavery in the American South; it was already a result of bloodline. I always understood that the people who received the Torah at Mount Sinai were already an ethnically distinct group.

Incidentally, this is why a person cannot convert out of Judaism. You are born a Jew or you are not. We are almost as much a race as we are a religion.

The concept of sin in Judaism is very different from in Christianity. The word for sin means "missing the mark." It is like an archer who doesn't hit the target – a mistake, not a condemnation. There is a three-step process for clearing such a mistake from your record: you apologize to G-d, you apologize to the person you wronged, and you pass up an opportunity to do the same thing again. This is called t'shuvah, meaning repentance. It is as if each person has a plaster-board, and when you sin, a pin is pushed into your board. Apologizing to G-d removes the pin, apologizing to the person fills the hole, and passing up a future opportunity paints over it so it is entirely gone. The only unforgivable sins are the ones where you cannot perform full t'shuvah, like if the person is dead. There is a tradition in the Torah of arguing with G-d when He proposes to do things like destroy cities; our righteous patriarchs plead with Him not to.

"Arguing with God? Can you tell me more about openness to dialoging with God?

Well, we don't really do it anymore. But then again, G-d doesn't exactly come to us and tell us he's going to wipe out cities anymore either. If He did, we know that we have the right (the responsibility!) to try to talk Him down from it – that's what Moses and Abraham did, and we take our cues from them. Jacob wrestles with an angel or possibly with G-d Himself, a literal wrestling match, and then is given his name, Yisrael. Yisrael, Israel, means "struggles with G-d." I was taught as a child that, to be a good Jew, one does not have to quietly believe everything one is told; one does not even have to believe in G-d. One just has to struggle with G-d. That's what "Israel" means. We are asked to think, to debate, to investigate the tradition and to work to understand it. Almost everything in Judaism eventually makes at least some kind of sense, if you struggle with it long enough.

"Didn't they believe in one God and avoided all physical representations of the divine, all foreign worship, all other gods"?

Yes, but! While we say it, we make the shape of the letter Shin on our forehead and eyes with our right hand. Shin stands for "Shaddai," the name for our nurturing Goddess! Polytheism strikes again!

"Very interesting! Can you tell me more about this"?

I don't know that there is that much more to tell...Shaddai has become one more name for G-d, not the name of a goddess, and people don't realize that this is who they are invoking when they make the shape of the Shin. There is a service we hold at the end of the Sabbath, Saturday at sundown, called Havdalah. It brings us back into the every-day world of the rest of the week and out of the holy time of the Sabbath. We talk a lot about the Shechinah in connection with that service. We draw Her in, we ask Her to be with us for the week, we honor Her. There are a few quiet, folk-y songs that Reform Jews sing in their services that talk about the Shechinah as being all around us, like the love of a mother. But we don't actually discuss Her all that much. She is just one more aspect of G-d, and not that important a one in the tradition, because ultimately Jews worship El, who is a male god of thunder. Let's not forget the Shechinah! All little Jewish children are taught about the Shechinah, feminine aspect of G-d. We are not taught that She is a protectoress and that we have other Goddesses for other feminine attributes, but we are taught that there is a Divine Feminine.

Also note: Christians read the creation story as saying that Adam and Eve did not have sex until after they had been kicked out of the Garden. This is a mistranslation due to a poor understanding of biblical Hebrew grammar. It does not read "and Adam knew Eve," but rather, "and Adam *had known* Eve," an unusual construction at that point in the story. From this we learn that Eve conceived Cain while still in the Garden.

"What can you share with me about the 'whaling Wall'?"

The Wall is the only remaining section of our ancient Temple. The Temple, of course, was our holiest place, and the center of Jewish life. The Wailing Wall is now the focus of the Jews' grief at our Diaspora, and the destruction of the Temple, and all the persecution we have suffered over centuries simply because we are different. We no longer have a Temple; we cannot observe all the commandments that require the Temple; we are dispersed throughout the Earth and in exile from our homeland that G-d Himself gave to us. And so we go to the Wall and we leave our prayers and we weep.

In order for an animal to be kosher, even if it is an inherently kosher animal, it must be killed in a way in which it feels no pain. This involves severing the head at a particular spot on the neck, which cuts both pipes at once and kills instantly. A giraffe is a kosher animal, but we cannot find the spot on the neck and so can't kill it right, and thus cannot eat giraffe (even if we wanted to).

"The Aramaic language has many meaning for each word. For example *"**Ru Hah...**"* (spirit) when placed into English translation meaning "Holy Spirit" could mean all of the following: breath-wind-air-atmosphere. There is no separate Word for body-soul-spirit-emotions—each is a part of the other. There can be both extreme and welcomed presentations of each of these "Ru Hah..."

In Hebrew, the word is "Ru-ach", and in modern Hebrew it still has all these meanings.

We know this because we are taught that we were all present at Mount Sinai. This comes up every year during the observance of Passover; we are asked to be thankful for the exodus from Egypt and the giving of the Torah as ones who were present at the time. This can be viewed as preexistence of the soul and mystical presence at the Mount, or as evidence of a Jewish belief in reincarnation.

A Sanhedrin that executed more than one criminal in a period of seven years (I may have this number wrong, it may have been a much longer time) was considered an evil court.

Glossary

Alaha, (Aramaic) Sacred Unity, Oneness, the Ultimate Power or Potential, the One without an Opposite, that which moves toward no end; also the negation of anything. "...both the Aramaic form *Alaha* and the Arabic *Allah* emphasize Unity without qualification or limit."[1036]

Adonai Hebrew for "my Lord." One of the names of God. Because the name is considered holy by religious Jews, they substitute *Hashem* ("the Name") in everyday usage, pronouncing "Adonai" only at prayer or during the reading or study of the Bible.[1037]

Ain Sof. God or the "Infinite", from which all forms in the Universe are created. Kabbalists teach that *Ain Sof* created the Ten *Sefiroth* as a link from man to Him.[1038]

Alma (often translated as eternity). Also means age, generation, era. Based on a root that means youth or newness, everything that constantly arises in diversity in the worlds of forms.[1039]

Apocrypha "The Greek word *Apocrypha*...the term means "things hidden away,..."[1040] "Books not included in the Hebrew Bible but included in Roman Catholic and Greek Orthodox canon..."[1041]

Bar nasha (son of man) "bar" means *son*, "...nasha means any human being, man or woman, and derives from the Hebrew-Aramaic root NSH, which points to something weak and subject to change."[1042]

Bisha (evil) "...has fallen out of rhythm with Sacred Unity...the being or act in question has been delayed in its purpose and is not yet ready for the purpose for which it is meant."[1043] Unripe, not fit for its intended purpose, not ready, out of rhythm.

Davenen (in Yiddish) is the Jewish way of praying. "Traditional Jewish *daveners* often move their bodies rhythmically back and forth or from side to side, and in some

---

[1036] Douglas-Klotz, Neil. *The Hidden Gospel*, 28.
[1037] Stephanie M adds: "Adonai" is the god of mercy. "Elohim" or "Elohainu" is the god of justice (interesting to note that this word is actually plural, "gods" not "god"). "Shechinah" is the feminine protectoress. "Shaddai" is the feminine nurturer (the word literally means "breast"). Sound like a list of gods and goddesses to you?
[1038] Sheinkin. Op. cit., 39.
[1039] Douglas-Klotz. *The Hidden Gospel*, 122.
[1040] Davis. Op. cit., 319.
[1041] *Dictionary of the Jewish Religion*.
[1042] Douglas-Klotz. *The Hidden Gospel*, 164.
[1043] Ibid., 132.

Jewish-renewal circles there are moments when all in the congregation are asked to get up, move to the melodies…stretch, dance, or otherwise involve their whole beings…"[1044]

Enunah Translating from Hebrew to Greek to English the word *faith* translates to the Greek word *pistis* (a function of the mind). In Hebrew **enunah,** "meant the capacity to trust, the courage to act, the willingness to commit…It dealt with *being* far more than it dealt with *doing*."[1045]

Fourchette to not participate in sex or one's virginity is maintained.

Gnosis has been described as knowledge, a revelation of the higher world. Gnostics scholar Jean Doresse, says:
This "gnosis,"…is to be not so much a "knowing" as a remembering; it is to awaken the neophyte [a novice], to recall him to what was his original nature…to restore to him the everlasting part of his being…[1046]

Hamartia the Greek word for the word translated a "sin." The original Greek meaning of *hamartia* means "to miss the mark."[1047]

Hataha (sin) Error, failure, mistake; what misses the mark; frustrated hopes; figuratively, tangled threads. Derives from the verbs meaning to dig out or sew—both having to do with an effort (CH) made against resistance (T).

Ha-tzelah in Hebrew means the side of Adam.[1048]

"heresy" is derived from a Greek word *hairesis* that means 'choice!'[1049]

Koinonos—Greek for "intimate companion, consort," used in the *Gospel of Philip* to describe Mary Magdalene, the "consort" of the Savior.[1050]

Khanokh is the Hebrew name for Enoch also it is another word for education or knowledge.[1051]

Lilith name is a derivative of the Hebrew word *lailah*, meaning night, for she was a creature of the night.[1052] "Lilith was Adam's first wife, who preceded Eve….Lilith is created from the earth, as Adam was. In the Talmud…Lilith was also made out of dust…she balked at the way Adam wished to make love, with the man on top. When

---

[1044] Lerner. Op. cit., 395.
[1045] Spong. *This Hebrew Lord*, 22-23.
[1046] Doresse, Jean. *The Secret Books of the Egyptian Gnostics*, 113.
[1047] Lerner. Op. cit., 370.
[1048] Blech, Benjamin and Doliner, Roy. *Sistine Secrets*, U.S News & World Report (Special Edition, copyright 2008), 76.
[1049] Evrett, Ferguson, Michael P. McHugh, & Fredrick W. Norris, *Encyclopedia of Early Christianity* (New York & London: Garland Publishing, 1990), 420.
[1050] Starbird. *Magdalene's Lost Legacy*, 128.
[1051] Hanson, Kenneth, Ph.D, *Secrets of the Lost Bible*, 50.
[1052] Ibid., 81.

Adam refused Lilith's demand that she be regarded as his equal, she walked out on him."[1053] "Originally the lily was the flower of Lilith, the first of Adam's wives."[1054]

monogenes means "of a single kind." The word "only" in English is a mistranslation of this Greek word. *Monogenes* describes a quality of Jesus, his uniqueness.[1055] The Greek word *monogenes* was incorrectly translated as "only begotten." The scriptures do not say that Jesus Christ was the *only* son of God. The same word was used to describe Isaac in Hebrews 11:17 meaning Isaac held a "special and precious" place to Abraham not to be translated as the only son. We know that Abraham had other sons.[1056]

Nepes [or nefesh] "...the Old Testament uses the Hebrew word **nepes** [or **nefesh**] which comes from the verb "*to breath*" as their closest approach to the concept of soul." *Nepes* means that breath sustains life but *nepes* does not make a differentiation between "life" and "soul." So when God "breathed into his nostrils the breath of life" (Genesis 2:7) it is close to say that the soul (or life) of man comes from God. All that this means is in any of the sayings of Jesus which have been translated as "soul," the word "life" can be used.[1057]

Nephesh Our English words *soul* and *spirit* are our efforts to translate the Greek word **psyche** into English. In Greek *psyche* means the mind or the spirit; that is, the nonphysical aspect of our life.[1058] predating this Greek word are two Hebrew words, **nephesh** and **ruach** (also Aramaic); having no connection with the nonphysical view of life! *Nephesh* can be translated as breath like the breath of God and r*uach* means the wind of God.

Paraclete a Greek word that means Holy Ghost. It comes from the Greek word *Parakletos* which means "the Comforter" or the "one called to help" from *para* meaning "to the side of" and *kalein* meaning "to call."

Parthenos a Greek word used to translate the Hebrew word **almuh**—**meaning a young woman**[1059] in Hebrew. "The Hebrew word for virgin is **betulah.** *Almuh* never means 'virgin' in Hebrew."[1060] In other words, the early Christians writers translated the Hebrew word *alma* (young woman) in Isaiah 7:14 into the Greek word *parthenos* (virgin), so that the people would recognize their savior (born of a virgin[1061]).

[1053] Davis, op. cit., 55.
[1054] Godwin, Malcolm. *Angels: An Endangered Specie*, 45.
[1055] Moore. *Christianity and the New Age Religion*, 172.
[1056] Ibid. , 173.
[1057] Moore. *The Christian Conspiracy*, 160.
[1058] Spong. *This Hebrew Lord*, 18.
[1059] In other translations it meant a young woman who has not yet borne a child.
[1060] Moore. *Christianity and the New Age Religion*, 176.
[1061] Bruce Childon writes: "Mary was either Christianity's immaculate virgin or the Talmud's common whore who had slept with a Roman soldier (in the Babylonian Talmud, see Sanhedrin 67a)." *Rabbi Jesus: An Intimate Biography*, 8.

Partzufim (a kabbalistic notion) in every age God may have different *partzufim*, ways of becoming known or appearing to human beings. This is not because there are different gods, but because human beings need different forms of representation in different eras.[1062]

"Resurrection first appears in the Hebrew Bible as a metaphor, symbolizing the rebirth of the nation of Israel."[1063]

"Shelama!" the Aramaic equivalent of *shalom*, "peace," in Hebrew.

Samayim Translating **"kingdom of heaven,"**[1064] in Hebrew, the word *samayim*[1065] is plural though in English it is often translated in the singular.

Saphra The Hebrew word for "corner-stone or foundation rock."

Satan In Judaism, a very loyal servant of God who enables human free will to exist through offering the option of evil.[1066]

Sophia Holy Wisdom, the Greek personification of the Holy Spirit, the "consort" or "mirror" of God.

Taba (good) Ripe, fit for a particular purpose, ready. Its root points to something that maintains its integrity and health (T) by inner growth and harmony with what surrounds it (B).

Teshuvah Repentance, or more broadly, return and ascent to one's divine source of origin. *Teshuvah* is said to have existed before the Creation of our universe.[1067] Also, "a complete "turning", a total reorientation of attitude or action."[1068] *"Tavu, teblu limshebaq dehovatkon!* (Repent, immerse for release of your sins!)" Aramaic

To be saved in Hebrew means to *"breathe freely."*

teivah in Hebrew means a "box" it does not mean a boat or sailing vessel.

In the Hebrew Bible, in the apocryphal Book of Sirach that ***instruction and prophecy*** flow like a stream from Holy Wisdom, "whose thoughts are deeper than the sea, whose counsels are deeper than the great abyss" (Sirach 24.27). The sea and the

---

[1062] Lerner. Op. cit , 409.

[1063] Vermes, Geza. *A Matter of Faith*, U.S. News & World Report, (Special Edition, *Secrets of the Bible*, copyright 2008), 67.

[1064] "The Old Testament often mentions heaven; but in Hebrew, the word *samayim* is plural though in English it is often translated in the singular." Moore, *The Christian Conspiracy*, 94. Rabbi Weinstein says the word should be spelled, *"shamayim."*

[1065] Rabbi Weinstein says the word should be spelled, *"shamayim."*

[1066] Sheinkin. op. cit., 194.

[1067] Ibid., 195.

[1068] www.adl.org/main_Interfaith/nostra_aetate.htm?Multi_page_sections=sHeading_4.

abyss were both "feminine" in ancient philosophical systems: The *Mary* in its many forms comes from the word for "oceans...'"

The Hebrew meaning for the word that was later translated as **_light._** To Hebrew people it meant "knowledge" and what can be called enlightenment today.

Zohar The "Book of Splendor," which first appeared in the late thirteenth-century Spain. It is the "bible" of the Kabbalah and its most influential work...scholars today attribute it to Moses de Leon, who is said to have composed most of it in the 1280s and 1290s.[1069]

A Study of the Aramaic Language

In Aramaic the word **_"abwoon"_** means connecting our breath with Holy Breath the Unity of All.

The word **_"adam"_** in Aramaic means to carry the essence of the cosmos. It contains both masculine and feminine created at the same time!

Yeshua uses the word **_"a-la-'ha"_** which also is "elohim" in old Hebrew and **_"e (a)-'lat (lot)"_** in Canaanite and **_"allah"_** in Arabic. They all mean "Sacred Unity."

In Aramaic **_"Ameyn"_** (Amen) means "may this be the earth from which our new growth come."

The word "Kingdom" in Aramaic was more correctly translated as *kingship*. Not a piece of land or territory. A relation-*ship* to come.

In Egyptian the word **_"amet"_** refers to the sacred ground that held the bones of the ancestors—the foundation of being.

Asyya an Aramaic word meaning physician and corresponded to the Greek word *essenoi*.[1070]

The Aramaic word for "carpenter" is translated in Jewish commentaries on the law, it means a learned man.[1071]

The word **_"evil"_** in Aramaic means "unripeness" or "not in its right place and time—too early or too late. It can mean not appropriate to present circumstances.

extra ecclesiam nulla salus "There is no salvation outside the Church" Origen formulated this dogma.

Homoousios Having to do with early church discussions (fourth century) regarding the relationship of God and Jesus. *Homoousisos* is a Greek word meaning "identical to," or "of one substance" with the Father and *homoiousios* means similar to the Father. *Homoousios* was chosen at the Ecumenical Councils to describe the relationship of the Father (God) and the Son (Jesus).[1072]

[1069] Sheinkin. Op. cit., 195.

[1070] Gardner. op. cit., 24.

[1071] Tully. op. cit., 76.

[1072] Moore. *The Christian Conspiracy*, 135.

Kanon A Greek word that literally means a "cane used as a measuring rod" or loosely translated as a "rule" or a "standard."[1073]

"Perfect" in Aramaic means to be as completely aware as you can. To be completely human, to be balanced. The *Didache* offers a different meaning than found in Matthew that expects one to "be perfect." It suggests "bearing the whole yoke of the Lord" or obeying the whole law, also more balanced concept, "If you cannot [be perfect], do what you can."[1074]

"Ru Hah…" Spirit. In both Hebrew and Aramaic, the same word—*ruha* in Aramaic, *ruach* in Hebrew—must stand for several English words: spirit, wind, air, atmosphere and breath. There is no separate word for body-soul-spirit-emotions.

In ancient Egypt there was no word that meant "religion" and no word that meant "belief."

Unam Sanctam (1302) Boniface VIII asserts that outside the Church there can be neither salvation nor remission of sins.

[1073] Ibid., 34.
[1074] Pagels. *Beyond Belief*, 16.

Bibliography

Acharya, S. *The Christ Conspiracy: The Greatest Story Ever Sold*. Illinois: Adventures Unlimited Press, 1999.

Armstrong, Karen. *A History of God*. New York: Ballantine Books, 1993.

Baigent, Michael. *The Jesus Papers: Exposing the Greatest Cover-up in History*. New York: HarperSanFrancisco, 2006.

Baignet, M., Leigh, R. and Lincoln, H., *The Holy Blood and the Holy Grail*. London, 1982.

-------. *The Messianic Legacy*. New York: Dell Publishing, 1986.

Baldock, John. *The Alternative Gospel: The Hidden Teaching of Jesus*. Boston, MA: Element Books Limited, 1997.

Baring, Anne and Cashford, Jules. *The Myth of Goddess: Evolution of an Image*. New York: Penguin Books USA Inc., 1993.

Bolen, Jean Shinoda. *Goddesses in Older Women: Archetypes in Women Over Fifty*. New York: HarperCollins Publishers Inc., 2001.

Borg, Marcus J. *Jesus A New Vision*. San Francisco: Harper & Row, 1987.

-------. *Jesus at 2000*. Colorado: Westview Press, 1998.

Braden, Gregg. *The God Code: the Secret of our Past, the Promise of our Future*.

--------. *The Isaiah Effect: Decoding the Lost Science of Prayer*. New York: Harmony Books, 2000. California: Hay House, Inc., 2004.

Bradley, Michael. *The Secrets of the Freemasons*. New York/London: Sterling, 2008.

Bramley, William. *Jesus Goes to Hollywood: the Alternative Theories About Christ*. California: Dahlin & Associates, 2005.

Campbell, Joseph. *The Inner Reaches of Outer Space*. New York: Harper & Row, Publishers, 1986.

--------.*Myths to Live By*. New York: Penguin Compass, 1972.

Ch'en, Kenneth K. S. *Buddhism: The Light of Asia*. New York: Barron's Educational Series, Inc., 1968.

Chilton, Bruce. *Rabbi Jesus: An Intimate Biography*. New York: Doubleday, 2000

Chilton, B., Evans, C., and Neusner, J. *The Missing Jesus: Rabbinic Judaism and the New Testament.*, Boston, MA: Brill Academic Publishers, Inc., 2002.

Crossan, J. and Reed, J. *Excavating Jesus: Beneath the Stones, Behind the Texts*. New York: HarperSanFrancisco. 2001.

Davis, Kenneth C. *Don't Know Much About the Bible*. New York: Perennial, 2001.

Doresse, Jean. *The Secret Books of the Egyptian Gnostics*. New York: MJF Books, 1986.

Douglas-Klotz, Neil. *Blessings of the Cosmos: Benedictions From the Aramaic Words of Jesus*. Boulder, CO: Sounds True, 2006.

-------. *The Hidden Gospel: Decoding the Spiritual Message of the Aramaic Jesus*. Wheaton, IL: Quest Books, 1999.

-------. *Prayers of the Cosmos: Meditations on the Aramaic Words of Jesus*. New York: HarperSanFrancisco, 1990.

Eagle, Rainbow. *Native American Spirituality: A Walk in the Woods*. Zanesfield, OH: Rainbow Light & Company, 2003.

Eisler, Riane. *The Chalice and the Blade*. New York: HarperCollins Publishers, Inc., 1987.

Fideler, David. *Jesus Christ, Sun of God: Ancient Cosmology and Early Christian Symbolism*. Illinois: Quest Books, 1993.

Fox, Matthew. *The Coming of the Cosmic Christ*. San Francisco: Harper & Row, Publishers, 1988.

Freer, Neil. *God Games: What Do You Do Forever?* Escondido, CA: The Book Tree, 1998, 1999.

Funk, Robert W. *Honest to Jesus: Jesus for the New Mellennium*. New York: HarperSanFrancisco, 1996.

Funk, Robert W., Hoover Roy W. and the Jesus Seminar. *The Five Gospels: The Search for the Authentic Words of Jesus*. New York: Scribner, 1993.

Funk, Robert W and the Jesus Seminar. *The Gospel of Jesus: according to the Jesus Seminar*. California: Polebridge Press, 1999.

Greenberg, Gary. *The Bible Myth: The African Origins of the Jewish People*.

Secaucus, NJ: Carol Publishing Group, 1996.

Gruber, Elmer R., Kersten, Holger. *The Original Jesus: The Buddhist Sources of Christianity.* Rockport, MA: Element Books Limited, 1995.

Gardner, Laurence. *Bloodline of the Holy Grail.* Great Britain: Element Books Ltd., 1996.

Hanson, Kenneth. *Secrets from the Lost Bible.* San Francisco/Tulsa: Council Oak Books, 2004.

Hoover, Row W. *Profiles of Jesus.* California: Polebrideg Press, 2002.

Isaacson, Ben. *Dictionary of the Jewish Religion.* New York: Bantam Books, 1979.

Jenkins, Philip. *Hidden Gospels: How the Search for Jesus Lost Its Way.* New York: Oxford University Press, 2001.

Kersten, Holger. *Jesus Lived in India.* England: Element Book Ltd., 1986.

Leloup, Jean-Yves. *The Gospel of Mary Magdalene.* Rochester, Vermont: Inner Traditions, 2002.

Lerner, Michael. *Jewish Renewal: A Path To Healing and Transformation.* New York: First HarperPerennial, 1994.

Lippman, Thomas W. *Understanding Islam: An Introduction to the Muslem World.* New York: Penguin Group, 1982.

Mack, Burton L. *The Lost Gospel: The Book of Q & Christian Origins.* New York: HarperSanFrancisco, 1993.

McIntosh and Twyman, MD. *The Archko Volume.* Connecticut: Keats Publishing, Inc., 1975.

Messadie, Gerald. *A History of the Devil.* New York: Kodansha International, 1996.

Meyer, Marvin. *The Gospels of Mary: The Secret Traditions of Mary Magdalene, The Companion of Jesus.* New York: HarperCollins Publishers, 2004.

Moore, L. David. *Christianity and The New Age Religion.* Atlanta, GA: Pendulum Plus Press, 1992.

-------. *The Christian Conspiracy: How the Teachings of Christ Have Been Altered by Christians.* Jasper, GA: 1994.

Pagels, Elaine. *Adam, Eve, and the Serpent.* New York: Vintage Books, 1988.

-------. *Beyond Belief: The Secret Gospel of Thomas.* N. Y.: Vintage Books, 2003.

-------. *The Gnostic Gospels.* New York: Vintage Books, 1979.

-------. *The Gnostic Paul: Gnostic exegesis of the Pauline letters.* Valley Forge, PA: Trinity Press International, 1975.

-------. *The Origin of Satan.* New York: Random House, 1995.

Pearson, Simon. *The End of the World: From Revelation to Eco-Disaster.* New York: Carroll & Graf Publishers, 2006.

Pelikan, Jaroslav. *Jesus Through the Centuries: His Place in the History of Culture.* New Haven and London: Yale University Press, 1985.

Phipps, W. E. *The Sexuality of Jesus.* Cleveland, Ohio: The Pilgrim Press, 1996.

Picknett, Lynn. *Mary Magdalene: Christianity's Hidden Goddess.* New York: Carroll & Graf Publishers, 2003.

Picknett, Lynn and Prince, Clive. *The Templar Revelation: Secret Guardians of the True Identity of Christ.* New York: Simon & Schuster, 1997.

Ploski, Cynthia Berresse. *Chasing The Magdalene: A Personal Journey of Discovery In Provence and Languedoc.* Lamar, MO: Little Eagle Publishing, 2005.

Rambsel, Yacov. *The Genesis Factor: The Amazing Mysteries of the Bible Codes.* Beverly Hills, CA: Lion's Head Publishing, 2000.

Rovin, Jeff. *Fascinating Facts from the Bible: The New Testament.* Boca Raton, FL: American Media Mini Mags, Inc., 2001.

Sanford, Charles B. *The Religious Life of Thomas Jefferson.* Charlottesville, VA: University Press of Virginia, 1984.

Schweitzer, Albert. *The Quest of the Historical Jesus.* New York: Macmillan, 1968; first published in German in 1906, and in English in 1910.

Sheinkin, David. *Path of the Kabbalah.* New York: Paragon House, 1986.

Shlain, Leonard. *The Alphabet Versus The Goddess.* New York: Penguin/Compass, 1999.

Spong, John Shelby. *A New Christianity for a New World.* New York: HarperSanFrancisco, 2001.

-------. *Born of a Woman: A Bishop Rethinks the Virgin Birth and the Treatment*

Of Women by a Male-Dominated Church. New York: HarperSanFrancisco, 1992.

-------. *Jesus For the Non-Religious.* New York: HarperSanFrancisco, 2007.

-------. *Liberating the Gospels: Reading the Bible with Jewish Eyes.* New York: HarperSanFrancisco, 1996.

-------. *Living in Sin: A Bishop Rethinks Human Sexuality.* New York: HarperSan Fancisco, 1988.

-------. *Rescuing The Bible From Fundamentalism: A Bishop Rethinks the Meaning Of Scripture.* New York: HarperSanFancisco, 1991.

-------. *The Sins of Scripture: exposing the Bible's texts of hate to reveal the Love of God.* New York: HarperSanFrancisco, 2005.

-------. *This Hebrew Lord: A Bishop's Search for the Authentic Jesus.* New York: HarperSanFrancisco, 1988.

-------. *Why Christianity Must Change or Die: A Bishop Speaks to Believers in Exile.* New York: HarperCollins, 1999.

Strong, James. *Strong's Exhaustive Concordance of the Bible.* Nashville, TN: Abingdon, 1890.

Starbird, Margaret. *Magdalene's Lost Legacy: symbolic numbers and the sacred Union in Christianity.* Vermont: Bear & Company, 2003.

-------. *The Feminine Face of Christianity.* Illinois: Quest Books, 2003.

-------. *The Woman with the Alabaster Jar: Mary Magdalen and the Holy Grail.* Santa Fe, NM: Bear & Company Publishing, 1993.

Stone, Merlin. *When God Was a Woman.* Barnes & Noble, Inc., 1976.

Telushkin, Rabbi Joseph. *Jewish Wisdom: Ethical, Spiritual, and Historical Lessons from the Great Works and Thinkers.* New York: William Morrow And Company, Inc., 1994.

The Archko Volume: or,The Archelogical Writings of the Sanhedrin and Talmuds of The Jews. Translated by Drs. McIntosh and Twyman. Connecticut: Keats Publishing, Inc., 1975.

The Complete Gospels. Santa Rosa, CA: Polebridge Press, 1992.

The Five Gospels. New York: SCRIBNER, 1993.

The Other Bible. New York: HarperSanFrancisco, 1984.

Tully, Mark. *Four Faces: A Journey in Search of Jesus the Divine, the Jew, the Rebel, the Sage.* Berkeley CA: Ulysses Press, 1997.

Vayro, Ian Ross. *Tears in Heaven.* Queensland Australia: Joshua Books, 2008.

Waldman, Steven. *Founding Faith: How Our Founding Fathers Forged a Radical New Approach to Religious Liberty.* New York: Random House Trade Paperbacks, 2009.

Winkler, Gershon. *Sacred Secrets: The Sanctity of Sex in Jewish Law and Lore.* Northvale, NJ: Jason Aronson, Inc., 1998.

Wylen, Stephen M. *The Jews in the Time of Jesus: An Introduction.* New York/Mahwah, N.J.: Paulist Press, 1996.

Zinn, Howard. *A People's History of the United States.* New York: HarperCollins Publishers, 1980.

Index

A

Abraham, 17, 81, 93, 183, 200-1, 208, 221, 250, 330
Adam, 51, 64, 65, 102, 160, 162-4, 186, 243, 274, 324, 325-9, 342
adapt, 29, 82
adopt, 6, 29, 59, 82, 211, 360
adoption, 131, 136, 164, 228
adoption (ed), 5, 30, 44
adversary, 134, 198, 202
Africa, 74, 75, 181, 240, 256, 293
Ahura Mazda, 235
Ain Sof, 323-5, 328, 329
alabaster, 27, 51, 166, 205, 343
Alaha, 200
Albigensian, 20, 21
almuh, 193
Amen, 46
Americanizing, 95
androgynous, 252
angels, 59, 87, 107, 108, 133, 147, 194, 233
ankh, 242
Anointed, 234, 270, 271
anthropos, 302, 303
apocalypse (apocalyptic), 51, 56, 66-7, 179, 225, 270, 300, 306
Apocrypha, 27, 52, 53, 365
apokalypsis, 66
apologist, 50
apprenticeship, 109, 128, 129
Arian, 256
Arimathea, 25, 216, 217, 338
Ark (...Covenant), 65, 66, 186, 317
Armageddon, 104, 234, 235
Aryan, 230, 234, 240, 245-8, 249, 250, 256
Asherah, 236, 243, 244
Ashoreth, 236
assumption, 85, 270, 276, 348
atheist, 33, 73, 76, 77
Atonement, 78, 169, 174, 187, 223
Augustine, 28, 162, 163, 176, 341

Augustus, 155

B

Babylon (ian), 64, 110, 222-3, 235
baggage, 3, 89, 114, 173, 175
balance, 4, 7, 9, 15, 46-7, 69, 82-3, 84, 93, 96, 98-9, 107, 113, 117-8, 127, 138, 145, 203-4, 206, 218-9, 220-2, 242, 253, 278, 295, 302-3, 310, 340
baptism, 102, 122, 134, 152, 155, 158, 234, 290
Baptist, 72
Baptist, John the, 50, 178, 205, 206
baptize, 127, 151, 152, 173, 178, 233, 234, 282, 290
Barabbas, 215
Barbarian, 256, 258
being human, 89, 121, 165, 169, 302
being saved, 41, 62, 273, 282
Bethlehem, 147
betrayal, 14, 192, 353
Bible Belt, 1, 12, 283
Bibles, The
  Alexandrian, 285, 286, 288; Alexandrianus, 286; Aramaic, 55
  Bezae, 286, 288; Greek (Septuagint), 27, 52; Hebrew, 27, 51, 53, 55, 56, 93, 175, 179, 181, 195, 198, 225, 330; Hebrew (Old Testament), 342; Jefferson transformed, 77; Jeffersonian, 76, 77, 78; King James Version, 38, 46, 79, 80, 102, 116, 147, 178, 288; King Solomon, 236; Latin (Vulgate), 27, 53; Old Testament, 81; Septuagint (Greek), 56; Sinai (Sinaiticus), 53, 285, 286, 287; St. Jerome, translation, 217; The Oxford Companion, 221; Vatican, 286, 288; Vulgate (Latin), 27, 217
bimah, 220, 221, 358
biographies, 37, 38, 225

birth, 2, 46, 52, 57, 64, 111, 122-3, 124, 126, 133, 147-8, 152, 156, 170, 174-5, 177-8, 184, 193-4, 195, 196, 204, 206, 223-4, 229, 232-3, 235, 238, 243, 262, 276-7, 284, 286, 330, 332; virgin, 36, 77, 343
bloodline, 23, 27, 28, 129, 130, 138, 249, 287, 330
boarding school, 2, 4, 141
boat, 65, 186, 296
body, 10, 24, 37, 54, 63, 67, 69, 102, 109, 121-2, 144, 149, 160, 169, 170, 187, 198-9, 216, 219, 230, 234-5, 237-8, 274-5-7, 283, 304, 311-2, 314, 322, 326, 328, 332, 339
Book of the Dead, 232
boundaries, 72, 98, 100, 113, 115-6, 127, 149, 161, 209, 279, 308
Bramley, William, 38, 349, 333
breaking bread, 230, 290
bride, 81, 167, 224
Buddha, 22, 175, 193, 233-4, 346, 351
Buddhism, 35, 97, 172, 174-5, 207, 246
Buddhist, 172, 175, 207, 246, 337

C

Caesar, 49, 50, 154, 155
Caiaphas, 211, 212, 272, 273
Campbell, Joseph, 17, 35, 65
Canon (s), 37, 56, 256, 288, 293, 333, 341
canonical, 27, 57, 200, 221, 229, 334
carpenter, 229, 370
caste, 86, 205, 240, 246, 317
catacombs, 42, 102, 116, 171
Cathars, 20, 21, 22, 134, 346
Catherine, 53, 285, 286
Catholic--Orthodox, 139; Roman, 21, 27, 37, 44, 58, 71, 79, 81, 103, 128, 139, 141, 160, 198, 218, 245, 258, 288, 338, 343-4, 346, 348-9, 350, 365
Catholic Encyclopedia, 28, 32, 37-8, 46, 145, 153-4, 174, 195, 287-8

Catholic Popes
  Innocent IV, 58; Pope Adrian IV, 140; Pope Alexander VI, 144; Pope Clement, 350; Pope Clement XII, 350; Pope Clement XIV, 348; Pope Gregory, 27; Pope Gregory IX, 346; Pope Innocent II, 347; Pope Innocent III, 21, 346; Pope Innocent IV, 347; Pope John Paul II, 305, 342, 344, 345, 349, 351; Pope John XXIII, 351; Pope Leo XIII, 351; Pope Lucius III, 346; Pope Paul III, 30, 347; Pope Paul IV, 347; Pope Paul VI, 347, 348, 349; Pope Pius IX, 348; Pope Pius VII, 348; Pope Pius X, 338; Pope Urban II, 346
CBS, 33, 264
celibacy, 23, 166, 204, 207, 349
celibate, 104, 141, 165, 166, 346
ceremony, 1, 55, 106, 109, 117, 119, 120, 124, 126, 128, 136, 163, 244, 290
charity, 59, 208, 209, 273
Chava (a name for Eve), 324, 326, 327
Cherokee, 126, 138
Chi rho, 154
Choctaw, 1, 2, 3, 5, 7, 8, 95, 107, 126, 262
Chosen (chosen people), 25, 59, 60, 62, 80, 102, 105, 137-8, 170, 183, 184, 194, 230, 249, 292, 325, 330, 331, 333
Christianizing, 95
circumcision, 223, 319
citizenship, 129, 158
clans, 113, 118
cleanse (ing), 122, 169
CNN, 46, 66, 150, 193, 216, 229, 244, 276, 282, 340
colonization, 30, 70, 71, 125
commandments, 162, 183-4, 188, 220, 264, 332, 355-6, 358-9
communion, 134, 144, 155, 230, 320

confession, 59, 89, 119, 128, 176, 307, 320, 347
Confucius, 98
Conservadox, 182, 183, 353
consort, 236, 243, 244, 247, 250
conspiracy, 217, 242
Constantinople, 48-9, 159, 170, 260, 269, 271, 272, 285, 346
Constitutum Constantini, 159
contraries, 97, 117, 131
Coptic (s), 52, 244, 251, 254, 285, 333, 334, 339, 343
corpse, 32, 216
cosmos, 45, 161, 206, 241, 243, 308, 322
Council of Nicaea, 37, 150, 151, 154, 158, 201, 289
cousins, 269, 277, 353
covenant, 100, 187, 223
Covenant, Ark of the, 26, 236, 317, 318
Coyote, 219
Creator, 8, 9, 18, 35, 40, 43, 59, 60, 63, 94, 99, 100, 105-7, 110, 114, 115, 117-8, 120-4, 130, 136-8, 161, 163, 174, 176, 196, 203-4, 242, 262, 266, 275, 280, 284, 295-6, 302, 305, 308, 314-5, 327
Creed (s), 22, 73, 103, 156, 200, 270, 280, 288, 348, 351
crucifix, 42, 102, 171
crucifixion (s), 18, 25, 48-9, 51, 103, 116, 134, 147-8, 154, 189, 196, 213-6, 217-8, 226, 272, 312-3, 337-9
crusade (s), (ers), 20, 21, 139, 346, 352
curse, 69, 102, 122
cycle (s), 70, 100, 110, 120, 122, 124, 174, 175, 232, 235, 240, 241, 242, 243, 276, 278, 308

D

Dark Ages, 255, 256, 257
Dead Sea Scrolls, 31, 51, 205-6, 340, 343

death, 18, 20, 41, 48, 50, 55, 70, **75**, 81, **96**, **98**, 105, 128-**9**, **136**, 144-5, 148, 150, 153, 158, **161**, 162-4, 178, 183, **185**, 186, 193, **202-4**, 205, **207**, 220, 223, **225**, 236, 241-2, 245, 248, 253-4, 262, **263**, 275, 282, 289, 290, 296-8, 304, 312-4, **323**, 326, 331,
debt (s), **31**, 129, 166, 200-1 , 296
December 25th, **146**, **149**, 150, **152**, **154**, 222
denomination (s), 1, 16, 29, 31-2, 37, 39, 57, 59, 68, 97, 99, 101, 111, 114, 122-3, 129, 139, 174, 198, 264, 300, 328-9
Devil, 5, **21**, 60, 80, 100, 126-8, 178, 188-9, 190-1, 291, 343; Satan, **63**, 78, **83**-4, 126-8, **136**, 178, 188-9, 190-2, 194, 197, 224, 232-3, 350
Didache, 47, **85**, 219, 288, 352
disciple (s), 12, 55, 76, 99, **109**, 131, 136, 142, **156**, 171, 184-5, 187, 206, 216, 222, 255, **259**, 262, **271**, 284, 297, 323
discipleship, 99, 104, **136, 175**
diversity, 45, 108, **137**, 140, 143-4, 154, 215, 270, 347
Divi filius, **42**
divinity, **72**, 75, 90, **95**, 103, 111, 139, 168, **169**, **184**, **186**-7, **220**, 236, 243-4, 254, **270**, 278, 309, 323, 327, 333
divorce, 8, 213
doctrine, 21, 33, 56, 64, 72, **75**, 97, 99, 100, 126, 129, 138, 150-1, **155**, 162-3, **163**, 166, 168-9, **169**, **172**, 219, 258-9, **263**, 266, 287, 298, 326, 331
Doctrine of Discovery, 29, 65-6, 68, 328, 330
doctrine, Calvinist, 72
dogma, 21, 32-3, 54, 56, 58, 82, 84, 89, 117, 132, 140, 143, 145, 151, 156, 161, 164, 167, **169**, 189, 192, 217, 242, 251-3, 264, 266, 274, 278, **334**, 351
Dominus Jesus, 152

donkey skins, 51, 272
Douglas-Klotz, Neil, 13, **43-4**, **60**, **78**, **84**, **107**, **116**, **127**, **153**-4, **170**, **189**, **198**, 267, **283**, **287**, **347**, 354
Doyle, Father Thomas, **243**, 243-7,

E

Earth, **22**, **29**, **31**, 32-3, 39, **44**, **46**, **59**, 60, **64**, 69, 97-9, 100-3, 108-10, 115-6, 118, 127, 129, **136-7**, 139, **142**, 151, **153**-5, 161, 169, 172, 175, 180, **186**, 188, 194, 197, 208, **220**, 227, 229, 230-1, **237**, 240, 250, 255-6, 261, 266, 268-9, 282, 289, 290-3, 295, 299, 300, 302, 310, 320, **325**, 329, 333, 342-3, 346, 348, 351
Easter, 74
Edict of Milan, 145-6
Egypt (Egyptian), 12, 17, 25, 41, **47**, **50**, **51**, **59**, 83, **95**, **104**, **106**, 141, **149**, **152**, 157-8, **161**, **165**, **166**, **170**, **174**, 175, 186-7, 192-3, **207**, 210, 213, **217**, 219, **220-1**, 225, **226**, **229**, 230, **232**, 235, 238-9, 241, **268**, **271**, 272, **278**, 314, 320, 323, **325**, **327**, 332-3, 342, 344, 346, **348**, 351-2
elder, 1, **2**, 8, 15, 39, 41, 47, 90-2, 96, 100, 102, 105, **106**, 109, 110, 120, 122-3, 132, **136**, 156, 160, **164**, 194, 202, 220, 230, 251, 253, 269, 281-4, 287, 306, 309, 320,
Elijah, 185, 202
elohim, **347**, 351
Emperor, 36, **42**, 47, 53, **63**, **98**, 141, 144-6, **149**, 246, 319, 327; Augustus, 141, 148; Claudius, 49; Constantine, 36, 42-3, **63**, 144-7, **146**, **149**-152, 207, 298;Diocletian, 146; Galerius, 146; Licinius, 146; Maxentius, 146
end times, 63, 100, **137**, 223-4, 267
England, 24, 61, 69, **70**, **72**, 73, 75, 332, 342
enunah, 265-6, 348

362

Epistle of Barnabas, 271
Essenes, 49, 157, 194-7, 296, 303, 332
eternal, 33, 97, 105, 109, 130, 156-7, 189, 211, 236-7, 239, 264, 266, 287, 298
Ethiopia, **190**, 228,
Eucharist, 244, 246-7
Eve, 61-2, **62**, 98, 109, 117, **155**, 165, 178, **203**, 308, 310, **312**, **325-6**, 344, 346, 348
evil, 19, 23-4, **58**, **60**, 62, 80, 83-4, 89, 98, 100, 109, 116-7, **126-8**, 162, **164**, **187**, 188-9, 190, 192-4, 196, 204, 223, 225, 236, 262-3, 269, 287, 289, 291, 312-3, 316, 319, 341, 343-4, 236-7, 350, 351
excommunicate, 329
Exodus, 59, 157, 191-2, 201, **211**, 216, **218**, 267, 314, 320, **325**, 344, 346,

F

faith, 6, 12, 31-2, 36, 41, 46, **48**, 55, **68-9**, **72**, **84**, 90, 114, 155, 157, 163, 179, **182**, **185**, 187, **191**, 202, 216, 257, 264-6, 287, 295, 301, **314**, 326, 328, 348, **350**
fear, 3, 18, 30, 39, **89**, 94, 164, 189, 192, 224, 244-5, 281, 282, 293, 297, 334, 343
feather, 104, 221, **229**
feminine, **20**, 21, **25-6**, **35**, **49**, **95**-6, 104, 120-1, 150, 157, **159**, 179, **185**, 188, **206**, 208-9, **210**-11, **221**, 226-7, 230-1, 235, 239, 286, **307**-8, **321**, **329**, 346, **347**, 351
Finland, 9, **133**-5
first century, **16**, 18, **25**, **27**, 36, **38**, 43, 47, **50**, 52, 55, **96**, 153, 172, 176-7, 201, **205**, 212-3, **213**, 237, 242, 250, 254, 260, 274, 277, 282-3, 287, 298, 301-2, 304, 324, 331
Flood, 3-4, 24, 57, 63, **105**, **325**, **326**, 339
forgery, **27**, 152, 185

forgive (ness), 58-9, 79, 92, 129, **198**, **200**, 242, 290, 329
forty, 15, 22, 145, 146, 187, 190, 210, 213, 291
France, 20, 21, 25, 26, 27, 28, 249, 254, 256, 337, 346
Frankl, 83
Franklin (Ben), 76
Freemason, 26, 76, 232, 249, 349, 350, 351, 352
Funk, 35, **36**-7, **256**,

G

Gandhi, 90, 265
Garden of Eden, **61-2**, 84, 97-8, 109, 117, **129**, 292, 308, 310-11, 314, 325, **326**
Gardner, Laurence, **22**, **25**, 33, **49**, **149**, **169**, **188**, 195-6, **322-3, 326,**
genocide, 79, 92
Gentile (s), 48, 55, 144, 183, 225, 241, 275, 302, 339
German (y), 22, 75, **100**, **142**, 162, **233**, 272, 321, 340
ghettos, 207
Gilgamesh, **105**
Glastonbury, 24
Gnostic (s), 25, **30**, 32, **35**, 49, **50**, **142**, 157, **161**, 187, 193, 211, 216, 221, **230**, **232**, 239, 267-8, **268**, 271, 289, **322**, 323, 348
Goddess (es), 35, **61**, 100, 158, **190**, **217**, **221**, 224, 226-9, **231**, 232, **235**, **237**, 238-9, **268**, 301, 345-6
Gospel of
    Mark, **36**, 63, **84**, 156, 170-1, **183**, 186, **206**, 255, **256**, 257, 264, **273**, 277, 318
    Mary Magdalene, 59, 160, 206, 232, 271, 289, 292, 295
    Matthew, **36**, 54, 95, **116**, 126, 140-1, 154, 170, 183, 184, 186, 188, 216, 255, **256**, 277, 288, 319, 352
    Philip, 160, 171, 193, 290-1, 295, 312, 348

Gospel of "Q", 54-5, 267, 271
Thomas, **27**, 37, **50**, 54, **64**, 101, 109, **141**, 142, 156, **159**, 167, 170, 216, 248, 249, 254, 255, 262, 267, 271, 274, 277-8, 280, 285, 286, 288, 291, **292**, 293, 317-18
Grace, 31, 98, 109, 163, 211, 237, 239, 309
Grandmother (s), 9, 21, 95-6, 110, 118, 120-1, 123, 135, 160
Great Mystery, **8**, 41, 60, 84, 90, 96, 101-3, 110, 129, 130, 132, 136, 154, 230, **249**
Growing space, 94, 120-1, 137, 294
guilt (y), 18, **31**, 33, 39, 84, 86-7, 98, 109, 136, 156, **164**, 165, 167, 251, 293, 312,

H

Haftarah, 179, **303**
Hamartia, 58-9, 348
Hand over, 183
Harlotized (harlots), **259**, 326
Harmony. 44, 69, 103, 107-8, 115, 136, 194, 208-9, **269**, 270, 294-5, 300, 311, 350
Hayye, **180**, 290
Heal (ed)(ers)(ing), 30, 67, 79, 92, **114**, 156, 160, 175, 180, 195-6, 222, 253, 261, 316, 341-3
Heaven (ly), 3, 31, 39, 58, 60, 64, **96**, 97-9, **100**, 105, 109, **116**, 127-8, 136, **142**, 145, **148**, 153-4, 162-3, **164**, 170-1, 178-9, 180, 189, 197, 219, 220, **237**, 245, 249, 254, 255-6, **263**, 264, 267-8, 273, 280, 286, 288-9, 292-3, 319, 324, 338, **350**
Helena (Saint), **146-7**
Hell, 64, 96, 98-9, **99**, 100, 105, **128**, 136, **148**, **164**, 178, **189**, 221, 245, 264, 280, 289, 290-1, 293, 325, 326, 338
Heretic (s)(cal), 21, 50, **56**, 68, 151, 162, 243, 258, 274, 286, 327, 329, 330, 334
Herod, 140, 273

Hero (ic)(es), 43, 103-4, **105**, 220, 241
Hieroglyphics, 17, 238, **327**
High Priest (s), **161**, 179, 201-3, 213, 302, 339
Himalayas, **26**, 234, 321
Hindu (ism)(s), 22, 93, 126, **151**, 165, 166, 169, **218**, 234
Hitler, 233
Hogan, 329
Holocaust (s), 77, 340
Hologram, 310, 315
Holy of Holies, 161, 179, **202**, 302, 339
Holy Spirit, 52, **148**, 231, 239, 346, 350
Honest, 12, 81, 85, 87, 144, 209, 253, 288
Horus, **217**, 220-2, 333
Human nature, 84, 116, 126, 137, 155-6, 259, 289
Huna, **128,** 188

I

Illegitimate, 270, 305
Immaculate(Conception)(virgin), 331, 349
Incarnation (reincarnation), 21, 25, 96, 157, 162-4, 167, 169, **220**, 280, 314, 338, 346
India, 21-2, 101, **151**, 166, 197, 206, 216, 219, **223**, 233, 234-5, **321**
Indian (s), 1-4, 28-9, 39, 40, **42**, 70-1, 90-1, 125, **128**-9, 132, 194, 321, 331
Indulgence (s), 20, **31**, **330**
Inquisition, 56, 77, 152, 328, 330-1
Intercourse, 23, 157, 159, 207, 291
Invaders, **223**, 233, 234, 235, 243,
Ireland, 77, 173; Irish, 95, 322
Irv Romans (Peace Shield), 102, 109
Isaac, **77**, 156, 174, 190-1, 210, 315, 337, 341, 344, 349
Isis, **104**, **149**, **217**, 220-2
Islam (ic), 13, **22**, 92, 96-7, 126, **148**, 162, 169, 173, 223, 237, 239, 306, 322

Israel (ites), 13, 26, 49, 59, **77**, 83, 148, 157, **185**, 195, **198**, 203, **204**, 211-14, 219, 220, 224-5, 227, **231**, 236-7, 239, **257**, 267, 296, 297-8, 301-2, 305-6, 314-154, 320, 323, 325, 327, 335, 339, 344, 345, 350
Issa, 21, **22**, 228, **321**
Italy, 47, 61, 243, 245, 329

J

Jackson (President), 91
Jefferson (President), 72-3, **74**, 75, 169, 172, 270
Jesus Seminar, 37, 254-5, 257, 317-319
Johannite Church, 187
Joseph, 24, 37, 77, **183**, 188, 206, 222, 256, 263, **263**, 305, 320, 322
Josepus, 48, 194, **195**, 327, 332
Jubilees, 190, 192
Judas, 50, 75, **183**, **271**
Judgment Day, 100, 109, 223
Justin, 48, 151, 275

K

Kabbalah, 175, 192, **197**, 294, **306**, 310-12, 315, 343, 351
Kabbalist (ic)(s), 52, 156, 159, 162, 260, 305, **308**, 316, 341, 343, 347, 350
Kahuna, 128, 188
Karma, 86, 164-7
Kashmir (ian), **22**
King David, 35, 77, 198, 273, 315, 344
Kingdom, 20, 31, 44, 54, **63-64**, 68-9, 142, 154, **159**, 163, 179, **195**, 197, **225**, 238, 240, **246**, 256, 276, 280, 286, 288-9, 291-2, 296, 300, 333, 350-1
Koran, 96, 107, **169**, 263, 265, **322**
Koser, 13, 129, 174, 303, 335-9, 346
Kurgans, 233
Kushner (Rabbi), 176-7, 268, 269

L

Lactees, 203
Lakota, 93, 101, 112
Lalli, 133-5
Law, 24, 48, **52**, 53, 57, 58, 70, 80, 97, 109, 117, 119, 120, 124, 127-8, 135-6, 141, **145**, 149, 151, 154, 158, 160, 165, 173, 176, 178, 182, 191, 193-4, 201-5, 211, **218**, **221**, 222, 226, **229**, 250-1, 258-9, 265, 268-9, **270**, 275, 288, 290, 295, 302-3, 309, 324, 329, 336-8, 342-4, 352

M

Maat, 221, **229**, 230
Madonna, **217**
Mamzer, 304-5
Manger, 140, **149**, **185**, 222, 263
Married, 1, 5-6, 23-4, 26, 27, 116, 158, 178, **235**, 306, 322, **324**, 329, **329**, 343
Masculine, 18, 102, 104, 119, 121, 128, 150, 159, 208-9, 227-8, 231, 235, 238-9, 288, 308, 351
Massacre, 19, 70, 140, 340
Mastema, 190-2
Mediterranean, 25, 35, 140, **206**, 225, 297
Melchizedek, **50**, 62,
Menstrual, 117, 304, 341
Merovingian, 27, 332
Messiah, 172, **195**, 198, 254-5, 257, 344
Metanoia, 199, 200, **230**
Metanois (awakening), 199
Mexico, 281, **331**
Michelangelo, 31, 61-3
midianites, 175, 342-3
midrash, 180-4, 188, 214, 296, 306, 308
mistakes, 36, 58, 86, 93, 136, 165, 171, 312, 331
Mithras (ism), **130**, 146-7, 148, **149**, 150, 185

Mitzvah, 13, 316, 335, 337-8, 341
Moari, 103
Modernists, 321-2
Money changers, 186
Monk, 24, 47, 158
Monogenes, 172, 349
Moon time, 118
Moore, 33, 98, 100, 129, **145**, 146, 151-2, 156, 166, 170, 172, 178, 215, 246, 253, 258, 261, 322, **325**, 330-1, 349, 350, 351
Moses, **22**, 51, 53, 62, 75, 168, 180, **190**, 191, 216, **218**, 234, 259, 267, **308**, 314, 325, 332, 338, 345, 351
Moshe, **51**
moshia, 177, 267
Mother Mary, 184, **186**, 329, 331
Mount Sinai, 157, 268, 314, 344-6
Muhammad, **169**
Muslim, 6, 19, 27, **52**, 77, **97**, 263, **271**, 325, 328,
mystery, **8**, 17, 19, 25, 30-1, 41, 60, 84, 87, 90, 93, 95-6, 101-**4**, 110, 129-30, 132, 136, 154, 159, 168, **190**, 197, 217, **218**, 230, **249**, 262, 265, 279, 285, 291, 295, 306, 328,
Mysticism, **198**, **218**, 292, 294, 305-6, 308, 310-1, 313-4, 334
myth, **17**, **34-5**, 44, **61-2**, 72, 75, 93, 101, 104, **148-9**, **214**, 216, **220-1**, 235, 257, 307, 323, 325, 343,
mythology, 34, 185, 221, 225, 226, **229**,

N

Nag Hammadi, **30**, **50**, **59**, **78**, **160**, **171**, **232**, **240**, 268, **291**, 322-4, 327
naked, 69, 77, 109, 311,
Native American (s), 1-2, 5, 11, 15-7, 19, 28, 38-9, 42, 46, **51**, 56-7, **62**, 67, 89, 91, **102**, 105-8, 110, 112, 120, 128, 130, 132, 135, 139, 159, 161, 173, 179, 194, 197, 223, 229, 230, 249-51, 261, 265, 269, 276, 283-4, 290-3, 295, 299, 312, 324, 327, 329, 331,

Nativity, **146**, 150,
Nazareth, 47, 29, 140, 200, 218, 304,
neighbor, 14, **20**, **72**, 85, 289, 336
Noah, 63, 77, 315, 332
NPR, 72-**4**,
nun, 26, **77**,

O

obedience, 33, 43, 58, 59, 97-8, 103, 110, 116, 127, 136, 156, 158, 160-1, 165, 199, 264, 277, 187-8, 293, 326
only son, 100, 152, 170, 172, 191, 215, 344, 349
Origen, 48, 186-7, **187**, 278, **351**
original sin, 33, 126, 129, 152, **155**, 156, 287, 326, 331
Osiris, **104**, 187, 218, 220, 222

P

pagan, 12, 14, 19, 35, 49, 61, 70, **98**, **101**, **130**, 134, 146, **148**-9, 150, **163**, 168, **172**, 174, **218**, **223**, 333, 335-7, 341-2
Pagels (Elaine), 11-2, **40**, **50**, **83**, **155**, **161**, 186, **189**, **239**, 268, 274, **275**-7, 323, **352**
Palestine, 43, 97, 257, 321
papyi,
Papal (Bull, decreed), 20, 29, 56, 65, 152, 158, **233**, 245, 327-8, 329, 331, **333**
paradise, 62, 98, 109, 129, **159**, 162
Parakletos, 52, 349
Passover, 157, 186, 192, **203-5**, 210, **256**, **273**, 314, 323, 340-1, 346
patriarchy, 211, 226,
patriotism, 29, 124,
Paul, **36-7**, **50**, 63-4, 74, 141, 169-70, 172, 183, 248, 251, 272, 297, 324,
PBS, **31**,
peace, 60, 71, 90, 124, 193, **194**, 254, 295, 350
Peace Shield, 16, **102**, 109-11, 121, 173, 253, 299, 306, 311

Pentateuch, 75, 306,
Pentecost, **273**,
Persia, **51**, 146-8, 218, **223**, 234, 241
Peshitta, **267**,
Peter, 37, 55, 59, 126, 141, **147**, 160, 171, 187, **193**, 232, 225, **329**, **330**
Pharaoh, 148, 192, 221, **229**, 230, 320, 325
Pilate, 221, **323**
Pistis Sophia, 221, 323
plagues, 17, 325
poverty, 280, 296
pregnancy (nant), 120, 263, **304**
priest (s), 21, 49, 57, **63**, 70, 74, 99, 136, 147, 158, 159, **161**, 179, 186, **195**, **201-3**, 212-3, **216**, 219, 225, 232-4, **243**, 246, 259, 268, 301-2, 321, 329, 331, 339, 340, 344,
priesthood, 30, 46, 158, 213, 234
priestess (es), 213, 226
prophecy, 28, 41, **50**, 67, 102, 104, 148, 182, 214, 218, 291, 315, 350,
prophet, **21-2**, 48, 49, 103, 105, **169-70**, 171, 179, **198**, **206**, **210**-11, 218, **234**, 275, 296-7, 299, **303**, 306, 321
Prostitute (s), 26, **56**, 77, 213, 226, **257**, 258, **326**
Protectoress, 239, 346, **347**
Protestant, 31, 68, **74**, 330, 332
Purgatory, 163, 179
Purification, 114, 116-7, 161, 163, 223, 304
Puritians, 69-70
Purity, 41, 114, 116,-7, 178, 194, 212, 234, 302-4
Pyramid, **331**
Pythagoras, 226

Q

Quakers, 69-70
Queens, 211
Qumran, 49, **195**, 324, 327

R

Rabbi,
 Akibah, 14, 289, 336; Emden, **23;** Ohad, **197;** Kook, Abraham Isaac, 198; Kushner, Lawrence, **176**, 177, 268-9; Moshe, **23;** Rosen, David; 89, 173; Serzosky, 179, 250; Telushkin, Joseph, **202**, **224;** Teplitz, Saul, 179; Weinstein, **52, 57**, 127, **128**, **174**, **179**, 191, **204**, 205, 213, **303**, **350;** Winkler, 22
Rabbi (s), 13, 14, 22-3, **24, 49**, 58, 98, **96**, 173, 175-6, 178, 180-2, 190, **198**, 210, 214, 229, 268, 269, 306-7, 311-13, 315, **316**, 324, 341-2,
Rabbinic, 22, 36, 61, **96**, 172, 176, 178, 182, 201, 213, **282**, 303, 307, 330, 336
rapture, **100,** 137,
Reformation, 215, 330, 333
regret, 86, 198
reincarnation, 21, **96**, 157, 162-4, 167, **220**, 280, 314, 338, 346
repent (ed)(s), 58, 70, 165, 192, **198**, 200, 292, 350
repentance, 57-9, 98, 199, 200, 338, 340, 350
respect (ed)(ful)(ing), 3, 10, 12, 15, 27, 39-41, 44, 85-6, **89**, 90, 92, 94, 96, 99-100, 108-9, 112-3, 122, 125, 134, 139, 140, 161, 179, 197, 209, 210, **225**, **235**, 253, 289, 293, 310, 307, 312
rest, 8, 45, 53, 67, **74**, 95, 149, 160, **161**, 179, 180, **189**, 191, 208, **249**, 256, 269, 289, 291, 302, 316, 341, 343, 345
resurrection, **35**, 50, 55, 64, 74, 98, 142, 183, 185, **188**, **207**, 213, 220, 273, 297-8, 312, 314-6, 350
Rex Mundi (god of evil), 128
ritual (s), **35**, 71, 108, 114-5, 117, 122, 127, 150, 160, 173-4, 202, 209, 212, 219, 247, 253, 259, 275, 298, 301, 303-4, 307, 332, 337-8, 340-1, 344

ruha, 52, 352

S

Sabbath, 14, 23, 53, **145**, 149, 160, 174, 191, 194, 302-3, 336-7, 342-3, 345
Sabbath Joy, 23, 160, 343
Sacred (breath,self, spirit), 15, 60, 103, 261, 290, 293, 300
Sacred Unity, **60**, 154, **190**, 264, 287, 347, 351
Sacrifice (ed)(s), 33, 39, 77, 81, 104, 129-30, 136, **148**, 150, 163, 190-1, 212, 218, 223-4, 244, 246-7, 256, 259, 287, 301-2, 322, 326, 344
Sage (s), 52, 61, 89, **141**, 285, 301
Saint Bernard, 21
Saint Sarah, 25
salvation, **72**, **75**, 97, 99, 109, 129, 142, 148, 151, 163, 167-8, 172, 237, 246, 250, 254, 266-270, 276, 286-7, 289, 326, 330-1, 351-2
samayim, 179, **350**
Sanhedrin, 47, 201-4, 206, **256**, 259, 269, 346
Sanskrit, **223**
savior, 40, 59, 60, 99, 136, **159**, 184-5, 217, 233, 238, 252, 267, 272, 348-9; Saviour, 148, **149**
Schweitzer, **28**, 89, 171-2, 185, 247, **279**, 321
Second Vatican, 207
Sefiroth, 175, 310, 314, 347
Semitic, 52, **76**, 127, 234-5, **267**, **325**
Serpent, 189, **310**, **325**
Servant (s), 71, 99, 186, 192, 201, 207, **246**, 296-7, 350
Seth, **220**
Seventh Fire, 106, 306
Sex (sexual)(ist)(ism), 20, 23-4, 27, 83, 109, 115-6, 157-62, 178, 188, 207, 209, 210-1, 213, 242, **243**, 259, 262, 291, 304-5, **312**, 326, **329**, 340-4, 346, 348
sexuality, 23, 109, 137, 157-9, 162, 212, 263, 289, 291, 295, 310, 312

Shechinah, 159, 242, 345-6, **347**
sherara, 107, **269**, 283
Shinto, 62
Sin (ful)(ing) (s),18, 20, 23, **31**, 57-9, 85, 98, 100, 104, 109, 115-7, 126, 129, 130, 136-7, 155-7, 161, 165, 167, 178, 197-9, 200, 201, 211-2, 216, 222, 250-2, 254, 256, 270, 287, 291, 298, 311-2, 329, 338, 340-1, 344-5, 348, 350, 352
sinner (s), **31, 56,** 124, 198, 242, 258, 270, **259**
slaves (enslave-ment)(slavery), 29, 65, 70-2, 77, 82-3, 155, 158, 164, 201, **204**, 226, 276, 314, 320, 325, 344
snakes, 7, 216, 293
Socrates, 193, **225**
Sodomy, 23
Sol Invictus, **146**, **149**, 150
Solomon ('s), 35, **63**, 77, 149, **161**, 182, 212, 224, 231-2, 263, 332
Solstice (s), 105, 115, 147, **149**, 220
Son of God, 42, 50, 99, 100, **146**, 148, 152, 169, 170, 172, 215, 243, **246**, 255, **256**, 273, 299, 349
Sophia, 25, 47, 211, 226, **230-1**, 239, 255, 323, 350
Soul (s), 23, 52, 64, 83, **99**, 100, 103, 132, 136, **148**, 156-7, 162-3, 166, 178, 189, **195**, 223, 226, **230**, 240, 260, **261**-2, 285, 288, 290, 295, 307, 311-12, 314, 316, 346, 349, 352
spiral, 198
spirit guide (s), 103, 136
Spong, 12, **27**, 56, 60, **62**, 65, **76-7**, 140, **156**, **164**, 165, 167, 170, 172, **181**-2, **183**, 184, 188, **214**, 216, 227, **249**, 254, **256**-7, 261-2, **263**, **274**, 290, 296, 304, **322**, 326
Starbird, 25, 49, 63, 95, 158, 185, 218
Storyteller(ing)(s), 8, 93
Sublimus Dei (1537 Papal Bull), 29
Suffer (ed)(ing)(s), 33, **56**, **79**, 80-1, 99, 117, 129, 130, 137, 155, 165, 258, 262, 265, 279, 296, 304, 326, 346
Sufi, 34, 154, **266**
Sufism, 13, 93,
suicide, 79, 225
Sumerian (s)(Sumar), 35, 49, **61**, 65, 105, 235, **326**, **331**
Sunday, 4, 12, 32, **145**, 150, 160
surrender, 33, 98, 130
survey, 32, **99**, 177, **189**
survival, 14, 43, 78, 95, 136, 150, 180, 335, 343
Syria, 47, **50**, 52
Szekely, 46, 196

T

Theodsius, 374
Talmud, 127, 162, **202-3**, 205, 255, 269, 330, 342, 348, **349**
targum, 53, 304
teacher, 3, 16, 21, **24**, 34, 48, 55, 59, 73, 98, 105, 109, 123, **141**-2, 160, 175-6, **178**, 196, 211, **218**, 246, 253, 255, 283, 285, 289, 292, 296, 306, 313, 335
Teacher of Righteousness, 195
technology, 300, 315-6,
Templar, 49, 152, 187-8, 215, 217, 234, **334**
Temple, 35, 49, 114, 117, 150, 157, **161**, 178-9, 182, 186, **194**, 202, 204, 212, 222, 224, 231, 237-8, 259, 263, 295, 298, 301-4, **302**, 332, 339-340, 346
Tertullian, 48, **275**-6
thirty pieces of silver, 35
tithes, 259
tobacco, 70, 123
tomb, **22**, 25, 74, **163**, 206, 222, 273
Torah, 14, 22, 49, 53, 63, 96, 127, 136, 157, 176, 179, 180-2, **183**, **190**-1, **194**, 201, 210, 212, 214, 216, 225, **303**, **308**, 310-11, 314-6, 336-39, 341-6
torture, 18, 56, 192, 330-1
Trail of Tears, 1, 91

Tree of (Life), 62, 175, 179, 196, 310
Trinity, 168-9, **169**, 170
twin, 1, 2, 5, 50, 223, 280
tzitzit, 304, 343

U

universe, 53, 154, 174, 176, **178**, **180**, 189-190, 196-7, 209, 229, 260, 290, 294, 301, 307, 309, **325**, 332, 337, 340, 347, 350
urim and thummim, 203

V

Vedic, 101, 223, 234
victim, 35, 78-87, 132, 137, **204**, 240, **243**, **322**
Vidui (confession), 56, 168, 305
virgin, **35**, 50, 74, **77**, 115, **146**, 152, **169**, 183-5, 188, 211-2, **214**, 217-18, 220, 222, 239, 248, **263**, 273, 327, 332, 348, **349**
vision, 9, 38, 45, 85, 90, 92-3, 96, **100**, 105-6, 108, 111-13, 119, 121, 125, 131-2, 136, 146-7, 156, 175, 209, **256**, 265, 288, 295-6, 299, 322, 324

W

Westar Institute, 319
Western Hemisphere, 123
wife, 6, 15, 29, **62**, 77, 79, 112, 118, 133-5, 145, 159-160, 175,191, 212, 220, 252, 276, 281, 291, **322**, **329**, 344, 348
wine, 187, 219, **231**, 259, 275
Wisdom, 10, 13, 15, 38, 41, 44, **50**, 55, **74**, 92-4, 101-3, **104**, 105, 122, 211, 226-7, **231**, 239, 249, 254, 267-8, 271, 284-6, 295, 299, 306, 311-2, 315, 317, 320, 333, 350
woman, 1, 13, 22, 26, **27**, **51**, 71, 117, 120, **128**-9, 141, 160, **164**-5, 172, **184**, **207**, 209-10, 213, 226-7, **231**, 239, 252, 263, 288, 307, 309-10, 313, 319, **322**, 326, 340-1, 347, **349**
womb, 87, 94-5, 120-1, 307
women, 18, **20**-1, **77**, 82-3, 95-6, 98, 100, 115, 117-121, 157-160, 162, 172, **204**, 207-213, 216, 226-7, 235, 238, 254, **259**, 273, 297, 304, **322**, 325-6, 328, 340-1, 344
worth (less), 10, 23, 29, 57, 67, **77**, 80, 83, 85, 124, 160, 246-7, 265, 268, 327

Y

Yahweh, 224, 227, 231-2, 234, 237
YHWH, 172, 191-2
yin and yang, 80, 132, 193
Yom Kippur, 56-7, 302, 339-40, 342
Young, Brigham, 324
Yuz Asaf (Issa, Jesus), 22, **185**

Z

Zeus, 185, 226-7
Zohar, **308**, 315, 351
Zoroaster, 21, 218, **223**-4, **329**
Zoroastrianism, 189, **223**, 234
Zoroastrians, 189

*Numbers in **bold** indicate information is in the footnote